Fullstack Vue

The Complete Guide to Vue.js and Friends

Hassan Djirdeh
Nate Murray
Ari Lerner

Fullstack Vue

The Complete Guide to Vue.js and Friends

Written by Hassan Djirdeh, Nate Murray, and Ari Lerner

ISBN: 978-1987595291

Cover Art by TJ Fuller.
Published in San Francisco, California by Fullstack.io.

Questions? Email us at: us@fullstack.io

Sample code download available at fullstack.io/vue/code

Contents

Book Revision 1
Bug Reports 1
Be notified of updates via Twitter 1
We'd love to hear from you! 1

Foreword 3

How to Get the Most Out of This Book 1
Overview 1
Vue 2.x 2
Running Code Examples 2
Code Blocks and Context 3
Instruction for Windows users 4
Getting Help 4
Emailing Us 5
Get excited! 5

I - Your first Vue.js Web Application 7
Building UpVote! 7
Development environment setup 8
JavaScript ES6/ES7 9
Getting started 9
Setting up the view 14
Making the view data-driven 16
List rendering 20
Sorting 24
Event handling (our app's first interaction) 25
Components 29
`v-bind` and `v-on` shorthand syntax 37
Congratulations! 38

II - Single-file components 39
Introduction 39
Setting up our development environment 40
Getting started 41

Single-File Components . . . 47
Breaking the app into components . . . 50
Managing data between components . . . 54
Simple State Management . . . 55
Steps to building Vue apps from scratch . . . 58
Step 1: A static version of the app . . . 59
Step 2: Breaking the app into components . . . 61
Step 3: Hardcode Initial States . . . 65
Step 4: Create state mutations (and corresponding component actions) . . . 76
The Calendar App . . . 101
Methodology review . . . 102

III - Custom Events . . . **103**
Introduction . . . 103
JavaScript Custom Events . . . 103
Vue Custom Events . . . 104
Event Bus . . . 116
Custom events and managing data . . . 124
Summary . . . 125

IV - Introduction to Vuex . . . **127**
Recap . . . 127
What is Flux? . . . 127
Flux implementations . . . 128
Vuex . . . 128
Refactoring the note-taking app . . . 129
Vuex Store . . . 132
Building the components . . . 138

V - Vuex and Servers . . . **147**
Introduction . . . 147
Preparation . . . 147
The Server API . . . 154
Playing with the API . . . 156
Client and server . . . 160
Preparing the application . . . 162
The Vuex Store . . . 170
`productModule` . . . 176
`cartModule` . . . 186
Interactivity . . . 196
Vuex and medium to large scale applications . . . 205
Recap . . . 210

VI - Form Handling **211**
Introduction 211
Forms 101 211
Preparation 211
The Basic Button 213
Text Input 218
Multiple Fields 226
Validations 230
Async Persistence 241
Vuex 248
Form Modules 261

VII - Routing **263**
What is routing? 263
URL 263
Single-page applications 265
Basic Vue Router 267
Dynamic Route Matching 290
The Server API 294
Starting point of the app 297
Integrating `vue-router` 300
Supporting authenticated routes 328
Implementing login 333
Vue `watch` 341
Navigation Guards 348
Recap and further reading 354

VIII - Unit Testing **355**
End-to-end vs. Unit Testing 355
Testing tools 356
Testing a basic Vue component 359
Setup 359
Testing `App` 364
`vue-test-utils` 371
More assertions for `App.vue` 375
Writing tests for a weather app 390
Store 427
Further reading 431

Book Revision

Revision 5

Bug Reports

If you'd like to report any bugs, typos, or suggestions just email us at: **vue@fullstack.io**.

For further help dealing with issues, refer to "How to Get the Most Out of This Book".

Be notified of updates via Twitter

If you'd like to be notified of updates to the book on Twitter, follow us at @fullstackio[1].

We'd love to hear from you!

Did you like the book? Did you find it helpful? We'd love to add your face to our list of testimonials on the website! Email us at: `vue@fullstack.io`.

[1] https://twitter.com/fullstackio

Foreword

Front-end web development has become astoundingly complex. If you've never used a modern JavaScript framework, building your first app that just displays "Hello" can take a whole week! That might sound ridiculous, but most frameworks assume knowledge of the terminal, advanced JavaScript, and tools such as the Node Package Manager (NPM), Babel, Webpack, and sometimes more.

Vue, refreshingly, *doesn't* assume. We call it the "progressive" JavaScript framework because it scales *down* as well as it scales up. If your app is simple, you can use Vue just like jQuery - by dropping in a `<script>` tag. But as your skills and needs grow more advanced, Vue grows with you to make you more powerful and productive.

Chris Fritz - Vue Core Team

Hassan provides a catalyst for that growth in this book. Through project-driven learning, he'll guide you from the simplest examples through the necessary skills for large-scale, enterprise applications. Along the way, you'll learn not only how to solve a variety of problems with Vue, but also the concepts and tools that have become industry standards – no matter what framework you use.

Welcome to the community, have fun, and enjoy the Vue!

– Chris Fritz, @chrisvfritz[2], Vue Core Team

[2]https://twitter.com/chrisvfritz

How to Get the Most Out of This Book

Overview

This book aims to be the **single most useful resource** on learning Vue.js. By the time you're done reading this book, you (and your team) will have everything you need to build reliable, powerful Vue applications.

Vue is built on the premise of simplicity by being designed from the ground up to be incrementally adoptable. After the first few chapters, you'll have a solid understanding of Vue's fundamentals and will be able to build a wide array of rich, interactive web apps with the framework.

But beyond Vue's core, there are tools and libraries that exist in the Vue ecosystem that's often needed to build real-world production scale applications. Things like client-side routing between pages, managing complex state, and heavy API interaction at scale.

This book can be broken down into two parts.

In Part I, we cover all the fundamentals with a progressive, example-driven approach. You'll first **introduce Vue through a Content Delivery Network (CDN)** before moving towards building within Webpack bundled applications. You'll gain a grasp of **handling user interaction**, **working with single-file components**, **understanding simple state management**, and **how custom events work**.

We bookend the first part by introducing Vuex and how Vuex is integrated to manage overall application data architecture.

Part II of this book moves into more **advanced concepts** that you'll often see used in large, production applications. We'll **integrate Vuex to a server-persisted app**, **manage rich forms**, build a multi-page app that uses **client-side routing**, and finally explore how **unit tests** can be written with Vue's official unit testing library.

First, know that you do not need to read this book linearly from cover-to-cover. **However**, we've ordered the contents of the book in a way we feel fits the order you should learn the concepts. Some sections in Part II assume you've acquired certain fundamental concepts from Part I. As a result, we encourage you to learn all the concepts in Part I of the book first before diving into concepts in Part II.

Second, keep in mind this package is more than just a book - it's a course complete with example code for every chapter. Below, we'll tell you:

- how to approach **the code examples** and
- **how to get help** if something goes wrong

Vue 2.x

In Sept. 2016[3], the Vue framework was rewritten and released as version 2.0. Vue 2.0 introduced new concepts such as the Virual DOM, render functions, and server-side rendering capabilities. In addition, version 2.0 was rewritten to provide significant performance improvements over v1.

This book covers, and will always cover, the latest release of Vue - **which is currently labelled as version 2.x**.

Running Code Examples

This book comes with a library of runnable code examples. The code is available to download from the same place where you purchased this book.

If you have any trouble finding or downloading the code examples, email us at **vue@fullstack.io**.

Webpack projects

For Webpack-bundled projects, we use the program `npm`[4] to run examples. You can install the application dependencies with:

```
npm install
```

And boot apps with one of the following commands:

```
npm run start
```

or

```
npm run dev
```

With every chapter, we'll reiterate the commands necessary to install application dependancies and boot example code.

After running `npm run start` or `npm run dev`, you will see some output on your screen that will tell you what URL to open to view your app.

If you're unfamiliar with `npm`, we cover how to get it installed in the "Setting Up" section in the second chapter.

If you're ever unclear on how to run a particular sample app, checkout the `README.md` in that project's directory. Every Webpack bundled sample project contains a `README.md` that will give you the instructions you need to run each app.

[3] https://medium.com/the-vue-point/vue-2-0-is-here-ef1f26acf4b8

[4] https://www.npmjs.com/

Direct `<script>` Include

For simpler examples, we've resorted to directly including the Vue library from a Content Delivery Network (CDN) to get the app up and running as fast as possible.

In this book, applications that introduce Vue from a CDN often consist of a single HTML file (`index.html`) for markup and a single JS file (`main.js`) for all Vue code. With these examples, we'll be able to run the app by opening the `index.html` file in our browser (e.g. right click `index.html` file and select `Open With > Google Chrome`). Since the Vue library is hosted externally in these cases, **these examples will require your machine to be connected to the internet**.

Code Blocks and Context

The majority of code blocks in this book is pulled from a **runnable code example** which you can find in the sample code. For example, here is a code block pulled from the first chapter:

upvote/app_5/main.js

```
new Vue({
  el: '#app',
  data: {
    submissions: Seed.submissions
  },
  computed: {
    sortedSubmissions () {
      return this.submissions.sort((a, b) => {
        return b.votes - a.votes
      });
    }
  },
  components: {
    'submission-component': submissionComponent
  }
});
```

Notice that the header of this code block states the path to the file which contains this code: `upvote/app_5/main.js`.

Certain code examples will resemble building blocks to get to a certain point and thus may not reflect a code block directly from the sample code. If you ever feel like you're missing the context for a code example, open up the full code file using your favorite text editor. **This book is written with the expectation that you'll also be looking at the example code alongside the manuscript.**

For example, we often need to `import` libraries to get our code to run. In the early chapters of the book we show these `import` statements, because it's not clear where the libraries are coming from otherwise. However, the later chapters of the book are more advanced and they focus on *key concepts* instead of repeating boilerplate code that was covered earlier in the book. **If at any point you're not clear on the context, open up the code example on disk**.

Code Block Numbering

In this book, we mostly build larger examples in steps. If you see a file being loaded that has a numeric suffix, that generally means we're building up to something bigger.

For instance, the code block above has the file path: `upvote/app_5/main.js`. When you see the `-N.js` syntax, that means we're building up to a final version of the file. You can jump into that file and see the state of all the code at that particular stage.

Instruction for Windows users

> All the code in this book has been tested on a Windows machine. If you have any issues running the code on Windows, send us an email[5] and we'll try to help you get it resolved.

Ensure Node.js and npm are installed

If you're on a Windows machine and have yet to do any web development on it, you can install the Node.js Windows Installer from the Node.js[6] website. With Node.js (and npm) appropriately installed, you should be able to start the Webpack-bundled Node.js projects in the book as expected.

See this tutorial[7] for installing Node.js and npm on Windows.

Getting Help

While we've made every effort to be clear, precise, and accurate you may find that when you're writing your code you run into a problem.

Generally, there are three types of problems:

- A "bug" in the book (e.g. how we describe something is wrong)
- A "bug" in our code

[5] vue@fullstack.io

[6] http://nodejs.org

[7] http://blog.teamtreehouse.com/install-node-js-npm-windows

- A "bug" in your code

If you find an inaccuracy in how we describe something, or you feel a concept isn't clear, email us! We want to make sure that the book is both accurate and clear.

Similarly, if you've found a bug in our code we definitely want to hear about it.

If you're having trouble getting your own app working (and it isn't *our* example code), this case is a bit harder for us to handle. If you're still stuck, we'd still love to hear from you.

Emailing Us

If you're emailing us asking for technical help, here's what we'd like to know:

- What revision of the book are you referring to?
- What operating system are you on? (e.g. Mac OS X 10.13.2, Windows 95)
- Which chapter and which example project are you on?
- What were you trying to accomplish?
- What have you tried already?
- What output did you expect?
- What actually happened? (Including relevant log output.)

The **absolute best way to get technical support** is to send us a short, self-contained example of the problem. Our preferred way to receive this would be for you to send us a Plunkr link by using this URL[8] as a template.

That URL contains a runnable, boilerplate Vue app. If you can copy and paste your code into that project, reproduce your error, and send it to us **you'll greatly increase the likelihood of a prompt, helpful response**.

When you've written down these things, email us at **vue@fullstack.io**. We look forward to hearing from you.

Get excited!

Writing web apps with Vue is *fun*. And by using this book, **you're going to learn how to build real Vue apps** fast. (Much faster than spending hours parsing out-dated blog posts.)

If you've written client-side JavaScript before or used existing JavaScript frameworks, you'll find Vue refreshingly intuitive. If this is your first serious foray into the front-end, you'll be *blown away* at how quickly you can create something worth sharing.

So hold on tight - you're about to become really proficient with Vue, and have a lot of fun along the way. Let's dig in!

---

[8]http://bit.ly/2orvQcd

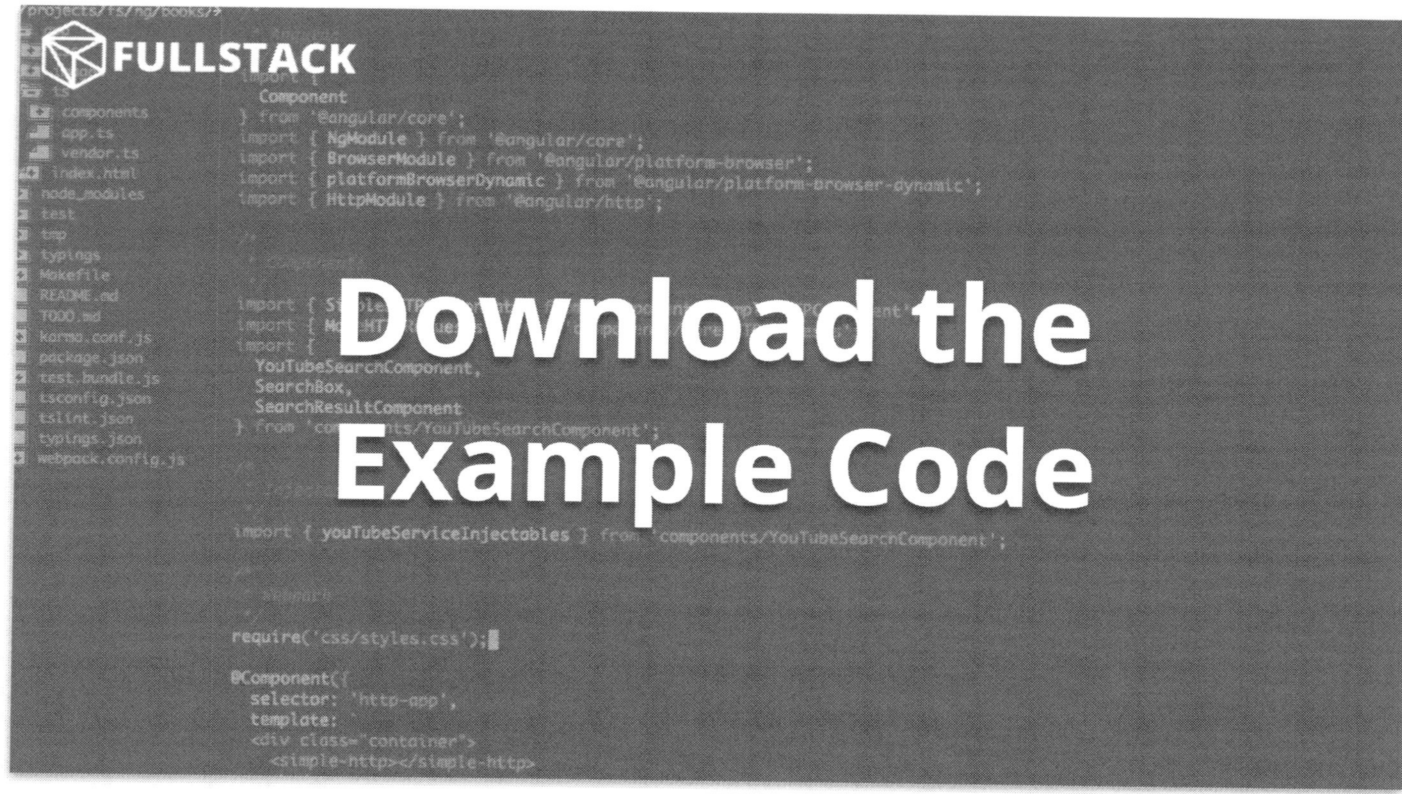

This book contains several example apps and code samples. Because you purchased the paperback version you can **download this code for free** at our website.

URL	https://fullstack.io/vue/code/
BOOK SERIAL CODE	`AMZ-82AJ`

To download the code, visit the URL above and enter your email and serial code and we'll email you the code download.

Learn more at: fullstack.io/vue/code

DOWNLOAD

I - Your first Vue.js Web Application

Building UpVote!

On our first step to learning Vue, we're going to build a simple voting application (named UpVote!) that takes inspiration from popular social feed websites like Reddit[10] and Hacker News[11].

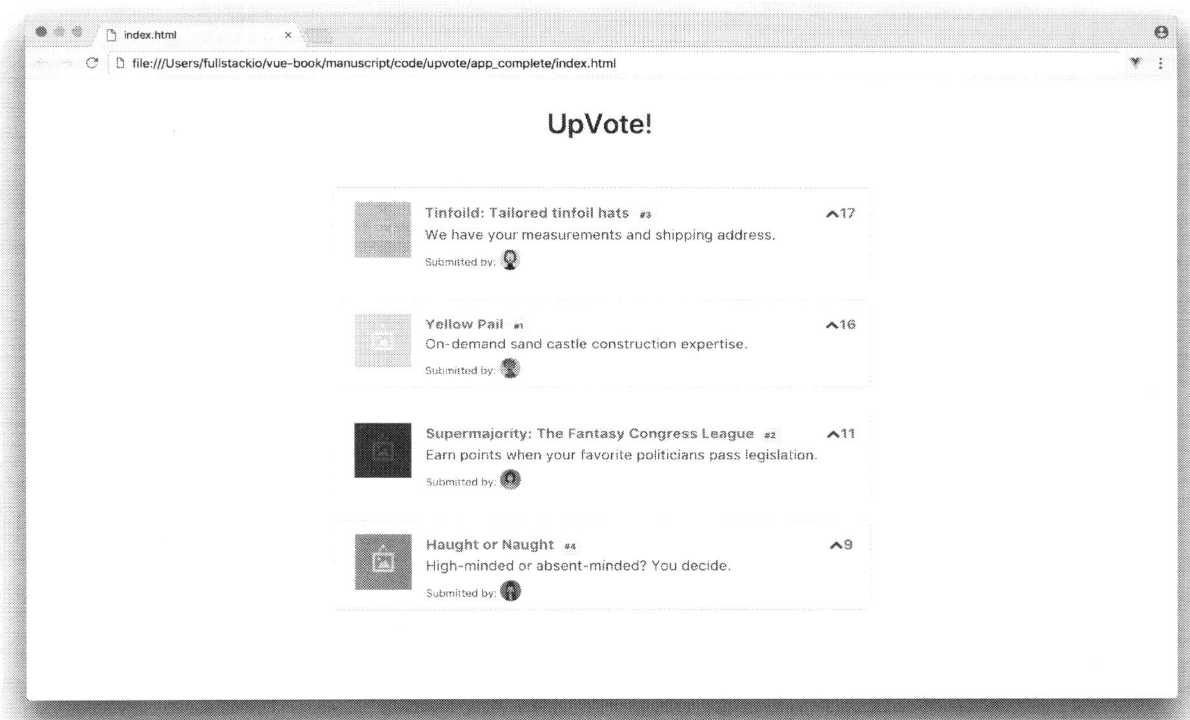

Completed version of the app

UpVote! focuses on displaying a list of submissions that users can vote on. Each submission will present some information about itself like an image, title, and description. All submissions are sorted instantaneously by number of votes. The up-vote icon in each submission will allow users to increase vote numbers and subsequently rearrange submission layout.

With UpVote!, we'll become familiar with how Vue approaches front-end development by understanding the basic fundamentals associated with the library. By the end of the chapter we'll be well

[10]https://reddit.com

[11]https://hackernews.com

on our way to building dynamic front-end interfaces thanks to Vue's simplicity!

Development environment setup

Code editor

Regardless of experience, whenever developing for the web, we'll need a code editor to write our application (this is true for all code in this book). It's most important to be comfortable with your code editor, so if you have one you like, stick with it. If not, we recommend Atom[12], Sublime Text 3[13], or Visual Studio Code[14].

Development Environment

For this chapter, we'll focus on getting our Vue app up and running as fast as possible, so we'll simply introduce Vue through a Content Delivery Network (CDN). We'll take a deeper look into installing all the necessary libraries for our development environment in the next chapter.

Browser

We highly recommend using the Google Chrome Web Browser[15] to develop Vue apps since we'll be using the Chrome developer toolkit[16] throughout this book. To follow along with our development and debugging, we recommend installing Chrome, if not installed already.

With Chrome, Vue provides an incredibly useful extension, Vue.js devtools[17] that simplifies debugging of Vue applications. We'll be using the devtools at separate points throughout the book so we encourage you to install it as well.

Note: With certain chapters in this book (like this chapter for example), we'll be working with applications opened via `file://` protocol. To make the Vue devtools work for these pages, you'll need to check "Allow access to file URLs" for the extension in Chrome's extension manager:

---

[12] http://atom.io

[13] https://www.sublimetext.com/

[14] https://code.visualstudio.com/

[15] https://www.google.com/chrome/

[16] https://developers.google.com/web/tools/chrome-devtools/

[17] https://github.com/vuejs/vue-devtools

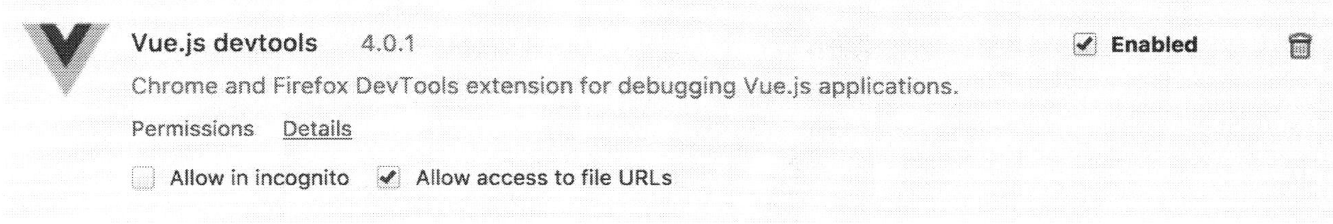

Allow access to file URLs

JavaScript ES6/ES7

JavaScript is the language of the web. It runs on many different browsers, including Google Chrome, Firefox, Safari, Microsoft Edge, and Internet Explorer. Different browsers have different JavaScript interpreters which execute JavaScript code.

Its widespread adoption as the Internet's client-side scripting language led to the formation of a standards body which manages its specification. The specification is called **ECMAScript** or ES.

The 5th edition of the specification is called ES5. We think of ES5 as a "version" of the JavaScript programming language. Finalized in 2009, ES5 was adopted by all major browsers within a few years.

The 6th edition of JavaScript is referred to as ES6. Finalized in 2015, the latest versions of major browsers are still finishing adding support for ES6 as of 2017. ES6 provides a significant update. It contains a whole host of new features for JavaScript, almost two dozen in total. JavaScript written in ES6 is tangibly different than JavaScript written in ES5.

ES7, a much smaller update that builds on ES6, was ratified in June 2016. ES7 contains only two new features.

To take advantage of the future versions of JavaScript, we want to write our code in ES6/ES7 today. We'll also want our JavaScript to run on older browsers until they fade out of widespread use.

This book is written using the JavaScript ES7 version. As ES6 ratified a majority of these new features, we'll commonly refer to these new features as ES6 features.

ES6 is sometimes referred to as ES2015, the year of its finalization. ES7, in turn, is often referred to as ES2016.

Getting started

Sample Code

All the code examples/snippets contained in this chapter (and all the other chapters) are available in the code package that came with the book. In the code package we'll see completed versions of the apps as well as boilerplates to help us get started. Each chapter provides detailed instruction on how to follow along on our own.

While coding along with the book is not necessary, we highly recommend doing so. Playing around with examples and sample code will help solidify and strengthen understanding of new concepts.

Previewing the application

We'll begin this chapter by taking a look at a working implementation of the UpVote! app.

Let's open up the sample code that came with the book and locate the `upvote/` folder with our machines file navigator (Finder for OS X or Windows Explorer on Windows) or through our code editor (e.g. Sublime). By opening the `upvote/` folder, we'll see all the sub-directories contained within the sample app:

```
upvote
    app/
    app_1/
    app_2/
    app_3/
    app_4/
    app_5/
    app_complete/
    public/
```

We've included each version of the app as we build it up throughout this chapter (`app_1/`, `app_2/`, etc). Each code block in this chapter references which app version it is contained within. We can copy and paste longer code insertions from these app versions into our local `app/` folder, the starting point of our application.

The `public/` sub-folder hosts all the images and custom styles we'll use within our application.

`app_complete` represents the completed state of our application. Opening the `app_complete` folder, we'll see there are just three files located inside:

```
app_complete
    index.html
    main.js
    seed.js
```

We can see the running application by right clicking on the `index.html` file and selecting `Open With > Google Chrome`.

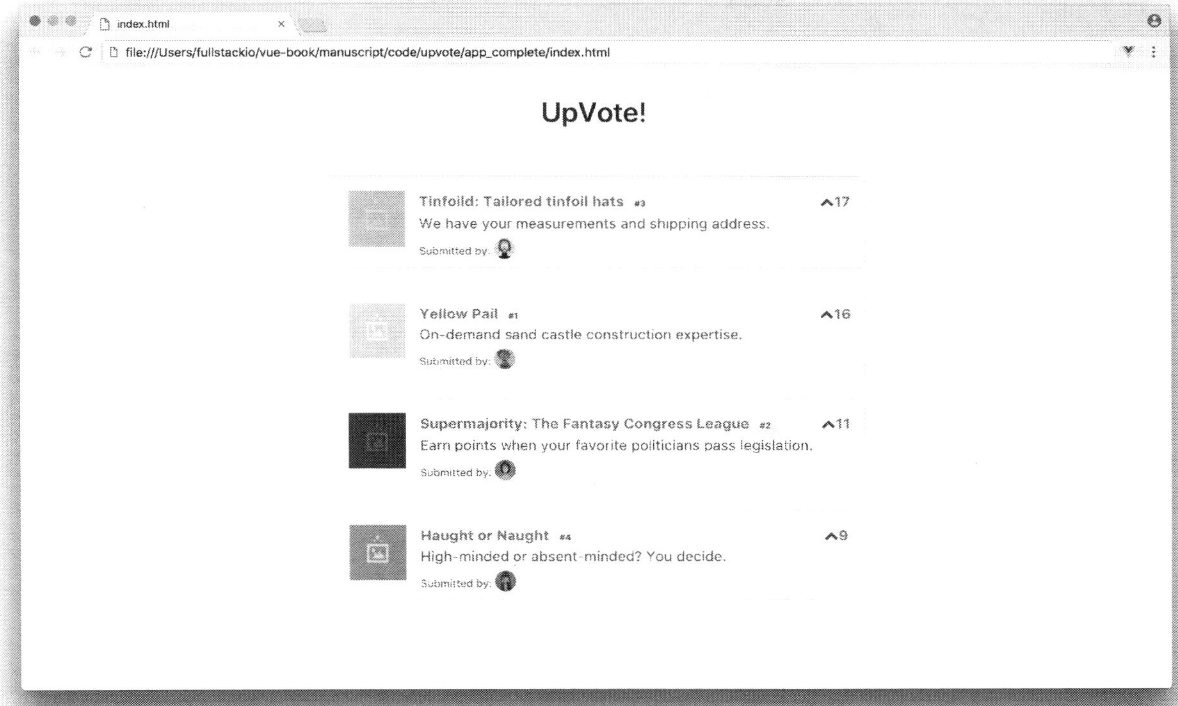

Completed version of the app

Notice how the submissions are all sorted from highest to lowest number of votes. The application will keep the posts sorted by number of votes, moving them around as the votes change *without* reloading the page.

Prepare the app

Let's begin building the application. We're going to be working entirely from the `app/` directory. By opening the files within `app/` in a text editor, we'll see some boilerplate code contained in the `index.html` and `seed.js` files, while `main.js` is left blank.

Let's begin by looking inside the `index.html` file:

upvote/app/index.html

```
<!DOCTYPE html>
<html>

<head>
  <link rel="stylesheet"
    href="https://cdnjs.cloudflare.com/ajax/libs/bulma/0.5.3/css/bulma.css">
  <link rel="stylesheet"
    href="https://use.fontawesome.com/releases/v5.0.6/css/all.css">
  <link rel="stylesheet"
    href="../public/styles.css" />
</head>

<body>
  <div id="app">
    <h2 class="title has-text-centered dividing-header">UpVote!</h2>
  </div>

  <script src="https://unpkg.com/vue"></script>
  <script src="./seed.js"></script>
  <script src="./main.js"></script>
</body>

</html>
```

In our `<head>` tag, there are three stylesheet dependancies we've included in our application:

upvote/app/index.html

```
<head>
  <link rel="stylesheet"
    href="https://cdnjs.cloudflare.com/ajax/libs/bulma/0.5.3/css/bulma.css">
  <link rel="stylesheet"
    href="https://use.fontawesome.com/releases/v5.0.6/css/all.css">
  <link rel="stylesheet"
    href="../public/styles.css" />
</head>
```

We've introduced Bulma[18] as our applications CSS framework, Font Awesome[19] for icons, and our own `styles.css` file that lives in our `public` folder.

[18]http://bulma.io/

[19]http://fontawesome.io/

For this project, we're using Bulma[20] for styling.

Bulma is a CSS framework, much like Twitter's popular Bootstrap[21] framework. It provides us with a grid system and some simple styling. We don't need to know Bulma in-depth in order to go through this chapter (or this book).

We'll always provide all the styling code that is needed. At some point, it's a good idea to check out the Bulma docs[22] to get familiar with the framework and explore how to use it in other projects we'll build in the future.

The heart of our application lives in the few lines within our `<body>` tag which currently looks like this:

upvote/app/index.html

```
<div id="app">
  <h2 class="title has-text-centered dividing-header">UpVote!</h2>
</div>
```

The `class` attributes refer to CSS styles and are safe to ignore in the context of our application. Not paying attention to those, we can see we have a title for the page (`h2`) and a `<div>` element with an `id` of `app`.

The `<div>` element with the `id` of `app` is where our Vue application will be loaded and *attached* onto the template. In other words, our Vue application will be **mounted** on to this particular element.

The next few lines tells the browser which JavaScript files to load:

upvote/app/index.html

```
<script src="https://unpkg.com/vue"></script>
<script src="./seed.js"></script>
<script src="./main.js"></script>
```

The first `<script>` tag loads the latest version of Vue from a Content Delivery Network (CDN) at unpkg[23]. Using the CDN to load the Vue dependency is the simplest and quickest way to introduce Vue to an application.

[20]http://bulma.io/

[21]http://getbootstrap.com/

[22]http://bulma.io/documentation/overview/start/

[23]https://unpkg.com

A Content Delivery Network (CDN) is a system of services that deliver content to users based on their geographical location and the content delivery server. Using CDN's have the benefit of decreasing server load and providing faster loading times to users who've already downloaded the content.

Most CDNs are used to deliver static content like common JavaScript libraries, fonts, CSS files, etc. We've also introduced Bulma and Font Awesome through CDNs in our `<head>` tag.

The other two `<script>` tags reference the internal JavaScript files we'll write in the `./seed.js` and `./main.js` files.

Setting up the view

Now that we have a good understanding of our boilerplate code, we can start diving in and writing some code. Let's first set up a template for how a single submission would look like. We'll adapt Bulma's media object[24] as it represents a good starting point.

In our `index.html` we'll insert the following template block right below our `h2` title:

upvote/app_1/index.html

```
    <div class="section">
      <article class="media">
        <figure class="media-left">
          <img class="image is-64x64"
            src="../public/images/submissions/image-yellow.png">
        </figure>
        <div class="media-content">
          <div class="content">
            <p>
              <strong>
                <a href="#" class="has-text-info">Yellow Pail</a>
                <span class="tag is-small">#4</span>
              </strong>
              <br>
                On-demand sand castle construction expertise.
              <br>
              <small class="is-size-7">
                Submitted by:
                <img class="image is-24x24"
                  src="../public/images/avatars/daniel.jpg">
```

[24] http://bulma.io/documentation/layout/media-object/

```
          </small>
        </p>
      </div>
    </div>
    <div class="media-right">
      <span class="icon is-small">
        <i class="fa fa-chevron-up"></i>
        <strong class="has-text-info">10</strong>
      </span>
    </div>
  </article>
</div>
```

This template is a slight modification of Bulma's media object[25].

We've added an encompassing `<div>` element over an `<article>` template block. The `<article>` template block is the view for a single submission and has three child DOM elements:

- `<figure>` with `media-left` class which will display the main image of the submission and is positioned to the left.
- `<div>` with `media-content` class which displays the additional details of the submission such as the title, id, description, and avatar of the submitted user.
- `<div>` with `media-right` class which shows a `fa-chevron-up` icon alongside the submission's number of votes.

If we open our `app/index.html` in our Chrome Browser (right click and select `Open With > Google Chrome`), we will see our newly built submission.

[25]http://bulma.io/documentation/layout/media-object/

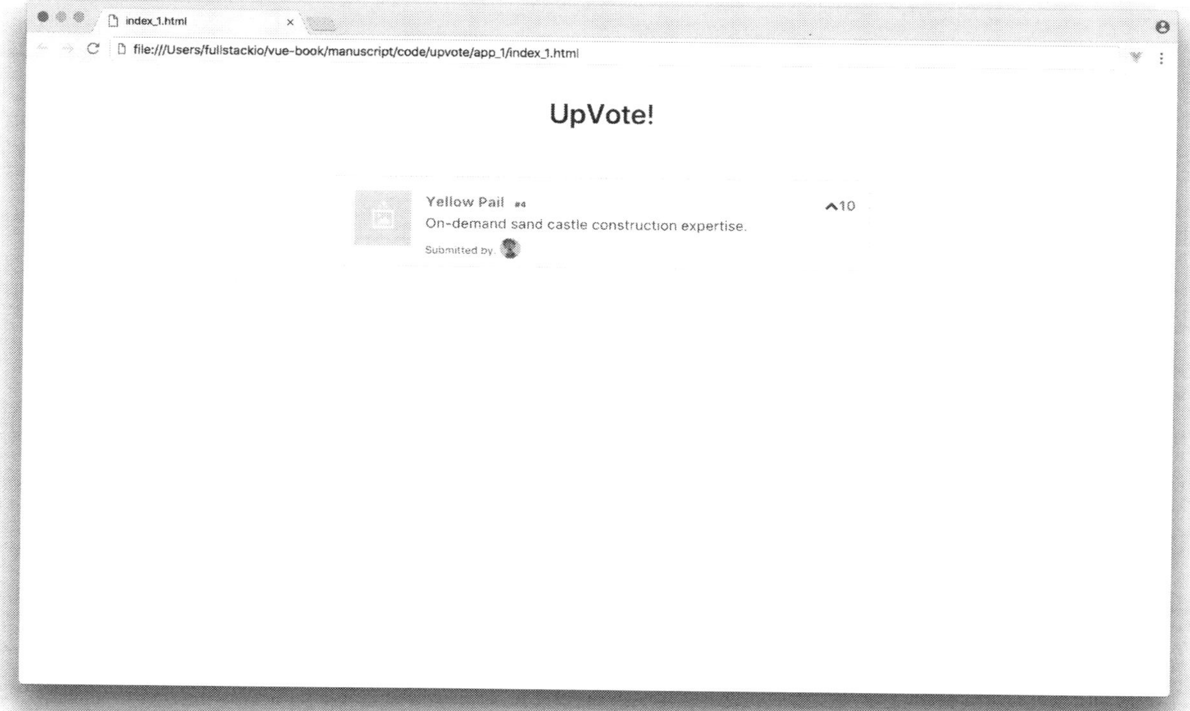

A single submission

Awesome. We won't write much more HTML markup than what we've just added.

While neat, at the moment our view is static. We've simply hard-coded the title, description and other details. To use this template in a meanigful way, we'll want to change it to be *reactive* (i.e. dynamically data-driven).

Making the view data-driven

Driving the template with data will allow us to dynamically render the view based upon the data that we give it. Let's familiarize ourselves with the applications data model.

The data model

Within our `app` directory, we've included a file called `seed.js`. `seed.js` contains sample data for a list of submissions (it *seeds* our application with data). The `seed.js` file contains a JavaScript object called `Seed.submissions`. `Seed.submissions` is an array of JavaScript objects where each represents a sample submission object:

```
const submissions = [
  {
    id: 1,
    title: 'Yellow Pail',
    description: 'On-demand sand castle construction expertise.',
    url: '#',
    votes: 16,
    avatar: '../public/images/avatars/daniel.jpg',
    submissionImage: '../public/images/submissions/image-yellow.png',
  },
  // ...
]
```

Each submission has a unique `id` and a series of properties including `title`, `description`, `votes`, etc.

Since we only have a single submission displayed in our view, we'll first focus on getting the data from a single submission object (i.e. `submissions[0]`) on to the template.

The Vue Instance

The Vue instance is the starting point of all Vue applications. A Vue instance accepts an **options** object which can contain details of the instance such as its template, data, methods, etc. Root level Vue instances allow us to reference the DOM with which the instance is to be mounted/attached to.

Let's see an example of this by setting up the Vue instance for our application. We'll write all our Vue code for the rest of this chapter inside the `main.js` file. Let's open `main.js` and create the Vue instance using the `Vue` function:

```
new Vue({
  el: '#app'
});
```

We've just specified the HTML element with the id of `app` to be the mounting point of our Vue application, by using the `el` option and providing it a string value of `#app`. Anywhere within this element can Vue JavaScript code now be used.

The Vue instance can also return data that needs to be handled within the view. This data must be specified within a `data` object in the instance. This is how we'll arrange the connection between the data in our `seed.js` file and the template view.

Let's update the instance by specifying a new `data` object. In the object, we'll include a `submissions` key that will have the same value as the `Seed.submissions` array:

upvote/app_2/main.js

```
new Vue({
  el: '#app',
  data: {
    submissions: Seed.submissions
  }
});
```

In the HTML template, we can now reference all submission data by accessing `submissions`.

The `Vue` object constructor is available on the global scope since we've included the `<script />` tag, that loads Vue, in our `index.html` file. Without including this tag, the `Vue` function won't be available and we'll be presented with a console error stating `Uncaught ReferenceError: Vue is not defined`.

With our Vue instance created and containing submission data, we can now work towards synchronizing data in the model to the view. In other words, we can now **data bind** the instance's data to the DOM.

Data binding

The simplest form of data binding in Vue is using the 'Mustache' syntax which is denoted by double curly braces `{{}}`. We'll apply this syntax to bind all the text within our HTML (e.g. title, description, etc.).

The 'Mustache' syntax however cannot be used in HTML attributes like `href`, `id`, `src` etc. Vue provides the native **`v-bind`** attribute (this is known as a Vue directive) to bind HTML attributes. We'll use this directive to update the `src` attributes in our template.

The Vue syntax may take some brief time to get used to, both within template manipulation as well as on the JavaScript side.

We'll gain familiarity on syntax/semantics as we continue to write code within this book.

Let's swap the hard-coded data in the template to now reference the content in the first object in the `submissions` array, `submissions[0]`. This will make the newly added template block now look like this:

upvote/app_2/index.html

```
<div class="section">
  <article class="media">
    <figure class="media-left">
      <img class="image is-64x64"
        v-bind:src="submissions[0].submissionImage">
    </figure>
    <div class="media-content">
      <div class="content">
        <p>
          <strong>
            <a v-bind:href="submissions[0].url" class="has-text-info">
              {{ submissions[0].title }}
            </a>
            <span class="tag is-small">#{{ submissions[0].id }}</span>
          </strong>
          <br>
            {{ submissions[0].description }}
          <br>
          <small class="is-size-7">
            Submitted by:
            <img class="image is-24x24"
              v-bind:src="submissions[0].avatar">
          </small>
        </p>
      </div>
    </div>
    <div class="media-right">
      <span class="icon is-small">
        <i class="fa fa-chevron-up"></i>
        <strong class="has-text-info">{{ submissions[0].votes }}</strong>
      </span>
    </div>
  </article>
</div>
```

If we've bound everything appropriately, we should see no change in our view (since the hard-coded information was the same content in our `submissions[0]` object).

Let's refresh our browser and see our template be rendered again.

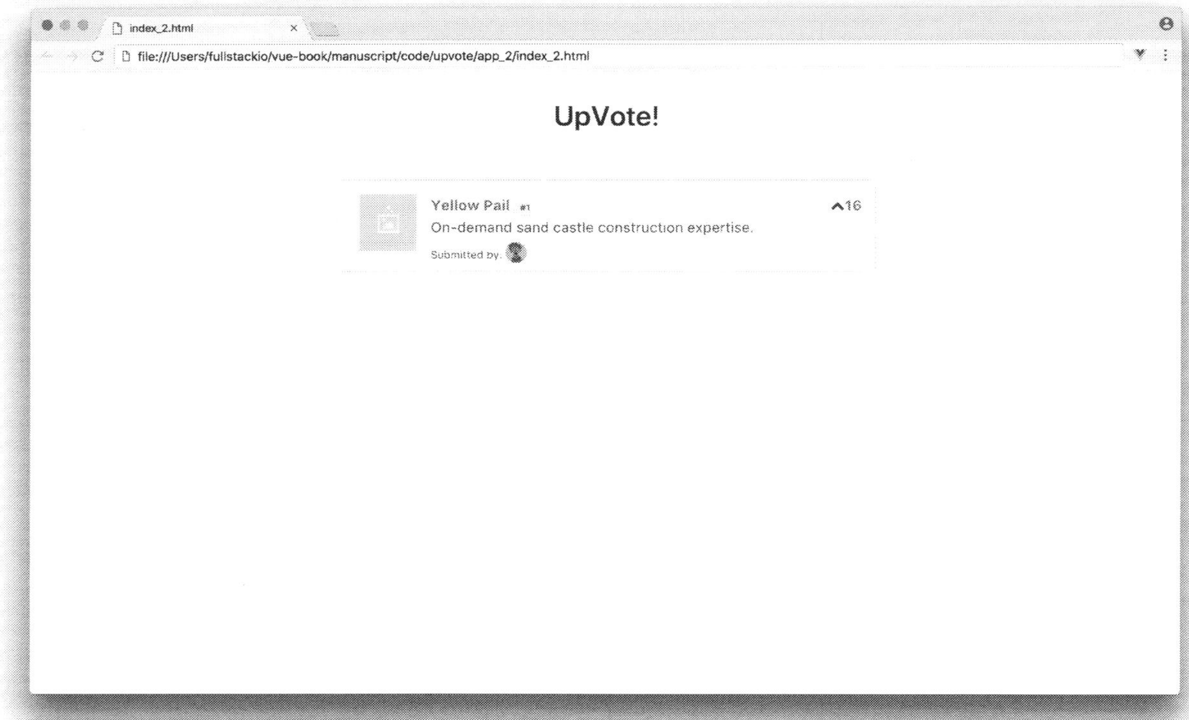

Submission with bound data

List rendering

We've successfully created our Vue instance and **bound** a single submission object in our view. Our next objective is to render all the submission objects to our view by displaying each submission object as a separate template block.

Since we're going to be rendering a *list* of submission objects, we're going to use Vue's native **`v-for`** directive.

`v-for` directive

The `v-for` directive is used to render a list of items based on a data source. In our case, we would like to render a submission post for each of the submission objects in our `Seeds.submission` array.

The `<article>` element in the `index.html` file, which is a standard HTML element, currently displays a single submission post:

```
<article class="media">
  <!-- Rest of the submission template -->
</article>
```

The `v-for` directive requires a specific syntax along the lines of `item in items`, where `items` is a data collection and `item` is an alias for every element that is being iterated upon:

In our template, since `submissions` is the data collection we'll be iterating over; `submission` would be an appropriate alias to use. We'll add the `v-for` statement to the `<article>` block like this:

```
<article v-for="submission in submissions" class="media">
  <!-- Rest of the submission template -->
</article>
```

key

It's common practice to specify a `key` attribute for every iterated element within a rendered `v-for` list. Vue uses the `key` attribute to create unique bindings for each node's identity.

To specify this uniqueness to each item in the list, we'll assign a `key` to every iterated submission. We'll use the `id` of a submission since a submission's `id` would never be equal to that of another submission. Because we're using dynamic values, we'll need to use `v-bind` to bind our key to the `submission.id`:

```
<article v-for="submission in submissions" v-bind:key="submission.id"
  class="media">
  <!-- Rest of the submission template -->
</article>
```

If there were any dynamic changes made to a `v-for` list *without* the `key` attribute, Vue will opt towards changing data within each element *instead* of moving the DOM elements accordingly. By specifying a unique `key` attribute to each iterated item, we're now telling Vue to reorder elements if needed.

The Vue docs[26] explains the importance of the `key` attribute in more detail.

In our template, let's now change the `submissions[0]` references and update it to use the iterated array instance variable `submission`:

upvote/app_3/index.html

```
    <div class="section">
      <article v-for="submission in submissions" v-bind:key="submission.id"
        class="media">
        <figure class="media-left">
          <img class="image is-64x64"
            v-bind:src="submission.submissionImage">
        </figure>
        <div class="media-content">
          <div class="content">
            <p>
              <strong>
                <a v-bind:href="submission.url" class="has-text-info">
                  {{ submission.title }}
                </a>
                <span class="tag is-small">#{{ submission.id }}</span>
              </strong>
              <br>
                {{ submission.description }}
              <br>
              <small class="is-size-7">
                Submitted by:
                <img class="image is-24x24"
                  v-bind:src="submission.avatar">
```

[26] https://vuejs.org/v2/guide/list.html#key

```
          </small>
        </p>
      </div>
    </div>
    <div class="media-right">
      <span class="icon is-small">
        <i class="fa fa-chevron-up"></i>
        <strong class="has-text-info">{{ submission.votes }}</strong>
      </span>
    </div>
  </article>
</div>
```

Refreshing our browser, we should now expect to see a list of submissions. This is due to the `v-for` directive now dynamically creating a submission `<article>` element for each submission in the seed file.

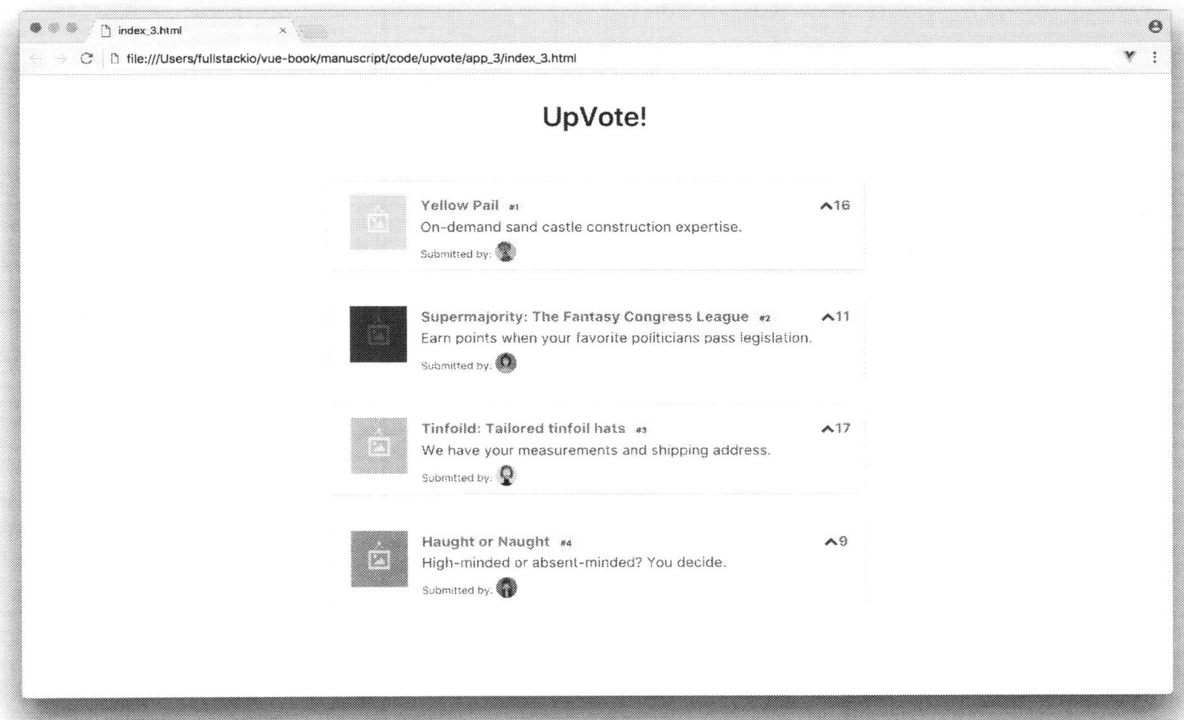

List of submissions

Sorting

In traditional social feeds (like Reddit[27] and Hacker News[28]), we often see number of votes as the measuring stick that controls the position of different submission posts. Submissions with the highest number of votes appear at the top of the web page with lower voted submissions being positioned at the bottom.

If we go back to our `v-for` statement in the template, we see an iteration of `submission in submissions`. `submissions` is the standard data object that is being used in our view, retrieved from our data source.

Wouldn't it be great if we can somehow specify an iteration like `submission in sortedSubmissions` where `sortedSubmissions` returns a *sorted* array of `submissions` all the time? This is where Vue's `computed` properties come in.

Computed properties

Computed properties are used to handle complex calculations of information that need to be displayed in the view. Below the `data` property in our Vue instance (back in the `main.js` file), we'll introduce a `computed` property `sortedSubmissions` that returns a sorted array of `submissions`:

```
new Vue({
  el: '#app',
  data: {
    submissions: Seed.submissions
  },
  computed: {
    sortedSubmissions () {
      return this.submissions.sort((a, b) => {
        return b.votes - a.votes
      });
    }
  }
});
```

Within a Vue instance, we're able to reference the instance's `data` object with `this`. Hence `this.submissions` refers to the `submissions` object we've specified in our instance's `data`. For sorting we're simply using the native Array object's sort method[29].

In our template where we have our `v-for` expression, we can now replace `submissions` with `sortedSubmissions` as the array to iterate over.

---

[27] https://reddit.com

[28] https://hackernews.com

[29] https://developer.mozilla.org/en-US/docs/Web/JavaScript/Reference/Global_Objects/Array/sort

```
<article v-for="submission in sortedSubmissions" v-bind:key="submission.id"
  class="media">
  <!-- Rest of the submission template -->
</article>
```

Refreshing our browser, we see the same list of submissions but now appropriately sorted by the number of votes!

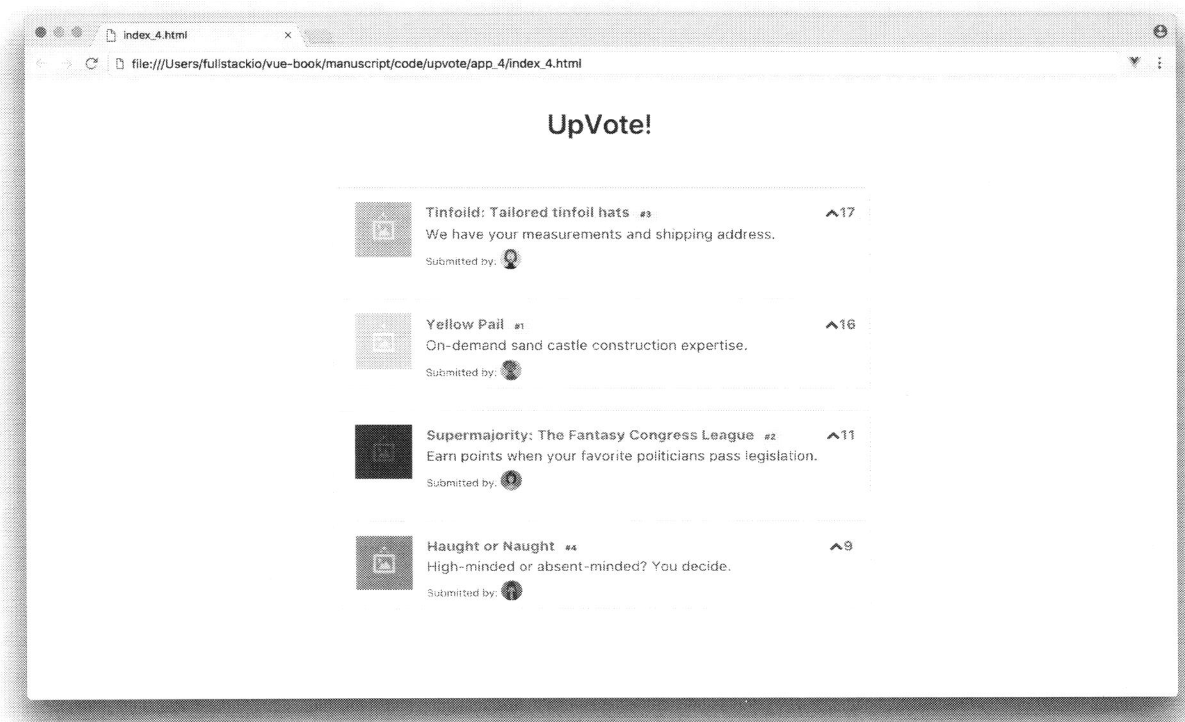

Sorted list of submissions

Event handling (our app's first interaction)

When the up-vote icon on each one of the submissions is clicked, we expect it to increase the `votes` attribute for that submission by one. To handle this interaction, we'll be using Vue's native **`v-on`** directive.

The `v-on` directive

The `v-on` directive is used to create event listeners within the DOM.

As all web browsers are event driven, we'll use these events to trigger interaction in our Vue application. For instance, in native JavaScript (i.e. without Vue), we can attach an event listener to a DOM object using the `addEventListener()` method.

const ele = document.getElementById('app'); ele.addEventListener('click', () => console.log('clicked'))

In Vue, we can use the `v-on:click` directive to implement a click handler. We can specify this click handler on an up-vote icon of a submission. We'll set this click event handler to call an `upvote(submission.id)` method whenever the up-vote icon is clicked. We'll pass in the `submission.id` as an argument to be used within the method. This updates the `div` element that encompasses the up-vote icon to this:

```
<div class="media-right">
  <span class="icon is-small" v-on:click="upvote(submission.id)">
    <i class="fa fa-chevron-up"></i>
    <strong class="has-text-info">{{ submission.votes }}</strong>
  </span>
</div>
```

Since we've specifed the click event, we now need to define the `upvote(submissionId)` method in our Vue instance.

A `methods` property exists in a Vue instance to allow us to define methods bound to that instance. Methods behave like normal JavaScript functions and are only evaluated when explicitly called. Below the `computed` property in our instance, let's introduce the `methods` property and the `upvote` method:

```
new Vue({
  el: '#app',
  data: {
    submissions: Seed.submissions
  },
  computed: {
    // ...,
  },
  methods: {
    upvote(submissionId) {
      const submission = this.submissions.find(
        submission => submission.id === submissionId
      );
      submission.votes++;
    }
  }
});
```

The up-voting logic involves using the native JavaScript `find()` method to locate the submission object with the `id` equal to the `submissionId` parameter. The `votes` attribute of that submission is then incremented by one.

Reactive state

We need to note an **important** aspect of Vue here. With a library like React, the above method implementation is problematic since state is often treated as *immutable*. State within Vue, on the other hand, is *reactive*.

Reactive state is one of the key differences that makes Vue unique. State (i.e. data) management is often intuitive and easy to understand since modifying state often directly causes the view to update.

We'll be seeing more and more on how Vue data responds reactively throughout the book. For now, keep in mind Vue has an unobtrusive system to how data is modified and the view reacts.

Our app is now responsive to user interaction. Let's save the `index.html` and `main.js` files, refresh the browser, and start clicking the up-vote icons.

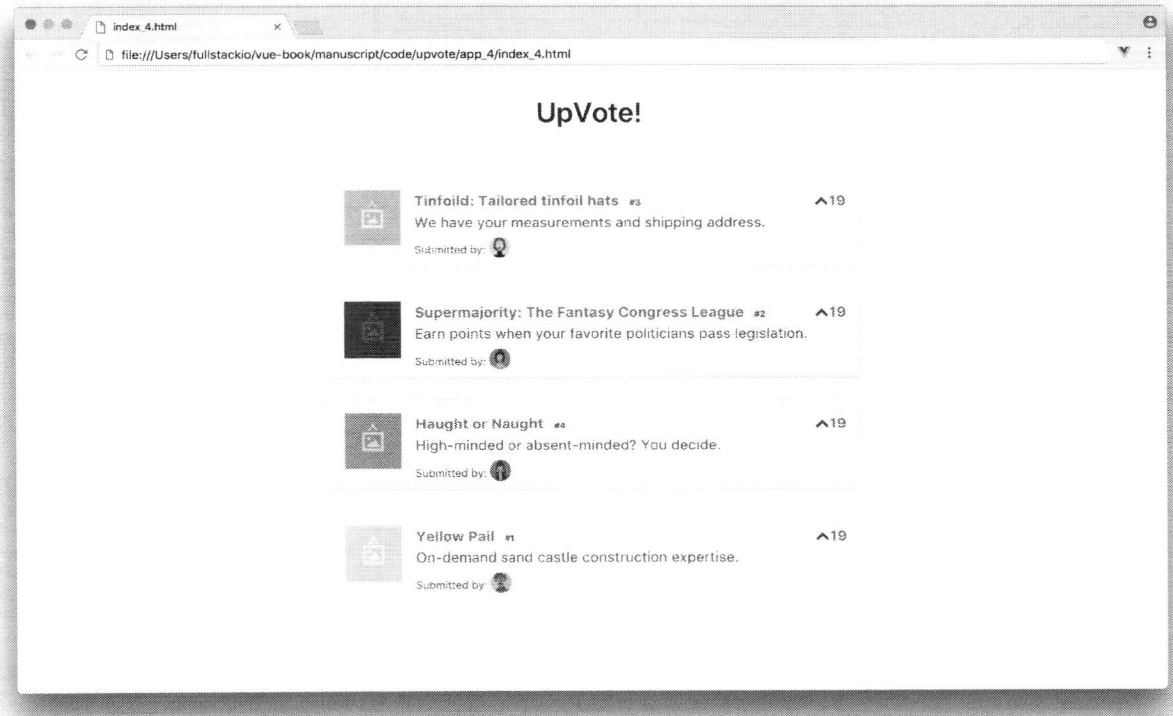

They work! Try up-voting a submission multiple times. Do you notice how it immediately jumps over other submissions with lower vote counts? This functionality works thanks to Vue's reactivity system.

As we up-vote a submission, we are directly modifying the `this.submissions` data array. Our computed property `sortedSubmissions` depends on `this.submissions`, so as the latter changes, so does the former.

Our view is reactive to `sortedSubmissions`. When changes happen to our computed property, our view re-renders to display that change!

Class bindings

Our application has implemented almost all the functionality we expected from the beginning.

Before we dive in and try to improve how our code is laid out, let's add a conditional class that displays a special blue border around a submission when said submission reaches a certain number of votes (let's say 20 votes).

We have the class `blue-border` already set up in our custom `styles.css` file. Our conditional class binding will basically dictate: the presence of the `blue-border` class depends on the truthiness of `submission.votes >= 20`. We'll use the `v-bind` directive to dynamically enable the class when the submission votes exceeds 20:

```
<article v-for="submission in sortedSubmissions"
  v-bind:key="submission.id"
  class="media"
  v-bind:class="{ 'blue-border': submission.votes >= 20 }">
  <!-- Rest of the submission template -->
</article>
```

Pretty simple huh? There's many ways to specify inline conditional class and style bindings with which we'll investigate deeper throughout the rest of the book!

Now, if we go ahead and up-vote a submission to twenty or more votes, we'll see a blue border appear.

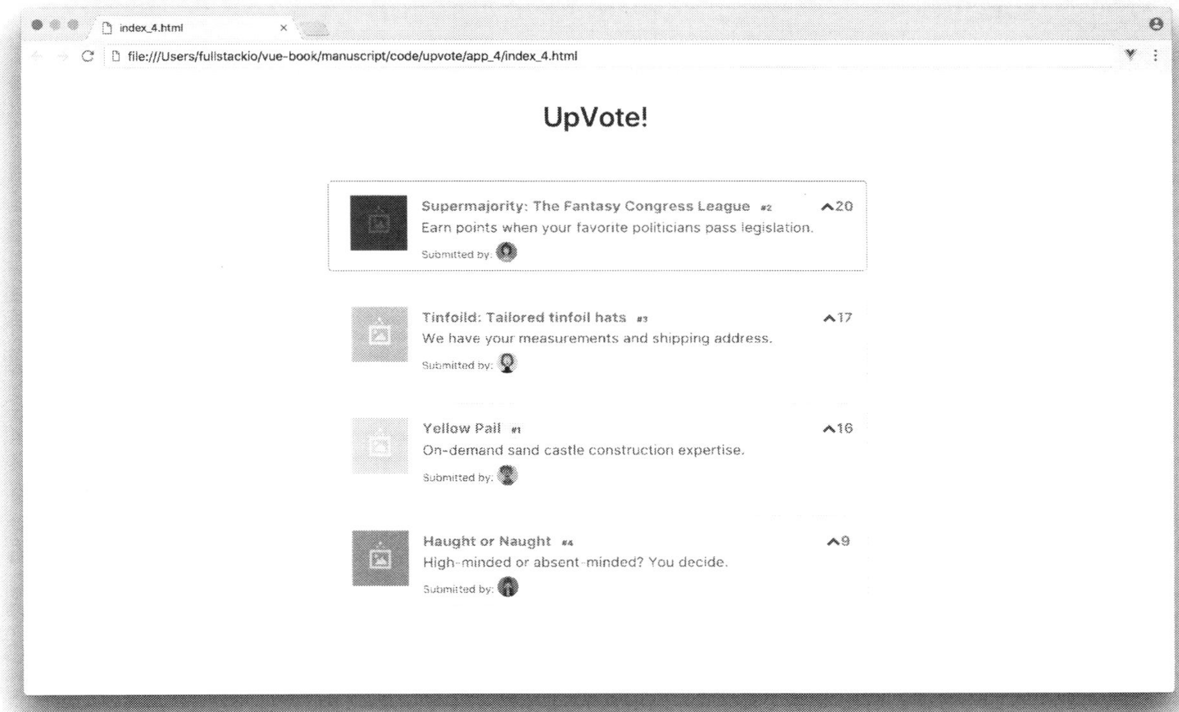

Yay! We've introduced all the features we initially had in mind for UpVote!. Our application is dynamically data-driven with external data, sorts all the submissions based on the number of votes, and listens for user interaction on up-voting.

Let's assume we had much larger plans on scaling the front end of UpVote!. New features could be added in like having a navigation header, a sidebar for submitting new submissions, a footer, etc. If we continue building our application the same way we've been going about it, we'll be introducing a lot more data/methods/properties to our Vue instance.

This will bloat our DOM, eventually making changes to our code unmanageable. This is where the concept of **isolated components** come in.

Components

Vue, like other modern-day JavaScript frameworks, provides the ability for users to create isolated components within their applications. **Reusability** and **maintainability** are some of the main reasons as to why components are especially important.

Components are intended to be **self-contained** modules since we can group markup (HTML), logic (JS) and even styles (CSS) within them. This allows for easier maintenance, especially when applications grow much larger in scale.

Let's create a new component for our application. As a result, we'll break apart the interface of our app into two separate entities:

- The parent component which encompasses all the separate submissions - this will be the existing Vue instance.
- The new submission component which represents a single submission.

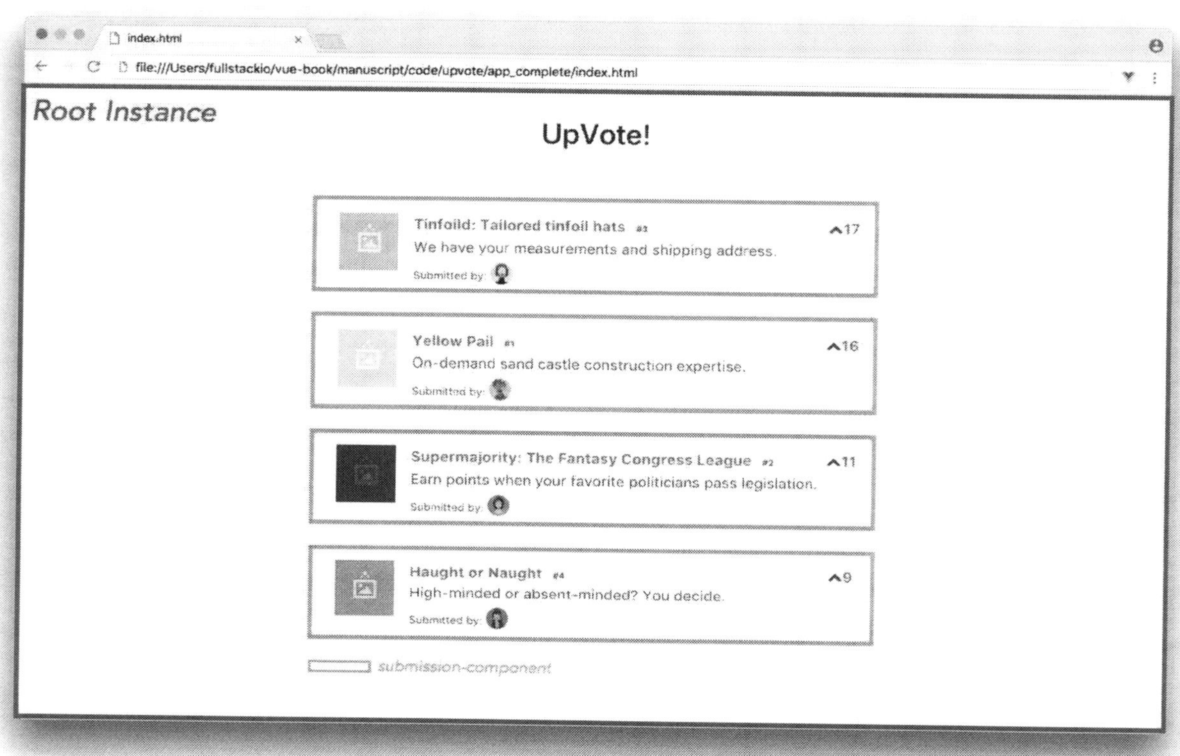

Our app's components

The standard method for creating a global Vue component is handled by using the `Vue.component` constructor method:

```
Vue.component('submission-component', {
    // options
});
```

Though this would work, we'd want our component properly defined within the scope of our application instance. Instead, let's assign our newly created `submission-component` to a constant variable and register it as part of the `component` option in our Vue instance.

In our `main.js` file, let's specify a `submissionComponent` object that references a new component. We'll declare this object right above the root Vue instance:

```
const submissionComponent = {

};

new Vue({
  // ...
});
```

template

Vue components *are* Vue instances. The majority of properties (except for a few root-specific options) that exist in a root Vue instance (`data`, `methods`, etc.) can exist in a component as well.

In Vue instances, a `template` option exists that allows us to define the template of that instance. The simplest way of defining a template is within strings. Here's an example:

```
const submissionComponent = {
  template: '<div>Hello World!</div>'
}
```

If we wanted to define a template over multiple lines, we'll have to use ES6's template literals[30] (specified with the use of backticks). This is because JavaScript doesn't allow strings to span over multiple lines.

```
const submissionComponent = {
  template:
  ` <div>
      Hello World!
    </div>`
}
```

We're specifying templates for a Vue application that *isn't* being precompiled. In the next chapter[31], we'll be exposed to a different way of defining component templates since that chapter's application will be precompiled during build.

In the `submissionComponent`, the `template` property will reflect all the items contained within a single submission. Let's update the `submissionComponent` to reflect this:

---

[30]https://developer.mozilla.org/en-US/docs/Web/JavaScript/Reference/Template_literals

[31]components

```
const submissionComponent = {
  template:
  `<div style="display: flex; width: 100%">
    <figure class="media-left">
      <img class="image is-64x64"
        v-bind:src="submission.submissionImage">
    </figure>
    <div class="media-content">
      <div class="content">
        <p>
          <strong>
            <a v-bind:href="submission.url" class="has-text-info">
              {{ submission.title }}
            </a>
            <span class="tag is-small">#{{ submission.id }}</span>
          </strong>
          <br>
            {{ submission.description }}
          <br>
          <small class="is-size-7">
            Submitted by:
            <img class="image is-24x24"
              v-bind:src="submission.avatar">
          </small>
        </p>
      </div>
    </div>
    <div class="media-right">
      <span class="icon is-small" v-on:click="upvote(submission.id)">
        <i class="fa fa-chevron-up"></i>
        <strong class="has-text-info">{{ submission.votes }}</strong>
      </span>
    </div>
  </div>`
};
```

There's a few things to address here.

1. The template of a component **must** be enclosed within a single root element. This is a **strict** limitation to declaring Vue templates. Because of this, we've wrapped everything within a `<div style="display: flex; width: 100%"></div>` element. We've added some additional styling to comply with this new root element.

2. The `submission` object in this template is currently `undefined`. When this component is declared, we're going have to pass data from the parent component (i.e. the root instance) down to this child component. We're going to use Vue **props** to pass data from the root instance to this component.
3. The `upvote()` click listener method needs to be mapped to a method within the `submissionComponent` for it to work. As a result, we're going to have to transfer the `upvote()` method from the Vue instance to this component.

Before we look into points (2) and (3), let's reference the newly created component in the DOM. In the `index.html` file; we'll first remove the submission template code within the `<article>` element. We'll then replace this inner content with a single `<submission-component>` element:

```
<article v-for="submission in sortedSubmissions"
  v-bind:key="submission.id"
  class="media"
  v-bind:class="{ 'blue-border': submission.votes >= 20 }">
  <submission-component></submission-component>
</article>
```

Our Vue instance currently doesn't recognize this `<submission-component>` element. In order to give the Vue instance awareness of our new component, we'll define it as a key in a `components` property of our Vue instance in the `main.js` file:

```
new Vue({
  // ...,
  components: {
    'submission-component': submissionComponent
  }
});
```

In the `components` options of the root Vue instance, we've mapped a `submission-component` declaration to the `submissionComponent` object.

Props

Vue gives us the ability to pass data from a parent component down to a child component with the help of **props**. In Vue, **props** are attributes that need to be given a value in the parent component and have to be explicitly declared in the child component. As a result, `props` can only flow in a single direction (parent to child), and never in the opposite direction (child to parent).

The `v-bind` directive is used to bind dynamic values (or objects) as props in a parent instance.

In the `index.html` file, we're going to pass both the iterated `submission` object and the `sortedSubmissions` array as `props` to `submission-component`. The `submission` object will be used in the template of the `submission-component` while `sortedSubmissions` will be used in the `upvote()` method of that component.

This makes our `<article>` element be updated to this:

upvote/app_5/index.html

```
<div class="section">
  <article v-for="submission in sortedSubmissions"
    v-bind:key="submission.id"
    class="media"
    v-bind:class="{ 'blue-border': submission.votes >= 20 }">
    <submission-component
      v-bind:submission="submission"
      v-bind:submissions="sortedSubmissions">
    </submission-component>
  </article>
</div>
```

We've set the `submission` object to a prop of the same name and we've set the `sortedSubmissions` array to a prop labelled as `submissions`.

For a child component to use the props provided to it, it needs to explictly declare the props it receives with the `props` option. Let's introduce a `props` option in the `submissionComponent` object and specify the `submission` and `submissions` props being passed in:

```
const submissionComponent = {
  template:
  `
    // ...
  `,
  props: ['submission', 'submissions']
};
```

Now the `submission` object and the `submissions` array can safely be used within the template of `submissionComponent`. All that's left for us to do is migrate the `upvote()` component from the Vue instance to the `submissionComponent` object.

This will update the `submissionComponent` object to:

upvote/app_5/main.js

```
const submissionComponent = {
  template:
  ` <div style="display: flex; width: 100%">
      <figure class="media-left">
        <img class="image is-64x64"
          v-bind:src="submission.submissionImage">
      </figure>
      <div class="media-content">
        <div class="content">
          <p>
            <strong>
              <a v-bind:href="submission.url" class="has-text-info">
                {{ submission.title }}
              </a>
              <span class="tag is-small">#{{ submission.id }}</span>
            </strong>
            <br>
              {{ submission.description }}
            <br>
            <small class="is-size-7">
              Submitted by:
              <img class="image is-24x24"
                v-bind:src="submission.avatar">
            </small>
          </p>
        </div>
      </div>
      <div class="media-right">
        <span class="icon is-small" v-on:click="upvote(submission.id)">
          <i class="fa fa-chevron-up"></i>
          <strong class="has-text-info">{{ submission.votes }}</strong>
        </span>
      </div>
    </div>`,
  props: ['submission', 'submissions'],
  methods: {
    upvote(submissionId) {
      const submission = this.submissions.find(
        submission => submission.id === submissionId
      );
      submission.votes++;
```

```
    }
  }
};
```

And the Vue instance will now look like the following:

upvote/app_5/main.js

```
new Vue({
  el: '#app',
  data: {
    submissions: Seed.submissions
  },
  computed: {
    sortedSubmissions () {
      return this.submissions.sort((a, b) => {
        return b.votes - a.votes
      });
    }
  },
  components: {
    'submission-component': submissionComponent
  }
});
```

If we save the `main.js` file and refresh our browser, everything should remain as is and all functionality should work as expected!

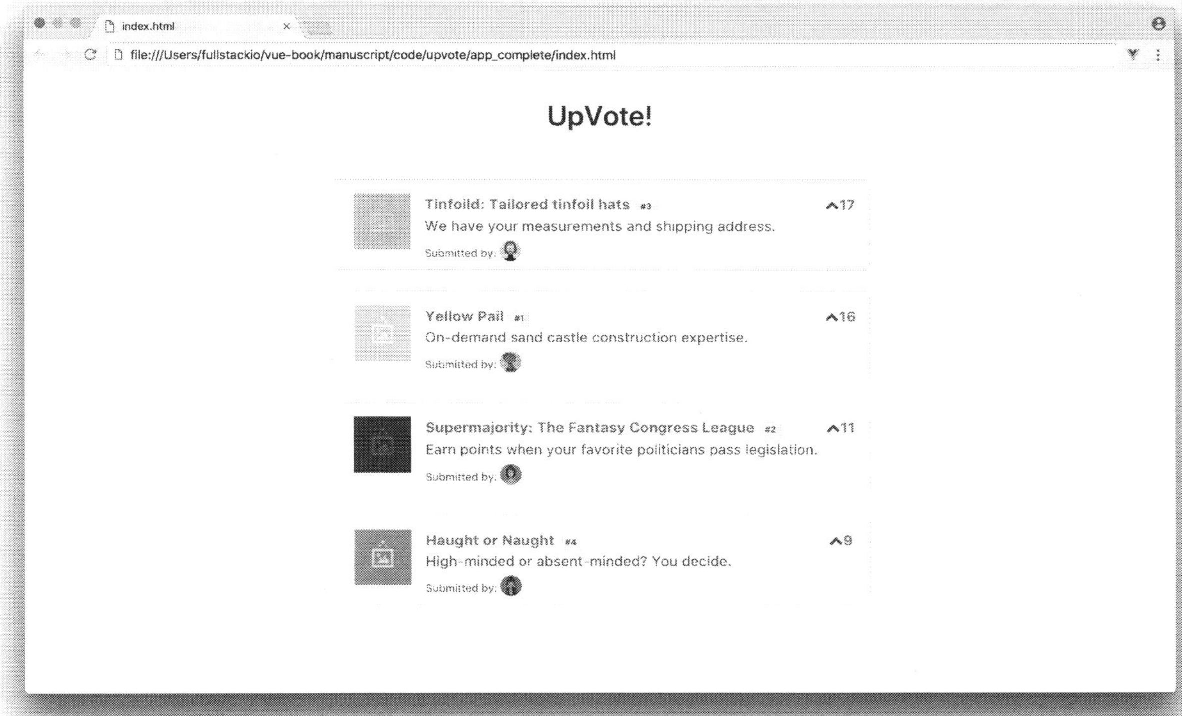

`v-bind` and `v-on` shorthand syntax

Before we conclude this chapter, let's discuss another feature that Vue provides.

The `v-` prefix in Vue directives is a visual indicator that a Vue template attribute is being used. For simplicity, Vue provides shorthands for the commonly used `v-bind` and `v-on` directives.

The `v-bind` directive can be shortened with the `:` symbol:

```
// the full syntax
<img v-bind:src="submission.submissionImage" />

// the shorthand syntax
<img :src="submission.submissionImage" />
```

And the `v-on` directive can be shortened with the `@` symbol:

```
// the full syntax
<span v-on:click="upvote(submission.id)"></span>

// the shorthand syntax
<span @click="upvote(submission.id)"></span>
```

This shorthand syntax is completely optional but allows us to use the `v-bind` and `v-on` directives without explicitly typing out the full syntax.

> For the rest of the book we'll stick to using the shorthand syntax for `v-bind` and the `v-on` directives.

For the UpVote! application, you'll be able to see the use of the shorthand syntax in the `upvote/app_-complete/` folder. **The rest of the code remains the same with the only changes replacing the `v-bind` and `v-on` syntax with `:` and `@` respectively**.

Congratulations!

We just wrote our first Vue app. We've gone through the easiest foray to getting started and there are plenty of powerful features we haven't covered yet. With this chapter, we've managed to understand the core fundamentals that we'll be building on throughout the book.

Recap

1. The Vue instance is the starting point of all Vue applications. The instance can have options like the `data`, `computed` and `methods` properties and is often mounted/attached to a DOM element.
2. The 'Mustache' syntax can be used for data binding. The `v-bind` directive is used for binding HTML attributes.
3. Vue directives such as `v-for` can be used to manipulate the template based on the data provided. The `v-on` directive is used as an event handler to listen to DOM events.
4. We think and organize our Vue apps with components.

Onward!

II - Single-file components

Introduction

In the last chapter we briefly covered how Vue lets us organize our app into components which can be used and manipulated in the view.

In this chapter, we'll be diving in deeper into building components with Vue. We'll investigate a pattern that we'll be be able to use to scale Vue apps from scratch. We'll be using this pattern to create an app interface that manages events within a weekly calendar.

In our weekly calendar app, a user can add, delete, and edit day to day events within a week. Each event corresponds to a particular task/to-do item that the user would like to keep track of:

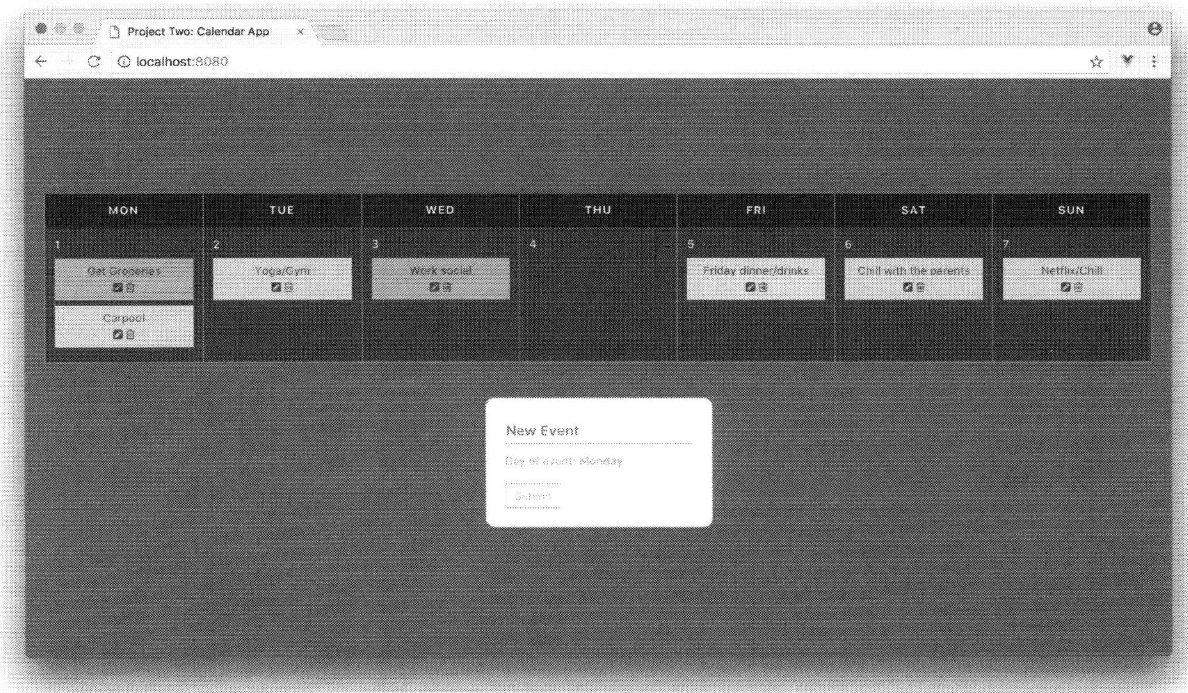

Setting up our development environment

Node.js and npm

For this project (and the majority of projects) in this book, we'll need to make sure we have a working Node.js[32] development environment along with the Node Package Manager (`npm`).

There are a couple different ways we can install Node.js so please refer to the Node.js website for detailed information: https://nodejs.org/download/[33].

It's also possible to install Node.js using a tool like nvm[34] or the n[35] tool. Using a package like these allow us to maintain multiple version of node in our development environment.

If you're on a Mac, your best bet is to install Node.js directly from the Node.js[36] website instead of through another package manager (like Homebrew). Installing Node.js via Homebrew is known to cause some issues.

If you're on a Windows machine, you would need to install Node.js through the Windows Installer from the Node.js[37] website.

The easiest way to verify if Node.js has been successfully installed is to check which version of Node.js is running. To do this, we'll open a terminal window and run the following command:

```
$ node -v
```

npm is installed as a part of Node.js. To check if npm is available within our development environment, we can list the version of our npm binary with:

```
$ npm -v
```

In either case, if a version number is not printed out and instead an error is emitted, make sure to download a Node.js installer that includes npm and ensure that the `PATH` is set appropriately.

[32]http://nodejs.org
[33]https://nodejs.org/download/
[34]https://github.com/creationix/nvm
[35]https://github.com/tj/n
[36]http://nodejs.org
[37]http://nodejs.org

Vue syntax highlighting

In this chapter, we'll be introducing Vue single-file components. These components allow us to write Vue code within a new file format - `.vue`. Depending on your code editor, you may need to install a syntax highlighting plugin to simplify the readability of these components. Here are some popular Vue code highlighting plugins for the following editors:

- Sublime Text: vue-syntax-highlight[38]
- Atom: language-vue-component[39]
- Vim: vim-vue[40]
- Visual Studio Code: Vetur[41]

Getting started

As with all chapters, we begin by making sure that we've downloaded the book's sample code and have it at the ready.

Previewing the app

Before we start writing any code, let's see a complete implementation of the app.

In the terminal, let's change into the `calendar_app` directory using the `cd` command:

```
$ cd calendar_app
```

We'll use npm to install all the application's dependencies. These dependencies allow us to write our application using ES6/ES7 as well as include the Vue library. Instead of using the CDN version of Vue, we'll embed the dependency into our application.

Let's install the applications' dependencies:

```
$ npm install
```

Now we can start the server using the `npm run dev` call (which starts the application in development mode):

---

[38]https://github.com/vuejs/vue-syntax-highlight

[39]https://atom.io/packages/language-vue-component

[40]https://github.com/posva/vim-vue

[41]https://marketplace.visualstudio.com/items?itemName=octref.vetur

```
$ npm run dev
```

Our browser will automatically launch with the URL `http://localhost:8080`. Spend a few minutes playing around with the app to get an understanding of what we'll be building.

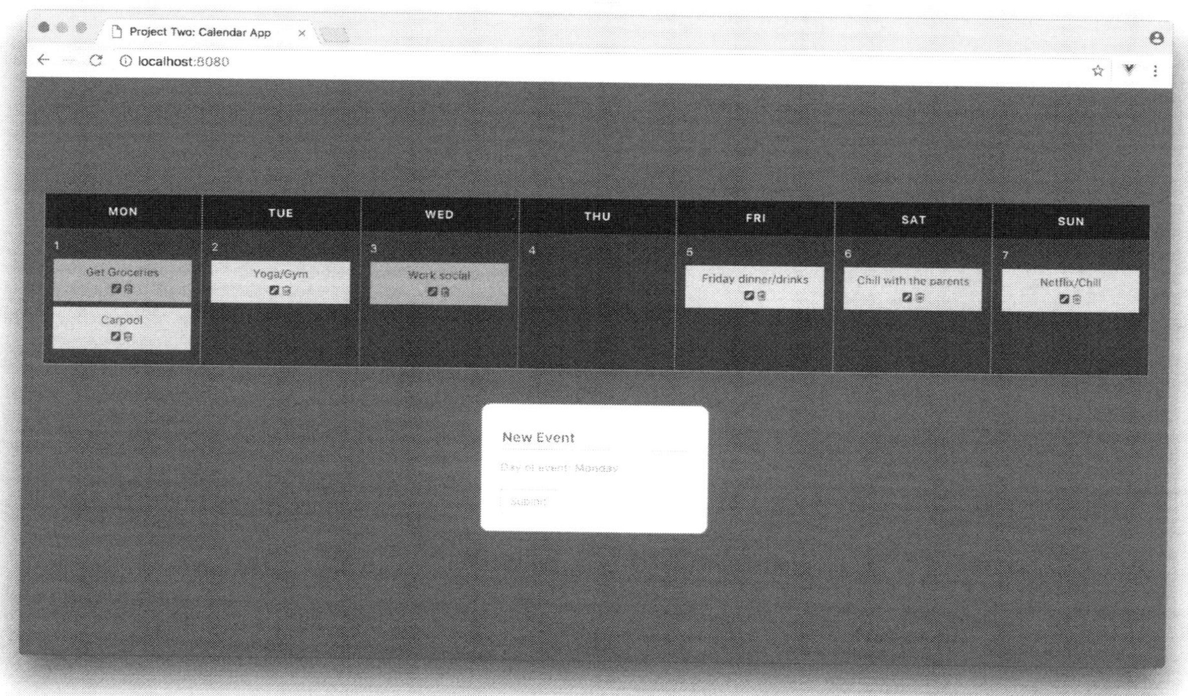

Prepare the app

In our terminal, let's run `ls` to see the project's layout:

```
$ ls
README.md
index.html
node_modules/
package.json
public/
src/
webpack.config.js
```

In addition, we have the hidden files `.babelrc` and `.gitignore` files in the project directory.

There are significant changes in the structure of this project as compared to our first app. We'll break down each file and directory in the section below.

If you're not familiar with Javascript Webpack projects, don't be deterred from continuing with this chapter. The configuration is good to understand but we'll only be working within the `src/` folder of the application.

`README.md`

All extra information/run steps are listed in the `README.md` file.

`index.html`

The `index.html` file is the root markup page of our application. This file is where we specify the external stylesheet dependencies as well as the DOM element where the Vue instance is to be mounted.

The `index.html` file:

calendar_app/index.html

```
<!DOCTYPE html>
<html lang="en">
  <head>
    <meta charset="utf-8">
    <title>Project Two: Calendar App</title>
    <link rel="stylesheet" href="./public/bulma/bulma.css">
    <link rel="stylesheet" href="./public/font-awesome/css/font-awesome.min.css">
  </head>
  <body>
    <div id="app"></div>
    <script src="/dist/build.js"></script>
  </body>
</html>
```

The `<script src="/dist/build.js"></script>` line within `index.html` dictates the bundled `build` file that our Webpack configuration provides, for the purpose of deployment.

`node_modules`

The `node_modules` directory refers to all the different JavaScript libraries that have been installed in our application with `npm install`.

package.json

The `package.json` file lists all the locally installed npm packages in our application for us to manage. The `scripts` portion dictates the `npm` commands that can be run in our application.

For our app, we'll be running `npm run dev` in our terminal to run our local server (`webpack-dev-server`). Thanks to the `--open` and `--hot` options specified in this script, our Webpack server will automatically launch the app in the browser and *hot-reload* component instances when changes are made to the app.

Though we won't be deploying our application in this chapter, `npm run build` will use Webpack to bundle certain files (dictated in `webpack.config.js`) to static assets within a `dist/` folder. This prepares the `dist/` folder to be ready for deployment.

Let's quickly address the dependencies that have been installed in our application.

We have the `vue` library as the main dependency:

calendar_app/package.json

```
"dependencies": {
  "vue": "^2.4.4"
},
```

And a series of build libraries as the `devDependencies`:

calendar_app/package.json

```
"devDependencies": {
  "babel-core": "^6.26.0",
  "babel-loader": "^7.1.2",
  "babel-preset-env": "^1.6.0",
  "babel-preset-stage-3": "^6.24.1",
  "cross-env": "^5.0.5",
  "css-loader": "^0.28.7",
  "file-loader": "^1.1.4",
  "sass-loader": "^6.0.6",
  "vue-loader": "^13.0.5",
  "node-sass": "^4.5.3",
  "vue-template-compiler": "^2.4.4",
  "webpack": "^3.6.0",
  "webpack-dev-server": "^2.9.1"
}
```

`babel-core`, `babel-loader`, `babel-preset-env` and `babel-preset-stage-3` are the packages needed to work with Webpack to transpile ES6 JavaScript down to ES5.

`cross-env` is used to extend the declaration of environment variables with `NODE_ENV=` to work with Windows machines.

`css-loader`, `file-loader`, `sass-loader` and `vue-loader` are the loaders we use in the `webpack.config.js` file.

`node-sass` helps compile SCSS to CSS within a node development environment (also referenced in `webpack.config.js`).

`vue-template-compiler` is an auto-generated package to help compile Vue 2.0 templates into render functions.

Finally, the `webpack` package is used to bundle JavaScript files for the browser to use and `webpack-dev-server` is needed to run a development server.

In a Node.js environment, `devDependencies` are the packages needed *only* during development while `dependencies` are often needed for both development and production.

`public/`

The `public/` folder hosts the `bulma/`[42] and `font-awesome/`[43] libraries that we'll use in our application.

`src/`

The `src/` directory contains the JavaScript files that we'll be working directly with:

```
$ ls src/
app/
app-1/
app-2/
app-3/
app-4/
app-5/
app-6/
app-7/
app-complete/
main.js
```

We'll be building our app inside `app/`. Each significant step we take along the way is included here: `app-1/`, `app-2/`, and so forth.

[42] https://bulma.io/

[43] http://fontawesome.io/

Like the last chapter, code examples in the book are titled with the file in which the example is defined.

Our `main.js` file dictates the starting point of our application. `main.js` is where we mount our Vue instance to the DOM element with an id of `#app`, the declared DOM element in our `index.html` file.

We also import and specify the main component `App.vue` to be rendered in our instance with `render: h => h(App)`.

calendar_app/src/main.js

```
import Vue from 'vue'
import App from './app-complete/App.vue'

new Vue({
  el: '#app',
  render: h => h(App)
})
```

Our first step is to ensure we're not referencing the `app-complete` sub folder anymore. Instead, we'll import `App` from `./app/App.vue` to load the application from a starting point:

```
import Vue from 'vue'
import App from './app/App.vue'

new Vue({
  el: '#app',
  render: h => h(App)
})
```

Vue's `render` function is an alternative to templates and is basically what Vue does under the hood. Since our application is **runtime only** build, we can't declare `<App></App>` in a `template` option like we did in the first chapter. All our component templates have to be specified in a `.vue` file with which we'll see shortly. The Vue docs explain Vue's `render`[44] function as well as the difference between runtime and compiler+runtime builds[45] in more detail.

[44]https://vuejs.org/v2/guide/render-function.html

[45]https://vuejs.org/v2/guide/installation.html#Runtime-Compiler-vs-Runtime-only

webpack.config.js

The `webpack.config.js` file contains all information with regards to build configuration, loaders, etc. We specify `./src/main.js` as the main entry file which contains the root Vue instance.

Webpack loaders can be seen as tasks or transformations that need to be done to target files in the build process. We have three *loaders* defined in the `webpack.config.js` file:

- `babel-loader` to help transpile ES6 code
- `vue-loader` to write components in a single-file format
- `file-loader` to emit required file types as public URLs.

Another responsibility of Webpack is to *build* the app for deployment purposes. In this app, Webpack achieves this by outputting the bundled code to a `build.js` file located within a `dist/` folder. This bundling and output only happens when we run the `build` script specified in the `package.json` file.

.babelrc

Babel[46] is a JavaScript transpiler that transpiles ES6 syntax to older ES5 syntax for any browser to understand. The `.babelrc` file is used to configure the Babel presets and plugins for the `babel-loader` package in our application. This package/setup allows us to transpile all of our `.js` files, which allows us to write with ES6.

.gitignore

`.gitignore` dictates the files in our repository that we don't want Git to check into Github. This file is often used to ignore certain files such as build products (`node_modules/`) or local configuration settings.

Front end configuration with build tools like Webpack/Browserify is known to be an arduous task often labelled as *JavaScript fatigue*.

This project is adapted from the `webpack-simple` template generated with `vue-cli`[47] (the Vue command line interface) to have all the necessary build tools set up right away.

Single-File Components

Before we start building our application, we'll address and talk about a powerful Vue feature known as **single-file components**.

In the last chapter, we touched on how `Vue.component` can be used to define global components. Instead of using `Vue.component`, we assigned our created components to constant variables and declared them in the `components` option of the Vue instance, like this:

[46] https://babeljs.io/

[47] https://github.com/vuejs/vue-cli

```
const submissionComponent = { // ... };
new Vue({
  el: '#app',
  components: {
    'submission-component': submissionComponent
  }
})
```

With either `Vue.component` or components assigned to constant variables, we have to write our component templates using ES6's template literals (by using backticks) to obtain a presentable multiline format.

```
const submissionComponent = {
  template: `<div>
                <p>Component Template</p>
              </div>`,
}
```

The above does a good job for small to medium sized projects. However, as an application grows, global components create limitations by not allowing us to specify unique CSS within them and not having appropriate syntax highlighting within their template.

As a result, Vue provides the option to use **single-file components** to reduce this disorganization. Vue's single-file components focus heavily on coupling logic by giving us the ability to define HTML/CSS and JS of a component all within a single **`.vue`** file.

A **single-file component** consists of three parts:

- `<template>` which contains the component's markup in plain HTML
- `<script>` which exports the component object constructor that consists of all the JS logic within that component
- `<style>` which contains all the component styles

Here's an example of a **single-file component** called `MyComponent.vue`:

appendix/components/MyComponent.vue

```
<template>
  <h2>{{ getGreeting }}</h2>
  <p>This is the Hello World component.</p>
</template>

<script>
export default {
  name: 'MyComponent',
  data () {
    return {
      reversedGreeting: '!dlrow olleH'
    }
  },
  computed: {
    getGreeting() {
      return this.reversedGreeting.split("").reverse().join("");
    }
  }
}
</script>

<style lang="scss" scoped>
h2 {
  width: 100%;
  text-align: center;
}
</style>
```

Our template displays the returned value of the `getGreeting` computed property declared in the `<script>` tag. `getGreeting` simply reverses the `reversedGreeting` data property to return "Hello World!" in the template.

The `<style>` tag specifies `lang="scss"` which dictates the use of the SCSS preprocessor in our styles. `scoped` dictates these styles will be applied to this and only this component.

Single-file components in Vue are made possible due to build tools like Webpack and Browserify. These tools work alongside the `vue-loader` or `vueify` packages respectively to compile `.vue` components to plain JavaScript modules that can be understood in browsers.

With the single-responsibility principle, we'll be able to componentize our application with the help of single-file components.

Breaking the app into components

Just like we did in the last chapter, we'll start by breaking the app down into its components. Visual components can be tightly mapped to their respective **single-file components**.

With the components of our application in mind, let's address the interface of the app again:

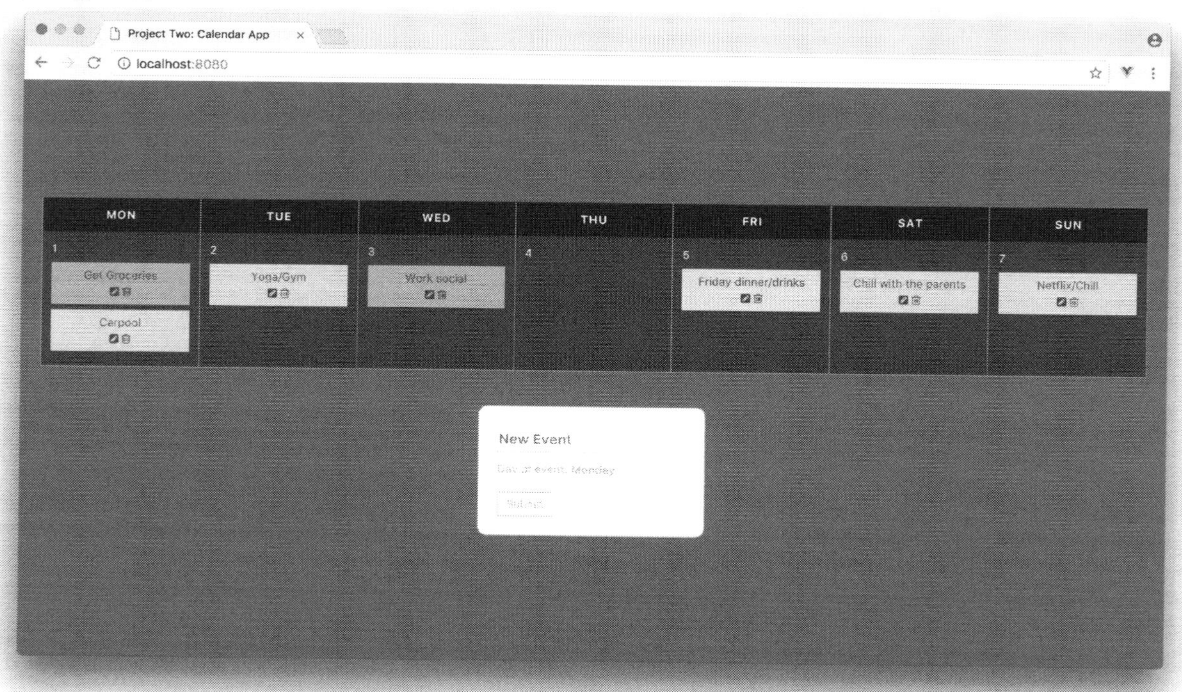

We can first separate the application to three main components - **`App`** (the overarching parent component), **`CalendarWeek`**, and **`CalendarEntry`**.

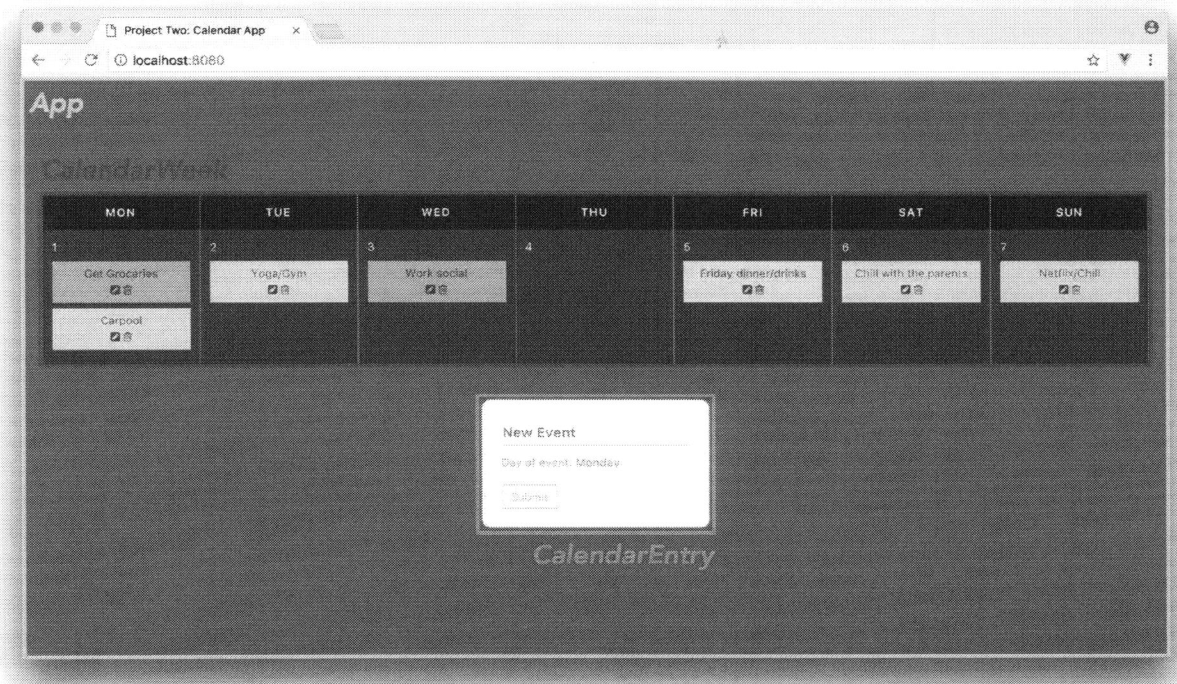

Within `CalendarWeek`, we can spot a pattern between the different columns (i.e. days). From this, we can say the `CalendarWeek` component is the parent of different **`CalendarDay`** components.

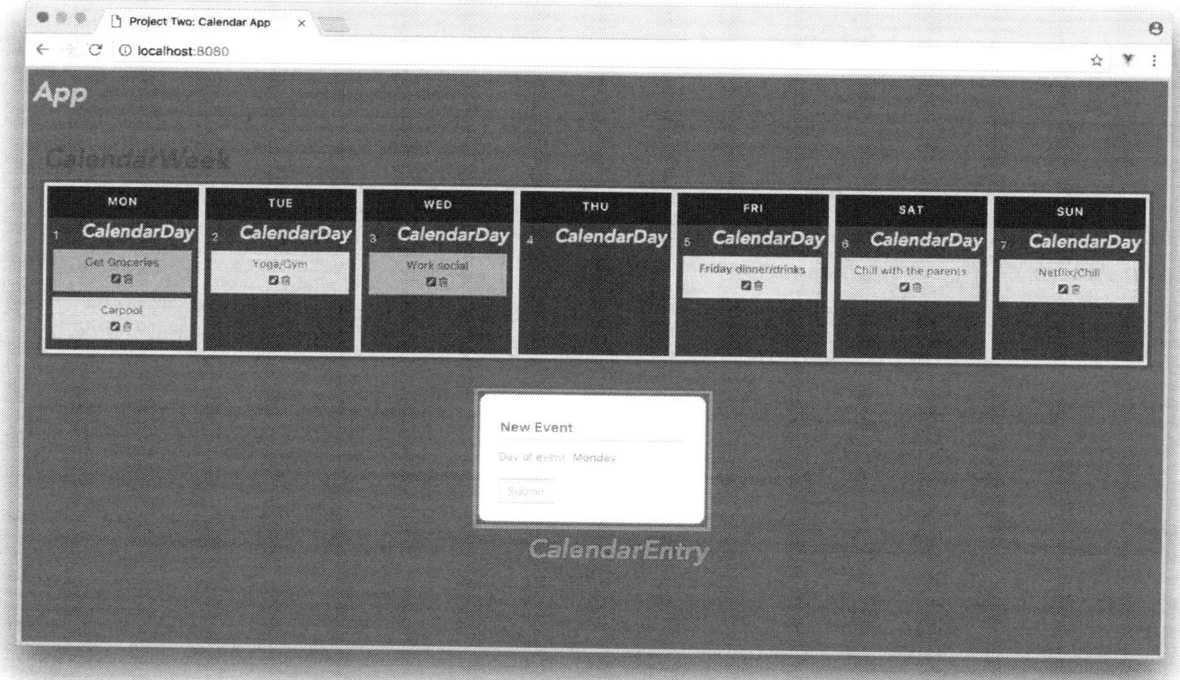

We can also take this a step further and declare `CalendarDay` to be the parent component of multiple **`CalendarEvent`** components.

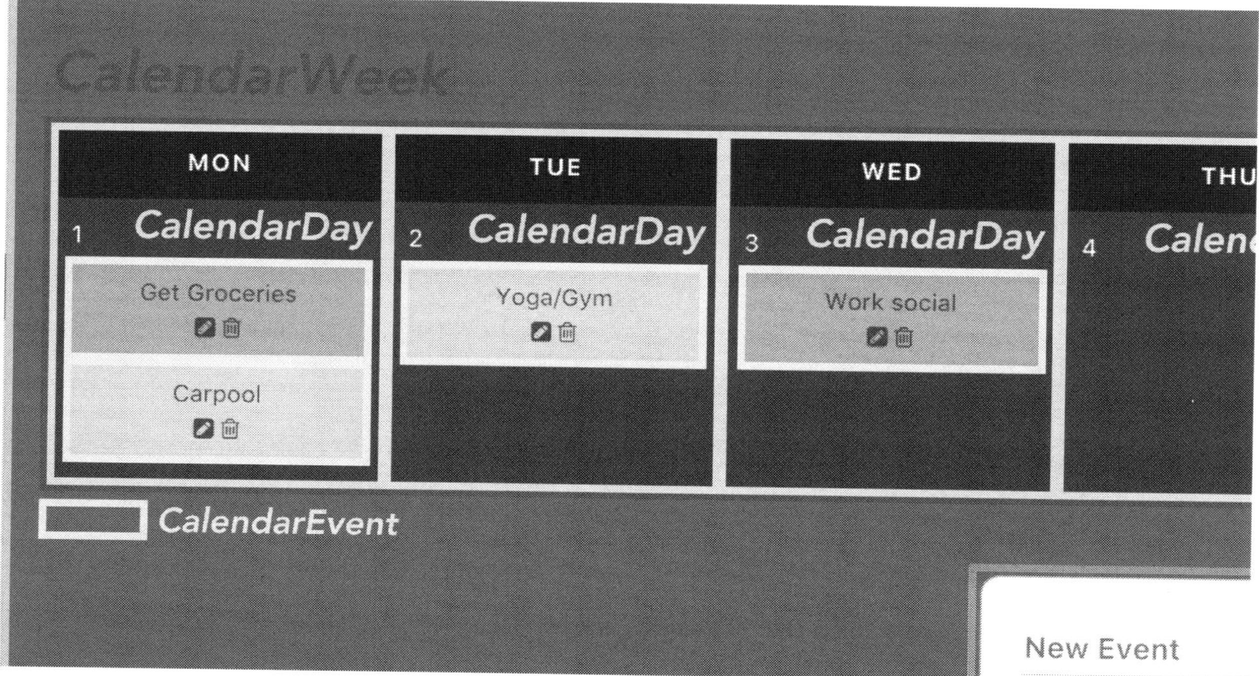

The naming of our components is up to us, but having some consistent rules around language will greatly improve code clarity.

Our final component hierarchy:

- `App`: Parent container
  - `CalendarWeek`: Displays a row of calendar days
    - `CalendarDay`: Displays a list of day events
      - `CalendarEvent`: Displays a given event
  - `CalendarEntry`: Displays a form

Our hierarchy represented with a simple graphical tree:

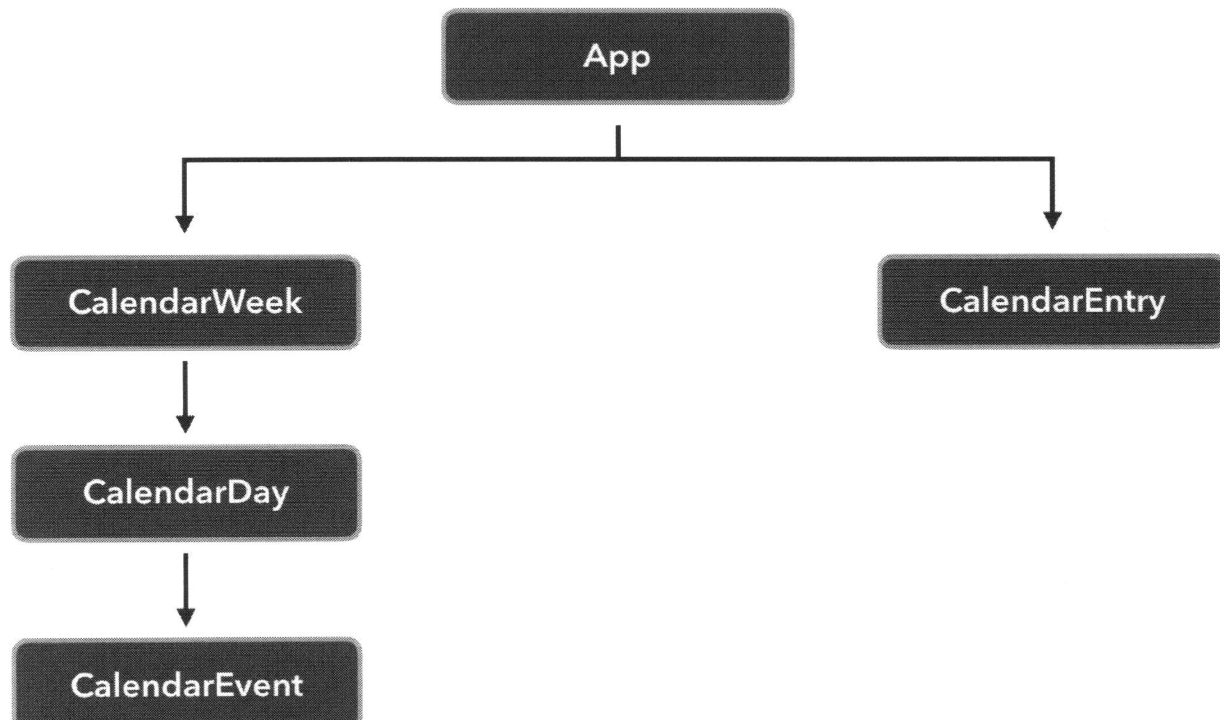

When it comes to Component-Based Architecture, levels of granularity depends upon how we wish to encapsulate individual pieces of an interface.

Different teams/developers have different ways of laying out components, but the underlying goal is maintainability and/or reusability. It's a good idea to define the approach across all developers explicitly.

Managing data between components

We've stressed that components should be as self-contained and isolated as much as possible. Taking into account the scope of our application - we know that there should be some level of communication between the components (e.g. submitting an event entry in `CalendarEntry` should surface an event on `CalendarDay`). This brings us to component communication and/or state management.

Parent-Child Components

Since every component has it's own isolated scope, child components can never (and should never) reference data *directly* from parent components. For a child component to access data from a parent, data has to flow from the parent down to the child with the help of **props**. This design greatly simplifies the understanding of an applications data flow since child components will never be able to mutate parent state directly.

We'll use **props** to pass data from `CalendarWeek` to `CalendarDay` to `CalendarEvent`, since a linear hierarchy exists between these components.

Child-Parent Components

Since **props** can only flow in a single direction from parent to child, children components can only *directly* communicate with a parent through **custom events**. Vue's custom events work by triggering events within a particular component, `$emit(nameOfEvent)`, and listening for that event in another component, `$on(nameOfEvent)`. Data can also be passed through these events.

Though custom events work well, we won't have the need to use it in this chapter. We'll be going through custom events in detail in Chapter 3.

Sibling Components

Managing data between sibling components are more difficult than that of parent-child (or child-parent). **Props** cannot be used since sibling components are independent of one another (i.e. a sibling component isn't rendered within another sibling component).

In our application, we need to pass information from `CalendarEntry` to its sibling component `CalendarDay`.

Managing data between sibling components in Vue can be categorized in three main buckets:

- Using a global event bus
- Using a simple, shared store object (for simple state management)
- Using the state management library Vuex

Global Event Bus

A global event bus builds on top of using Vue's simple custom events by making events *global* to the entire application. This is often a simple way of passing information between any components regardless of their relationship (parent-child, child-parent or sibling-sibling).

It's important to note, however, a global event bus is not often the *recommended* way of managing data between components, since it doesn't conform to a predictable and manageable way to handle application state. [Since it's a good concept to grasp due to its simplicity, we'll be building a global event bus in Chapter 3].

Vuex

Vuex builds upon having a simple state object by introducing *explicitly defined* getters, mutations, and actions. A gradual understanding of this and the benefits of **Vuex** comes from first understanding how **simple state management** works, which is exactly what we'll be doing in this chapter. We need not worry! We'll be introducing how to integrate Vuex in Chapter 4.

Vue style guide suggestions Despite its boilerplate, the Vue style guide suggests Vuex as the preferred method for global state management in large scale applications. The Non-Flux State Management[48] section of the style guide addresses application state management and provides some useful examples.

Simple State Management

Simple state management can be performed by creating a store pattern that involves *sharing* a data store between components. The store manages this state with its actions/mutations/etc. and simply passes the same data to multiple components.

> *State* basically means data. State management often refers to the management of **application level data.**

To give an example: assume we had a `store.js` file that exports a `store` object (which contains a `state` object within):

[48]https://vuejs.org/v2/style-guide/#Non-flux-state-management-use-with-caution

appendix/store/simpleStore/store.js

```
export const store = {
  state: {
    numbers: [1, 2, 3]
  },
  // ...
}
```

Let's say we had a single-file component, named `NumberDisplay.vue`, that displays the entire array from the `numbers` property in our store:

appendix/store/simpleStore/NumberDisplay.vue

```
<template>
  <div>
    <h2>{{ storeState.numbers }}</h2>
  </div>
</template>

<script>
import { store } from './store.js';

export default {
  name: 'NumberDisplay',
  data () {
    return {
      storeState: store.state
    }
  }
}
</script>
```

Assume we needed to provide functionality to add a new number, one at a time, to the rendered array shown in `NumberDisplay.vue`. We will need a method that takes an input value and simply pushes that value to that array.

All actions that mutate/change store data should always be within the store itself to ensure proper centralization of application state.

With this method in mind, we can update the store with the following code:

appendix/store/simpleStore/store.js

```
export const store = {
  state: {
    numbers: [1, 2, 3]
  },
  pushNewNumber(newNumberString) {
    this.state.numbers.push(Number(newNumberString));
  }
}
```

We can now introduce a separate component `NumberSubmit` that simply calls the `pushNewNumber` action in our store. In other words, the `NumberSubmit` component *dispatches* the store *mutation*, `pushNewNumber`, which subsequently *mutates* the store (application) state.

The `NumberSubmit` component (defined in a `NumberSubmit.vue` file) can handle this functionality like so:

appendix/store/simpleStore/NumberSubmit.vue

```
<template>
  <div>
    <input v-model="newNumber" type="number" />
    <button @click="pushNewNumber(newNumber)">Add new number</button>
  </div>
</template>

<script>
import { store } from './store.js';

export default {
  name: 'NumberSubmit',
  data () {
    return {
      newNumber: 0
    }
  },
  methods: {
    pushNewNumber(newNumber) {
      store.pushNewNumber(newNumber);
    }
  }
}
</script>
```

We're using the `v-model` directive in the example above to specify two-way data binding between the `input` element and the `newNumber` data property. We explain the `v-model` directive in detail later in this chapter.

Thanks to Vue's reactivity, whenever the data within store state is manipulated - the relevant DOM (`<template>` of `NumberDisplay`) automatically updates.

Important Note: Components are not allowed to change state directly. Instead they need to dispatch *events* for the store to listen and invoke a mutation within. This form of simple state management is a great precursor to understanding how the Flux architecture works.

Here's a diagram to better display how state was managed in the example provided above:

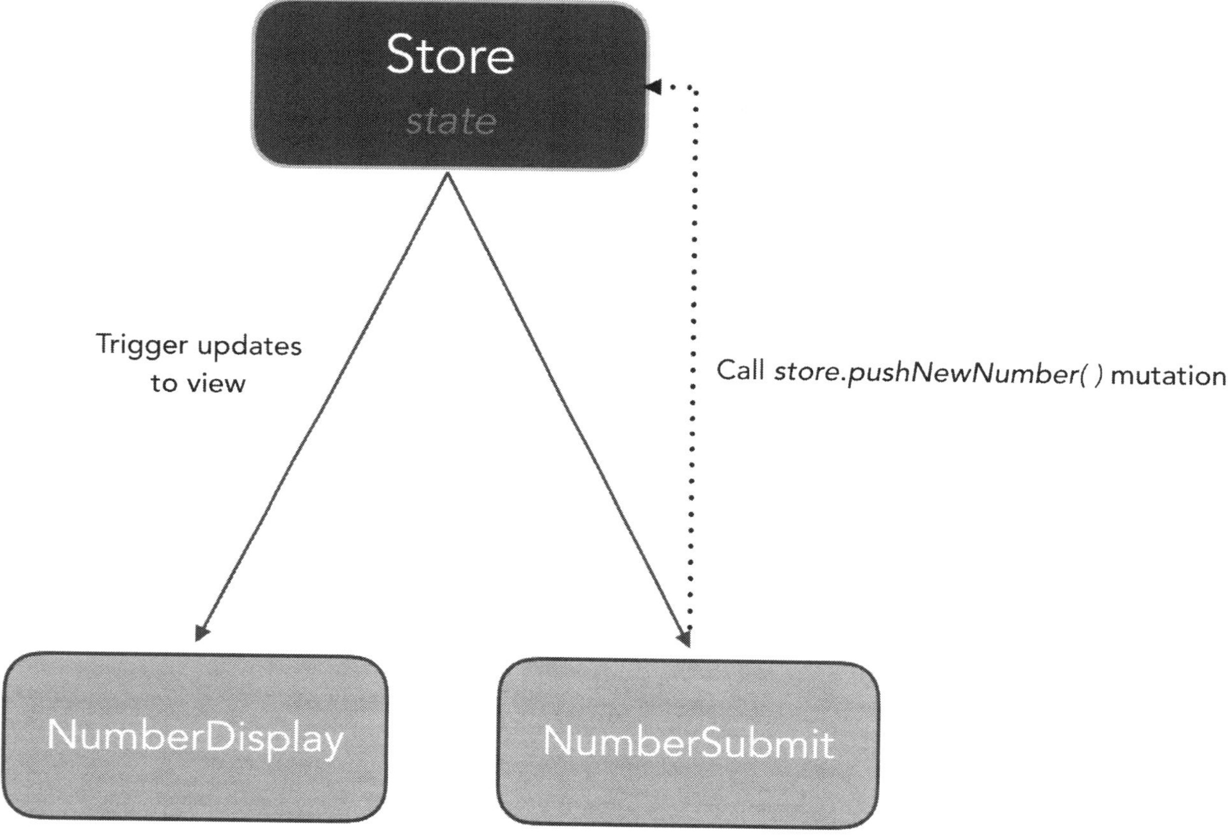

Steps to building Vue apps from scratch

Now that we have a good understanding of the composition of our components and how to set up simple state management, we're ready to start building our calendar app.

Like our last chapter, it simplifies things for us to start off with static components. Clicking on buttons won't yield any behavior as we will not have wired up any interactivity. This will enable us to lay the framework for the app getting a clear idea of how our components should be organized.

Next, we can determine the **state** for the app and in which component it should live. We'll just hard-code the state into the components instead of loading it from the server.

At that point, we'll have the data flow from **parent to child** in place. We can then address setting up our state mutations so one component can start manipulating the view in other components.

This follows from a simple, generic approach for developing an app from scratch:

1. Build a static version of the app
2. Break the app into components
3. Hard-code initial states with parent-child data flow
4. Create state mutations (and accompanying component dispatchers)

Let's start with Step (1).

Step 1: A static version of the app

App.vue

As mentioned, all our Vue code for this chapter will be inside `src/app/`. By opening up the existing `App.vue` file in `src/app/`, we'll see a single file component with a *large* amount of markup and css.

A summarized `App.vue` looks like the following:

```
<template>
  <div id="app">
    <div id="calendar-week" class="container">
      <!-- Markup for calendar week -->
    </div>
    <div id="calendar-entry">
      <!-- Markup for calendar entry -->
    </div>
  </div>
</template>

<script>
export default {
  name: 'App'
}
</script>
```

```
<style lang="scss">
html, body {
  height: 100%;
}

#app {
  <!-- SCSS for app -->
}

#calendar-week {
  <!-- SCSS for calendar week -->
}

#calendar-entry {
  <!-- SCSS for calendar entry -->
}
</style>
```

The markup for `App.vue` consists of a parent `<div>`, `#app`, with two child elements - `#calendar-week` and `#calendar-entry`.

The `<div id="calendar-week"></div>` element displays a series of columns for each day within a week with two hard-coded calendar events, on Monday and Friday respectively.

The `<div id="calendar-entry"></div>` element displays an input section where users will be able to submit events to any particular day.

The `<script>` tag simply creates an export of the file with the name of `App`. The `<style>` element contains custom styling for the `#app`, `#calendar-week` and `#calendar-entry` elements.

Just like the first chapter, our focus will be primarily on the usage of Vue. All the styling needed in our application has already been prepared. As we start breaking our app into components, we'll transfer the necessary custom styles to each respective component.

Let's see the current static version of the app. We'll run the webpack-server (`npm run dev`) and open our browser to the url at `http://localhost:8080`:

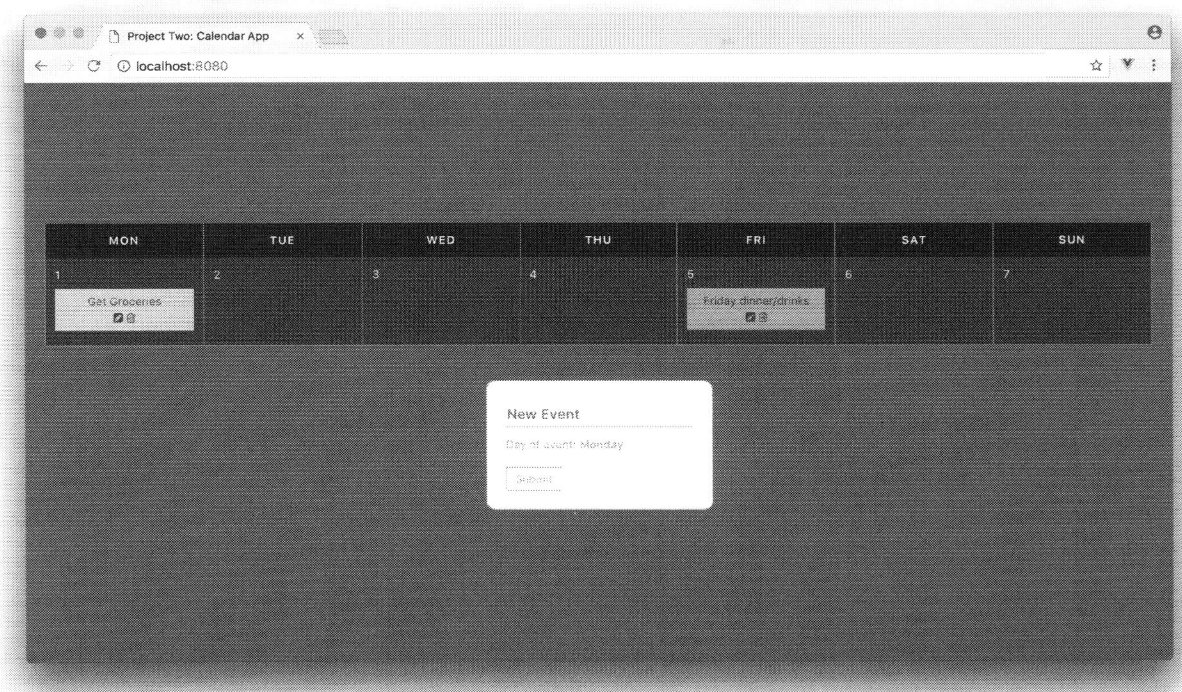

Static version of the app

Step 2: Breaking the app into components

Here's the component layout we created earlier by assessing the app UI:

- `App`: Parent container
  - `CalendarWeek`: Displays a row of calendar days
    - `CalendarDay`: Displays a list of day events
      - `CalendarEvent`: Displays a given event
  - `CalendarEntry`: Displays a form to create a new calendar event

Let's begin by creating the two main sibling components `CalendarWeek` and `CalendarEntry`. Within our `app/` folder we'll create a `components/` subfolder that consists of two new component files - `CalendarWeek.vue` and `CalendarEntry.vue`. To do so, we can run the following steps in our terminal:

```
$ mkdir src/app/components
$ touch src/app/components/CalendarEntry.vue
$ touch src/app/components/CalendarWeek.vue
```

Let's check out the structure now:

`src/app/`:

```
$ ls src/app/
App.vue
components/
seed.js

src/app/components/:

$ ls src/app/components/
CalendarEntry.vue
CalendarWeek.vue
```

Vue style guide suggestions

- With the exception of `App`, component names should generally be multi-word (e.g. `CalendarEntry`). Check out the Multi-word components[49] blurb of the Vue style guide for a deeper discussion about this.
- The filenames for single-file components should either be kebab-case (`calendar-entry.vue`) or PascalCase (`CalendarEntry.vue`) as stated in the Single-file component filename casing[50] section of the Vue style guide.

The HTML markup and scss within `App.vue` are conveniently segregated with `#app`, `#calendar-week` and `#calendar-entry`. We'll simply move the relevant markup/scss for `#calendar-week` to `CalendarWeek` and `#calendar-entry` to `CalendarEntry`.

A summary of the new `CalendarWeek.vue` component:

```
<template>
  <div id="calendar-week" class="container">
    <!-- Markup for calendar week -->
  </div>
</template>

<script>
export default {
  name: 'CalendarWeek'
}
</script>
```

[49] https://vuejs.org/v2/style-guide/#Multi-word-component-names-essential
[50] https://vuejs.org/v2/style-guide/#Single-file-component-filename-casing-strongly-recommended

```
<style lang="scss" scoped>
#calendar-week {
  <!-- SCSS for calendar week -->
}
</style>
```

Next, we'll take the same approach to building the `CalendarEntry` component. In the same manner, a summary of the new `CalendarEntry.vue` component:

```
<template>
  <div id="calendar-entry">
    <!-- Markup for calendar entry -->
  </div>
</template>

<script>
export default {
  name: 'CalendarEntry'
}
</script>

<style lang="scss" scoped>
#calendar-entry {
  <!-- SCSS for calendar entry -->
}
</style>
```

We're not displaying the entire markup/scss in the examples above for easier readability. As you follow along, include the necessary markup and scss within these components that are included in the final version of the application.

We now can update our root `App.vue` file to import and reference these newly created components:

calendar_app/src/app-1/App.vue

```
<template>
  <div id="app">
    <CalendarWeek />
    <CalendarEntry />
  </div>
</template>

<script>
import CalendarWeek from './components/CalendarWeek.vue';
import CalendarEntry from './components/CalendarEntry.vue';

export default {
  name: 'App',
  components: {
    CalendarWeek,
    CalendarEntry
  }
}
</script>

<style lang="scss">
html, body {
  height: 100%;
}
</style>

<style lang="scss" scoped>
#app {
  height: inherit;
  background: #6e6e6e;
  display: flex;
  flex-direction: column;
  align-items: center;
  -webkit-align-items: center;
  justify-content: center;
  -webkit-justify-content: center;
}
</style>
```

Notice how we have two `<style>` elements in `App.vue`. The `scoped` tag element (the one below) references the styles within our component while the other element adds the CSS property `height: 100%` to the global `html`/`body` elements.

Vue style guide suggestions It is recommended for components with no content to be self-closing (e.g. `<CalendarEntry />` instead of `<CalendarEntry></CalendarEntry>`) when declared in single file components. This is mentioned in the Self-closing-components[51] section of the Vue style guide.

Step 3: Hardcode Initial States

Let's move on to step 3: hard-coding initial states for our components.

`CalendarDay`

In our `app/` folder, we have a `seed.js` file just like we had in our first chapter. The `seed.js` exports a `seedData` array that contains information for every day of the weekly calendar:

```
export const seedData = [
  {
    id: 1,
    abbvTitle: 'Mon',
    fullTitle: 'Monday',
    events: [
      { details: 'Get Groceries', edit: false },
      { details: 'Carpool', edit: false }
    ],
    active: true
  },
  // ...,
}
```

To reference the seed data in our components, we'll do so in the store for our application. We'll create the `store.js` file in the root of our `app/` folder:

[51] https://vuejs.org/v2/style-guide/#Self-closing-components-strongly-recommended

```
$ ls src/app/
App.vue
components/
seed.js
store.js
```

Let's now set up our `store.js` file to export a constant `store` variable that contains a `state` object with the `seedData`.

calendar_app/src/app-2/store.js

```
import Vue from 'vue';
import { seedData } from './seed.js';

export const store = {
  state: {
    seedData
  }
}
```

We're using an ES6 property value shorthand to declare the `seedData` property in the `state` object. Expressing `state: { seedData }` is equivalent to explicitly stating `state: { seedData: seedData }`. This shorthand works only when the property value has the same name as the property identifier.

As we mentioned previously, the `CalendarWeek` component can render a *list* of `CalendarDay` components and a single `CalendarDay` component can render a *list* of `CalendarEvent` components. Let's use the seed data to create our nested `CalendarDay` and `CalendarEvent` components.

First we'll create the `CalendarDay.vue` and `CalendarEvent.vue` files in the `components` sub-directory:

```
$ ls src/app/components/
CalendarDay.vue
CalendarEntry.vue
CalendarEvent.vue
CalendarWeek.vue
```

In the `CalendarWeek.vue` file, we can see a repetition of markup associated with `<div class="day column"></div>` elements. We'll remove these sections and instead use `v-for` to render a list of `CalendarDay` components. Let's lay out how we'll do this step-by-step.

In the `<script>` element of the `CalendarWeek` component, we'll first import the `store` and reference the store state as a `sharedState` data property within the component:

```
<script>
import { store } from '../store.js';

export default {
  name: 'CalendarWeek',
  data () {
    return {
      sharedState: store.state
    }
  }
}
</script>
```

We'll then import `CalendarDay` and pass it in a `components` property:

calendar_app/src/app-2/components/CalendarWeek.vue

```
<script>
import { store } from '../store.js';
import CalendarDay from './CalendarDay.vue';

export default {
  name: 'CalendarWeek',
  data () {
    return {
      sharedState: store.state
    }
  },
  components: {
    CalendarDay
  }
}
</script>
```

With this, we can now dictate a list of `CalendarDay` components using the `v-for` directive. Recall the `v-for` directive requires the form of `[variable name] in [data]`, so our `CalendarDay` component can be repeated like so:

```
<CalendarDay v-for="day in sharedState.seedData" :key="day.id" />
```

We're using the `day id` value as the `key` for each iterated component.

We can also pass down a `prop`, the iterated `day` object within our list, down to every `CalendarDay` component. Since we're passing in data objects as props, we'll need to use the `v-bind` directive (with the `:` shorthand) to bind our iterated data objects to our props.

```
<CalendarDay v-for="day in sharedState.seedData"
  :key="day.id"
  :day="day"/>
```

Implementing all the above and removing all repetitive `day column` elements in `CalendarWeek`, the `CalendarWeek.vue` file will be updated to this:

calendar_app/src/app-2/components/CalendarWeek.vue

```
<template>
  <div id="calendar-week" class="container">
    <div class="columns is-mobile">
      <CalendarDay v-for="day in sharedState.seedData"
        :key="day.id"
        :day="day" />
    </div>
  </div>
</template>

<script>
import { store } from '../store.js';
import CalendarDay from './CalendarDay.vue';

export default {
  name: 'CalendarWeek',
  data () {
    return {
      sharedState: store.state
    }
  },
  components: {
    CalendarDay
  }
}
</script>

<style lang="scss" scoped>
#calendar-week {
  margin-bottom: 50px;
  .column {
    padding: 0 0 0 0;
  }
}
</style>
```

For our application to run, we'll now need to create the `CalendarDay` component.

`CalendarDay` should explicitly declare the `day` prop that it's receiving so that it can be used in the template. We'll set up a `<script>` element in the `CalendarDay.vue` file that specifies the name of the component as `CalendarDay` and declares a `day` attribute as a `prop` of the component:

calendar_app/src/app-2/components/CalendarDay.vue

```
<script>
export default {
  name: 'CalendarDay',
  props: ['day']
}
</script>
```

The `<template>` of `CalendarDay` will consist of a single `<div class="day column"></div>` element. With the use of the Mustache syntax, {{ }}, this element will display the `day.abbvTitle` and `day.id` properties:

calendar_app/src/app-2/components/CalendarDay.vue

```
<template>
  <div class="day column">
    <div class="day-banner has-text-centered">{{ day.abbvTitle }}</div>
    <div class="day-details">
      <div class="day-number">{{ day.id }}</div>
      <div class="day-event" style="background-color: rgb(153, 255, 153)">
        <div>
          <span class="has-text-centered details">Get Groceries</span>
          <div class="has-text-centered icons">
            <i class="fa fa-pencil-square edit-icon"></i>
            <i class="fa fa-trash-o delete-icon"></i>
          </div>
        </div>
      </div>
    </div>
  </div>
</template>
```

Moving the necessary CSS along, our entire `CalendarDay.vue` file will be laid out like so:

calendar_app/src/app-2/components/CalendarDay.vue

```
<template>
  <div class="day column">
    <div class="day-banner has-text-centered">{{ day.abbvTitle }}</div>
    <div class="day-details">
      <div class="day-number">{{ day.id }}</div>
      <div class="day-event" style="background-color: rgb(153, 255, 153)">
        <div>
          <span class="has-text-centered details">Get Groceries</span>
          <div class="has-text-centered icons">
            <i class="fa fa-pencil-square edit-icon"></i>
            <i class="fa fa-trash-o delete-icon"></i>
          </div>
        </div>
      </div>
    </div>
  </div>
</template>

<script>
export default {
  name: 'CalendarDay',
  props: ['day']
}
</script>

<style lang="scss" scoped>
.day {
  background-color: #4A4A4A;
  color: #FFF;
  border-left: 1px solid #8F8F8F;
  border-bottom: 1px solid #8F8F8F;
  font-size: 12px;
  cursor: pointer;

  &:hover {
    background: darken(#4A4A4A,3%);
  }

  .day-banner {
    background-color: #333333;
    color: #FFF;
```

```
    padding: 10px;
    text-transform: uppercase;
    letter-spacing: 1px;
    font-size: 12px;
    font-weight: 600;
  }

  .day-details {
    padding: 10px;
  }

  &:last-child {
    border-right: 1px solid #8F8F8F;
  }

  .day-event {
    margin-top: 6px;
    margin-bottom: 6px;
    display: block;
    color: #4C4C4C;
    padding: 5px;

    .details {
      display: block;
    }

    input {
      background: none;
      border: 0;
      border-bottom: 1px solid #FFF;
      width: 100%;

      &:focus {
        outline: none;
      }
    }
  }
}
</style>
```

If we run our application, we will see everything rendered with no errors. However, since our `CalendarDay` component always renders the same `<div class="day-event"></div>` element, we should expect to see the same event (`Get Groceries`) rendered multiple times.

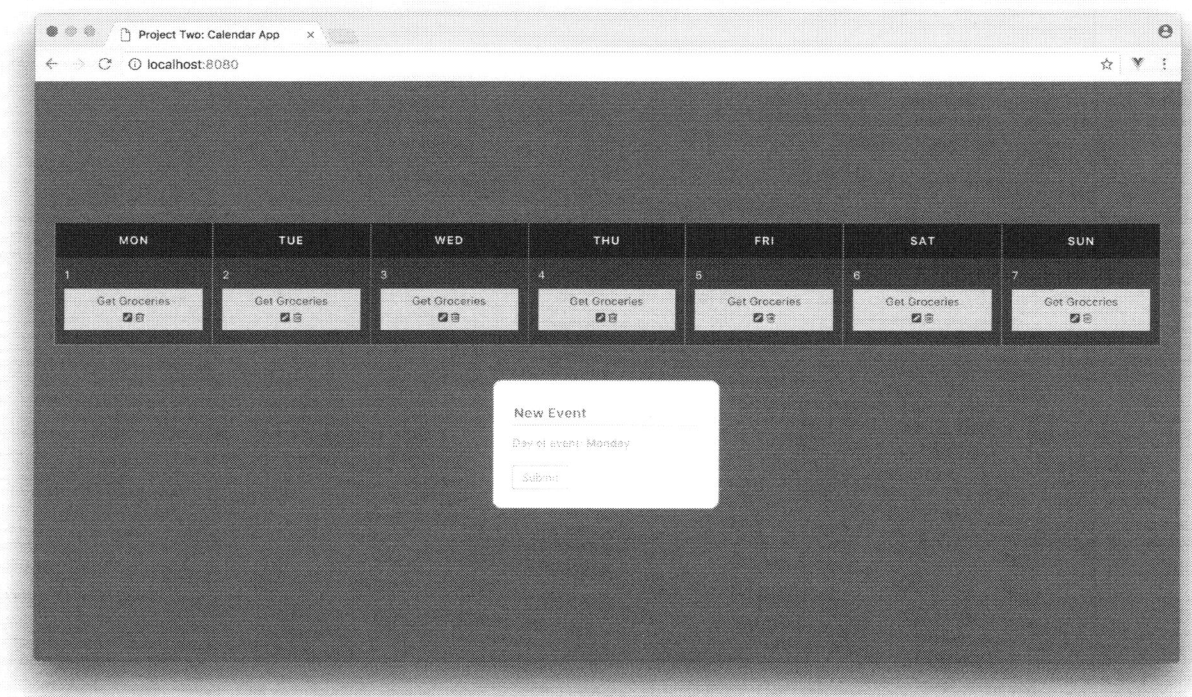

App with `CalendarDay` components

`CalendarEvent`

If we look back at our seed data, we'll notice that each `day` object has a list of `event` objects. Very similar to what we just did to render `CalendarDay`, we can invoke a `v-for` directive to render a new `CalendarEvent` component for every `event` in `CalendarDay`.

Assuming all event information (markup and css) is contained within `CalendarEvent`, our `CalendarDay.vue` file now becomes:

calendar_app/src/app-3/components/CalendarDay.vue

```
<template>
  <div class="day column">
    <div class="day-banner has-text-centered">{{ day.abbvTitle }}</div>
    <div class="day-details">
      <div class="day-number">{{ day.id }}</div>
      <CalendarEvent v-for="event in day.events"
        :key="day.events.indexOf(event)"
        :event="event"
```

```
        :day="day"/>
    </div>
  </div>
</template>

<script>
import CalendarEvent from './CalendarEvent.vue';

export default {
  name: 'CalendarDay',
  props: ['day'],
  components: {
    CalendarEvent
  }
}
</script>

<style lang="scss" scoped>
.day {
  background-color: #4A4A4A;
  color: #FFF;
  border-left: 1px solid #8F8F8F;
  border-bottom: 1px solid #8F8F8F;
  font-size: 12px;
  cursor: pointer;

  &:hover {
    background: darken(#4A4A4A,3%);
  }

  .day-banner {
    background-color: #333333;
    color: #FFF;
    padding: 10px;
    text-transform: uppercase;
    letter-spacing: 1px;
    font-size: 12px;
    font-weight: 600;
  }

  .day-details {
    padding: 10px;
```

```
  }

  &:last-child {
    border-right: 1px solid #8F8F8F;
  }
}
</style>
```

We're passing down both `day` and `event` objects to the `CalendarEvent` component. The `event` prop will be used to display information of the event while the `day` prop will be used in method handlers we'll create later. Since an `id` doesn't exist for each event object, we're using the index of the event within the events array as the `key` identifier.

We'll go ahead and build out the `CalendarEvent` component in the `CalendarEvent.vue` file. Within the `CalendarEvent` component, let's create a computed property called `getEventBackgroundColor` that returns a random color from an array to be used as the `background-color` for each event for styling.

This makes the `CalendarEvent.vue` file become:

calendar_app/src/app-3/components/CalendarEvent.vue

```
<template>
  <div class="day-event" :style="getEventBackgroundColor">
    <div>
      <span class="has-text-centered details">{{ event.details }}</span>
      <div class="has-text-centered icons">
        <i class="fa fa-pencil-square edit-icon"></i>
        <i class="fa fa-trash-o delete-icon"></i>
      </div>
    </div>
  </div>
</template>

<script>
export default {
  name: 'CalendarEvent',
  props: ['event', 'day'],
  computed: {
    getEventBackgroundColor() {
      const colors = ['#FF9999', '#85D6FF', '#99FF99'];
      let randomColor = colors[Math.floor(Math.random() * colors.length)];
      return `background-color: ${randomColor}`;
    }
```

```
  }
}
</script>

<style lang="scss" scoped>
.day-event {
  margin-top: 6px;
  margin-bottom: 6px;
  display: block;
  color: #4C4C4C;
  padding: 5px;

  .details {
    display: block;
  }

  input {
    background: none;
    border: 0;
    border-bottom: 1px solid #FFF;
    width: 100%;

    &:focus {
      outline: none;
    }
  }
}
</style>
```

At this point, we have our store created and the `App`, `CalendarWeek`, `CalendarEntry`, and `CalendarEvent` components all appropriately set up.

Saving our edited files and opening `http://localhost:8080` in our browser, we should see our application look like this:

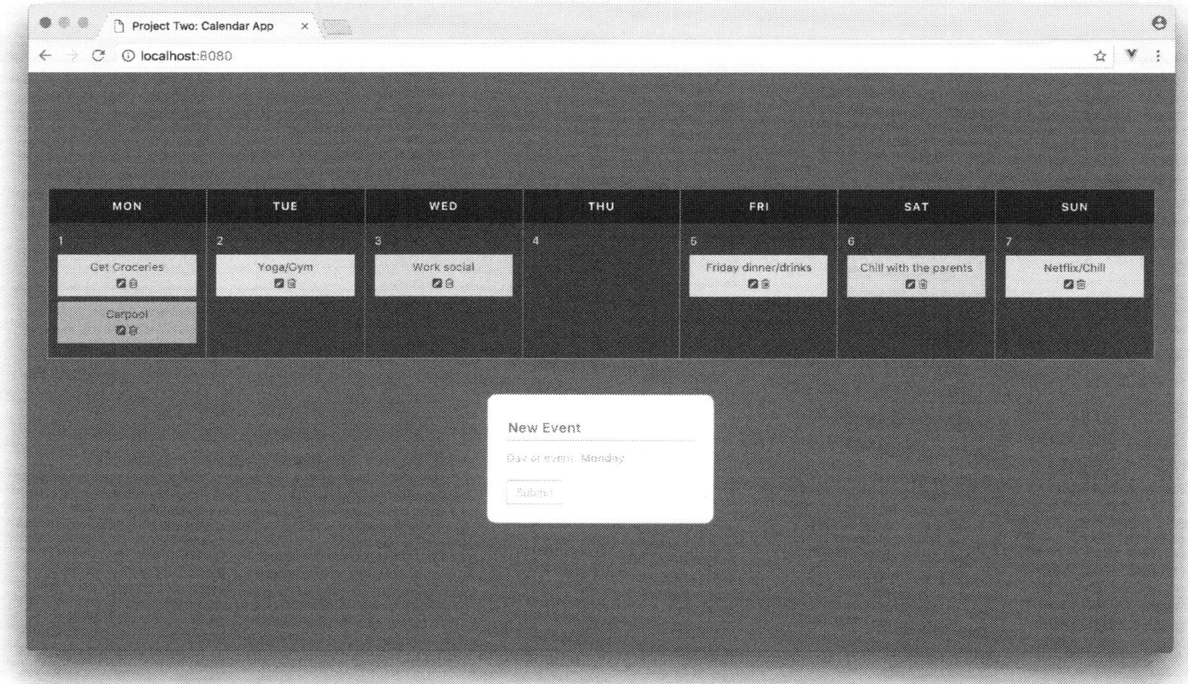

App with `CalendarEvent` components

Step 4: Create state mutations (and corresponding component actions)

We've done a good job in appropriately defining markup and CSS within their self-contained components. The messy and large single file we had started with is now a lot more easier to maintain.

We'll continue with this mindset by building and coupling interactions within their respective components.

Before we make our app interactive, we'll break down all the unique interactions our application should have before addressing each one of them:

1. When the user clicks a day within the calendar week, our `CalendarEntry` component should appropriately reference the correct day selected. (i.e. the user clicks *THU* - text in `CalendarEntry` becomes *Day of Event: Thursday*).

2. The user can submit a new event to a certain day by typing the details in the input within the `CalendarEntry` component and clicking `Submit`. (If the user clicks `Submit` with a blank input, an error message should appear stating blank inputs are invalid).

3. If the user clicks the edit icon on an event, an input is provided to allow the user to change the event details. When the user updates the event and clicks the confirm icon, the event details are

updated. (If the user clicks the edit icon, then the confirm icon with a blank input - the event details remains the same).

4. The user is able to completely remove an event by clicking the delete icon on an event.

We'll address each of these interactions one by one.

`getActiveDay` | `setActiveDay`

Let's take a look at a single `day` object within our seed data once again:

calendar_app/src/app/seed.js

```
{
  id: 1,
  abbvTitle: 'Mon',
  fullTitle: 'Monday',
  events: [
    { details: 'Get Groceries', edit: false },
    { details: 'Carpool', edit: false }
  ],
  active: true
},
```

We see the `active` property in each day object behaves as a boolean (`true`/`false`). This property is the primary indicator for our first interaction. This interaction will be seen as two separate pieces:

- `getActiveDay()`: return the day object that has `active: true`

  This method is used to display the title of the `active` day in `CalendarEntry`.
- `setActiveDay()`: sets the selected day to `active: true` and all other day objects to `active: false`

  This function will run when the user clicks on a particular day (`CalendarDay`), with which the user intends to make *active*.

As we mentioned earlier, all actions that mutate state should always be contained within the store. With this in mind, let's create our store methods.

We'll build the `getActiveDay()` function by using JavaScript's `find()` method on the `seedData` array. The `find()` method always returns the first value from the array that pass the test implemented.

```
export const store = {
  state: {
    seedData
  },
  getActiveDay () {
    return this.state.seedData.find((day) => day.active);
  }
}
```

Keep in mind we're simply laying out the store methods first. Nothing will change in our application until we create the `@click` listeners in our components to dispatch events to the store.

For the second piece, as the user clicks on a particular day, we'll use `day.id` as the argument to determine what day was selected. We'll use JavaScript's native `map()` method to iterate over the entire state object, set the intended day's `active` property to `true`, and set every other day to `active: false`.

We'll include the `setActiveDay()` method right below `getActiveDay()` making our `store` object now look like:

calendar_app/src/app-4/store.js

```
export const store = {
  state: {
    seedData
  },
  getActiveDay () {
    return this.state.seedData.find((day) => day.active);
  },
  setActiveDay (dayId) {
    this.state.seedData.map((dayObj) => {
      dayObj.id === dayId ? dayObj.active = true : dayObj.active = false;
    });
  }
}
```

We're using a `ternary` operator in the `setActiveDay()` method as a shortcut for an `if` statement. If this is unclear, check out the Conditional (ternary) Operator[52] section in the MDN web docs for details on how this works.

[52]https://developer.mozilla.org/en-US/docs/Web/JavaScript/Reference/Operators/Conditional_Operator

With our state getter/setter setup, we need to dispatch events in our components to call these actions.

For `CalendarEntry`, we'll use a simple computed property, `titleOfActiveDay`, to return the full title of the returned day from the `getActiveDay()` method.

We can update the `<template>` and `<script>` tags in the `CalendarEntry.vue` file to be:

calendar_app/src/app-4/components/CalendarEntry.vue

```
<template>
  <div id="calendar-entry">
    <div class="calendar-entry-note">
      <input type="text" placeholder="New Event" />
      <p class="calendar-entry-day">
        Day of event: <span class="bold">{{ titleOfActiveDay }}</span>
      </p>
      <a class="button is-primary is-small is-outlined">Submit</a>
    </div>
  </div>
</template>

<script>
import { store } from '../store.js';

export default {
  name: 'CalendarEntry',
  computed: {
    titleOfActiveDay () {
      return store.getActiveDay().fullTitle;
    }
  },
}
</script>
```

We now need to create the `@click` listener in the `CalendarDay` component to listen for the user click event on a particular day. The `day` prop is available in `CalendarDay` so we'll use this property to pass in the `day.id` into the click handler method.

We'll create the click handler on the encompassing `<div class="day column"></div>` element of `CalendarDay`:

```
<template>
  <div class="day column" @click="setActiveDay(day.id)">
    <!-- rest of the CalendarDay template -->
  </div>
</template>
```

Let's now set up the `setActiveDay()` method in `CalendarDay`'s `method` property to subsequently dispatch the `store.setActiveDay()` function when called:

calendar_app/src/app-4/components/CalendarDay.vue

```
<script>
import { store } from '../store.js';
import CalendarEvent from './CalendarEvent.vue';

export default {
  name: 'CalendarDay',
  props: ['day'],
  methods: {
    setActiveDay (dayId) {
      store.setActiveDay(dayId);
    }
  },
  components: {
    CalendarEvent
  }
}
</script>
```

Together, the `<template>` and `<script>` elements in the `CalendarDay.vue` file should look like this:

calendar_app/src/app-4/components/CalendarDay.vue

```
<template>
  <div class="day column" @click="setActiveDay(day.id)">
    <div class="day-banner has-text-centered">{{ day.abbvTitle }}</div>
    <div class="day-details">
      <div class="day-number">{{ day.id }}</div>
      <CalendarEvent v-for="event in day.events"
        :key="day.events.indexOf(event)"
        :event="event"
        :day="day"/>
    </div>
```

```
  </div>
</template>

<script>
import { store } from '../store.js';
import CalendarEvent from './CalendarEvent.vue';

export default {
  name: 'CalendarDay',
  props: ['day'],
  methods: {
    setActiveDay (dayId) {
      store.setActiveDay(dayId);
    }
  },
  components: {
    CalendarEvent
  }
}
</script>
```

Great! Running our application and clicking on the day columns, we will now see the *Day of Event:* text in our `CalendarEntry` component referencing the selected day!

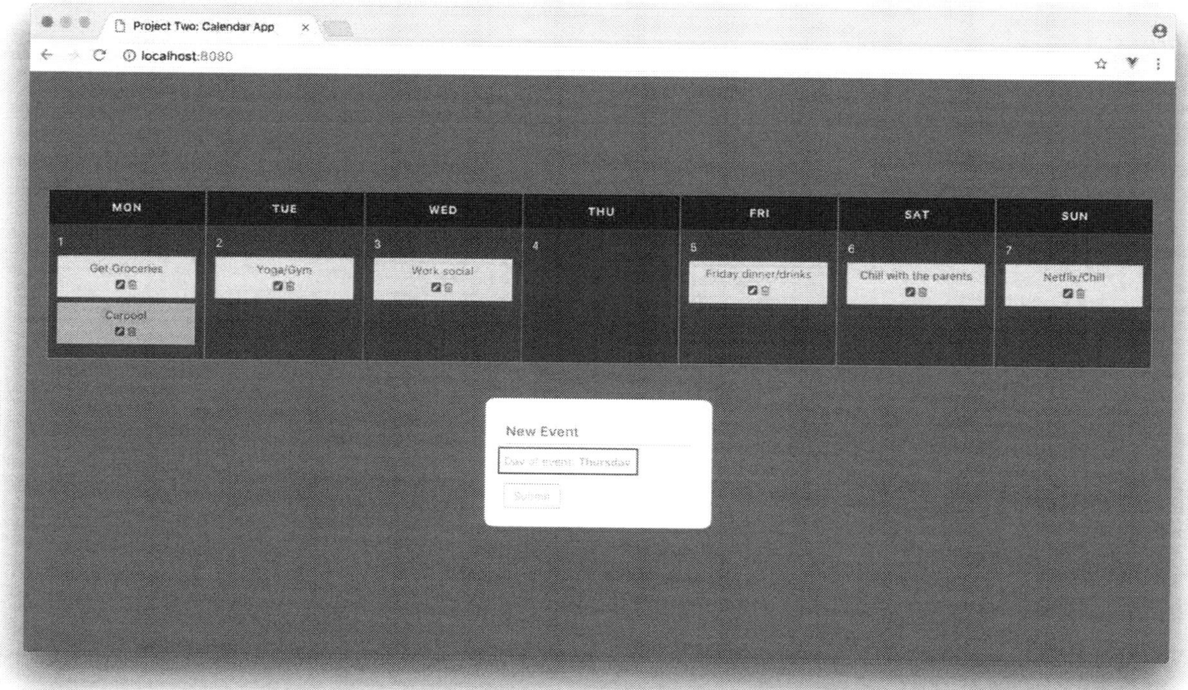

getActiveDay | setActiveDay

submitEvent

To address the interaction that involves submitting a new event to a certain day, we'll implement functionality that involves obtaining the information the user submits within the `CalendarEntry` input.

The day the user intends to submit an event to will have the `active` property set to true since the user must have clicked the day prior to typing the new event. With this in mind, let's set up a `submitEvent()` method in the `store.js` file that accepts an argument for the event details a user submits. The method will start by obtaining the active day with `getActiveDay()`:

```
export const store = {
// ...,
  submitEvent (eventDetails) {
    const activeDay = this.getActiveDay();
  }
}
```

Having the active day in our method, we can access the `events` array of that day with `activeDay.events`. We know a single `event` object within `events` has a `details` property and an `edit` property. We can push a new `event` object to the array by setting the `details` of the new object to the `eventDetails` argument and the `edit` property to `false`.

> We'll set the `edit` property of a new submitted event to `false` since this property will play a role in toggling UI with which we'll see later.

Our `submitEvent()` method now becomes:

calendar_app/src/app-5/store.js

```
export const store = {
  // ...
  submitEvent (eventDetails) {
    const activeDay = this.getActiveDay();
    activeDay.events.push({ "details": eventDetails, "edit": false });
  },
}
```

With the `submitEvent()` mutation prepared in our store, we need to create the component dispatcher. This component dispatcher will call `submitEvent()` and pass in the details a user types within the `input` field in `CalendarEntry`.

To capture the `input` value, we'll use the `v-model` directive to create two-way data binding between the form input and a data property in the component.

`v-model`

The `v-model` directive is used for two-way data binding with form inputs and textarea elements. In other words, `v-model` directly binds user input with a Vue object's data model (as one changes, the other gets updated).

In the `CalendarEntry` component, we've created the input field like below:

```
<input type="text" placeholder="New Event" required />
```

The `v-model` directive syntax takes an expression which is the name of the data property that the input is bound to. Specifying `inputEntry` to be the name of our input property, our `v-model` directive will be written as:

```
<input type="text" placeholder="New Event" v-model="inputEntry" required />
```

`inputEntry` now needs to be specified in the `CalendarEntry` data method. We'll set the initial value to be a blank string so the user is first presented with an empty field (remember, it's two-way data binded!):

```
<script>
import { store } from '../store.js';

export default {
  name: 'CalendarEntry',
  data () {
    return {
      inputEntry: ''
    }
  },
  // ...
}
</script>
```

In the `CalendarEntry` submit button, we can now add a click event listener to pass the `inputEntry` data value to a `submitEvent()` method:

```
<a class="button is-primary is-small is-outlined"
  @click="submitEvent(inputEntry)">
  Submit
</a>
```

When the user clicks the Submit button, this data property (`inputEntry`) will be passed to our component action as the new event details.

With the click listener specified in the template, we need to create the accompanying method in our component. This `submitEvent()` method will subsequently call `store.submitEvent()` and pass the user input appropriately. We'll also set `inputEntry` back to a blank string to clear out the user input:

```
<script>
import { store } from '../store.js';

export default {
  name: 'CalendarEntry',
  // ...,
  methods: {
    submitEvent (eventDetails) {
      store.submitEvent(eventDetails);
      this.inputEntry = '';
    }
  }
}
</script>
```

Things should be working well here. Before we test our application, let's introduce an `error` property within the component that:

1. Displays an error message if the user clicks submit without typing anything in the input
2. Prevents the action from calling the state mutation.

We'll first introduce the `error` property (initialized with `false`) in the component's data method:

```
<script>
import { store } from '../store.js';

export default {
  name: 'CalendarEntry',
  data () {
    return {
      inputEntry: '',
      error: false
    }
  },
  // ...
}
</script>
```

We can now specify a `<p>` tag in our `<template>` that renders *only if* the `error` property is set to true. This is where we'll use the `v-if` directive to *conditionally* display the `<p>` tag.

v-if

The `v-if` directive takes a data property as an expression and renders a particular code-block based on the truthiness of that data property. Here is how we'll implement the `<p>` tag using the `error` property as the condition to display the tag:

```
<p style="color: red; font-size: 13px" v-if="error">
  You must type something first!
</p>
```

We'll add the above tag as a sibling to the `<div class="calendar-entry-note"></div>` element, in the `<template>` of `CalendarEntry`:

calendar_app/src/app-5/components/CalendarEntry.vue

```
<template>
  <div id="calendar-entry">
    <div class="calendar-entry-note">
      <input type="text" placeholder="New Event" v-model="inputEntry" required />
      <p class="calendar-entry-day">
        Day of event: <span class="bold">{{ titleOfActiveDay }}</span>
      </p>
      <a class="button is-primary is-small is-outlined"
        @click="submitEvent(inputEntry)">
        Submit
      </a>
    </div>
    <p style="color: red; font-size: 13px" v-if="error">
      You must type something first!
    </p>
  </div>
</template>
```

Knowing that the error message should only show if the user attempts to submit with a blank string (i.e. when `error = true`), we'll dictate this in our components `submitEvent()` method. We'll also set a `return` statement to prevent the method dispatching the store action in this case:

calendar_app/src/app-5/components/CalendarEntry.vue

```
  methods: {
    submitEvent (eventDetails) {
      if (eventDetails === '') return this.error = true;

      store.submitEvent(eventDetails);
      this.inputEntry = '';
      this.error = false;
    }
  }
```

If `eventDetails` is blank, we've set the `error` property to `true` and return early. If `eventDetails` is not blank, we set the `error` property to `false` at the end of our method, after the store dispatcher, to remove any potential existing error messages in our template.

With all the above, our `CalendarEntry` component `<template>` and `<script>` will be laid out like this:

calendar_app/src/app-5/components/CalendarEntry.vue

```
<template>
  <div id="calendar-entry">
    <div class="calendar-entry-note">
      <input type="text" placeholder="New Event" v-model="inputEntry" required />
      <p class="calendar-entry-day">
        Day of event: <span class="bold">{{ titleOfActiveDay }}</span>
      </p>
      <a class="button is-primary is-small is-outlined"
        @click="submitEvent(inputEntry)">
        Submit
      </a>
    </div>
    <p style="color: red; font-size: 13px" v-if="error">
      You must type something first!
    </p>
  </div>
</template>

<script>
import { store } from '../store.js';

export default {
  name: 'CalendarEntry',
  data () {
    return {
      inputEntry: '',
      error: false
    }
  },
  computed: {
    titleOfActiveDay () {
      return store.getActiveDay().fullTitle;
    }
  },
  methods: {
    submitEvent (eventDetails) {
      if (eventDetails === '') return this.error = true;

      store.submitEvent(eventDetails);
      this.inputEntry = '';
      this.error = false;
```

```
    }
  }
}
</script>
```

We can now click any day in the calendar and submit events. Submit some events and try to submit events with blank inputs to see the error message. Here's a screen grab of three new events being submitted on Thursday:

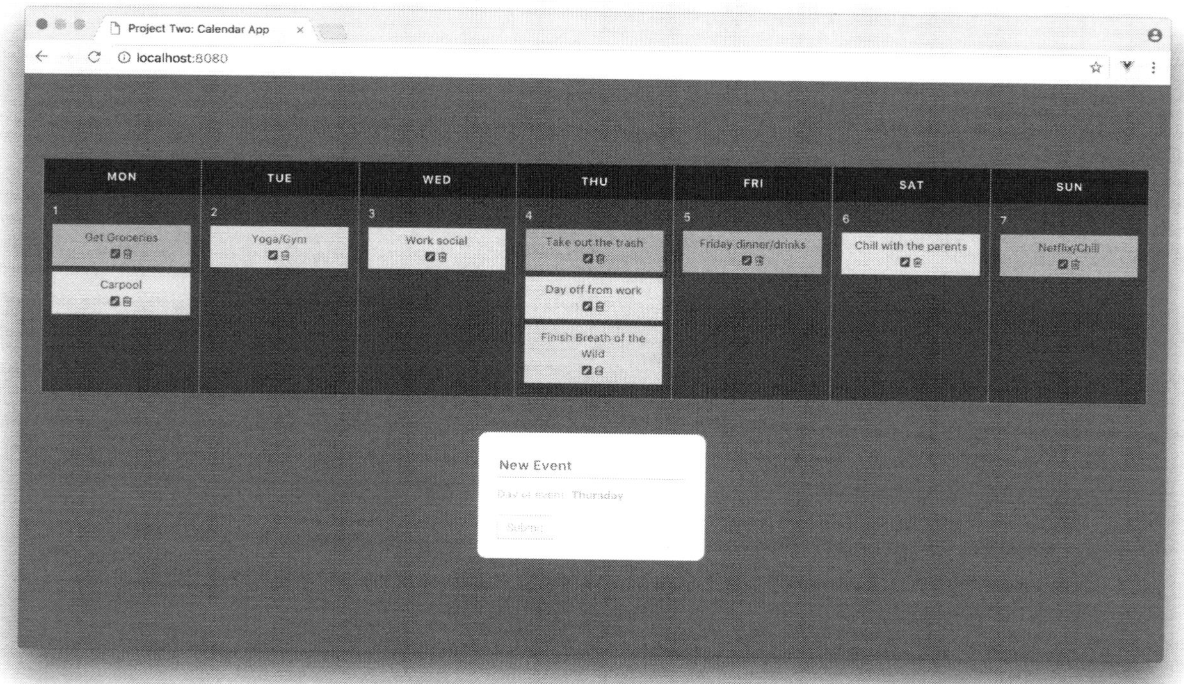

submitEvent

editEvent

Recall interacting with the completed app interface, a single event itself had a fair bit of functionality. The event can transform into an input to update the event details and clicking the trash icon deletes the event entirely.

We can regard displaying the event and editing the event as two distinct UI elements:

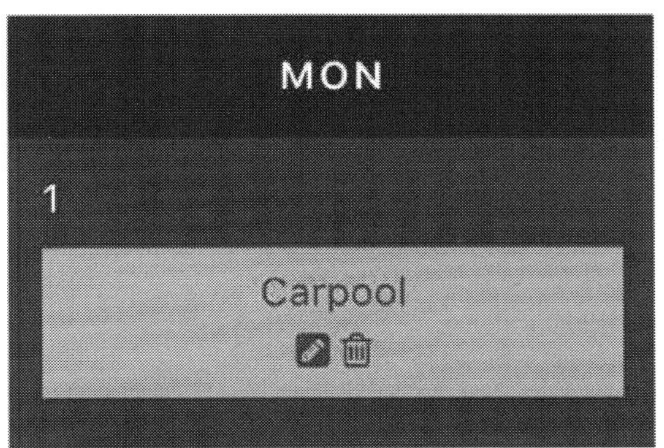

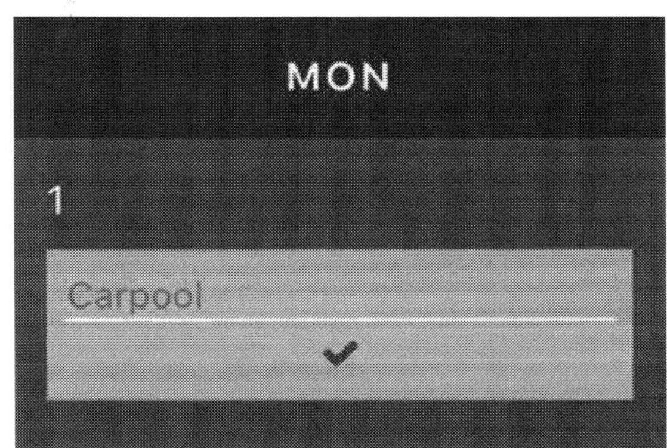

A single event: Displaying event (left) vs. edit event (right)

This is a case where we can take advantage of the event objects `edit` boolean to render one UI element in one condition and the other in the other condition.

Let's look at the `<template>` of what we have in the `CalendarEvent.vue` file:

calendar_app/src/app-5/components/CalendarEvent.vue

```
<template>
  <div class="day-event" :style="getEventBackgroundColor">
    <div>
      <span class="has-text-centered details">{{ event.details }}</span>
      <div class="has-text-centered icons">
        <i class="fa fa-pencil-square edit-icon"></i>
        <i class="fa fa-trash-o delete-icon"></i>
      </div>
    </div>
  </div>
</template>
```

We know `event.details`, `fa-pencil-square`, and `fa-trash-o` elements refer to the UI of an event that *isn't* being edited. Similar to how we conditionally displayed the error message in `CalendarEntry`, we can use the `v-if` directive to only render these elements when the event is not being edited (i.e. `!event.edit`).

```
<!-- ... -->
<div v-if="!event.edit">
  <span class="has-text-centered details">{{ event.details }}</span>
  <div class="has-text-centered icons">
    <i class="fa fa-pencil-square edit-icon"></i>
    <i class="fa fa-trash-o delete-icon"></i>
  </div>
</div>
<!-- ... -->
```

We still need to create the UI element that is displayed when the event *is* being edited (i.e. `event.edit`). The UI for this will have an input field (with a placeholder of the original event details) and a `fa-check` icon.

Let's specify this block right below the previous element making the entire `CalendarEvent` `<template>` element like so:

calendar_app/src/app-6/components/CalendarEvent.vue

```
<template>
  <div class="day-event" :style="getEventBackgroundColor">
    <div v-if="!event.edit">
      <span class="has-text-centered details">{{ event.details }}</span>
      <div class="has-text-centered icons">
        <i class="fa fa-pencil-square edit-icon"
          @click="editEvent(day.id, event.details)"></i>
        <i class="fa fa-trash-o delete-icon"></i>
      </div>
    </div>
    <div v-if="event.edit">
      <input type="text" :placeholder="event.details"/>
      <div class="has-text-centered icons">
        <i class="fa fa-check"></i>
      </div>
    </div>
  </div>
</template>
```

Our application now appears the same as it did before since all `event` objects have the `edit` attribute set to false. We'll need to create the click event listener to toggle between the non-edit and edit views.

Before we tackle that, let's create the necessary store method mutation.

The goal of our edit action/mutation is to simply allow the user to change the `edit` boolean of the intended event object from `false` to `true`. Since events are part of the `day` object, we can create a method that uses two `find()` calls to get the targeted event object:

- Filter `seedData`, based on `day.id`, to get the day that the event is being edited.
- Filter the events array of the targeted day, based on `event.details`, to get the targeted event.

Once the targeted event object is obtained, we can set its `edit` property to true. Let's introduce this `editEvent()` mutation to our store:

```
export const store = {
  // ...,
  editEvent (dayId, eventDetails) {
    const dayObj = this.state.seedData.find(
      day => day.id === dayId
    );
    const eventObj = dayObj.events.find(
      event => event.details === eventDetails
    );
    eventObj.edit = true;
  }
}
```

We now can create our component dispatcher to invoke the above mutation.

In the `<template>` of our `CalendarEvent` component, we'll introduce the `editEvent()` click-event listener on the `fa-pencil-square` `<i>` icon:

```
<i class="fa fa-pencil-square edit-icon"
  @click="editEvent(day.id, event.details)"></i>
```

Since we've attached the `editEvent()` click listener on the edit icon, we'll now introduce the method in our components `methods` option:

```
<script>
import { store } from '../store.js';

export default {
  name: 'CalendarEvent',
  // ...,
  methods: {
    editEvent (dayId, eventDetails) {
      store.editEvent(dayId, eventDetails);
    }
  }
}
</script>
```

At this moment, the events in our calendar app can switch from the first UI element (display event details) to the second UI element (edit event details) by clicking the edit icon.

Here's a screen grab of clicking the edit icon for all the events:

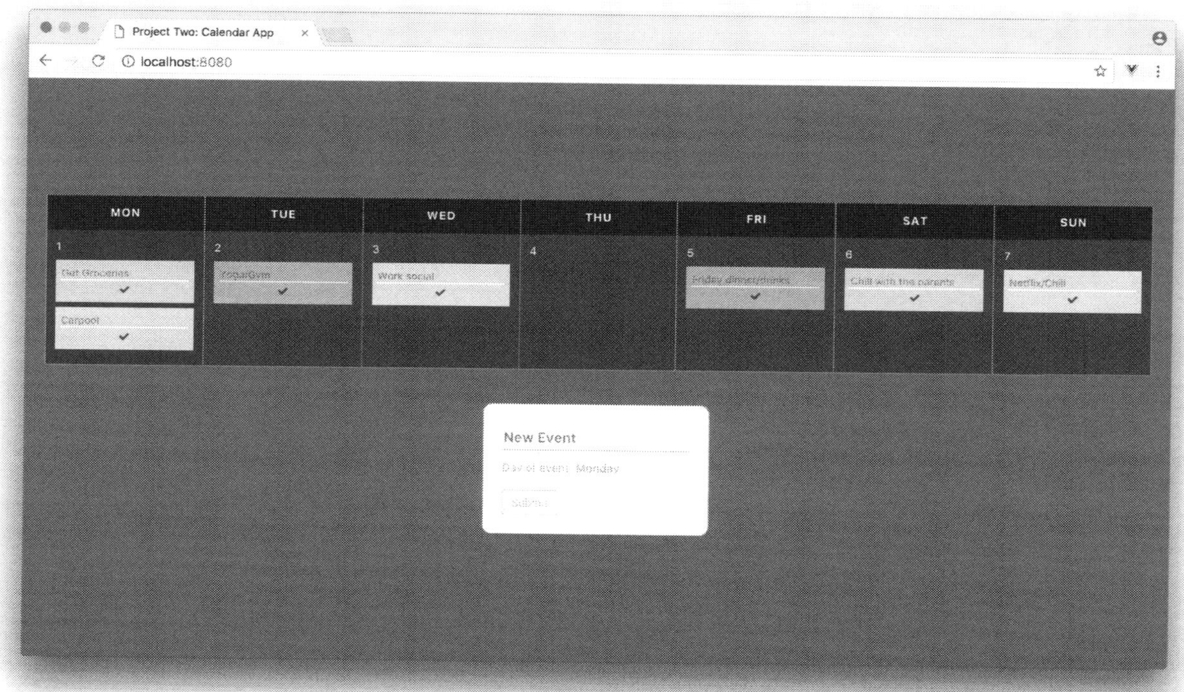

`editEvent`

Let's only allow the editing of one event at a time. This requirement means the `edit` boolean of all other events have to be set to `false`. To do handle this functionality, we can introduce a `resetEditOfAllEvents()` helper method in our store that sets all events to the non-edit state prior to toggling the targeted event.

In the `resetEditOfAllEvents()` method, we'll use the `map()` function to run through all the data and set all the events `edit` property to `false`:

```
export const store = {
  // ...,
  resetEditOfAllEvents () {
    this.state.seedData.map((dayObj) => {
      dayObj.events.map((event) => {
        event.edit = false;
      });
    });
```

```
  }
}
```

The `editEvent()` method can now call the helper `resetEditOfAllEvents()` prior to toggling the intended event `edit` property to `true`:

```
export const store = {
  // ...,
  editEvent (dayId, eventDetails) {
    this.resetEditOfAllEvents();
    const dayObj = this.state.seedData.find(
      day => day.id === dayId
    );
    const eventObj = dayObj.events.find(
      event => event.details === eventDetails
    );
    eventObj.edit = true;
  },
  resetEditOfAllEvents () {
    this.state.seedData.map((dayObj) => {
      dayObj.events.map((event) => {
        event.edit = false;
      });
    });
  }
}
```

Our application now only allows editing a single event at a time.

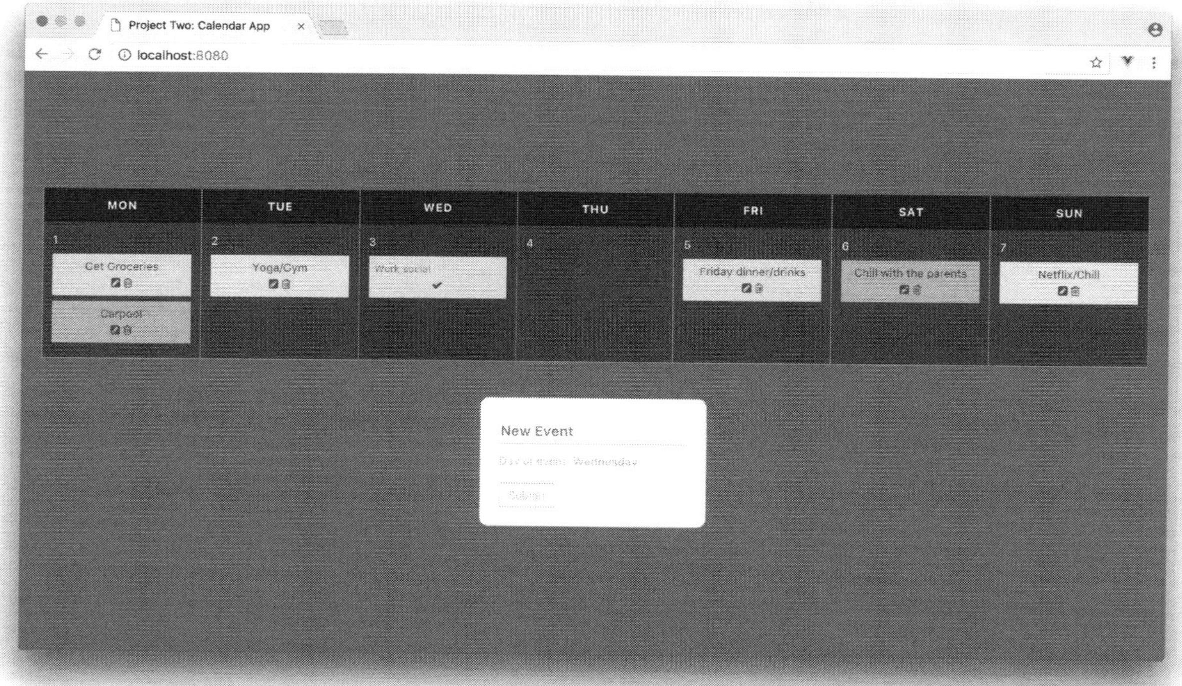

`editEvent`

`updateEvent`

We've established the first part of editing events within our calendar. Let's focus on the second part which involves updating event details with user input.

For this particular method, we'll create our component action first before setting up our state mutation. Lets look at the UI element and understand how we'll address capturing new event details.

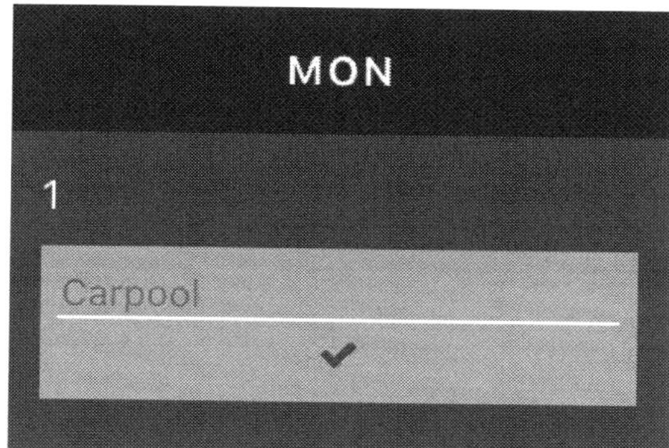

Update event details UI

There is no correct order in creating component actions and store mutations. Whether you find it easier to first set up the mutation or create the component action doesn't matter since you'll often find yourself frequently switching between them.

We'll use the `v-model` directive again to bind the user input to an attribute within the component's data object. We can then attach an `@click` event listener to our `fa-check` `<i>` icon and pass `day.id`, the current `event.details`, and the new user input to the method invoked when clicked. We'll call this method `updateEvent()`

The `v-if="event.edit"` section of `CalendarEvent` can now be updated to the following:

calendar_app/src/app-7/components/CalendarEvent.vue

```
    <div v-if="event.edit">
      <input type="text" :placeholder="event.details" v-model="newEventDetails"/>
      <div class="has-text-centered icons">
        <i class="fa fa-check"
          @click="updateEvent(day.id, event.details, newEventDetails)"></i>
      </div>
    </div>
```

Since we're binding a `newEventDetails` data property to the edit input, we need to create this property in the component's `data` object:

```
<script>
import { store } from '../store.js';

export default {
  name: 'CalendarEvent',
  // ...,
  data () {
    return {
      newEventDetails: ''
    }
  },
  // ...
}
</script>
```

It's important to understand that Vue **cannot** detect data property addition/deletion. This limitation is why a property must often be initialized in the data object for it to be considered *reactive*. Check out the Change-Detection-Caveats[53] docs for a deeper understanding of why this limitation exists.

[53]https://vuejs.org/v2/guide/reactivity.html#Change-Detection-Caveats

The new `updateEvent()` method now needs to be declared in the component to subsequently call the store action:

```
<script>
import { store } from '../store.js';

export default {
  name: 'CalendarEvent',
  // ...,
  methods: {
    editEvent (dayId, eventDetails) {
      store.editEvent(dayId, eventDetails);
    },
    updateEvent (dayId, originalEventDetails, updatedEventDetails) {
      store.updateEvent(dayId, originalEventDetails, updatedEventDetails);
    },
  }
}
</script>
```

In `updateEvent()`, we'll also specify that if `updatedEventDetails` is an empty string (i.e. the user input is left blank) - we'll assume the user aims to keep his original event details as is (i.e. `updatedEventDetails = originalEventDetails`):

```
updateEvent (dayId, originalEventDetails, updatedEventDetails) {
  if (updatedEventDetails === '') updatedEventDetails = originalEventDetails;
  store.updateEvent(dayId, originalEventDetails, updatedEventDetails);
},
```

The last thing we'll specify in our `updateEvent()` method is to set the **bound** input value back to an empty string. This clears out the user input upon submit:

calendar_app/src/app-7/components/CalendarEvent.vue

```
    updateEvent (dayId, originalEventDetails, updatedEventDetails) {
      if (updatedEventDetails === '') updatedEventDetails = originalEventDetails;
      store.updateEvent(dayId, originalEventDetails, updatedEventDetails);
      this.newEventDetails = '';
    }
```

Now that we have this set up, we'll need to create the necessary follow up method in the store.

We'll mimic the store's `editEvent` method to find the intended event object to update and set the event details of the event to the new user input. In addition, we can set the event `edit` attribute to false to revert the display out of the 'edit' UI element.

Our new store `updateEvent()` action:

```
export const store = {
  // ...,
  updateEvent (dayId, originalEventDetails, newEventDetails) {
    // Find the day object
    const dayObj = this.state.seedData.find(
      day => day.id === dayId
    );
    // Find the specific event
    const eventObj = dayObj.events.find(
      event => event.details === originalEventDetails
    );
    // Set the event details to the new details
    // and turn off editing
    eventObj.details = newEventDetails;
    eventObj.edit = false;
  },
  // ...
}
```

In both `editEvent()` and `updateEvent()`, we're following the same format to obtain the event object that's being edited/updated. We'll seperate that functionality on to a helper method to keep our code D.R.Y.

In the store, let's add a new helper method, called `getEventObj()` that we'd be able to use in our `editEvent()` and `updateEvent()` methods:

```
export const store = {
  // ...,
  getEventObj (dayId, eventDetails) {
    const dayObj = this.state.seedData.find(
      day => day.id === dayId
    );
    return dayObj.events.find(
      event => event.details === eventDetails
    );
  },
  // ...
}
```

`editEvent()` and `updateEvent()` can now use this helper method:

calendar_app/src/app-7/store.js

```
editEvent (dayId, eventDetails) {
  this.resetEditOfAllEvents();
  const eventObj = this.getEventObj(dayId, eventDetails);
  eventObj.edit = true;
},
updateEvent (dayId, originalEventDetails, newEventDetails) {
  const eventObj = this.getEventObj(dayId, originalEventDetails);
  eventObj.details = newEventDetails;
  eventObj.edit = false;
},
getEventObj (dayId, eventDetails) {
  const dayObj = this.state.seedData.find(
    day => day.id === dayId
  );
  return dayObj.events.find(
    event => event.details === eventDetails
  );
},
```

Saving our files and heading to `http://localhost:8080` in the browser, we can now edit our events!

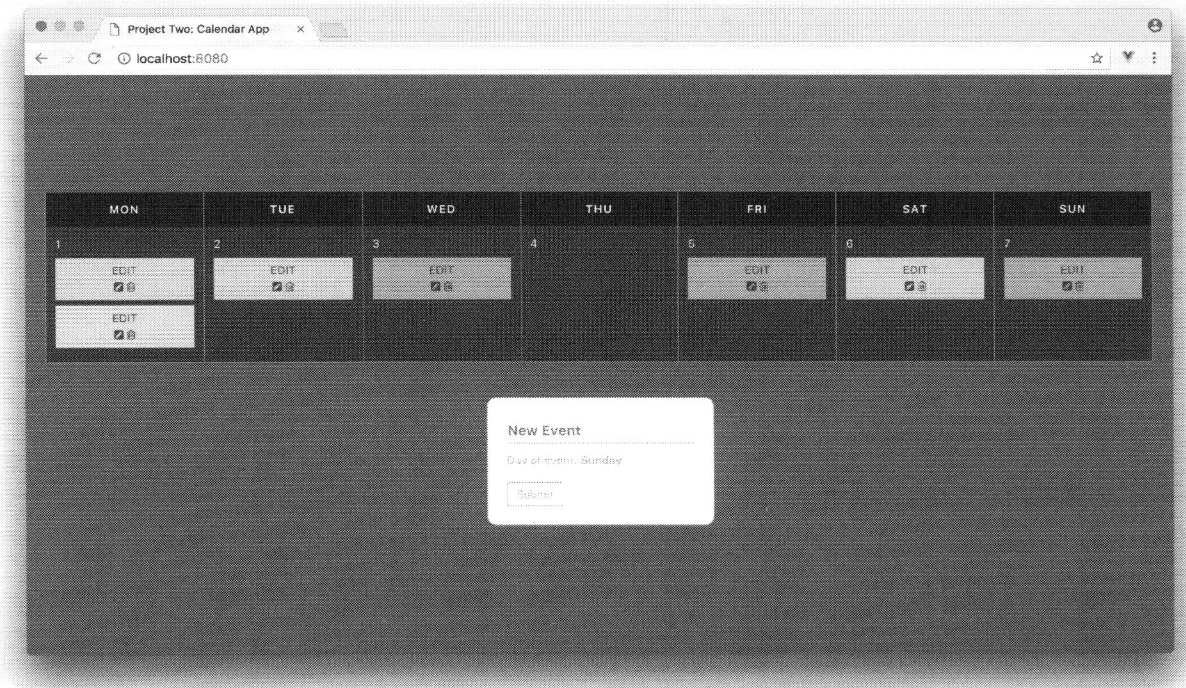

updateEvent

deleteEvent

We've almost completed the functionality of our application! The only other feature we want to introduce is the ability to completely delete events from the calendar.

Similar to our `editEvent()` method, we'll pass in `day.id` and `event.details` to a new dispatcher, `deleteEvent()`, in the `CalendarEvent` component.

We'll introduce the `deleteEvent()` click-event listener on the `fa-trash-o` <i> icon element in the `CalendarEvent.vue` file:

```
<i class="fa fa-trash-o delete-icon"
  @click="deleteEvent(day.id, event.details)"></i>
```

Let's set up the accompanying component method declaration:

```
<script>
export default {
  name: 'CalendarEvent',
  // ...,
  methods: {
    // ...,
    deleteEvent (dayId, eventDetails) {
      store.deleteEvent(dayId, eventDetails);
    }
  }
}
</script>
```

The `deleteEvent()` store mutation will use JavaScript's native `findIndex()` method on the `Array` object to return the index of the event to be deleted, based on its `event.details`. We'll then use Array's `splice()` function to remove the event from the `events` array.

We'll create `deleteEvent()` in the `store.js` file like so:

calendar_app/src/app-complete/store.js

```
export const store = {
  // ...
  deleteEvent (dayId, eventDetails) {
    const dayObj = this.state.seedData.find(
      day => day.id === dayId
    );
    const eventIndexToRemove = dayObj.events.findIndex(
      event => event.details === eventDetails
    );
    dayObj.events.splice(eventIndexToRemove, 1);
  },
  // ...
}
```

Ideally, we'd be using a more unique identifier (e.g. `id`) to parse through the events of a day and remove the event the user aims to delete. Since our `event` objects don't have unique `id`'s; we'll stick with using the event `details`.

Saving our changes, we can see that we're now able to delete events entirely.

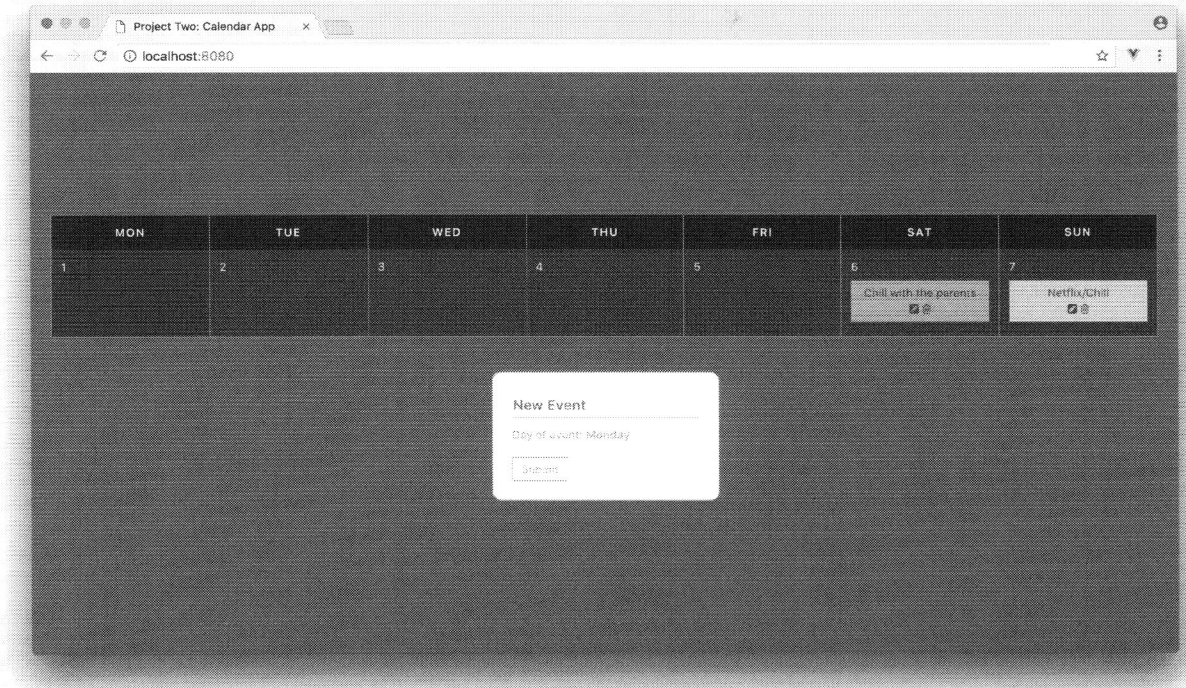

`deleteEvent`

The Calendar App

We can create, update and delete events in our application! This is excellent progress. With that being said, we'll address two important topics that limit the scale/capability of our app.

Persistence of data

When we refresh our browser, we lose all our application data. In other words, our app does not have any *data-persistence*.

A server can give us persistence. When our app loads, it will query the server and construct our data `store` based on the data the server provides (as opposed to using a static `seedData` object).

We'll then have our Vue app notify the server about any state changes/mutations, like when we delete a calendar event entirely.

Communicating with a server is a big major building block we'll need to develop and distribute real-world web applications with Vue.

State management

The **store pattern** we've set up worked fairly well for our application by allowing us to share data between components, and query and update our seed data. We employed good convention by keeping all our store actions centralized and had our components dispatch events to the store.

What if we want to scale our application state and appropriately track and replay changes to our state as they were happening? This feature is one primary benefit behind using Vue's official State Management library - **Vuex**.

We'll introduce Vuex in Chapter 4 and in Chapter 5 we'll see how **Vuex** can work with a server to ensure *persistence*. So get ready to level-up!

Methodology review

While building our calendar app, we learned and applied a methodology for building simple Vue apps. As a recap, these steps are:

1. Build a static version of the app

   Our application starting point was a static implementation of the app. This is always a great start to building any Vue application.
2. Break the app into components

   We mapped out the component structure of our app by examining the app's working UI. We then used Vue's single-file components and the single-responsibility principle to break components down so that each had minimal viable functionality.
3. Hard-code initial states with parent-child data flow

   By determining in which component each piece of state should live; we passed and referenced props from higher level components down to their children.
4. Create state actions (and corresponding component dispatchers)

   To make our app interactive, we created and centralized all state actions within the app store. We then created our component event listeners to dispatch events to the store which reactively updated our app.

III - Custom Events

Introduction

In the last chapter, we briefly touched upon what Vue Custom Events are and how they can be used to communicate from a child component back to a parent component. We also talked about how a *global event bus* can be used to make events global to all components.

When building our calendar app, we didn't find the need to use custom events since we set up a simple state pattern to manage our data. In this chapter, we'll build a simple application that takes advantage of the Vue event system to manage information between multiple components.

JavaScript Custom Events

As browsers are event-driven, events and event handling play a core role in JavaScript development by notifying our application when certain user actions occur.

Common JavaScript events we use all the time include the `onclick` event (when an element is clicked by a user), the `onload` event (when a page has completed loading), and the `onsubmit` event (when a form's submit button has been clicked).

We can create *event listeners* to provide additional methods/functionality to work with these events when the browser calls the callback.

In addition, JavaScript provides a `CustomEvent` API to allow us to create our *own custom events.*

Here's an example of how a custom event can be created, dispatched and listened to with native JavaScript:

```
// Creating the event
let event = new CustomEvent("customEvent", {
  detail: { book: "FullStack Vue " }
});

// Dispatching the event
element.dispatchEvent(event);

// Listening for the event
element.addEventListener("customEvent", e =>
  console.log("This book is " + e.detail.book)
);
```

Vue Custom Events

Vue implements its own events interface that works similarly to JavaScript's `addEventListener` and `dispatchEvent`. Though similar, it's **important** to note that Vue's event system is different than JavaScripts event system for DOM communication.

> Vue's event system is *primarily* used for **communication between components**, as opposed to communication between DOM nodes.

We know props have to be passed from parent to child components to pass data downwards through our component tree. Vue custom events are mainly used to create communication in the *opposite* direction, communication from the child up to the parent component.

Preparing the app

Let's build a very simple note-taking application to get an understanding of how custom events work in Vue.

Our note-taking app will have a simple input field that allows a user to enter notes. We'll assume there isn't a need for a submit button, so only when the user presses the `Enter` key, would the user input and the current timestamp gets captured and displayed to the view.

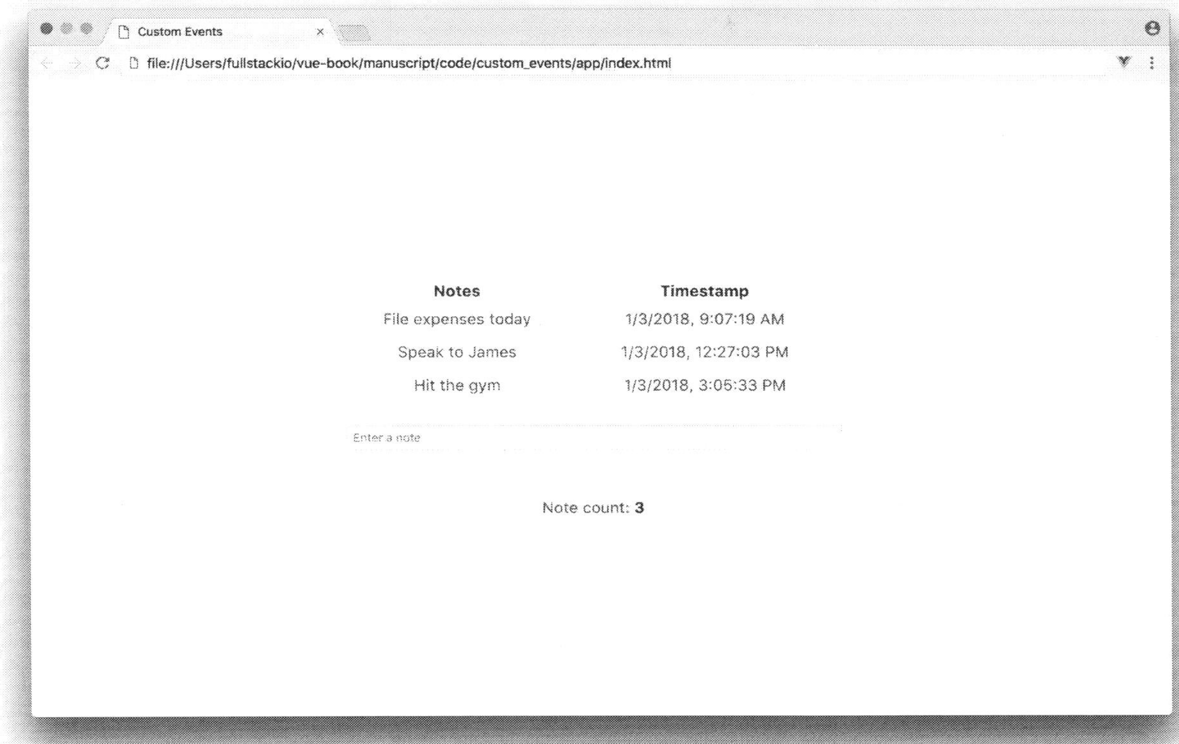

Let's open up the sample code that came with the book and locate the `custom_events/` folder. Opening the `custom_events/` folder, we'll see all the sub-directories contained within:

```
custom_events/
  app/
  app-1/
  app-2/
  app-complete/
  public/
```

We'll be working solely within the `app/` folder. We've included each version of the app as we build it through the chapter, in the `app-1/`, `app-2/`, and `app-complete/` folders.

The `public/` folder hosts the internal stylesheet, `styles.css`, of our application.

If we take a look within the `app/` directory, we'll see there's only two files located inside, `index.html` and `main.js`.

```
app/
  index.html
  main.js
```

Let's first take a look inside the `index.html` file.

custom_events/app/index.html

```
<!DOCTYPE html>
<html>

<head>
  <link
    rel="stylesheet"
    href="https://cdnjs.cloudflare.com/ajax/libs/bulma/0.5.3/css/bulma.css">
  <link rel="stylesheet" href="../public/styles.css" />
  <title>Custom Events</title>
</head>

<body>
  <div id="app">
    <div class="notes-section">
      <div class="columns">
        <div class="column has-text-centered">
          <strong>Notes</strong>
        </div>
        <div class="column has-text-centered">
          <strong>Timestamp</strong>
        </div>
      </div>
      <input-component></input-component>
    </div>
  </div>

  <script src="https://unpkg.com/vue"></script>
  <script src="./main.js"></script>
</body>

</html>
```

The `index.html` file has a similar set-up to the application we built in the first chapter. We're including Bulma[54] as our app's CSS framework and referencing an internal stylesheet `styles.css` in our `<head>` tag.

[54] http://bulma.io/

In our `<script>` tags, we're including Vue from a Content Delivery Network (CDN, for short) at unpkg[55] and specifying `./main.js` as the internal JavaScript file where we'll write our JavaScript.

Within the `<body>` of our HTML, we can see an encompassing `<div>` with an `id` of `app`, two separate columns of static text (Note and Timestamp), and a declaration of a custom child component `<input-component></input-component>`.

Let's open up our `main.js` file next:

custom_events/app/main.js

```
const inputComponent = {
  template: `<input class="input is-small" type="text" />`
}

new Vue({
  el: '#app',
  components: {
    'input-component': inputComponent
  }
})
```

We can see the template of `<input-component>` is a simple input field and the Vue instance specifies the element with the id of `app` as the element our application is to be mounted on.

When we open the `app/index.html` file in our Chrome Browser (right click and select `Open With > Google Chrome`), we will see a static view with no interactivity:

[55] https://unpkg.com

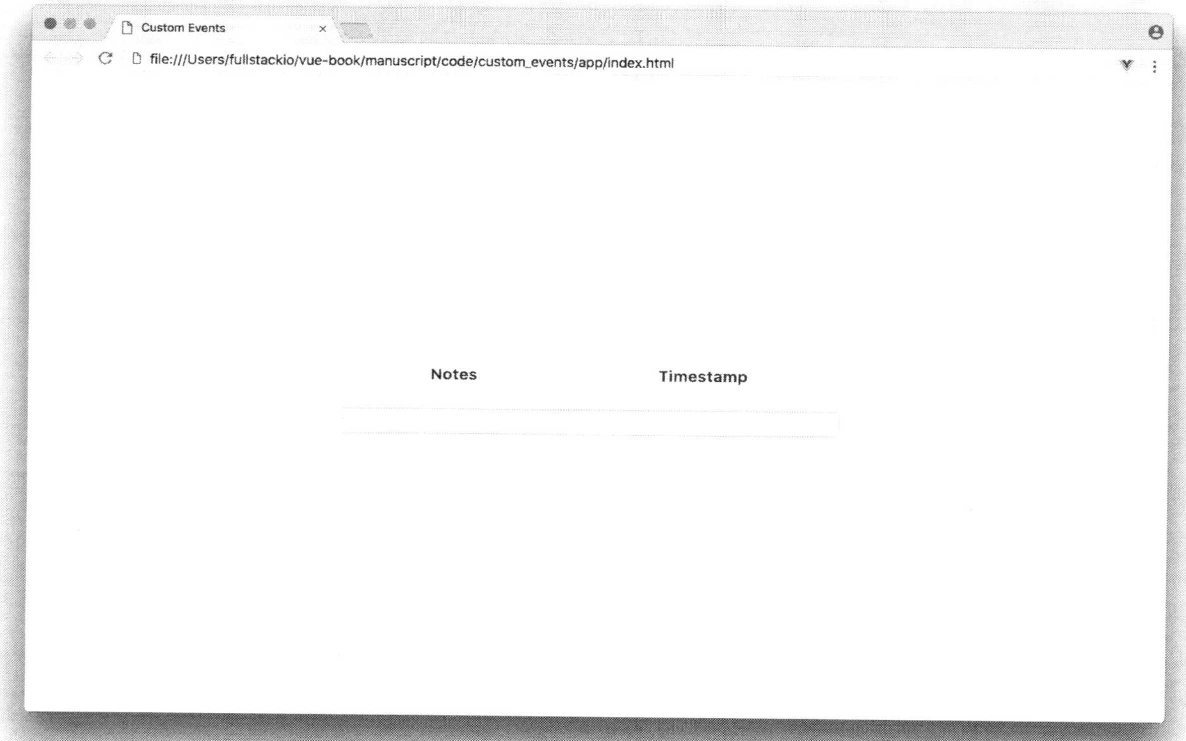

Components of the app

Before we begin adding interactivity into our application, let's lay out the actions we'll need to implement in order to have a complete working application. From our starting point, let's note that our application has a parent component (the root instance `#app`) and a single child component `input-component`.

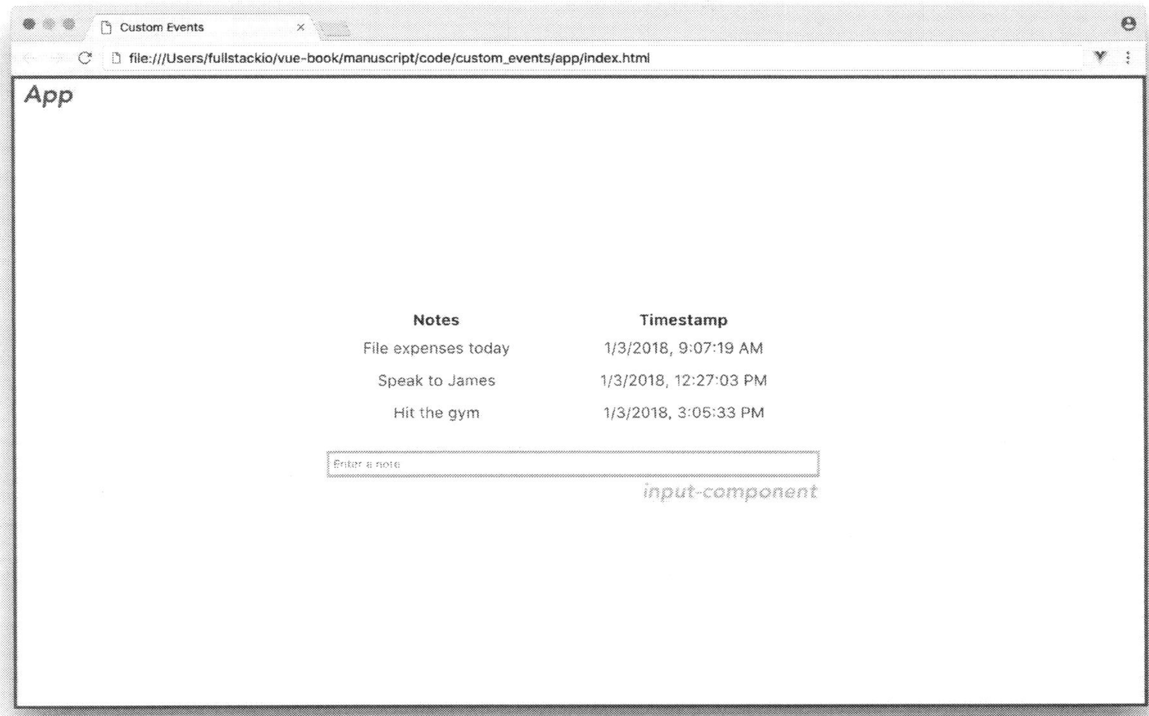

When the user types information and presses the `Enter` key, the user input should be displayed in the **Notes** column and the timestamp of that submission should be seen in the **Timestamp** column.

The input field is part of the `input-component` and the information displayed under **Notes** and **Timestamp** is part of the parent component (the root instance). We need an *action* to occur in the `input-component` that *notifies* the parent with the relevant data, so the parent can display that information.

Building the app

Since we know **Notes** and **Timestamps** are part of the Vue instance, lets create the necessary properties `notes` and `timestamps` within the instance's data object. We'll set blank arrays as their initial values. We'll also specify a `placeholder` property that we'll pass down to `input-component`.

In the `main.js` file, let's create the `data` object in our Vue instance:

custom_events/app-1/main.js

```
new Vue({
  // ...
  data: {
    notes: [],
    timestamps: [],
    placeholder: 'Enter a note'
  },
  // ...
})
```

With our `placeholder` property declared in our instance, let's bind this value as a `placeholder` prop for `<input-component></input-component>` to consume, in the `index.html` file:

```
<input-component :placeholder="placeholder"></input-component>
```

Let's declare the `placeholder` prop in `inputComponent` and bind it to the input placeholder attribute in its template. In our `main.js` file, let's update the `inputComponent` definition object to:

```
const inputComponent = {
  template: `<input
        :placeholder="placeholder"
        class="input is-small" type="text" />`,
  props: ['placeholder']
}
```

The input field now has a placeholder with a dynamic value declared in the Vue instance.

`<input-component></input-component>` refers to the declaration of the component in the application template. `inputComponent` refers to the component variable in the `main.js` file.

Our input in `inputComponent` needs to be dynamically-bound to a data value to allow it to communicate with the parent instance. To bind a data value, we'll set up the `v-model` directive with `input` as the name of the input property:

```
const inputComponent = {
  template: `<input
        :placeholder="placeholder"
        v-model="input"
        class="input is-small" type="text" />`,
  props: ['placeholder'],
  data () {
    return {
      input: ''
    }
  }
}
```

We're now in a good spot to create our first event handler. We know the input is only submitted when the `Enter` key is released. With this interaction in mind, we'll need to use JavaScripts `keyup` event listener.

When we listen for certain keyboard button triggers in vanilla JavaScript, we usually need to check the code for the event key that was triggered (e.g. `event.code === '13'`).

Vue allows us to specify the key code within the `keyup` directive declaration (e.g. `@keyup.13`). For even further simplification, Vue provides aliases for the most common keys (e.g. `@keyup.enter` will trigger only when the `Enter` key is released).

The Key Modifiers[56] section in the Vue docs provides further details on the different modifiers we can apply to the `keyup` event.

We'll use `@keyup.enter` to call a `monitorEnterKey()` method that we'll create in our component shortly. Let's add this keyup event listener to the `<template>` of `inputComponent`:

custom_events/app-2/main.js

```
  template: `<input
        :placeholder="placeholder"
        v-model="input"
        @keyup.enter="monitorEnterKey"
        class="input is-small" type="text" />`,
```

Just like we've done with most of our event listeners, we're using the `@` shorthand instead of `v-on:`.

[56] https://vuejs.org/v2/guide/events.html

With our `keyup` listener in place, we now need to create the `monitorEnterKey()` method. This function is where we'll be *emitting* the input the user enters from the component to the Vue instance.

Vue custom events are triggered using `$emit` while specifying the name of the custom event:

```
this.$emit('nameOfEvent');
```

The `$emit` function allows for a second *optional* argument that allows the caller to pass arbitrary values along with the emitted event:

```
this.$emit('nameOfEvent', {
  data: {
    book: 'FullStack Vue'
  }
});
```

Though listening for custom events in Vue can be done with `$on`, the `v-on` directive **must** be used in parent templates to listen to events emitted by children. We'll address `$on` when we set up event communication between unrelated components.

In our `monitorEnterKey()` method, let's set up a custom event `$emit` with an event name of `add-note`.

In this custom event, we'll pass in a data object that consists of two properties:

- the user input
- the timestamp.

The user input is the bound data value of the input field. We'll get the timestamp using the `new Date().toLocaleString` method, which returns a language appropriate representation of the current date in a string.

Let's define the `monitorEnterKey()` method in a `methods` property of the component:

```
const inputComponent = {
  // ...,
  methods: {
    monitorEnterKey() {
      this.$emit('add-note', {
        note: this.input,
        timestamp: new Date().toLocaleString()
      });
    }
  }
}
```

Directly after the declared event emitter, we'll set the input field value to an empty string to clear out user input.

```
const inputComponent = {
  // ...
  methods: {
    monitorEnterKey() {
      this.$emit('add-note', {
        note: this.input,
        timestamp: new Date().toLocaleString()
      });
      this.input = '';
    }
  }
};
```

With the event emitter created, we need to find a way to notify our root instance when the `add-note` event is triggered.

Just like how we've specified our `keyup` event listener on the DOM, we can declare custom event listeners on the template DOM as well. Since the `add-note` custom event is triggered within the `input-component`, we have to create the event listener on the `<input-component></input-component>` declaration in the application template. This event listener can trigger a method in the root instance to update the parent.

Let's create the event listener on the `<input-component></input-component>` declaration, in `index.html`, to call an `addNote()` method when triggered:

custom_events/app-2/index.html

```
      <input-component
        @add-note="addNote" :placeholder="placeholder"></input-component>
```

Now we can create the `addNote()` method in our root instance. With the `event` object present, the `addNote()` method pushes the `event.note` and `event.timestamp` to the instance's `notes` and `timestamps` arrays respectively:

custom_events/app-2/main.js

```
new Vue({
  // ...
  methods: {
    addNote(event) {
      this.notes.push(event.note);
      this.timestamps.push(event.timestamp);
    }
  },
  // ...
});
```

By default with JavaScript, the event object is automatically passed down as the first argument without the need for us to declare it in the template.

We can render a list of notes and timestamps in the view now that we have our event system wired up. We'll use `v-for` to render a list of `<div>` elements for each note and timestamp in their respective arrays.

Setting the `v-for` lists right below the `<strong>` titles, the `<div class="columns"></div>` section of our `#app` template, in the `index.html`, will look like this:

custom_events/app-2/index.html

```
      <div class="columns">
        <div class="column has-text-centered">
          <strong>Notes</strong>
          <div v-for="note in notes" class="notes">
            {{ note }}
          </div>
        </div>
        <div class="column has-text-centered">
          <strong>Timestamp</strong>
          <div v-for="timestamp in timestamps" class="timestamps">
```

```
        {{ timestamp }}
      </div>
    </div>
  </div>
```

With this implementation, we've just crafted our first custom event using Vue's event system.

Saving our files and refreshing our browser, we should be able to submit notes by typing information and releasing the 'Enter' key.

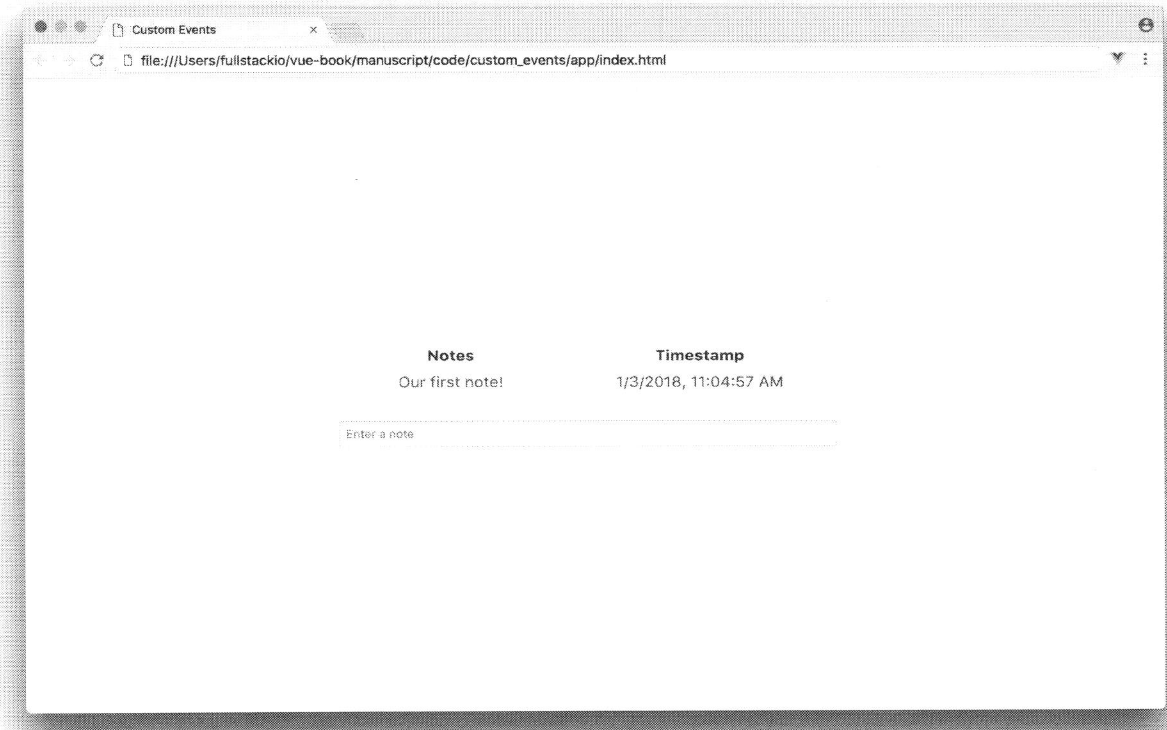

Let's summarize what we did to make this work:

- On `input-component`, the `keyup.enter` event listener is triggered when the 'Enter' key is released and calls `monitorEnterKey()`.
- The `monitorEnterKey()` method emits the custom `add-note` event and clears the input field.
- The `add-note` event listener declared on `<input-component></input-component>` listens for the event trigger and calls the root instance `addNote()` method.
- The `addNote()` method then updates the instance's data property which reactively rerenders the view

Here's a simple graphical representation of how that worked:

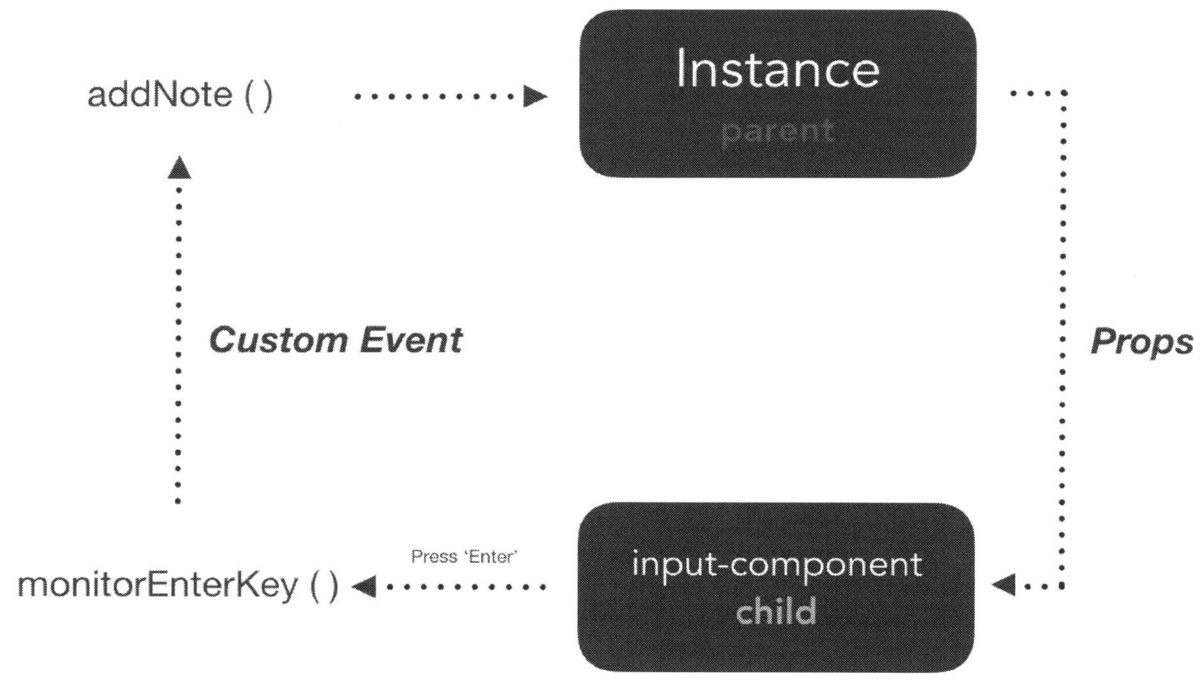

Event Bus

With props and custom events, we've become accustomed to understand simple component communication depends on hierarchy. Parents pass props down and custom events send events up.

With our application, assume we want to introduce a single new feature that displays the number of notes a user has entered. We'll introduce this feature through a new `<note-count-component></note-count-component>` as a sibling to `<input-component></input-component>` and a child of the root instance.

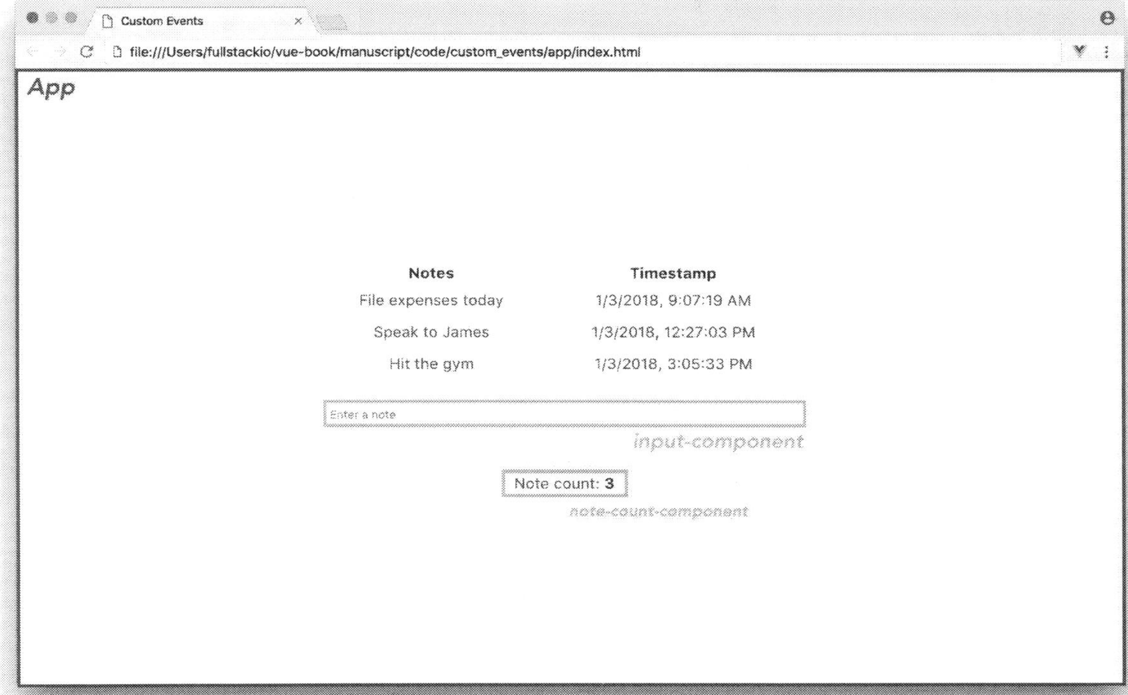

There are two ways we can go about creating this component's functionality.

- We can specify a new data property `noteCount` on the root instance which gets incremented with the `addNote()` method and pass it down as props to `note-count-component`.
- The second approach is to directly *trigger* an event from `input-component`, to increment a `noteCount` property within `note-count-component`.

We'll go with the latter approach to explain how an **Event Bus** can achieve this.

`input-component` and `note-count-component` are independent of one another. We can say they are unaware of each other's existence since neither explicitly registers the other. As a result, `note-count-component` will not be able to directly *listen* for an event trigger that occurs in `input-component`. This case is where we need a mechanism to transfer events between components, or in other words, an Event Bus.

> An **Event Bus** is a Vue instance that is used to enable isolated components to subscribe and publish custom events between each other.

In Vue, we can create an Event Bus by instantiating a new `Vue` instance.

```
const EventBus = new Vue();
```

An Event Bus is often made global to make it available everywhere in your app. For very simple project scaffolds, this can be done with:

```
window.EventBus = new Vue();
```

And for projects with import/export available:

```
import Vue from 'vue';
const EventBus = new Vue();
export default EventBus;
```

We know every Vue instance implements an events interface to allow the instance to trigger and listen for events. An EventBus has its own events interface that can be used within multiple components. Emitting events remain the same with `$emit`:

```
EventBus.$emit('nameOfEvent', {
  data: {
    book: 'FullStack Vue'
  }
});
```

Listening for events anywhere in our applications can now be handled using the `$on` method:

```
EventBus.$on("nameOfEvent", e =>
  console.log("This book is " + e.data.book)
);
```

Refactoring `this.$emit` to `Eventbus.$emit`

Let's refactor our existing custom event to instead use an Event Bus. First, let's declare the Event Bus at the top of our main.js file so we can use it within the rest of our application.

custom_events/app-complete/main.js

```
const EventBus = new Vue();
```

In the `monitorEnterKey()` method within `inputComponent`, we'll change from using the components events interface to that of the Event Bus to trigger the `add-note` event:

custom_events/app-complete/main.js

```
methods: {
  monitorEnterKey() {
    EventBus.$emit('add-note', {
      note: this.input,
      timestamp: new Date().toLocaleString()
    });
    this.input = '';
  }
}
```

Since we're using the Event Bus, a completely separate Vue instance, to trigger the event, we're now unable to listen to the event with `v-on` directly on the template. Instead, we have to specify `EventBus.$on()` within the component we want to listen.

Let's introduce the `EventBus.$on()` call method somewhere in our root instance to listen on and subsequently call the `addNote()` method when the event is triggered.

We'll implement this callback within the component's **`created`** lifecycle hook.

The Vue instance lifecycle

Lifecycle hooks, within a Vue instance are named functions that occur throughout the *lifecycle* of the instance. The lifecycle refers to the time an instance has been created, mounted, updated, and even destroyed. Vue gives us the ability to create actions whenever a lifecycle hook has been run.

An example of such a lifecycle hook is the `created` hook. The `created` hook is run when the instance has just been *created* and the instance data and events are active, and when the instance can be accessed.

If we wanted to alert the browser with information about an instance's data property upon launch, the `created` hook will work well:

```
new Vue({
  el: '#app',
  data: {
    book: 'FullStack Vue'
  },
  created () {
    alert('This book is ' + this.book);
  }
});
```

The `updated` hook can be used to apply an action whenever there are any data changes to a Vue instance causing it to re-render. Here's a simple case where `updated` can be used to log a data property when a data change has been made:

```
new Vue({
  el: '#app',
  data: {
    count: 'FullStack Vue'
  },
  updated () {
    console.log('The count is ' + this.count);
  },
  methods: {
    updateCount () {
      this.count++;
    }
  }
});
```

The Vue instance lifecycle is an important concept to understand since it allows us to run actions in specific stages of a Vue instance. We'll be explaining the hooks we use throughout the book, as we use them.

If you'd like to see all the possible lifecycle hooks one can use, the Lifecycle Diagram[57] section of the Vue docs provides a great graphical summary.

created

The `created` hook is triggered the moment a Vue instance has been created and the instance data and events can be accessed.

Since this hook refers to the *moment* of creation, it's the perfect time to set up our event listener (`EventBus.$on`). We'll first do this in the root instance.

Once the instance is created, the EventBus listener will be prepared to listen for an event trigger *throughout* the life of the instance. When the event is triggered, the listener will call the `addNote()` method and pass down the `event` object.

Let's see this in practice. We'll add this `created` hook to the Vue instance like so:

[57] https://vuejs.org/v2/guide/instance.html#Lifecycle-Diagram

```
new Vue({
  // ...,
  created() {
    EventBus.$on('add-note', event => this.addNote(event));
  },
  // ...,
});
```

We can now remove the event listener that's been declared on `<input-component></input-component>` in the parent template making our `<input-component></input-component>` declaration only have a placeholder prop:

custom_events/app-complete/index.html

```
      <input-component :placeholder="placeholder"></input-component>
```

We've now refactored our `add-note` event to be part of the `EventBus` as opposed to the internal `input-component`. Saving our files and running our application, everything should remain the same since we haven't changed anything else:

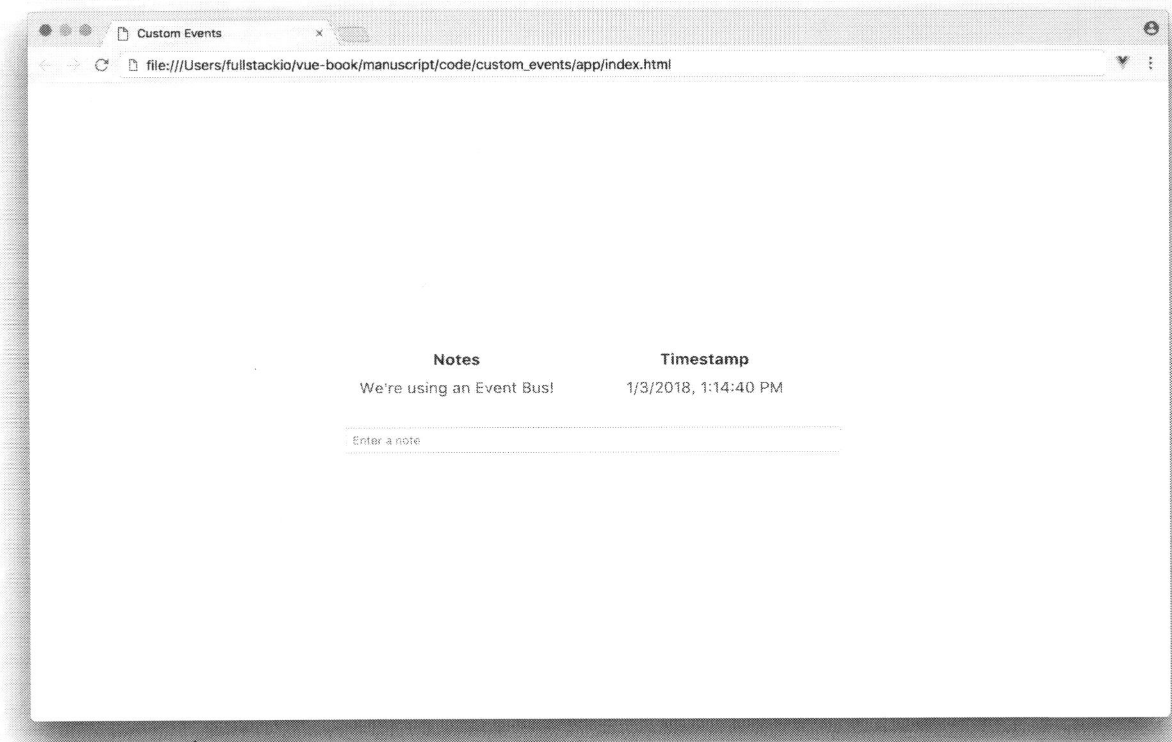

note-count-component

With our Event Bus appropriately set up, it's now simple to build our `note-count-component` and create an event listener within this new component.

Let's create the `<note-count-component></note-count-component>` declaration at the bottom of our parent template in the `index.html` file:

```
<div id="app">
  <div class="notes-section">
    <!-- The notes-section -->
  </div>
  <note-count-component></note-count-component>
</div>
```

To allow the use of the component declaration in the parent instance, we need to register this component within the scope of the parent. We'll do this by defining it in the `components` property of the parent instance, in the `main.js` file:

```
new Vue({
  // ...,
  components: {
    'input-component': inputComponent,
    'note-count-component': noteCountComponent
  }
});
```

Now we can set up the `noteCountComponent` component object. The template for this component is to be a simple `<div>` element that displays a `noteCount` data property. We'll create the `noteCount-Component` object right above the Vue instance:

```
const EventBus = new Vue();

const inputComponent = {
  // ...
};

const noteCountComponent = {
  template:
    `<div class="note-count">Note count: <strong>{{ noteCount }}</strong></div>`,
  data () {
    return {
```

```
      noteCount: 0
    }
  }
};

new Vue({
  // ...
});
```

We know the add-note event is triggered whenever a single note is entered. The simplest way we can count the number of notes submitted is to trigger an increment to the noteCount data value whenever the add-note event is emitted.

Just like how we set up the event listener in the created hook of the root instance, we'll do the same in this component. In this component's created hook, when the add-note event is triggered, the noteCount property value will be incremented by one:

custom_events/app-complete/main.js

```
const noteCountComponent = {
  template: `<div class="note-count">
      Note count: <strong>{{ noteCount }}</strong>
    </div>`,
  data() {
    return {
      noteCount: 0
    };
  },
  created() {
    EventBus.$on('add-note', event => this.noteCount++);
  }
};
```

That's it! Notice how easy it is to create event listeners now, regardless of whether components are dependant/independent of one other. Saving the files and running our application we'll be able to see a count of the number of notes submitted:

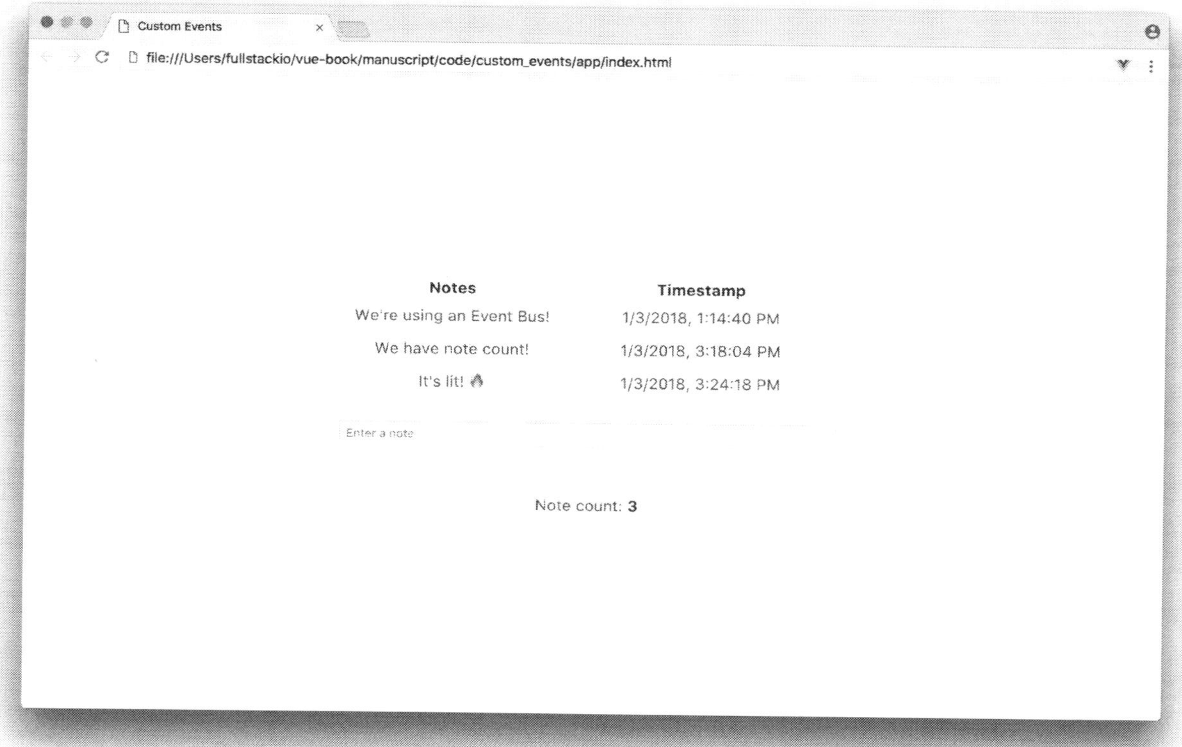

Custom events and managing data

With this simple note-taking app, we've obtained a good understanding of how custom events work and how an Event Bus can be used to communicate between all the components in an application.

Reviewing our work thus far, custom events can be used to notify a parent whenever a child component performs a certain action. An Event Bus on the other hand is geared towards setting up a standard method for all components to communicate with each other.

In much larger Vue applications, the global Event Bus can be extracted to its own separate file (e.g. `event-bus.js`) and imported whenever needed. The Event Bus itself can also be modified to have more internal logic to communicate with a server or a real-time backend. This set-up is useful since all events will be handled within a *central* location.

Different developers have different use cases for different applications. However, as mentioned in the previous chapter, a global Event Bus is not the *recommended* way of managing data between components[58].

Though incredibly easy to set-up, things get difficult to track *really quickly*. Having a large number

[58]https://vuejs.org/v2/style-guide/#Non-flux-state-management-use-with-caution

of event emitters/listeners sporadically placed in your components can make code frustrating to maintain and can become a source of bugs.

The main pain-point arises from the **tight coupling between user interactions and data changes**. For complex web applications, oftentimes a single user interaction can affect many different, discrete parts of the state.

This is where the advantage of using Vuex[59], the Flux-like library for state management, comes in. Vuex is the preferred method for managing data within applications, with which we'll be seeing in detail in the next chapter!

Summary

1. Vue custom events, though similar to native JavaScript custom events, are used primarily for a child component to notify its parent. `$emit` is used to create the event emitter within the child component and the `v-on` directive used on the template listens to the emitted events.
2. Vue lifecycle hooks can be used for us to create actions when an instance has gone through its lifecycle. `created`, `mounted`, `updated` and `destroy` are some of the more commonly used lifecycle hooks.
3. An Event Bus can use its internal events interface to create event emitters/listeners that any component relationship (parent-child, sibling-sibling) can adhere to.

---

[59]https://vuex.vuejs.org/

IV - Introduction to Vuex

Recap

In the second chapter, we used a basic methodology to build a Vue app. After setting up our static components, we created a store pattern to manage the application state for all components.

We kept all store actions centralized within the store object and had components dispatch events to the store. The components that displayed store information reactively rendered whenever a relevant change to store data was made.

The pattern we've just explained brings us very *close* to the popular and widely used **Flux** architecture.

What is Flux?

Flux[60] is a design pattern created by Facebook. The Flux pattern is made up of four parts, organized as a one-way data pipeline:

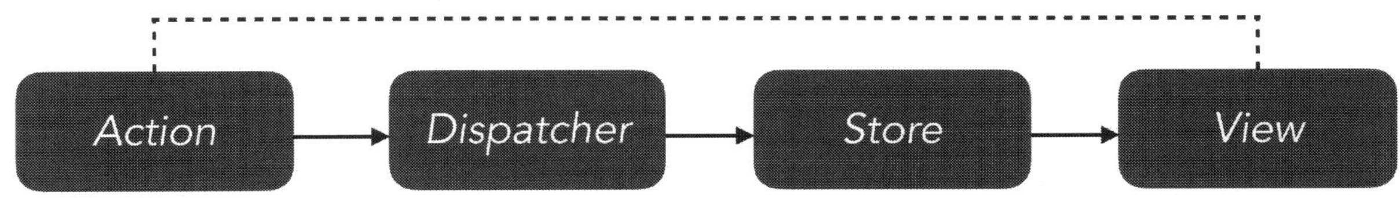

General Flux diagram

The **view** dispatches **actions** that describe what happened. The **store** receives these actions and determines what state changes should occur. After the state updates, the new state is pushed to the view.

In addition to decoupling interaction handling and state changes, Flux also provides the following benefits:

Breaking up state management logic

Flux allows us to naturally break up state management into isolated, smaller, and testable parts.

[60]https://facebook.github.io/flux/

Components are simpler

Certain component-managed state is fine, like activating certain buttons on mouse hover. However, by managing all other state externally, Vue components become simple HTML rendering functions. Detaching the data storage from the view makes them smaller, easier to understand, and more composable.

Mismatch between the state tree and the DOM tree

Oftentimes, we want to store our state with a different representation than how we want to display it. For example, we might want to have our app store a timestamp for a message (`createdAt`), but in the view we want to display a human-friendly representation, like "23 minutes ago."

Instead of having components hold all this computational logic for *derived data*, we can let Flux perform these computations *before* providing state to Vue components.

Flux implementations

Flux is a design pattern, not a specific library or implementation. Facebook has open-sourced a library they use[61]. This library provides the interface for a dispatcher and a store that we can use in our application.

Facebook's implementation is not the exclusive option. Since Facebook started sharing Flux with the community, the community has responded by writing tons of different Flux implementations[62].

Redux[63] has been made incredibly popular within the React ecosystem (and can be used in a Vue application, with minor configuration changes).

Within the Vue community, however, Vuex[64] is the most-widely used state management library.

Vuex

Unlike other Flux libraries, Vuex was created by the Vue team and built *solely for use* with Vue. Vuex provides a more fluid and intuitive development experience when integrated to an existing Vue app.

Vuex builds on top of having a simple store pattern by introducing:

- Explicitly defined getters, mutations and actions
- Integration with the Vue devtools for time-travel debugging and state snapshot import/export

[61]https://github.com/facebook/flux
[62]https://github.com/voronianski/flux-comparison
[63]https://github.com/reactjs/redux
[64]https://github.com/vuejs/vuex

Vuex does come with more boilerplate that may not be necessary for all applications. However, once we get beyond the initial hurdle of setting up Vuex, there are numerous benefits in conforming to a strong Flux-like pattern.

In the following chapters, we'll see how using Vuex as the backbone of our application equips our app to handle increasing feature complexity.

Though Vuex is primarily a Flux-like library, it also takes inspiration from the Elm Architecure[65] of building web apps.

Vuex's key ideas

Throughout this chapter, we'll become familiar with each of Vuex's key ideas. Those ideas are:

- All of our application's data is in a single data structure called the **state**, which is held in the **store**
- Our app reads the **state** from this **store**
- The **state** is never mutated directly outside the **store**
- The **views** dispatch **actions** that describe what happened
- The **actions** commit to **mutations**
- **Mutations** directly mutate/change store state
- When the **state** is mutated, relevant components/views are re-rendered

We've already implemented some of these ideas previously by using a simple store pattern. Over the course of this chapter, we'll work through them even deeper within the context of using Vuex.

> Just like how Vue differs from React, Vuex differs from Redux by mutating the state **directly** as opposed to making the state immutable and replacing it entirely. This idea ties with Vue's ability to automatically understand which components need to be re-rendered when state has been changed.

Refactoring the note-taking app

In the last chapter, we built a simple note-taking application with the help of an Event Bus:

[65]https://guide.elm-lang.org/architecture/

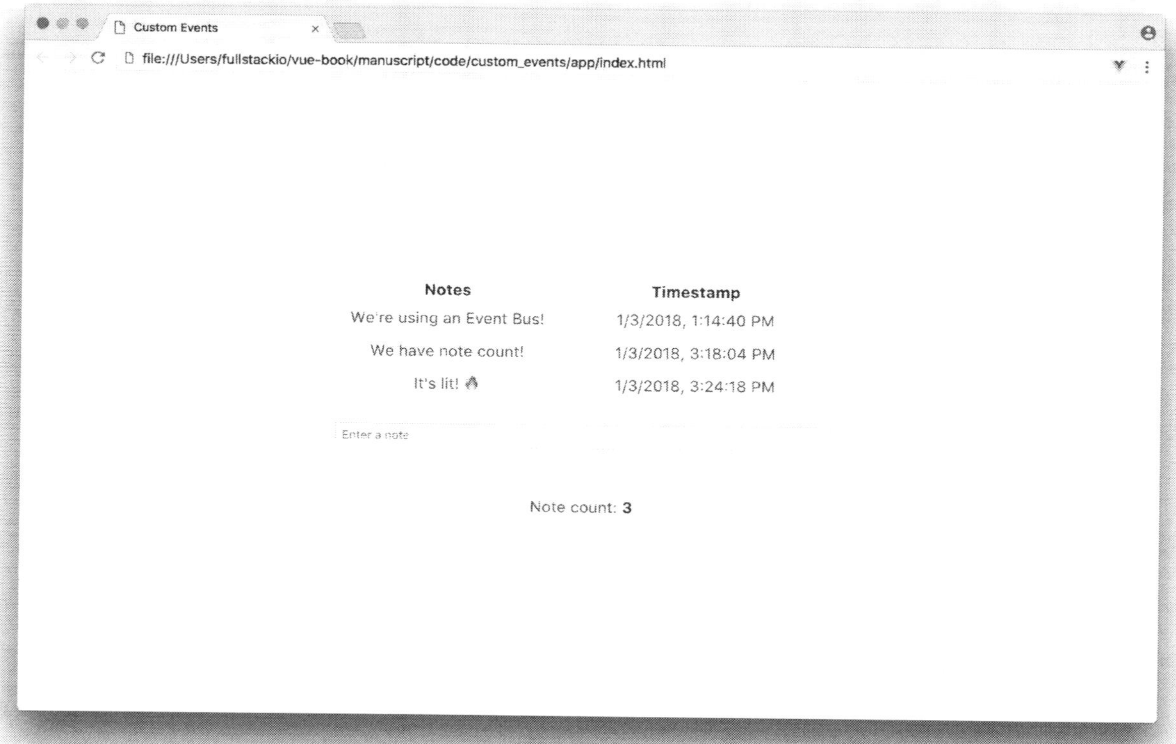

We're going to explore Vuex's core ideas by *refactoring* how data was managed in this app.

Despite adding a bit of overhead (especially for such a simple app), the focus of this chapter is to gain a solid understanding of the context of Vuex before moving to more complex applications.

This work is a good starting point in getting into Vuex, so let's take the time to absorb all the new information!

Preparation

Inside of the code download that came with this book, navigate to `vuex/note_taking`:

```
$ cd vuex/note_taking
```

Like always, we'll be working directly from the `app/` directory with the completed implementation being in `app-complete/`.

The initial set-up of `app/` is almost exactly the same as that of the last chapter:

```
$ ls app/
index.html
main.js
```

The only difference is the introduction of Vuex with the unpkg[66] CDN, in the `index.html` file:

vuex/note_taking/app/index.html

```
<script src="https://unpkg.com/vuex"></script>
```

Like the last chapter, we'll be writing all our JavaScript code within the `main.js` file.

Since everything else remains the same, refer to preparing the app section of Chapter 3 for a breakdown of the initial code.

Overview

Before we start to build and implement Vuex to the application, let's get a refresher of the components and interactions needed in the note-taking app.

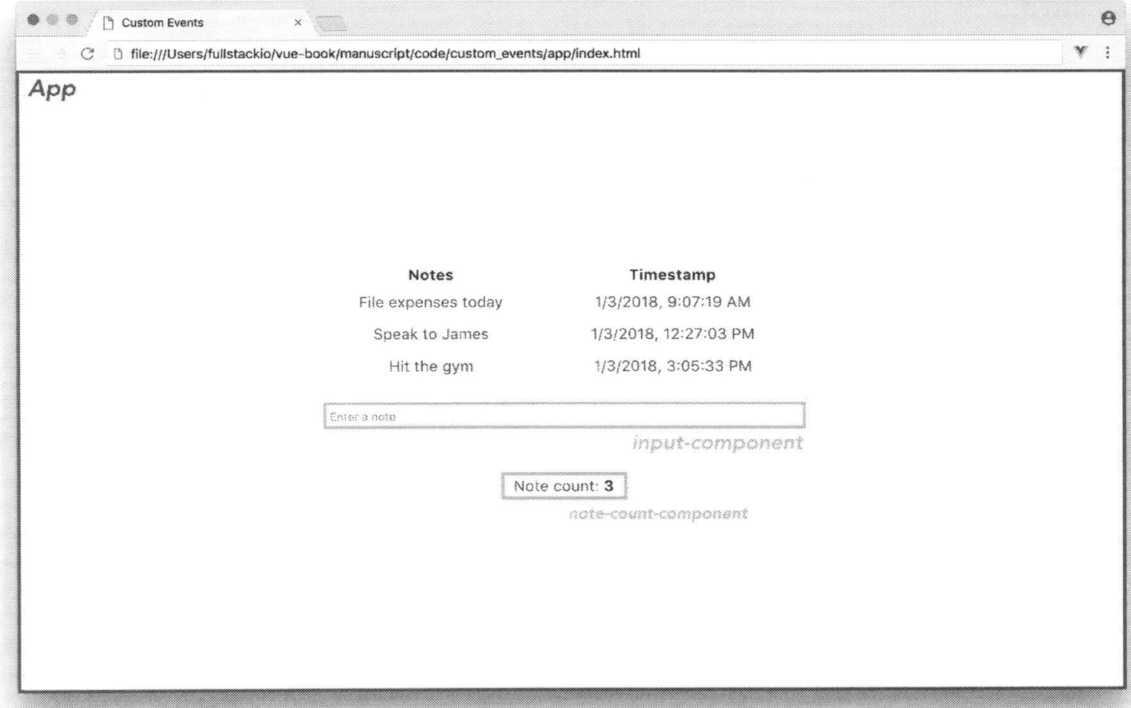

[66]https://unpkg.com

- The instance `#app` is the parent of two child components, `input-component` and `note-count-component`.
- When the user types information in the input field of `input-component` and presses and releases the `Enter` key, the user input will be displayed in the **Notes** column along with the timestamp of that submission in the **Timestamp** column.
- The `note-count-component` displays the total number of notes submitted.

Vuex Store

Just like how the core of a Vue application is it's Vue instance, the heart of a Vuex implementation is the Vuex **store**. The store is where the application data, (i.e. **state**) is kept.

State can never be mutated directly and can only be modified by calling **mutations**. **Actions** are often responsible in calling mutations and are themselves dispatched within components. A Vuex store also allows us to define **getters**, methods that involve receiving computed state data.

We've just defined all the pieces that make up a Vuex store

- **state**
- **mutations**
- **actions**
- **getters**

We're going to build each of these pieces before wiring everything together into a Vuex store.

State

To build the **state** of an application, it's important to understand and segregate component level and application level data. Application level data is the data that needs to be shared between components; which *is* the state.

Looking at our completed note-taking app from the last chapter, we can see two lists of data that are stored as part of the root instance, `notes` and `timestamps`. Instead of having these properties as part of the parent instance, we'll wire them up to be part of the application state.

In the top of our `main.js` file, let's define a new state object with the properties `notes` and `timestamps`. We'll initialize them with empty arrays:

vuex/note_taking/app-complete/main.js

```
const state = {
  notes: [],
  timestamps: []
}
```

Mutations

There are two changes we'll make to the state object (i.e. mutations) during the lifetime of our application. We'll need to be able to:

- Push a new note to the state `notes` array
- Push a new timestamp to the state `timestamps` array

To create a mutation, we'll simply need to define functions. In fact, when we say **mutation**, we really simply mean a function that's responsible in mutating store state.

In Vuex, **mutations** need to be explicitly defined. A mutation consists of a string type and a handler. In Flux architectures, mutation string types are often declared in capital letters to distinguish them from other functions and for tooling/linting purposes.

With this in mind, let's create our two mutation function handlers as `ADD_NOTE` and `ADD_TIMESTAMP` within a `mutations` object.

```
const mutations = {
  ADD_NOTE () {

  },
  ADD_TIMESTAMP () {

  }
}
```

When the mutation function is run, the first argument passed in is the `state`. It's important to reiterate that **mutations always have access to `state` as the first argument**. In addition, when an action calls a mutation, it may or may not pass a **payload** to the mutation.

The payload is an optional argument and, in some cases we can safely ignore it. However, in our case the mutations need access to the new note and timestamp objects to update the state arrays. These data objects will therefore be passed as the second argument to each mutation function.

The ability to always have access to `state` arises from how a Vuex store is wired together. The optional argument (`payload`) exists only when an action subsequently passes it to the mutation, with which we'll see shortly.

With the appropriate payloads, the `ADD_NOTE` and `ADD_TIMESTAMP` mutations will involve pushing the payload object to the `notes` and `timestamps` state arrays respectively.

With this functionality implemented, our `mutations` object now becomes:

vuex/note_taking/app-complete/main.js

```
const mutations = {
  ADD_NOTE (state, payload) {
    let newNote = payload;
    state.notes.push(newNote);
  },
  ADD_TIMESTAMP (state, payload) {
    let newTimeStamp = payload;
    state.timestamps.push(newTimeStamp);
  }
}
```

It's important to remember that mutations have to be **synchronous**. If asynchronous tasks need to be done, actions are responsible in dealing with them prior to calling mutations.

Actions

Actions are functions that exist to call mutations. In addition, actions can perform asynchronous calls/logic handling before committing to mutations.

Our example application is simple enough that our actions will consist of just calling the mutations directly.

Let's set up an `actions` object in the `main.js` file with an `addNote` and `addTimestamp` action.

```
const actions = {
  addNote () {

  },
  addTimestamp () {

  }
}
```

Similar to mutations, actions automatically receive an object as the first argument. In actions, this object is regarded as the `context` object which allows us to access the state with `context.state`, access getters with `context.getters`, and call/commit to mutations with `context.commit`.

Just like mutations, an optional payload object is passed in as a second argument to the function (optional because we can safely ignore it as an argument, if we don't need it). In our case, we'll be passing this payload on to our mutations.

Using `context.commit` to call the mutations, we can update our `actions` object:

vuex/note_taking/app-complete/main.js

```
const actions = {
  addNote (context, payload) {
    context.commit('ADD_NOTE', payload);
  },
  addTimestamp (context, payload) {
    context.commit('ADD_TIMESTAMP', payload);
  }
}
```

Getters

Getters are to an application store what computed properties are to a component. Getters are used to derive computed information from store state. We can call getters multiple times in our actions and in our components.

Getters aren't *required* to work with Vuex since information from store state can be directly obtained. For instance, a way to fetch the state `notes` array within a component might look like this:

```
computed: {
  getNotes () {
    return this.$store.state.notes;
  }
}
```

However, if this functionality is required in multiple places and to avoid repetition and ease testing; getters can be used to streamline this everywhere.

In our application, we'll use Vuex getters to get all the information we need in our components. We'll need three getter functions from our store; get all notes, get all timestamps, and get a count of the total number of notes.

Our `getters` object will initially be laid out like this:

```
const getters = {
  getNotes () {

  },
  getTimestamps () {

  },
  getNoteCount () {

  }
}
```

Getter functions receive state as their first argument. Knowing this, we can update our getter methods to pluck the appropriate data off the state object:

```
const getters = {
  getNotes (state) {
    return state.notes;
  },
  getTimestamps (state) {
    return state.timestamps;
  },
  getNoteCount (state) {
    return state.notes.length;
  }
}
```

Since we're returning a single expression for each method, we can use ES6 arrow functions (omitting the brackets and the `return` keyword) to simplify our `getters` object:

vuex/note_taking/app-complete/main.js

```
const getters = {
  getNotes: state => state.notes,
  getTimestamps: state => state.timestamps,
  getNoteCount: state => state.notes.length
}
```

Store

With the state, mutations, actions, and getters all set-up, the final part of integrating Vuex into our application is creating and integrating the **store**.

Creating the store means we'll need to wire everything together. The store object is how our mutations and getters get access to the state object and how actions can directly commit to mutations with `context.commit`.

The Vuex library provides a declaration for creating stores, `Vuex.Store({})`. At the minimum, this declaration requires `state` and `mutations` objects. Knowing that we've set-up our `state`, `mutations`, `actions`, and `getters` properties, our store can be instantiated like this:

vuex/note_taking/app-complete/main.js

```
const store = new Vuex.Store({
  state,
  mutations,
  actions,
  getters
})
```

> In ES6-land, adding an object with just a command is a convenient way to define both a key and a value.
>
> For instance, the example above is exactly the same as calling it like so:
>
> const store = new Vuex.Store({ state: state, mutations: mutations, actions: actions, getters: getters })

To inject the store to the entire application and have it accessible within all components, we need to pass the store object to the application's Vue instance:

```
new Vue({
  el: '#app',
  store,
  components: {
    'input-component': inputComponent
  }
})
```

With this previous instantiation, we have pretty much summed up everything we need to integrate Vuex into our application. We can now build our components to retrieve store state and have methods that simply dispatch to the actions we've created. Our store takes care of the rest!

Building the components

Let's get back to our demo application and convert it to use the Vuex store we just set up.

input-component

Just like we did in the last chapter, we'll dynamically bind the `input` field in `input-component` to an `input` data property. We'll specify a `keyup.enter` event listener to call a `monitorEnterKey` method when the `enter` key is released:

This makes the `inputComponent` object set up like this:

```
template: `<input
      placeholder='Enter a note'
      v-model="input"
      @keyup.enter="monitorEnterKey"
      class="input is-small" type="text" />`,
data () {
  return {
    input: '',
  }
},
methods: {
  monitorEnterKey () {

  }
}
```

When an input is entered by the user, we want two actions to be dispatched: `addNote` and `addTimestamp`. Store actions are dispatched simply with `store.dispatch('nameOfAction', payload)`. With our payloads being the `input` value for `addNote` and the current date/timestamp for `addTimestamp`, we can update our `monitorEnterKey` method:

```
monitorEnterKey () {
  store.dispatch('addNote', this.input);
  store.dispatch('addTimestamp', new Date().toLocaleString());
  this.input = ''; // set input field back to blank
}
```

Though this would work if we've defined our store object above our component object, this doesn't reference the injected store in our entire application. To reference the injected store object, we'll update it to use the `this.$store` object:

vuex/note_taking/app-complete/main.js

```
    monitorEnterKey () {
      this.$store.dispatch('addNote', this.input);
      this.$store.dispatch('addTimestamp', new Date().toLocaleString());
      this.input = '';
    }
```

note-count-component

The `note-count-component` is solely responsible for displaying the number of notes entered. We'll introduce this component by having a computed `noteCount` property that simply references the `getNotes` getter method from the store, to get the total number of entered notes.

Our `noteCountComponent` object can now be updated to reflect this additional functionality:

vuex/note_taking/app-complete/main.js

```
const noteCountComponent = {
  template:
    `<div class="note-count">
      Note count: <strong>{{ noteCount }}</strong>
    </div>`,
  computed: {
    noteCount() {
      return this.$store.getters.getNoteCount;
    }
  }
}
```

Vuex provides additional helpers that allow us to neatly map store getters (or state, actions) to components (`mapGetters`, `mapState`, `mapActions`). Though we won't be using these in this chapter, we'll be explaining and using them in the next chapter!

Let's now make sure we specify the `noteCountComponent` as a component property in the Vue instance so that it can get access to the `this.$store` property:

```
new Vue({
  el: '#app',
  store,
  components: {
    'input-component': inputComponent,
    'note-count-component': noteCountComponent
  }
})
```

And be referenced in the template of the root instance (`#app`), in the `index.html` file:

```
<div id="app">
  <div class="notes-section">
    <!-- Notes section -->
  </div>
  <note-count-component></note-count-component>
</div>
```

Root Instance

The root instance needs to display the list of notes and timestamps to the view. Very similar to `note-count-component`, we can introduce two computed properties, `notes` and `timestamps`. These properties can return the values that the `getNotes` and `getTimestamps` getter functions return.

Let's update our instance definition to include these two properties:

vuex/note_taking/app-complete/main.js

```
new Vue({
  el: '#app',
  store,
  computed: {
    notes() {
      return this.$store.getters.getNotes;
    },
    timestamps() {
      return this.$store.getters.getTimestamps;
    }
  },
  components: {
```

```
    'input-component': inputComponent,
    'note-count-component': noteCountComponent
  }
})
```

In our parent template, we need to set the `v-for` directives to render the list of `notes` and `timestamps`. Let's update the `<div class="columns"></div>` section of the `index.html` template to the following:

custom_events/app-complete/index.html

```
      <div class="columns">
        <div class="column has-text-centered">
          <strong>Notes</strong>
          <div v-for="note in notes" class="notes">
            {{ note }}
          </div>
        </div>
        <div class="column has-text-centered">
          <strong>Timestamp</strong>
          <div v-for="timestamp in timestamps" class="timestamps">
            {{ timestamp }}
          </div>
        </div>
      </div>
```

That's it! We've completed our Vuex application! Saving the `main.js` and `index.html` files and opening `index.html` in Chrome, we'll see everything work as expected:

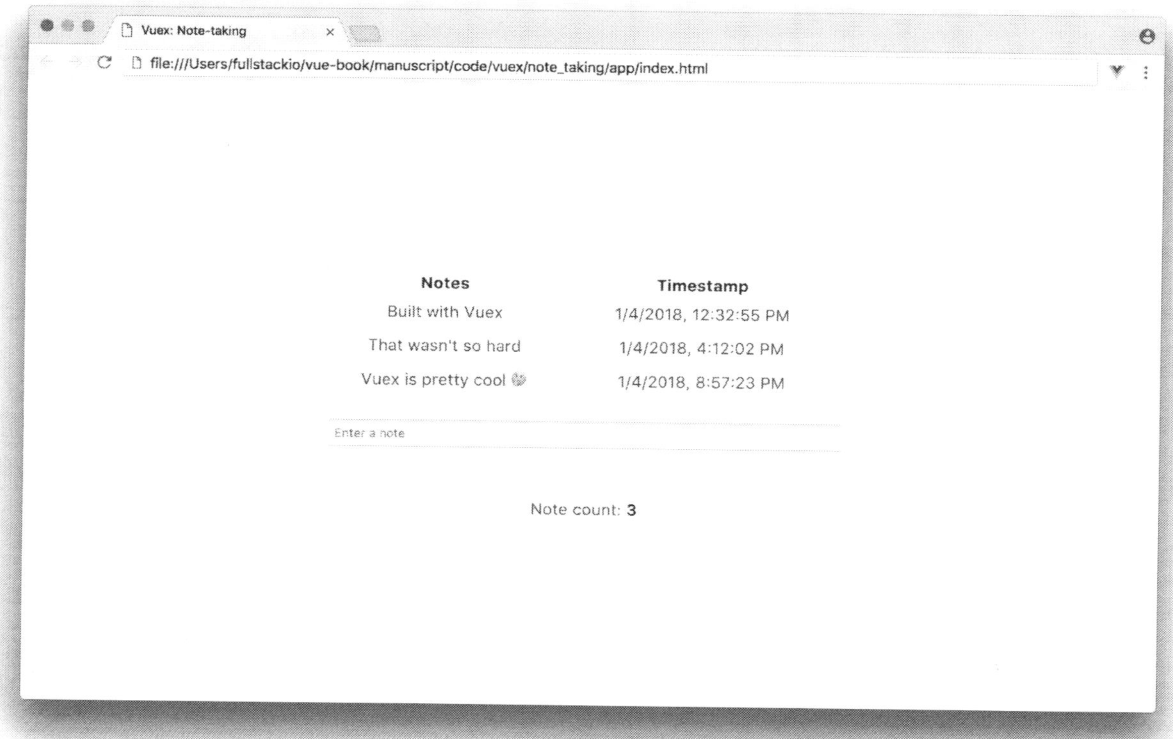

Notice how easy it was to create our components once our Vuex store was built? The Vuex store often makes the bulk of an application, since components become a lot simpler and focus primarily in displaying the view. Component methods will often now directly dispatch to an action letting the Vuex store deal with everything else.

Vuex and Vue devtools

In addition to a structured Flux-like pattern for data management, another primary benefit of using Vuex is its integration with Vue's official devtools[67] to provide 'time-travel' debugging. 'Time-travel' debugging allows us to track and replay changes to the state with *each and every mutation.*

Let's see this in practice. With the application launched in our browser, we'll open up the Vue devtools and select the **Vuex** tab in the top right corner:

[67] https://github.com/vuejs/vue-devtools

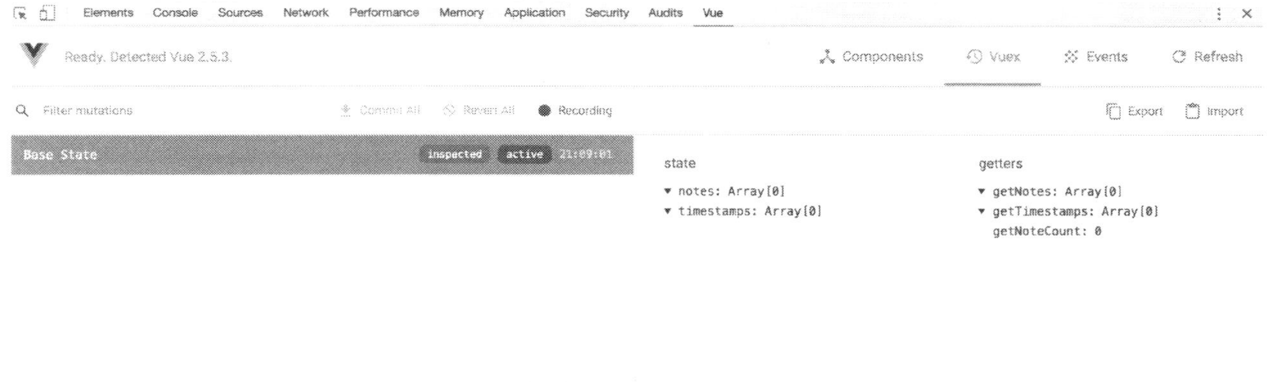

Base State

Mutations are tracked on the left hand side. For each selected mutation, information about the store is displayed on the right. In the `Base State`, we can see our store state and getters all consisting of and returning empty arrays.

Let's enter a few notes into the application. We'll notice both the `ADD_NOTE` and `ADD_TIMESTAMP` mutations being added as we invoke the `monitorEnterKey` method in our UI.

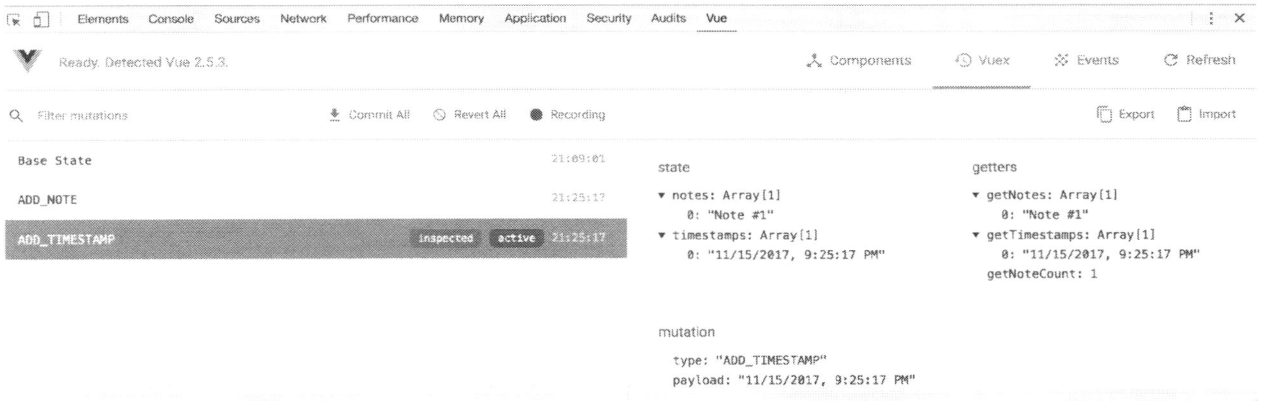

ADD_TIMESTAMP

In the image above we're inspecting the latest `ADD_TIMESTAMP` mutation. We can see the payload in this mutation, the state *after* the mutation is complete, and all the getters in the store. If we click the other mutation, we can *inspect* it by seeing the store information at that point.

When we click the `Time Travel` option within a mutation, we can actually 'time-travel' the UI back to when that mutation was called! Here's a screen grab of 'time-travelling' to when the `ADD_NOTE` mutation occured but before the `ADD_TIMESTAMP` mutation took into effect:

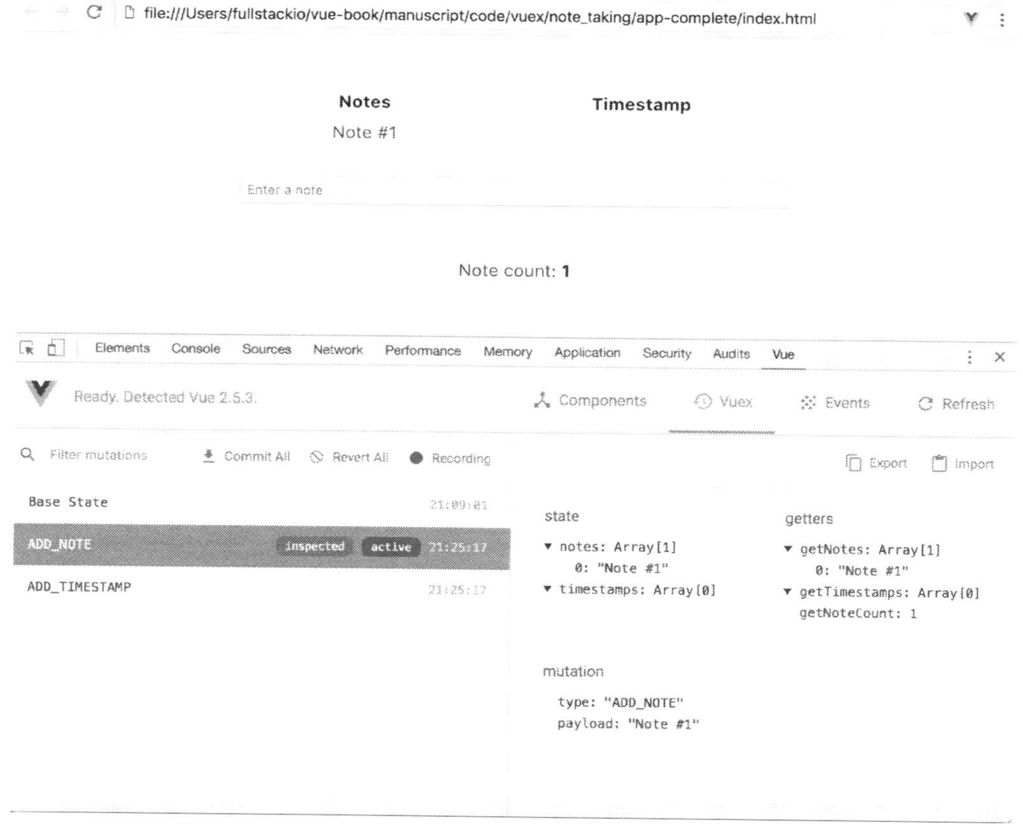

ADD_NOTE

Notice how the UI displays the note message without the timestamp? This is the moment *right before* the `ADD_TIMESTAMP` mutation was committed. This example is a good display of how mutations are all **synchronous**. They happen one after the other.

'Time-travel' debugging provides huge benefits towards solving application bugs or issues. Though not intended to replace standard debugging practices, debugging in this manner provides an extra layer towards inspecting the various parts of a Vuex store.

Recap

Let's recap how our Vuex store works:

1. The root instance and the `note-count-component` obtain state data with the help of **getters**.
2. When an input is entered, the `input-component` will *dispatch* the `addNote` and `addTimestamp` actions with the appropriate payloads.
3. These **actions** then *commit* to the relevant mutations, `ADD_NOTE` and `ADD_TIMESTAMP`, further passing in the necessary payloads.
4. The **mutations** mutate and modify the state causing the components that have the modified state data (root instance and `note-count-component`) to *re-render*.

Regardless of how large/small an application is, this pattern of data management remains the same. This form of unidirectional data flow and restriction of state changes to mutations keeps a front-end application *consistent* and *maintainable* as things continue to scale.

In the next chapter, we'll see how this pattern remains the same even as we build a much larger Vuex application!

V - Vuex and Servers

Introduction

In the last chapter, we learned about Vue's most widely used Flux implementation, **Vuex**. By building our own Vuex store from scratch and integrating the store to the application Vue instance, we got a feel for how data flows through a Vuex-powered Vue app.

In this chapter, we build on these concepts by using Vuex to build a functional shopping cart application that persists data to a server. All the applications we've built thus far had hard-coded initial state and the state only lived as long as the browser window was open.

In this chapter, however, the server will be in charge of persisting the data.

Our shopping cart app will begin to look like a real-world Vuex/Vue app as we explore strategies for handling more complex state management.

Preparation

Previewing the App

Like we've done for all our chapters, we'll start by previewing a completed implementation of the app.

In the terminal, let's change into the `vuex/shopping_cart` directory using the `cd` command:

```
$ cd vuex/shopping_cart
```

We'll use npm to install all the application's dependencies:

```
$ npm install
```

When all dependencies have been installed, we'll boot the application with `npm run start`:

```
$ npm run start
```

We'll see the following in our terminal:

```
$ npm run start

Compiled successfully in ####ms

Compiled successfully in ####ms

Your application is running here: http://localhost:8080
```

We'll now be able to visit `http://localhost:8080` to see our app running in the browser:

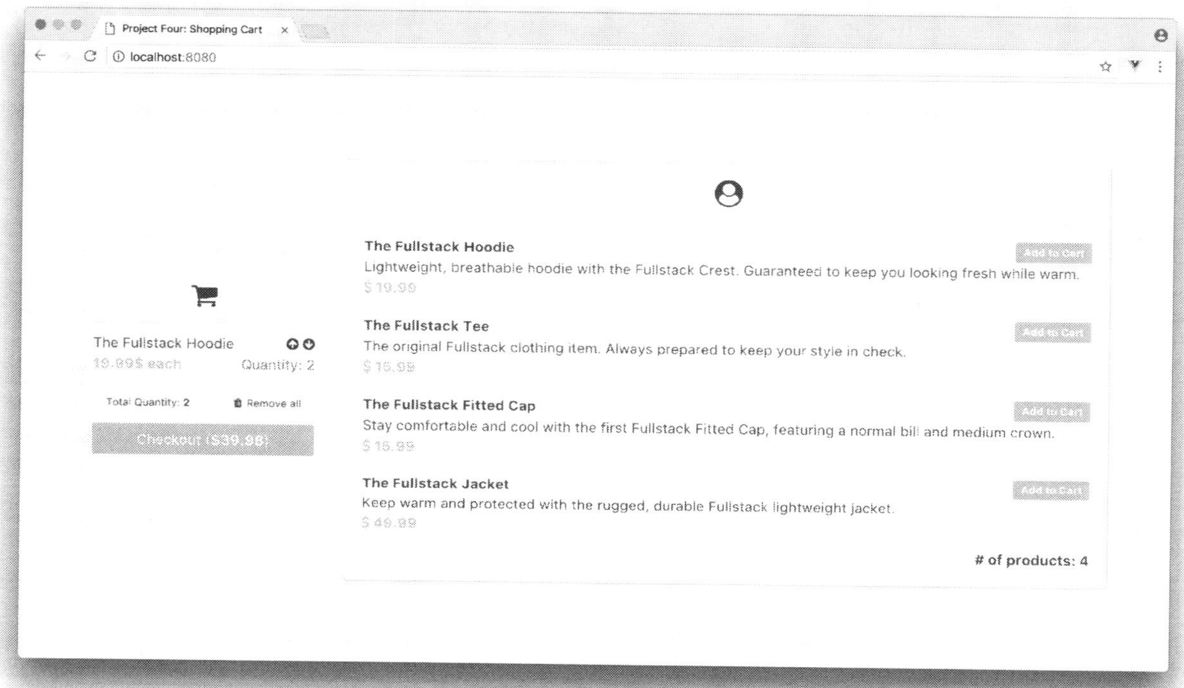

The Fullstack Shopping Cart

The premise of the shopping cart is the Fullstack team's first foray into selling clothing online! Spend some time playing around with the completed app to get an understanding of what we'll be building. Add items, remove items, refresh, and note that everything is persisted. You can even make changes to your app in one browser tab and see the changes propagate to another tab.

Preparing the App

In the terminal, let's run `ls` to see the project's layout:

```
$ ls
README.md
build/
config/
index.html
node_modules/
package.json
public/
server-cart-data.json
server-product-data.json
server.js
src/
```

In addition, we have the hidden files `.babelrc` and `.gitignore` in the project directory.

Let's address the responsibilities of each of these directories/files:

`README.md`

The `README.md` file summarizes the instructions on how to run the application.

`build/`

The `build/` directory hosts the Webpack details for build configuration, loaders, etc.

`config/`

`config/` contains the configuration details of the Webpack development environment.

`index.html`

The `index.html` file is the root markup of our application. `index.html` is responsible in specifying the application stylesheet dependencies (Bulma and Font Awesome) as well as the DOM element, `#app`, where the Vue instance is to be mounted.

vuex/shopping_cart/index.html

```
<!DOCTYPE html>
<html lang="en">
  <head>
    <meta charset="utf-8">
    <meta name="viewport" content="width=device-width,initial-scale=1.0">
    <title>Project Four: Shopping Cart</title>
    <link rel="stylesheet" href="/public/bulma/bulma.css">
    <link rel="stylesheet" href="/public/font-awesome/css/font-awesome.min.css">
  </head>
  <body>
    <div id="app"></div>
    <!-- built files will be auto injected -->
  </body>
</html>
```

node_modules/

The `node_modules` directory refers to all the different JavaScript libraries that have been installed in our application when we installed our dependencies using `npm install`.

package.json

The `package.json` file lists all the locally installed npm packages for us to manage.

The `scripts` portion dictates the `npm` commands that can be run in our application:

```
{
  // ...
  "scripts": {
    "start": "concurrently \"npm run server\" \"npm run client\"",
    "server": "node server",
    "client": "webpack-dev-server --inline --progress --config build/..."
  },
  // ...
}
```

We can use these different script commands to work with our application.

- `npm run start`: run both the client and server

- `npm run client`: run the client only
- `npm run server`: run the server only

We'll discuss these commands as we take a closer look into the server API.

Let's address the main dependencies that have been installed in our application:

```
{
  // ...
  "dependencies": {
    "axios": "^0.17.1",
    "vue": "^2.5.2",
    "vuex": "^3.0.1"
  },
  // ...
}
```

- `axios`: the ajax library used to make HTTP requests from the client to the server
- `vue`: the Vue npm library
- `vuex`: the Vuex npm library

The `devDependencies` in `package.json` constitute the packages needed for the build/configuration of the Vue application. We've discussed some of these in Chapter 2, but for the sake of brevity, we won't be going through the rest. Head to the vue-cli webpack template docs[68] for more information on this scaffold.

`public/`

`public/` holds the installed `bulma/` and `font-awesome/` libraries that we use in our application.

`server-cart-data.json` - `server-product-data.json`

These files are the root data files needed in the application server (`server.js`).

[68]http://vuejs-templates.github.io/webpack/structure.html

`server.js`

`server.js` is a Node.js server specifically designed for our shopping cart app.

You don't have to know anything about Node.js or about servers in general to work with the server we've supplied.

We'll provide the guidance that you need.

`server.js` uses both files `server-cart-data.json` and `server-product-data.json`.

- `server-product-data.json` acts as a read-only file holding product information for the server to display.
- `server-cart-data.json`, on the other hand, is where the server will read and write to persist data. Take a look at both files to see the data that exists.

  Note that we're using the `server-product-data.json` and `server-cart-data.json` files as a file-based database. In production, we could replace these files with a database like PostgreSQL or MySQL.

`src/`

`src/` contains the JavaScript files that we'll be working directly with:

```
$ ls src/
app/
app-1/
app-2/
app-3/
app-complete/
main.js
```

We'll be building our app inside the `app/` directory. `app-complete/` denotes the completed implementation of the application. Each significant step we take along the way is included in `app-1/`, `app-2/` and `app-3/`.

The `main.js` file represents the starting point of the application. This file is where the Vue instance is mounted to `#app`, the declared DOM element in our `index.html` file.

If we take a look in the `main.js` file, we can see the main component `App.vue` imported from the `app-complete/` directory and rendered in the Vue instance with `render: h => h(App)`. We also have a `store` instance being imported from `app-complete/` and passed into the instance:

vuex/shopping_cart/src/main.js

```
import Vue from 'vue';
import App from './app-complete/App.vue';
import store from './app-complete/store';

new Vue({
  el: '#app',
  store,
  render: h => h(App)
});
```

Our first step to building our own application is to ensure we're not referencing the `app-complete` sub folder anymore. Let's change the import of `App` from `./app-complete/App.vue` to `./app/App.vue` instead.

In addition, let's remove the `store` import and the store property declaration within the instance. We'll create this when we start building the store of our application.

This will update the `main.js` file to look like the following:

```
import Vue from 'vue';
import App from './app/App.vue';

new Vue({
  el: '#app',
  render: h => h(App)
});
```

We'll get a better understanding of the starting code within `app/` once we start building our application.

`.babelrc`

Babel[69] is a JavaScript transpiler that transpiles ES6 syntax to older ES5 syntax for any browser to understand. The `.babelrc` file is used to configure the Babel presets and plugins for the `babel-loader` package in our application.

[69] https://babeljs.io/

`.gitignore`

`.gitignore` dictates the files that we don't want git to check into our git repository. This `.gitignore` file is often used to ignore certain files such as build products (`node_modules/`) or local configuration settings.

To help us get familiar with the API for this project and working with APIs in general, the following section addresses making requests to the API outside of Vue.

The Server API

Our ultimate goal in this chapter is to understand how **Vuex manages data on a server**. We're not going to move all state management exclusively to the server. Instead, the server will maintain its state (in `server-cart-data.json` and `server-product-data.json`) and Vuex will maintain its own client-side state. We'll demonstrate later why keeping state in both places is desirable.

If we perform an operation on the server that we want persisted, then we also need to notify the Vuex store on that state change. This functionality keeps the two states in sync. We'll consider these our "write" operations. The write operations we want to send to the server are:

- Add an item to the shopping cart
- Remove an item from the shopping cart
- Remove all items from the shopping cart

We'll have two read operations, which focus on fetching data from the server:

- Get all items in the product list
- Get all items in the shopping cart

HTTP APIs

This section assumes some familiarity with HTTP APIs. If you're not familiar with HTTP APIs, you may want to read up on them[70].

However, don't be deterred from continuing with this chapter for the time being. Essentially what we're doing is making a "call" from our browser out to a remote web-server server (in this case, on our local development machine) and conforming to a specified format.

[70]http://www.andrewhavens.com/posts/20/beginners-guide-to-creating-a-rest-api/

curl

We'll use a tool called `curl` to make more involved requests from the command line.

OSX users should already have curl installed. Windows users can download and install curl here: https://curl.haxx.se/download.html[71].

JSON endpoints

`server-cart-data.json` and `server-product-data.json` are JSON documents. JSON is a format for storing human-readable data objects. We can serialize JavaScript objects into the JSON format and deserialize JSON files back into JavaScript objects. This format enables JavaScript objects to be stored in text files and transported over the network.

The `.json` files contain an array of objects. While not strictly JavaScript, the data in these arrays can be readily loaded into JavaScript.

In `server.js`, we see lines like this:

```
fs.readFile(CART_DATA_FILE, function(err, data) {
  const cartProducts = JSON.parse(data);
  // ...
});
```

`data` is a string, or in other words the contents of the file `CART_DATA_FILE`. We need to parse it into a JavaScript object. `JSON.parse()` converts this string into an actual JavaScript array of objects.

Let's break down all the calls that can be made to the server:

`GET /products`

Returns a list of all product items.

`GET /cart`

Returns a list of all cart items.

`POST /cart`

Accepts a JSON body with `id`, `title`, `description`, and `price` attributes and inserts that body as a new item object to the cart. If the cart item already exists, this call increments the quantity of the existing cart item by `1`.

`POST /cart/delete`

Accepts a JSON body with the attribute `id`. The server iterates through the cart store and decrements the quantity of the cart item with the matching `id` by `1`. If the quantity of that item is equal to `1` when the call is made, the cart item object is removed.

[71] https://curl.haxx.se/download.html

`POST /cart/delete/all`

Removes all items in the cart.

Playing with the API

Let's exit our application if we haven't stopped it previously. We'll now **only** boot the server with:

```
npm run server
```

With the server running, we can visit the `/products` and `/cart` endpoints at `http://localhost:3000/products` and `http://localhost:3000/cart` in the browser. When visiting these URLs, our browser makes a GET request to `/products` and `/cart` to see the JSON responses returned for each of these calls.

Here's a screenshot of visiting `http://localhost:3000/products` in our browser:

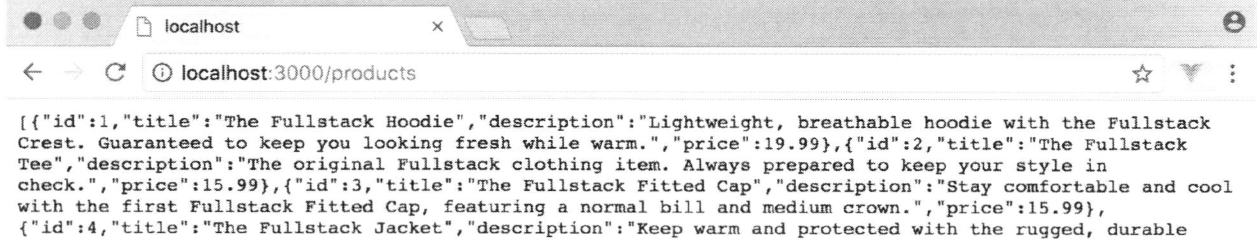

GET /products

Note that the server stripped all of the extraneous whitespace in `server-product-data.json`, including newlines, to keep the payload as small as possible. Those only exist in `server-product-data.json` to make it human-readable.

We can use a Chrome extension like JSONView[72] to "humanize" the raw JSON. JSONView takes these raw JSON chunks and adds back in the whitespace for readability:

[72] https://chrome.google.com/webstore/detail/jsonview/chklaanhfefbnpoihckbnefhakgolnmc

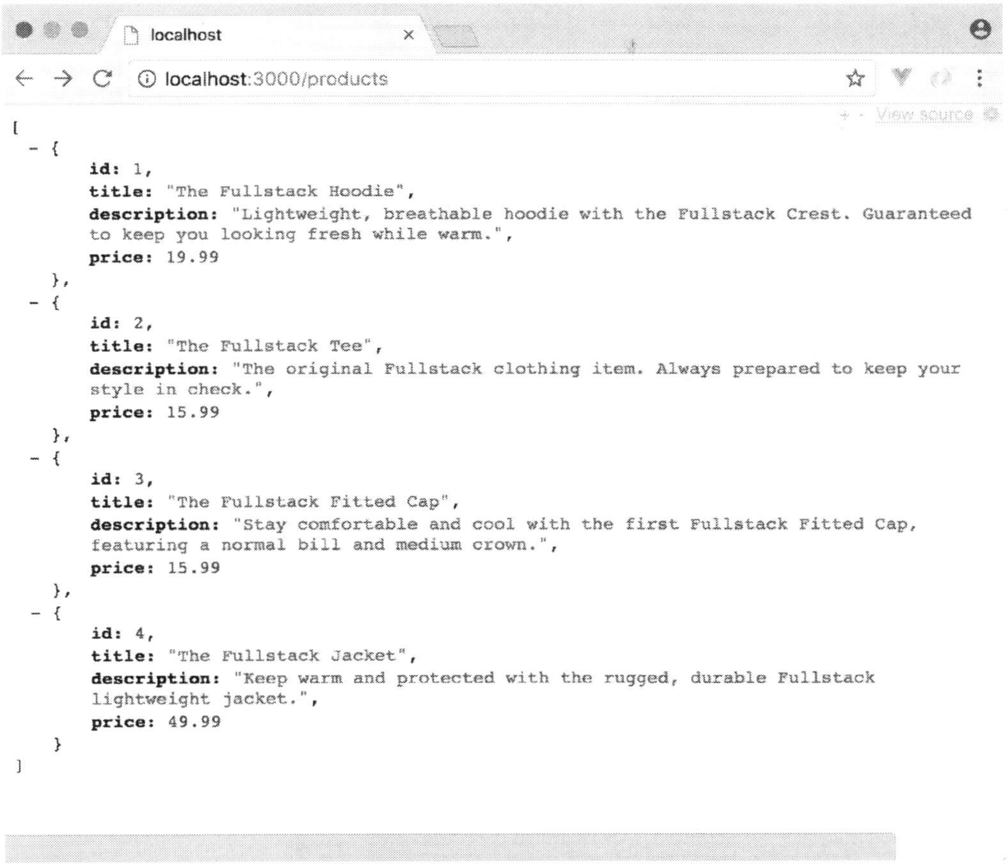

localhost

localhost:3000/products

View source


```
[
  - {
        id: 1,
        title: "The Fullstack Hoodie",
        description: "Lightweight, breathable hoodie with the Fullstack Crest. Guaranteed
        to keep you looking fresh while warm.",
        price: 19.99
    },
  - {
        id: 2,
        title: "The Fullstack Tee",
        description: "The original Fullstack clothing item. Always prepared to keep your
        style in check.",
        price: 15.99
    },
  - {
        id: 3,
        title: "The Fullstack Fitted Cap",
        description: "Stay comfortable and cool with the first Fullstack Fitted Cap,
        featuring a normal bill and medium crown.",
        price: 15.99
    },
  - {
        id: 4,
        title: "The Fullstack Jacket",
        description: "Keep warm and protected with the rugged, durable Fullstack
        lightweight jacket.",
        price: 49.99
    }
]
```


`GET /products` after installing JSONView

Visiting `http://localhost:3000/cart`, we can see the existing data within `server-cart-data.json` that shows the one item that currently exists in the shopping cart:

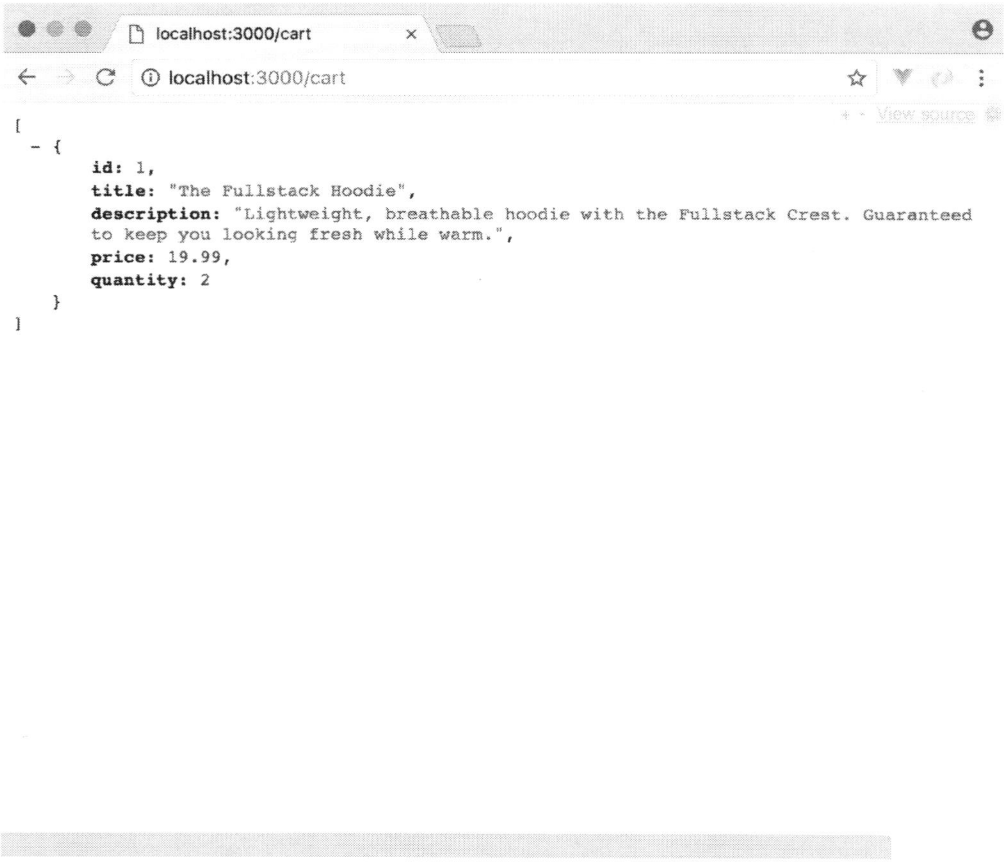

localhost:3000/cart

localhost:3000/cart

View source

```
[
  - {
        id: 1,
        title: "The Fullstack Hoodie",
        description: "Lightweight, breathable hoodie with the Fullstack Crest. Guaranteed
        to keep you looking fresh while warm.",
        price: 19.99,
        quantity: 2
    }
]
```

`GET /cart` after installing JSONView

The browser can only be used to make `GET` requests. For *writing* data — like removing an item from the cart — we'll have to make `POST`, `PUT`, or `DELETE` requests. For our application, the server uses `POST` for all *write* commands. Let's use curl to test this out.

Run the following command from the command line:

```
$ curl -X GET localhost:3000/cart
```

The `-X` flag specifies which HTTP method to use. It should return a response that looks a bit like this:

```
[{"id":1,"title":"The Fullstack Hoodie","description":"Lightweight, breathable
hoodie with the Fullstack Crest. Guaranteed to keep you looking fresh while
warm.","price":19.99,"quantity":2}]
```

We can insert a new item to the cart by issuing a `POST` request to the `/cart` endpoint. We need to send along a JSON body with `id`, `title`, `description` and `price` attributes as the new cart item:

```
$ curl -X POST localhost:3000/cart \
-H 'Content-Type: application/json' \
-d '{ "id":100,
      "title":"A New Cart Item",
      "description":"Adding a new cart item",
      "price":99 }'
```

Pasting the entire block above may cause some formatting issues in your terminal. To appropriately run the command, paste each line one by one or type it out.

The `-H` flag sets a header for our HTTP request, `Content-Type`. We're informing the server that the body of the request is JSON.

The `-d` flag sets the body of our request. Inside of single-quotes `''` is the JSON data.

The backslash `\` above is only used to break the command out over multiple lines for readability. This only works on MacOS and Linux. Windows users can just type it out as one long string.

When you press enter, curl will quickly return with an output. For this endpoint, the server will return all the cart items, with the newly included item:


```
[{"id":1,"title":"The Fullstack Hoodie","description":"Lightweight, breathable
hoodie with the Fullstack Crest. Guaranteed to keep you looking fresh while
warm.","price":19.99,"quantity":2},{"id":100,"title":"A New Cart Item",
"description":"Adding a new cart item","price":99,"quantity":1}]
```


If we open up `server-cart-data.json`, we'll also see the new item we've just added.

To bring back the `server-cart-data.json` to it's original state, we'll delete the added cart item with a POST request to the `/cart/delete` endpoint. We'll pass in the same JSON body since the `id` attribute is used in this case to find and remove the item:

```
$ curl -X POST localhost:3000/cart/delete \
-H 'Content-Type: application/json' \
-d '{ "id":100,
      "title":"A New Cart Item",
      "description":"Adding a new cart item",
      "price":99 }'
```

The endpoint will return showing that the added cart item was removed.

```
[{"id":1,"title":"The Fullstack Hoodie","description":"Lightweight, breathable
hoodie with the Fullstack Crest. Guaranteed to keep you looking fresh while
warm.","price":19.99,"quantity":2}]
```

We've tested most of the calls that can be made to the server. Feel free to play around with the other endpoints to get a feel for how they work. Just be sure to set the appropriate method with `-X` and to pass along the JSON `Content-Type` for the write endpoints.

For MacOS and Linux users, parsing and processing JSON on the command line can be greatly enhanced with the tool "jq". jq can pretty format responses as well do powerful manipulation of JSON (like iterating over all objects in the response and returning a particular field). You can find more about jq here: https://stedolan.github.io/jq/[a].

[a]https://stedolan.github.io/jq/

Client and server

The Vue Webpack server can be booted on `http://localhost:8080` with the following command:

```
$ npm run client
```

Our Node.js server runs on `http://localhost:3000` when we run:

```
$ npm run server
```

For our Vue application to make requests to the server, **we need to launch both the Webpack dev server and the API server simultaneously**. To do so, we'll use the `npm` library `concurrently`.

`concurrently`

`concurrently` is a npm utility for running multiple processes. The utility is already installed and set-up in our application, but we'll go through how it works.

`concurrently` works by passing multiple commands concurrently in quotes:

```
$ concurrently "command1" "command2"
```

In the `package.json` file, we have a `start` script that uses `concurrently` to boot both the Webpack and Node.js servers simultaneously:

```
"start": "concurrently \"npm run server\" \"npm run client\""
```

To get both servers running, we'll always run the `start` command in the terminal:

```
$ npm run start
```

At this point, the client would be able to make `GET/POST` requests to `http://localhost:3000` (i.e. the server running on our local machine).

This difference in web servers actually presents a browser security issue. Since our Vue app (hosted at `http://localhost:8080`) is attempting to load a resource from a different origin (`http://localhost:3000`), this will be performing **Cross-Origin Resource Sharing**[73]. The browser will prevent these types of requests from scripts for security reasons.

We essentially need our Webpack server to *proxy* requests intended for our API server.

API proxying

API proxying has already been set-up in our scaffold but we'll explain how it was done.

The `vue-cli` boilerplate we're using provides a mechanism for working with an API server in development. In the `config/index.js` file in our application, a new proxy rule has been introduced in the `dev.proxyTable` option:

```
proxyTable: {
  '/api': {
    target: 'http://localhost:3000/',
    changeOrigin: true,
    pathRewrite: {
      '^/api': ''
    }
  }
}
```

[73] https://developer.mozilla.org/en-US/docs/Web/HTTP/CORS

This rule dictates; if a request within our Vue Webpack server is made to `/api/`, it will be *proxied* to `http://localhost:3000/`. This will essentially allow us to make requests from our Vue client to the server with no issues! In our code, all our calls will be made to `/api` instead of `http://localhost:3000`.

Head to API Proxying During Development[74] of the Vue template docs to read more on API proxying.

Preparing the application

With a good understanding of the Node.js server and how our client can proxy requests to it, we can now start building our application.

Components

Let's break down the interface of the app to smaller pieces. From looking at the completed implementation, we can see at least two main components:

- A component that displays the list of cart items and the checkout button - we'll call this the `CartList` component
- A component that displays the list of items in the product list - we'll call this the `ProductList` component

[74]http://vuejs-templates.github.io/webpack/proxy.html

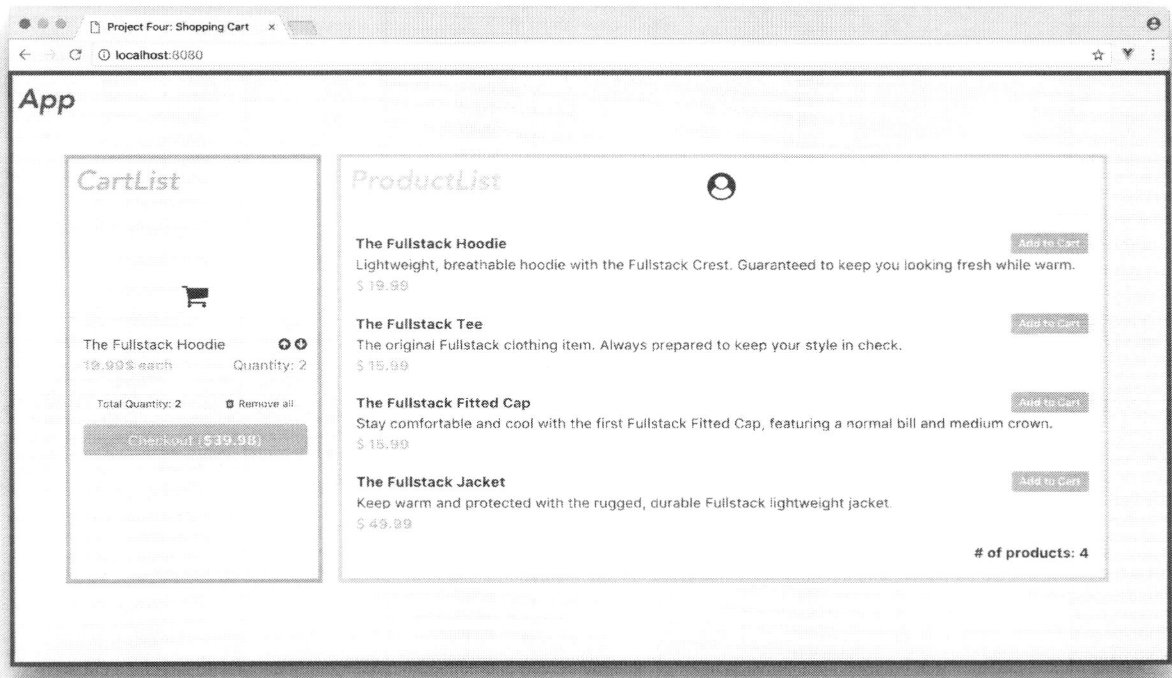

`CartList` and `ProductList` components

The `CartList` and `ProductList` components each display a list of cart items and product items respectively. Because of this, we can introduce these smaller list items as the `CartListItem` and `ProductListItem` components:

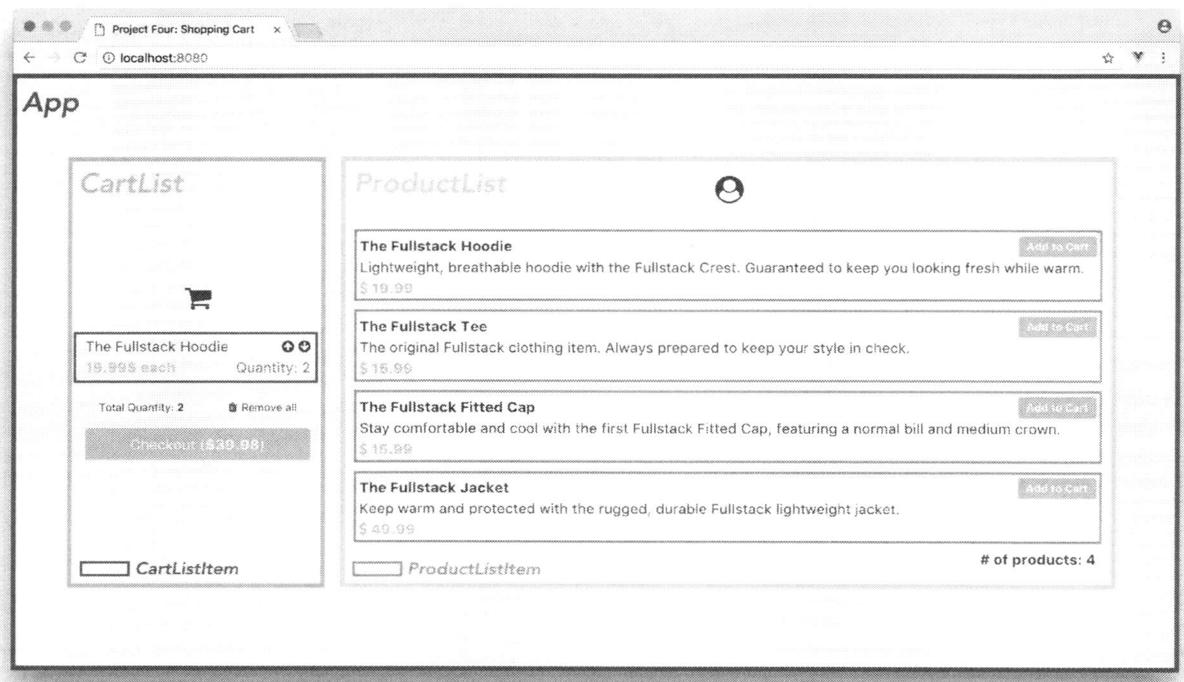

`CartList` and `ProductList` components

Our component hierarchy is:

- `App`: Parent container
  - `CartList`: Displays a list of cart items and the checkout button
    - `CartListItem`: Displays a single cart item
  - `ProductList`: Displays a list of product items
    - `ProductListItem`: Displays a single product item

Single-file components

In Chapter 2, we discussed how Vue allows us to create **single-file components** in a Webpack (or Browserify) bundled application. To reiterate, a single-file component is a Vue component that has its HTML, CSS and JS defined in a `.vue` file. A single-file component consists of three parts:

- `<template>` which contains the components markup in plain HTML.
- `<script>` which exports the component object constructor that consists of all the JS logic within that component.
- `<style>` which contains all the component styles.

All the components we build in this application will be single-file components.

Throughout this chapter, we'll often refer to pieces of a component that we'll be addressing at a time. For example, to modify the HTML of a component, we'll address and display *only* the `<template>` element of said component. To create a component's data, we'll *only* show how we update information in the `<script>` element of the `.vue` file. This helps in providing more concise code samples as we proceed through the chapter.

Component styles have already been prepared and exist within each component. For the sake of brevity, like always, we *won't* be addressing styles and CSS attributes since our focus is on the usage of Vue.

Static version of the app

All our Vue code for this chapter will be inside `src/`. We'll be focusing all our attention to `src/app/`. With that said, let's survey the existing files in `src/app/`:

```
$ ls src/app/
components/
App.vue
```

We can see a `components/` folder and a parent component `App.vue`. If we look inside the `components/` folder, we'll see two subfolders within - `cart/` and `product/`:

```
$ ls src/app/components/
cart/
product/
```

Within `cart/`, exists the main cart component `CartList.vue`:

```
$ ls src/app/components/cart/
CartList.vue
```

Within `product/`, exists the main product component `ProductList.vue`:

```
$ ls src/app/components/product/
ProductList.vue
```

Let's take a deeper look at the content within each of these files.

`App.vue`

In the `App.vue` file, we can see the `<template>` markup consists of a parent div `#app` that encompasses the `<CartList />` and `<ProductList />` component declarations in separate CSS columns:

vuex/shopping_cart/src/app/App.vue

```
<template>
  <div id="app">
    <div class="container">
      <div class="columns">
        <div class="column is-3">
          <CartList />
        </div>
        <div class="column is-9">
          <ProductList />
        </div>
      </div>
    </div>
  </div>
</template>
```

In the `<script>` tag of `App.vue`, the `CartList` and `ProductList` components are imported from the `components/` subfolder and declared in the `App`'s component property:

vuex/shopping_cart/src/app/App.vue

```
<script>
import CartList from './components/cart/CartList';
import ProductList from './components/product/ProductList';

export default {
  name: 'App',
  components: {
    CartList,
    ProductList
  }
};
</script>
```

`CartList.vue` and `ProductList.vue`

For both the `CartList.vue` and `ProductList.vue` files, the `<script>` tags currently export the constructor only containing the name of the components.

`<script>` of the `CartList.vue` file:

vuex/shopping_cart/src/app/components/cart/CartList.vue

```
<script>
export default {
  name: 'CartList',
}
</script>
```

<script> of the `ProductList.vue` file:

vuex/shopping_cart/src/app/components/product/ProductList.vue

```
<script>
export default {
  name: 'ProductList',
}
</script>
```

The `<template>` of the `CartList.vue` and `ProductList.vue` files display the markup of the cart list and product list component UIs. Each of these templates currently consist of *hard-coded* data of a single cart item and a single product item.

The `<template>` portion of the `CartList.vue` file looks like the following:

vuex/shopping_cart/src/app/components/cart/CartList.vue

```
<template>
  <div id="cart">
    <div class="cart--header has-text-centered">
      <i class="fa fa-2x fa-shopping-cart"></i>
    </div>
    <ul>
      <li class="cart-item">
        <div>
          <p class="cart-item--title is-inline">The Fullstack Hoodie</p>
          <div class="is-pulled-right">
            <i class="fa fa-arrow-circle-up cart-item--modify"></i>
            <i class="fa fa-arrow-circle-down cart-item--modify"></i>
          </div>
          <div class="cart-item--content">
            <span class="cart-item--price
                has-text-primary
                has-text-weight-bold">
```

```
          19.99$ each
        </span>
        <span class="cart-item--quantity
            has-text-grey
            is-pulled-right">
          Quantity: 2
        </span>
      </div>
    </div>
  </li>
  <div class="cart-details">
    <p>Total Quantity: <span class="has-text-weight-bold">2</span></p>
    <p class="cart-remove-all--text">
      <i class="fa fa-trash"></i>Remove all
    </p>
  </div>
</ul>
<button class="button is-primary">
  Checkout (<span class="has-text-weight-bold">$</span>)
</button>
</div>
</template>
```

The <template> of the ProductList.vue file looks like this:

vuex/shopping_cart/src/app/components/product/ProductList.vue

```
<template>
  <div id="products" class="box">
    <div class="products--header has-text-centered">
      <i class="fa fa-2x fa-user-circle"></i>
    </div>
    <div class="product-list">
      <div class="product-list--item">
        <div>
          <h2 class="has-text-weight-bold">The Fullstack Hoodie
            <span class="tag
                is-primary
                is-pulled-right
                has-text-white">
              Add to Cart
            </span>
          </h2>
```

```
          <p>Lightweight, breathable hoodie with the Fullstack Crest.
          Guaranteed to keep you looking fresh while warm.</p>
          <span class="has-text-primary has-text-weight-bold">
            <i class="fa fa-usd"></i> 19.99
          </span>
        </div>
      </div>
    </div>
    <div class="product-count has-text-right">
      <span class="has-text-weight-bold"># of products: 4</span>
    </div>
  </div>
</template>
```

To see the current static version of the app, we'll run the application (`npm run start`) and open the browser to the url at `http://localhost:8080`:

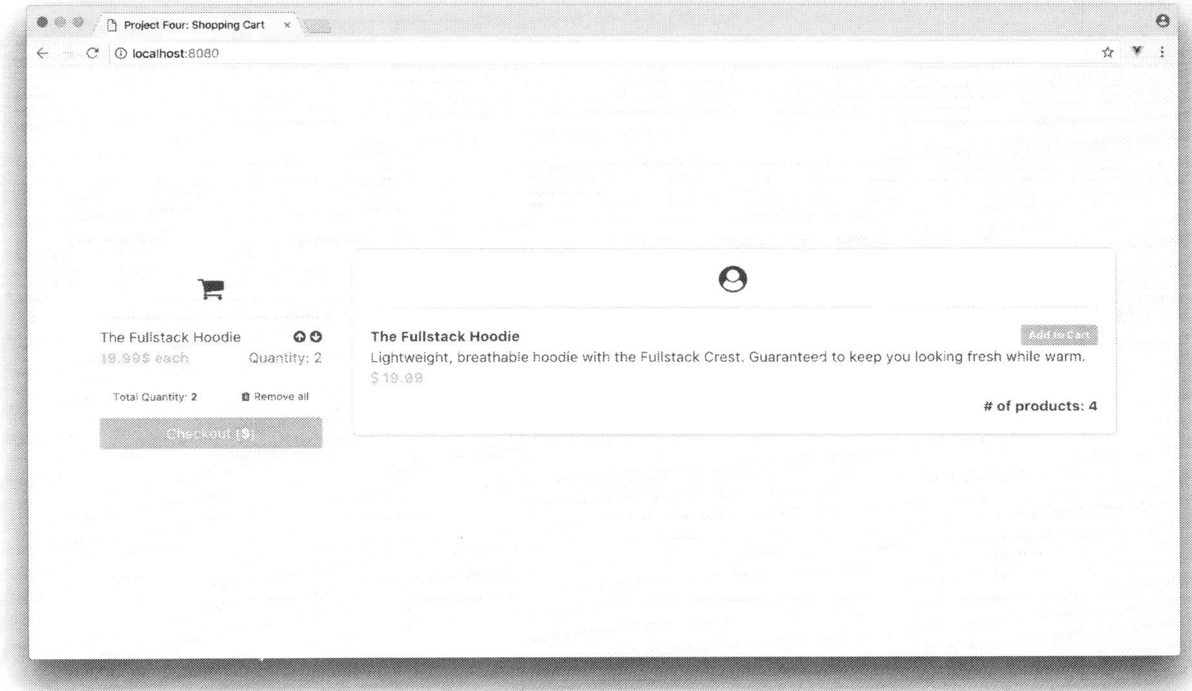

Static version of the app

All information currently displayed is hard-coded (*Total Quantity*, *# of products*, etc.). In the subsequent sections, we'll be making all application data dynamic and enabling interactivity.

The Vuex Store

We'll start building our application by first building the Vuex store. We know a fully-defined Vuex store is composed of 4 distinct pieces - **state**, **mutations**, **actions**, and **getters**. We'll set up the store in steps:

1. Create our state objects
2. Set up the mutations that will occur in our application
3. Create the actions that will *commit* to these subsequent mutations
4. Create getters for components to directly compute state data

In the last chapter, we had our entire store created and integrated within the same file we declared our components. We'll be structuring things a bit differently here.

Similar to how a `components/` folder exists, we'll set up a `store/` folder that hosts all the information pertaining to the Vuex store. This separation of concerns will help greatly in maintaining our app.

Let's create a `store/` subfolder and create an `index.js` file inside of it:

The `app/` directory will now have the following structure:

```
$ ls src/app/
components/
store/
App.vue
```

And the `store/` subfolder will have a single `index.js` file:

```
$ ls src/app/store/
index.js
```

This `index.js` file will be the heart of our Vuex application and where we declare `Vuex.Store({})`. In `index.js`, let's import the `Vue` and `Vuex` libraries at the top:

vuex/shopping_cart/src/app-1/store/index.js

```
import Vue from 'vue';
import Vuex from 'vuex';
```

> Our application already has the Vuex package installed. On a new npm project, `npm install vuex` needs to be run prior to importing it.

For Webpack and Browserify bundled Vue applications, global level functionality (plugins), like Vuex, need to be called with the `Vue.use()` global method.

In the `store/index.js` file, we'll apply Vuex by calling `Vue.use(Vuex)`.

```
import Vue from 'vue';
import Vuex from 'vuex';

Vue.use(Vuex);
```

And at the end of the file, we'll default export a `Vuex.store({})` declaration. This will allow us to import the store anywhere else in our application:

```
import Vue from 'vue';
import Vuex from 'vuex';

Vue.use(Vuex);

export default new Vuex.Store({})
```

The standard process would now be to build all the pieces of the Vuex store and specify them within the `Vuex.store({})` export. For this application, however, we'll be dividing our Vuex store into **modules**.

Vuex Modules

Vuex provides the ability to create **modules** to separate an application store into more manageable fragments. As an application scales, the store actions, mutations, and getters constantly evolve and grow. Modules exist primarily to avoid making an entire application store bloated and difficult to manage.

A module can be set up with the same pieces that make up the Vuex store. Here are examples of two module objects `moduleOne` and `moduleTwo`:

```
const moduleOne = {
  stateOne,
  mutationsOne,
  actionsOne,
  gettersOne
}

const moduleTwo = {
  stateTwo,
  mutationsTwo,
  actionsTwo,
  gettersTwo
}
```

When the store is instantiated, the module objects can then be introduced to the store's `modules` property:

```
const store = new Vuex.store({
  modules: {
    moduleOne,
    moduleTwo
  }
})
```

Anywhere in the application, the states of the separate modules can be accessed independently:

```
// accessing moduleOne state
this.$store.state.moduleOne;

// accessing moduleTwo state
this.$store.state.moduleTwo;
```

Though the states of the modules can be independently accessed; actions, mutations, and getters are registered to the global namespace by **default**. In other words, if you wanted to access getters from either `moduleOne` or `moduleTwo` you'd be able to do so without explicitly stating a module:

```
this.$store.getters;
```

This setup gets the `getters` from the entire store (i.e. for both modules). It's important to note that if the same getter method name exists in two modules, Vuex would not know which module it's referring to! To bypass this, Vuex allows us to **namespace** modules by specifying a `namespaced` property to true:

```
const moduleOne = {
  namespaced: true,
  stateOne,
  mutationsOne,
  actionsOne,
  gettersOne
}
```

Within components; namespaced mutations, actions, and getters have to be explicitly declared with the path the module is registered at. Here's an example of how an action is dispatched without a namespaced module and with a namespaced module:

```
// with namespacing
this.$store.dispatch('moduleA/nameOfAction')

// without namespacing
this.$store.dispatch('nameOfAction')
```

We won't have the need to namespace the modules we build in this application. For more reading on this, refer to the Modules[75] section of the Vuex docs.

`cartModule` - `productModule`

Since our application is separated into two distinct domains (`cart` and `product`), we can specify modules for each of these domains.

Within the `store/` directory, we'll create a `modules/` folder that contains a `cart/` and `product/` subfolders.

Let's create two directories (`cart/` and `product/`) and create an `index.js` file within them.

The `store/` directory will now look like this:

```
$ ls src/app/store/
modules/
index.js
```

With the `modules/` folder containing the new modules:

```
$ ls src/app/store/modules/
cart/
product/
```

The `modules/cart/` and `modules/product/` subfolders will each have an `index.js` file of their own:

The `modules/cart/` subfolder:

```
$ ls src/app/store/modules/cart/
index.js
```

The `modules/product/` subfolder:

[75] https://vuex.vuejs.org/en/modules.html

```
$ ls src/app/store/modules/product/
index.js
```

With our module directories set-up, let's create the pieces for each module and wire them to the global Vuex store.

In the `index.js` file for both the `cart/` and `product/` modules, let's create empty objects for `state`, `mutations`, `actions` and `getters`. With the empty objects, let's create and export `cartModule` and `productModule` in their respective files.

Our `store/module/cart/index.js` file should look like this:

vuex/shopping_cart/src/app-1/store/modules/cart/index.js

```
const state = {};

const mutations = {};

const actions = {};

const getters = {};

const cartModule = {
  state,
  mutations,
  actions,
  getters
}

export default cartModule;
```

Similarly, the `store/module/product/index.js` file becomes:

vuex/shopping_cart/src/app-1/store/modules/product/index.js

```
const state = {};

const mutations = {};

const actions = {};

const getters = {};

const productModule = {
```

```
  state,
  mutations,
  actions,
  getters
}

export default productModule;
```

Our main Vuex store now needs to import these modules and include them within the `modules` property. We'll update `store/index.js` to reflect this:

vuex/shopping_cart/src/app-1/store/index.js

```
import Vue from 'vue';
import Vuex from 'vuex';
import product from './modules/product';
import cart from './modules/cart';

Vue.use(Vuex);

export default new Vuex.Store({
  modules: {
    product,
    cart
  }
})
```

To have the store accessible in all our application's components, we need to inject it into the entire application.

In the `src/main.js` file, we'll import the entire store and pass it within the application's Vue instance. Our updated `src/main.js` file should look like this:

```
import Vue from 'vue';
import App from './app/App.vue';
import store from './app/store';

new Vue({
  el: '#app',
  store,
  render: h => h(App)
});
```

We can now begin building the pieces for both the `productModule` and the `cartModule`.

`productModule`

The `productModule` is solely responsible in obtaining a list of product items directly from the server. We'll build the interaction that involves adding a product item to the cart within the `cartModule`.

State

The application level state we need in `productModule` is simply an entire list (i.e. array) of product items. With this in mind, our `productModule` state will have a `productItems` property initialized with an empty array.

Let's update the `state` object in `store/modules/product/index.js` to be:

vuex/shopping_cart/src/app-2/store/modules/product/index.js

```
const state = {
  productItems: []
}
```

Mutations

When the application loads in the browser, we'll make a call from our client to the server to `GET` all items in `server-product-data.json`. When this call is made, we need to update the `state.productItems` property to reflect the information in `server-product-data.json`.

In essence, we need to *mutate* our `productModule` state to be equal to the state in the server. **This is how we keep our client state and our server state *in sync*.**

We'll create a mutation called `UPDATE_PRODUCT_ITEMS` that simply updates the state with the payload provided.

Remember, state is always the first argument of a mutation. The optional payload is the data we need here to update our state.

The `mutations` object in `store/modules/product/index.js` becomes:

vuex/shopping_cart/src/app-2/store/modules/product/index.js

```
const mutations = {
  UPDATE_PRODUCT_ITEMS (state, payload) {
    state.productItems = payload;
  }
};
```

Actions

We need to create an action that allows us to `GET` a list of product items from the server. We'll set this action up as the `getProductItems` action:

```
const actions = {
  getProductItems (context) {
    // action goes here
  }
}
```

We won't need to pass any argument into this function, so we can safely ignore the second argument in this action. Therefore, we only set the single `context` argument in the function definition.

The `context` object allows us to commit to a mutation in addition to accessing getters and state. Since we're not going to have a need for anything else but committing to a mutation with `context.commit`, we'll *destructure* the context argument to a `commit` property that we can call directly.

> Destructuring is a feature enabled by ES6 which allows us to pull out a specific key into a variable from a JavaScript object.
>
> For example, take the following functionality in ES5. First, let's assume we have an object like this:
>
> var obj = { a: 'A', func: function() {} }
>
> To get access to the `func` part of the object, we can create a variable:
>
> function(obj) { var func = obj.func }
>
> In ES6, we can destructure the `obj` object using the following line:
>
> function({ func }) {}

Using destructuring, we can change the `getProductItems` function to:

```
const actions = {
  getProductItems ({ commit }) {
    // action goes here
  }
}
```

With our `getProductItems` action set up, we'll need to create an async call to the server to retrieve the payload associated with a list of product items. This payload can then be passed to the `UPDATE_-PRODUCT_ITEMS` mutation to maintain the synchronicity between the client and the server.

Though numerous ajax libraries exist, we'll use the `axios` library for handling async API calls.

Prior to Vue 2.0, `vue-resource` was understood to be the 'official' ajax library for Vue applications. In Nov 2016, `vue-resource` was retired as a recommendation since other 3rd party ajax libraries provided fairly similar functionality. For more reading on this, here's a blog post[76] written by Evan You on discussing the retirement of `vue-resource`.

[76]https://medium.com/the-vue-point/retiring-vue-resource-871a82880af4

Just in case it's not apparent as to why it's important to keep the Vuex and server state in sync, let's explain it in a little more detail.

When the application loads for the first time, the `ProductList` component needs to display a list of product items from the server.

To list our product items on the server within a Flux-like pattern, the component needs to compute data directly from the Vuex state. The `getProductItems` action essentially needs to occur **right when** the application loads, to commit to the `UPDATE_PRODUCT_ITEMS` mutation that updates the Vuex state.

With the Vuex state updated, the `ProductList` component can then compute the product list directly from the state!

axios

`axios` behaves like other HTTP libraries to enable the client to make XMLHttpRequests requests. Since `axios` is promise-based, we dictate what happens when a call is made successfully with `.then()` or when a call fails with `.catch()`.

Here's an example of *fetching* and *posting* information with `axios`:

```
// Fetching information
axios.get('/api/book')
  .then((response) => {
    console.log('GET call successful :)', response)
  })
  .catch((error) => {
    console.log('GET call unsuccessful :(', error)
  });

// Posting information
axios.post('/api/book', { title: 'Fullstack Vue', edition: 1 })
  .then((response) => {
    console.log('Post call successful :)', response)
  })
  .catch((error) => {
    console.log('POST call unsuccessful :(', error)
  });
```

The `axios` library has already been installed in our application. We need to simply import it in the `store/modules/product/index.js` file for it to be used. We'll import it at the top of the file:

vuex/shopping_cart/src/app-2/store/modules/product/index.js

```
import axios from 'axios';
```

The call to the server to `GET` a list of product items is done with `/api/products`. With this in mind, we'll set up our asynchronous call in the `getProductItems` action and `commit` the response retrieved from the call.

vuex/shopping_cart/src/app-2/store/modules/product/index.js

```
const actions = {
  getProductItems ({ commit }) {
    axios.get('/api/products').then((response) => {
      commit('UPDATE_PRODUCT_ITEMS', response.data)
    });
  }
}
```

> The entire response object consists of information such as the `headers` of the HTTP call, the `status`, the `data` that was retrieved etc. Since the fetched data is the only relevant information for our mutation, we simply commit with `response.data` as the payload.

Within actions, it's important to commit to unique mutations under the conditions that an asynchronous call *fails*.

These mutations should update the state accordingly which would display information to the view specifying a call was unsuccessful. Though we won't create error cases for this application (for the sake of simplicity), this is an important note to remember.

Getters

The only getter we'll need in `productModule` is a method that gets the list of product items in our state. Calling this getter `productItems`, our `getters` object becomes:

vuex/shopping_cart/src/app-2/store/modules/product/index.js

```
const getters = {
  productItems: state => state.productItems
}
```

With everything set up, the `store/modules/product/index.js` file will be laid out like this:

vuex/shopping_cart/src/app-2/store/modules/product/index.js

```
import axios from 'axios';

const state = {
  productItems: []
}

const mutations = {
  UPDATE_PRODUCT_ITEMS (state, payload) {
    state.productItems = payload;
  }
};

const actions = {
  getProductItems ({ commit }) {
    axios.get('/api/products').then((response) => {
      commit('UPDATE_PRODUCT_ITEMS', response.data)
    });
  }
}

const getters = {
  productItems: state => state.productItems
}

const productModule = {
  state,
  mutations,
  actions,
  getters
}

export default productModule;
```

ProductList - ProductListItem

With a portion of our Vuex store complete, we can now make the `ProductList` component dynamic.

For us to retrieve information from the store, we first need to invoke the mutation that syncs the server data with the store. Since we need the mutation to occur at the moment the component is created, we'll dispatch the `getProductItems` action within the component's `created()` hook.

In the `<script>` tag of the `ProductList.vue` file, we'll set up the `created()` hook to dispatch the `getProductItems` action. Since the store is injected through the entire application, we can access it with `this.$store`:

```
<script>
export default {
  name: 'ProductList',
  created() {
    this.$store.dispatch('getProductItems');
  }
}
</script>
```

We can verify if the asynchronous call was successful and the store state was updated *before* we aim to display the information to the view. We can do this with the help of the Vue devtools.

With our application launched in the browser, let's open up Vue devtools and select the **Vuex** tab in the top right corner:

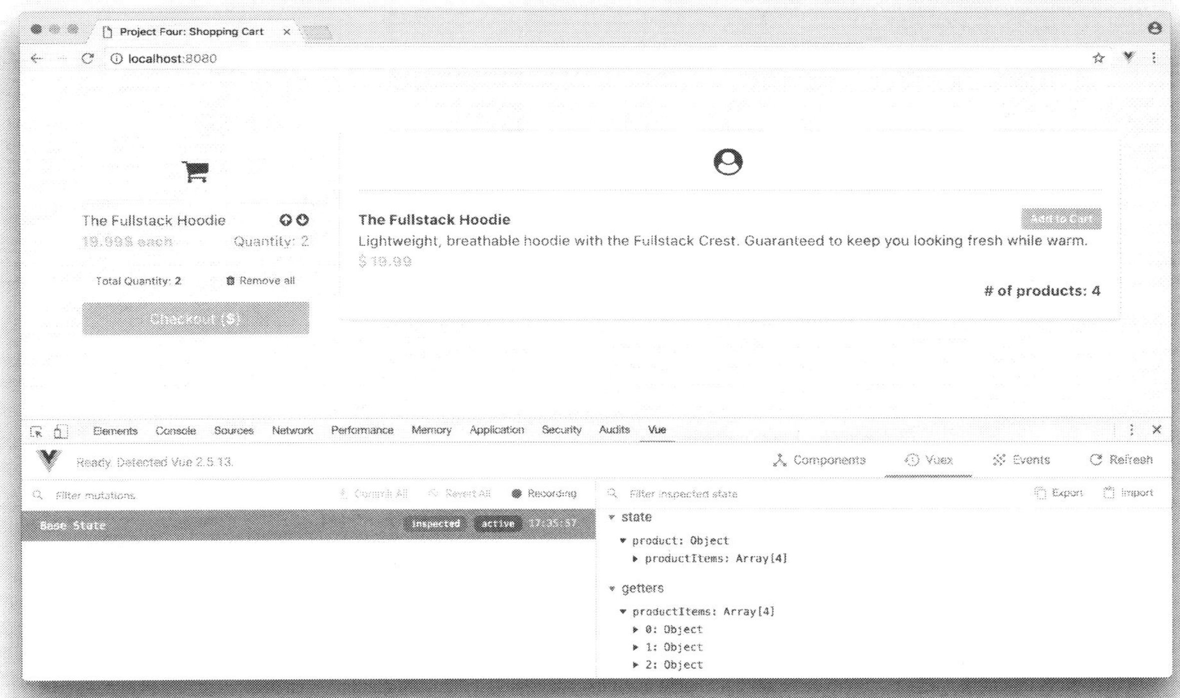

As we can see in the image above, our `productItems` state and getters are displaying the entire list of product item objects! The devtools validate that our `productModule` store is appropriately set up and can be used by components to compute information.

In our `ProductList.vue` file, we can create a computed property that calls the `productItems` getter method to retrieve the entire list of product items:

```
computed: {
  productItems() {
    return this.$store.getters.productItems;
  }
}
```

Though this computed property would work just fine, this can be simplified further. Vuex provides a `mapGetters` helper that directly maps store getters with component computed properties. This helper function helps avoid the continous reference of `this.$store.getters`.

We'll import `mapGetters` from the `vuex` plugin, and use it to mount the `productItems` getter to the scope of the component. The `<script>` of `ProductList.vue` will become:

```
<script>
  import { mapGetters } from 'vuex';

  export default {
    name: 'ProductList',
    computed: {
      ...mapGetters([
        // map this.productItems to this.$store.getters.productItems
        'productItems'
      ])
    },
    created() {
      this.$store.dispatch('getProductItems');
    }
  }
</script>
```

We're using the object spread operator (i.e. the three dots) to directly 'copy' the getters into the components computed property. This helper function allows us to define local computed properties above `mapGetters` if we wish to do so. If we wanted to reference *only* `mapGetters`, `computed` can also be written as:

```
computed: mapGetters({
  productItems: 'productItems'
})
```

In the `ProductList` component template; the content *within* `<div class="product-list"></div>` refers to a single product item:

```
<div class="product-list">
  <!-- Single product list item -->
  <div class="product-list--item">
    <div>
      <h2 class="has-text-weight-bold">The Fullstack Hoodie
        <span class="tag
            is-primary
            is-pulled-right
            has-text-white">
          Add to Cart
        </span>
      </h2>
      <p>Lightweight, breathable hoodie with the Fullstack Crest.
      Guaranteed to keep you looking fresh while warm.</p>
      <span class="has-text-primary has-text-weight-bold">
        <i class="fa fa-usd"></i> 19.99
      </span>
    </div>
  </div>
  <!--  -->
</div>
```

We can use the `v-for` directive to render a list of these divs for every product item in the computed `productItems` property.

Since we'll be creating a `ProductListItem` component that contains the information associated with a single product item, we can update the `<div class=product-list></div>` section of the `ProductList` component `<template>` to the following:

vuex/shopping_cart/src/app-2/components/product/ProductList.vue

```
    <div class="product-list">
      <div
        v-for="productItem in productItems"
        :key="productItem.id"
        class="product-list--item">
        <ProductListItem :productItem="productItem" />
      </div>
    </div>
```

We've passed each product item as a `productItem` prop for every iterated `ProductListItem` component. We've used `productItem.id` as the unique key identifier.

Assuming we'll create the `ProductListItem` component within the `components/product` folder, we'll need to import its respective file and reference it in `ProductList`'s component property.

The `ProductList` `<script>` tag now looks like:

vuex/shopping_cart/src/app-2/components/product/ProductList.vue

```
<script>
import {mapGetters} from 'vuex';
import ProductListItem from './productListItem';

export default {
  name: 'ProductList',
  computed: {
    ...mapGetters(['productItems'])
  },
  created() {
    this.$store.dispatch('getProductItems');
  },
  components: {
    ProductListItem
  }
};
</script>
```

Our application will error until we create the `ProductListItem` component. Within `components/product`, let's create a new `ProductListItem.vue` file:

```
$ ls src/app/components/product/
ProductList.vue
ProductListItem.vue
```

The `<template>` of `ProductListItem.vue` will contain the markup for a single product item. The `<script>` tag will explicitly declare the `productItem` props for it to be used in the template.

With this in mind, the completed `ProductListItem.vue` file will be:

vuex/shopping_cart/src/app-2/components/product/ProductListItem.vue

```
<template>
  <div>
    <h2 class="has-text-weight-bold">{{ productItem.title }}
      <span class="tag
          is-primary
          is-pulled-right
          has-text-white">
        Add to Cart
      </span>
    </h2>
    <p>{{ productItem.description }}</p>
    <span class="has-text-primary has-text-weight-bold">
      <i class="fa fa-usd"></i> {{ productItem.price }}
    </span>
  </div>
</template>

<script>
export default {
  name: 'ProductListItem',
  props: ['productItem']
}
</script>

<style scoped>
.tag {
  cursor: pointer;
}
</style>
```

Our application should now render a list of product items directly from our Vuex store. Saving all our files and refreshing our browser, we'll see a list of dynamic data in the product section:

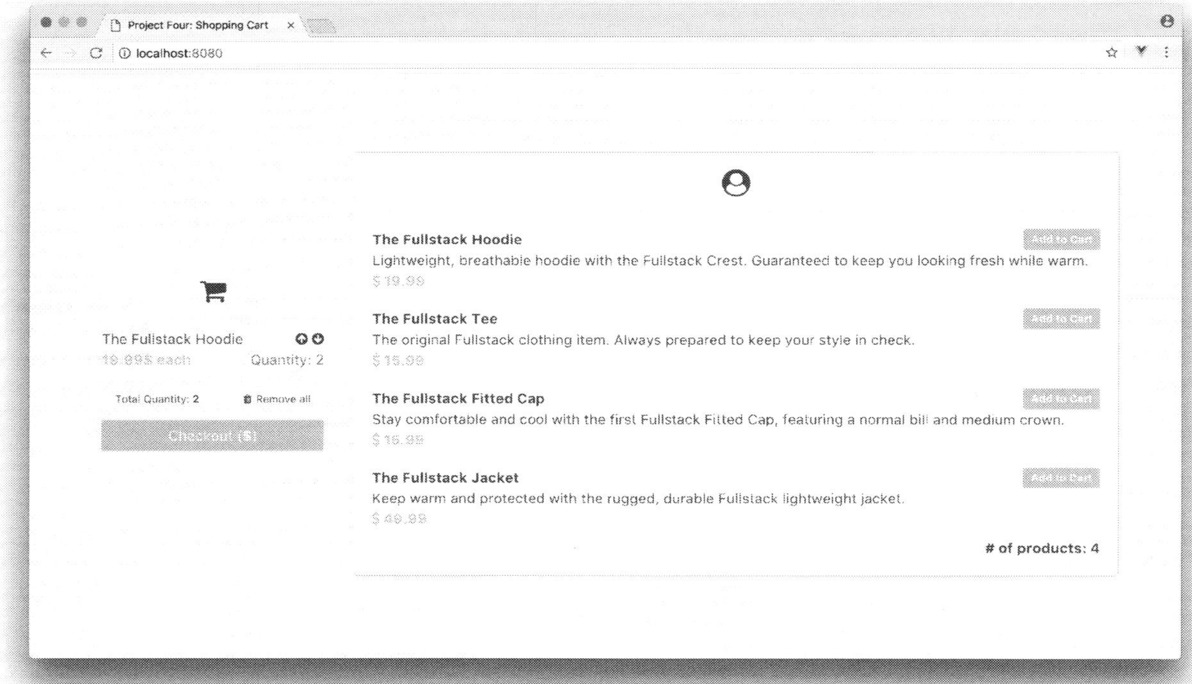

`cartModule`

The `cartModule` has more responsibilities than `productModule` by being responsible for the following functionality:

- Retrieving the list of cart items from the server
- Adding/persisting a new cart item to the server
- Deleting a single cart item from the server
- Deleting all cart items from the server

State

Though a number of interactions are to occur in `cartModule`, they are to act on a single source of data - the list of cart items. With this fact in mind, the state object in `cartModule` will contain a single `cartItems` property intialized with an empty array:

vuex/shopping_cart/src/app-3/store/modules/cart/index.js

```
const state = {
  cartItems: []
}
```

Mutations

We'll have a number of different actions that involve invoking changes to the server. Though our actions may have different purposes, their subsequent mutation will essentially do the same thing - update the `cartItems` state property with the payload provided to **keep the client and the server in sync**.

All our server calls return the *updated* server cart data when a call is made successfully thus all our actions will essentially be similar/do the same thing. We've seen examples of this when we tested out the API earlier - e.g. adding a cart item to the server *returns* a response of the updated cart list with the new item.

Because of this similarity, we can set up a single mutation, `UPDATE_CART_ITEMS`, that updates the state `cartItems` property with a provided payload.

Let's update our `mutations` object to contain this `UPDATE_CART_ITEMS` mutation:

vuex/shopping_cart/src/app-3/store/modules/cart/index.js

```
const mutations = {
  UPDATE_CART_ITEMS (state, payload) {
    state.cartItems = payload;
  }
}
```

Actions

We need to create actions for each of the changes we'd want to `GET` or `POST` to the server. Since every cart related call to the server returns the updated cart list items; each of the actions we'll create can commit to the same `UPDATE_CART_ITEMS` mutation.

To begin, we'll import the `axios` library at the top of the `store/modules/cart/index.js` file:

vuex/shopping_cart/src/app-3/store/modules/cart/index.js

```
import axios from 'axios';
```

Let's now create the `getCartItems` action that does a `GET` request to `/api/cart` to get a list of cart items. This action will then commit to the `UPDATE_CART_ITEMS` mutation to update the state:

```
const actions = {
  getCartItems ({ commit }) {
    axios.get('/api/cart').then((response) => {
      commit('UPDATE_CART_ITEMS', response.data)
    });
  }
}
```

The two POST calls to the server that involve adding a new item with `/api/cart` and deleting an item with `/api/cart/delete` each require a cart item object to be passed to the call. Let's create the actions for each of these as `addCartItem` and `removeCartItem`. Each of these actions will make a POST call with a `cartItem` object payload.

We'll update our `actions` object to reflect this:

```
const actions = {
  getCartItems ({ commit }) {
    axios.get('/api/cart').then((response) => {
      commit('UPDATE_CART_ITEMS', response.data)
    });
  },
  addCartItem ({ commit }, cartItem) {
    axios.post('/api/cart', cartItem).then((response) => {
      commit('UPDATE_CART_ITEMS', response.data)
    });
  },
  removeCartItem ({ commit }, cartItem) {
    axios.post('/api/cart/delete', cartItem).then((response) => {
      commit('UPDATE_CART_ITEMS', response.data)
    });
  }
}
```

The final call to the server involves the deletion of all cart items with a `POST` to `/api/cart/delete/all`. Since no object needs to be passed in to this call, we won't pass a second argument to `axios.post()`. We'll set up a `removeAllCartItems` method for this server call making our entire `actions` object now look like:

vuex/shopping_cart/src/app-3/store/modules/cart/index.js

```
const actions = {
  getCartItems ({ commit }) {
    axios.get('/api/cart').then((response) => {
      commit('UPDATE_CART_ITEMS', response.data)
    });
  },
  addCartItem ({ commit }, cartItem) {
    axios.post('/api/cart', cartItem).then((response) => {
      commit('UPDATE_CART_ITEMS', response.data)
    });
  },
  removeCartItem ({ commit }, cartItem) {
    axios.post('/api/cart/delete', cartItem).then((response) => {
      commit('UPDATE_CART_ITEMS', response.data)
    });
  },
  removeAllCartItems ({ commit }) {
    axios.post('/api/cart/delete/all').then((response) => {
      commit('UPDATE_CART_ITEMS', response.data)
    });
  }
}
```

The process of having multiple actions commit to a single mutation doesn't have to be enforced in Vuex-Vue apps. Different mutations are used to make *different* changes to an application state.

In our case, the server does a good job in returning the updated server data with every action - with which we're always able to use to update the module state.

Getters

There are three forms of computed data we would need to get from our `cartModule` state. The first being a method that gets the list of cart items in our state. We'll call this getter `cartItems`:

```
const getters = {
  cartItems: state => state.cartItems
}
```

We also need the total price of all items in the cart which we'll present in the `Checkout` button of our view. We can use JavaScript's native `reduce` method to compute this. The `reduce` will create the sum of `cartItem.quantity * cartItem.price` for every cart item. We'll label this getter `cartTotal`:

```
const getters = {
  cartItems: state => state.cartItems,
  cartTotal: state => {
    return state.cartItems.reduce((acc, cartItem) => {
      return (cartItem.quantity * cartItem.price) + acc;
    }, 0).toFixed(2);
  }
}
```

In addition, we'll use the `reduce` function again to determine the total quantity of items in the cart. The `getter` for this will be named `cartQuantity` making our `getters` object now become:

vuex/shopping_cart/src/app-3/store/modules/cart/index.js

```
const getters = {
  cartItems: state => state.cartItems,
  cartTotal: state => {
    return state.cartItems.reduce((acc, cartItem) => {
      return (cartItem.quantity * cartItem.price) + acc;
    }, 0).toFixed(2);
  },
  cartQuantity: state => {
    return state.cartItems.reduce((acc, cartItem) => {
      return cartItem.quantity + acc;
    }, 0);
  }
}
```

We've just set up the `cartModule`, which completes the application's Vuex store.

`CartList` - `CartListItem`

Similar to what we did in the `ProductList` component, we'll need to dispatch the `getCartItems` action in the `CartList` component to get a list of cart items from the server. We'll need to do this when the `CartList` component is *created*.

In the `<script>` tag of the `CartList.vue` file, we'll dispatch the `getCartItems` in the `created` hook:

```
<script>
export default {
  name: 'CartList',
  created() {
    this.$store.dispatch('getCartItems');
  }
}
</script>
```

With the action appropriately dispatched on page load, we're now able to get the necessary computed data from the state.

We'll use the `mapGetters` helper to map component computed `cartItems`, `cartTotal`, and `cartQuantity` properties to the respective store getters.

Importing `mapGetters` and creating the helper in the components computed property will make our `CartList.vue` file `<script>` tag be:

```
<script>
import { mapGetters } from 'vuex';

export default {
  name: 'CartList',
  computed: {
    ...mapGetters([
      'cartItems',
      'cartTotal',
      'cartQuantity'
    ])
  },
  created() {
    this.$store.dispatch('getCartItems');
  },
}
</script>
```

With the `cartItems` computed property, we can now render a list of cart items dynamically in the view. In the `CartList` component template, the `<li class="cart-item"></li>` element represents a single cart item:

```
<ul>
  <!-- single cart item -->
  <li class="cart-item">
    <div>
      <p class="cart-item--title is-inline">The Fullstack Hoodie</p>
      <div class="is-pulled-right">
        <i class="fa fa-arrow-circle-up cart-item--modify"></i>
        <i class="fa fa-arrow-circle-down cart-item--modify"></i>
      </div>
      <div class="cart-item--content">
        <span
          class="cart-item--price has-text-primary has-text-weight-bold">
            19.99$ each
        </span>
        <span
          class="cart-item--quantity has-text-grey is-pulled-right">
            Quantity: 2
        </span>
      </div>
    </div>
  </li>
  <!--  -->
  ...
```

We'll set up a CartListItem component that displays the markup of a single cart item shortly.

In CartList, we'll use the v-for directive to render a list of these CartListItem components for every item in the computed cartItems property. For every rendered CartListItem component, we'll pass in the respective cartItem as props.

This will change the <li class="cart-item"></li> portion of the template to the following:

```
<ul>
  <li v-for="cartItem in cartItems" :key="cartItem.id" class="cart-item">
    <CartListItem :cartItem="cartItem" />
  </li>
  ...
```

We can also reference the dynamic cartTotal and cartQuantity data in the CartList template. We'll reference cartQuantity in the <p> tag that displays 'Total Quantity':

```
<p>Total Quantity:
  <span class="has-text-weight-bold">
    {{ cartQuantity }}
  </span>
</p>
```

We'll apply `cartTotal` to the `Checkout` button tag:

```
<button class="button is-primary">
  Checkout (<span class="has-text-weight-bold">${{ cartTotal }}</span>)
</button>
```

With all these changes, the `<template>` section in the `CartList.vue` file will be updated to:

vuex/shopping_cart/src/app-3/components/cart/CartList.vue

```
<template>
  <div id="cart">
    <div class="cart--header has-text-centered">
      <i class="fa fa-2x fa-shopping-cart"></i>
    </div>
    <ul>
      <li v-for="cartItem in cartItems" :key="cartItem.id" class="cart-item">
        <CartListItem :cartItem="cartItem" />
      </li>
      <div class="cart-details">
        <p>Total Quantity:
          <span class="has-text-weight-bold">
            {{ cartQuantity }}
          </span></p>
        <p class="cart-remove-all--text">
          <i class="fa fa-trash"></i>Remove all
        </p>
      </div>
    </ul>
    <button class="button is-primary">
      Checkout (<span class="has-text-weight-bold">${{ cartTotal }}</span>)
    </button>
  </div>
</template>
```

Since we'll be building the `CartListItem` component within the `components/cart` folder, we'll import it from it's respective file and reference it in the `components` property of `CartList`. The `<script>` for `CartList` will update to reflect this:

vuex/shopping_cart/src/app-3/components/cart/CartList.vue

```
<script>
import {mapGetters} from 'vuex';
import CartListItem from './CartListItem';

export default {
  name: 'CartList',
  computed: {
    ...mapGetters(['cartItems', 'cartTotal', 'cartQuantity'])
  },
  created() {
    this.$store.dispatch('getCartItems');
  },
  components: {
    CartListItem
  }
};
</script>
```

We now need to create the `CartListItem` component. Within `components/cart`, let's create a new `CartListItem.vue` file:

```
$ ls src/app/components/cart/
CartList.vue
CartListItem.vue
```

The `<template>` of `CartListItem` will contain the markup for a single cart item. The `<script>` tag will explicitly declare the `cartItem` props for it to be used in the template. We'll remove the hard-coded data and appropriately reference the `cartItem` properties for the item title, price and quantity.

With all this in mind, the completed `CartListItem.vue` file will be laid out as so:

vuex/shopping_cart/src/app-3/components/cart/CartListItem.vue

```
<template>
  <div>
    <p class="cart-item--title is-inline">{{ cartItem.title }}</p>
    <div class="is-pulled-right">
      <i class="fa fa-arrow-circle-up cart-item--modify"></i>
      <i class="fa fa-arrow-circle-down cart-item--modify"></i>
    </div>
    <div class="cart-item--content">
```

```
      <span class="cart-item--price has-text-primary has-text-weight-bold">
        {{ cartItem.price }}$ each
      </span>
      <span class="cart-item--quantity has-text-grey is-pulled-right">
        Quantity: {{ cartItem.quantity }}
      </span>
    </div>
  </div>
</template>

<script>
export default {
  name: 'CartListItem',
  props: ['cartItem']
};
</script>

<style scoped>
.cart-item--modify {
  cursor: pointer;
}
</style>
```

If we save our files and refresh our browser, the cart items and other cart information would now be dynamically obtained from the server.

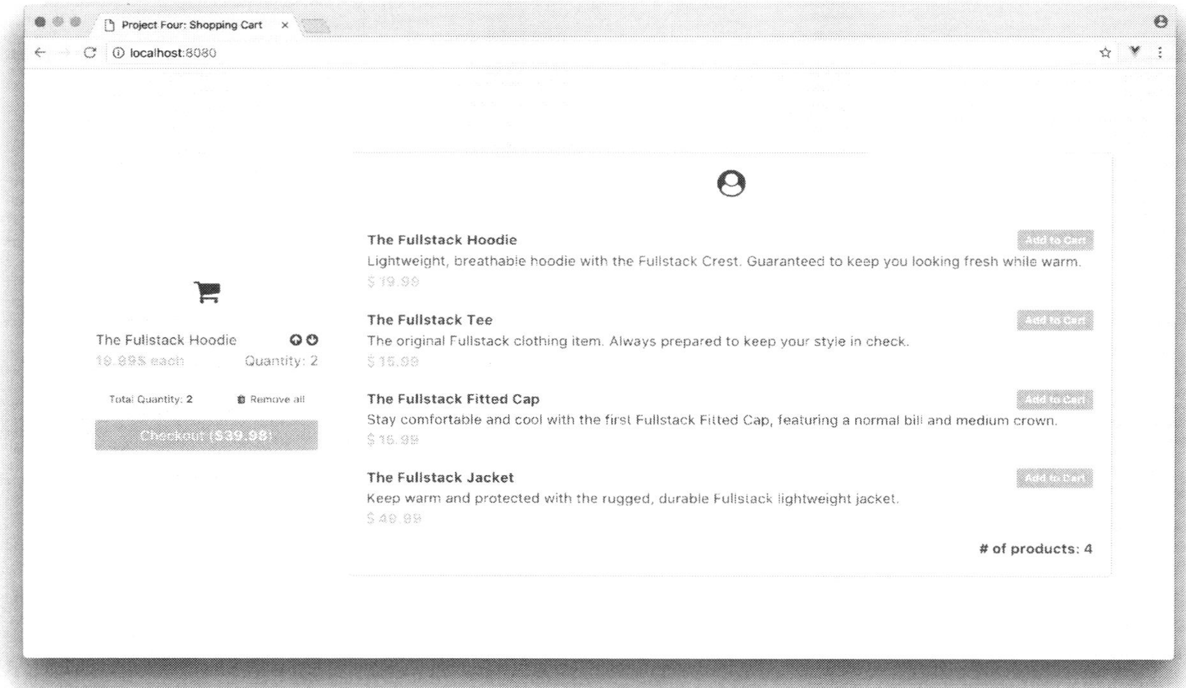

Dynamic cart data

Interactivity

We've managed to set up our application to display dynamic data directly from the server. The last thing we need to do is enable interactivity in the UI.

The following actions have already been created within our store:

- `addCartItem` - add an item to the cart list
- `removeCartItem` - remove an item from the cart list
- `removeAllCartItems` - remove all items from the cart list

Here's a diagram that shows where we need to invoke these actions:

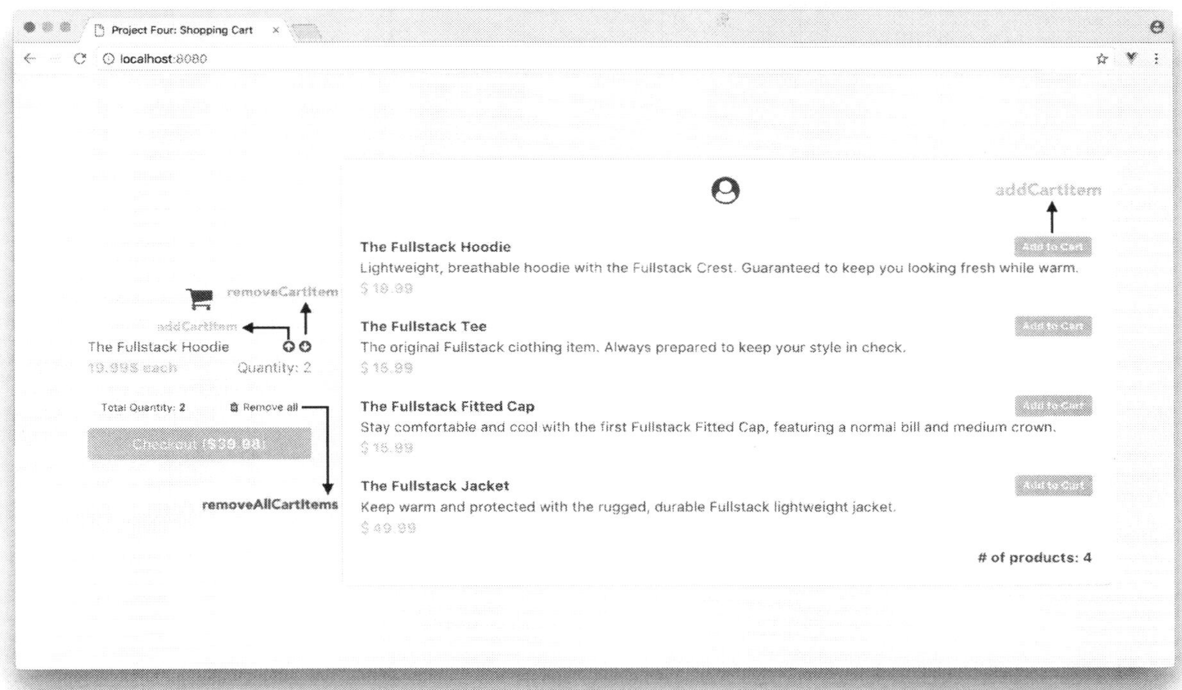

When these items are clicked, we'll need to create dispatchers within the components to call the relevant store actions. The Vuex store takes care of the rest!

ProductListItem

The 'Add to Cart' button in a single product item should dispatch the `addCartItem` action when clicked.

A single product item is reflected in the `ProductListItem` component. We'll create a click listener on the 'Add to Cart' button span, of `ProductListItem`, to call an `addCartItem` component method when triggered. When this method is called, we'll pass in the `productItem` prop since this object is needed in the `addCartItem` action.

We'll first create the click listener on the `<span>` of the 'Add to Cart' tag in the `ProductListItem.vue` file:

```
<span
  @click="addCartItem(productItem)"
  class="tag is-primary is-pulled-right has-text-white">
    Add to Cart
</span>
```

With the click listener created, we can create the `addCartItem` method in the `ProductListItem` component's `method` property to perform the dispatching with the `productItem` payload:

```
methods: {
  addCartItem (productItem) {
    this.$store.dispatch('addCartItem', productItem);
  }
}
```

However, just like how Vuex provides the `mapGetters` helper, we can use a `mapActions` helper that directly maps the component method action to the store action. `mapActions` works similarly to `mapGetters`, but also directly passes the intended payload without the need to specify it.

Importing `mapActions` and using it to map the `addCartItem` method, the `ProductListItem.vue` `<script>` tag becomes:

vuex/shopping_cart/src/app-complete/components/product/ProductListItem.vue

```
<script>
import { mapActions } from 'vuex';

export default {
  name: 'ProductListItem',
  props: ['productItem'],
  methods: {
    ...mapActions([
      'addCartItem'
    ])
  }
}
</script>
```

When we save our files and refresh the browser, we'll be able to add items from the product list to the cart:

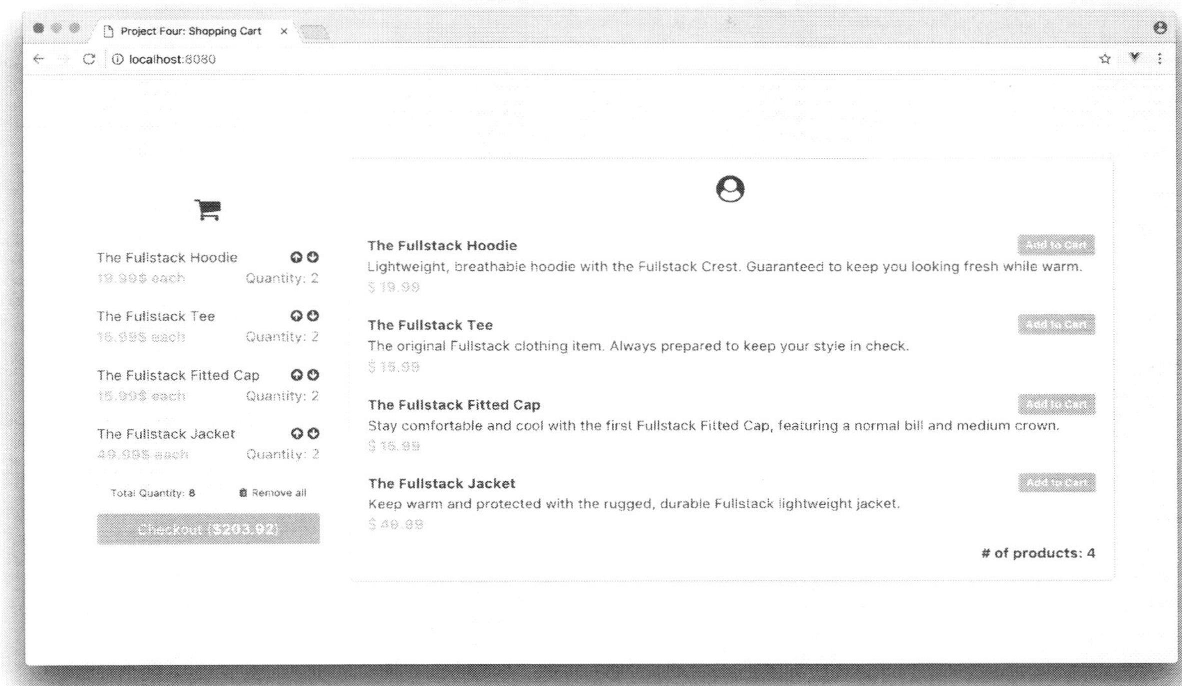

CartListItem

The arrow icons for a single cart item need to allow the user to add or remove cart items within the cart. Since the `CartListItem` component references a single cart item, we'll need to apply these methods within this component.

Adding and removing cart items are done with the `addCartItem` and `removeCartItem` actions respectively.

We'll introduce click listeners on the icons of the `CartListItem.vue` template to call `addCartItem` and `removeCartItem` component methods:

```
<div class="is-pulled-right">
  <i @click="addCartItem(cartItem)"
    class="fa fa-arrow-circle-up cart-item--modify"></i>
  <i @click="removeCartItem(cartItem)"
    class="fa fa-arrow-circle-down cart-item--modify"></i>
</div>
```

We'll import `mapActions` to this component and map these methods to the store actions. The `<script>` of `CartListItem` becomes:

vuex/shopping_cart/src/app-complete/components/cart/CartListItem.vue

```
<script>
import { mapActions } from 'vuex';

export default {
  name: 'CartListItem',
  props: ['cartItem'],
  methods: {
    ...mapActions([
      'addCartItem',
      'removeCartItem'
    ])
  }
}
</script>

<style scoped>
.cart-item--modify {
  cursor: pointer;
}
</style>
```

Launching the browser after saving the file, we'll be able to add and remove items from the cart within the cart component.

Here's a screenshot of removing all items from the cart:

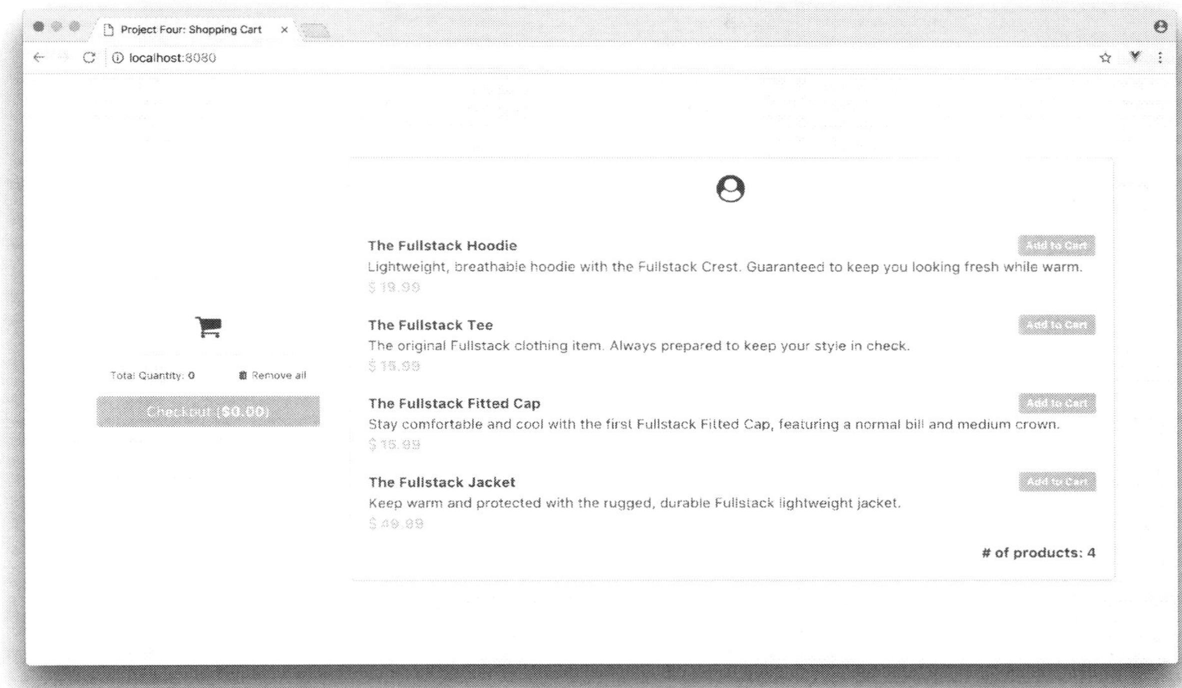

Though not necessary, it might be a good idea to notify the user to start adding items when no cart items are present. Let's set this up prior to dispatching the last remaining action, `removeAllCartItems`.

CartList

In the `CartList` template, we'll display a `<p>` tag that tells the user to 'Add some items to the cart' only under the condition that no cart items are present in the shopping cart.

We can do this by conditionally displaying the `<p>` tag with the `v-if` directive. We'll state that the tag will only be shown when the length of the `cartItems` property, in `CartList`, is equal to 0.

The `<p>` element will look something like this:

```
<p v-if="cartItems.length === 0"
  class="cart-empty-text has-text-centered">
  Add some items to the cart!
</p>
```

When this condition is met, we can also hide the 'Total Quantity' text and 'Remove all' icon within the cart. We'll specify to only show this cart information under the condition that at least a single item exists (`v-if="cartItems.length > 0"`):

```
<ul v-if="cartItems.length > 0">
  <li v-for="cartItem in cartItems" class="cart-item">
    <CartListItem :cartItem="cartItem" />
  </li>
  <div class="cart-details">
    <p>Total Quantity:
      <span class="has-text-weight-bold">{{ cartQuantity }}</span>
    </p>
    <p class="cart-remove-all--text">
      <i class="fa fa-trash"></i>Remove all
    </p>
  </div>
</ul>
```

We can also disable the checkout button if no cart items is present. We'll ensure this happens by binding the buttons `disabled` attribute to `cartItems.length === 0` (when this statement is true - the `disabled` attribute becomes true):

```
<button :disabled="cartItems.length === 0" class="button is-primary">
  Checkout
  (<span class="has-text-weight-bold">
    {{ cartTotal }}$
  </span>)
</button>
```

Let's now create the dispatcher to call the last remaining action, `removeAllCartItems`. We'll set up the click listener on the `fa-trash` icon to call a `removeAllCartItems` method when clicked:

```
<p @click="removeAllCartItems"
  class="cart-remove-all--text">
  <i class="fa fa-trash"></i>Remove all
</p>
```

With all this implemented, the finished `<template>` of the `CartList.vue` file looks like the following:

vuex/shopping_cart/src/app-complete/components/cart/CartList.vue

```
<template>
  <div id="cart">
    <div class="cart--header has-text-centered">
      <i class="fa fa-2x fa-shopping-cart"></i>
    </div>
    <p v-if="cartItems.length === 0" class="cart-empty-text has-text-centered">
      Add some items to the cart!
    </p>
    <ul v-if="cartItems.length > 0">
      <li v-for="cartItem in cartItems" :key="cartItem.id" class="cart-item">
        <CartListItem :cartItem="cartItem" />
      </li>
      <div class="cart-details">
        <p>Total Quantity:
          <span class="has-text-weight-bold">{{ cartQuantity }}</span>
        </p>
        <p @click="removeAllCartItems"
          class="cart-remove-all--text">
          <i class="fa fa-trash"></i>Remove all
        </p>
      </div>
    </ul>
    <button :disabled="cartItems.length === 0" class="button is-primary">
      Checkout (<span class="has-text-weight-bold">${{ cartTotal }}</span>)
    </button>
  </div>
</template>
```

To enable the final interactive piece of our application, we'll import `mapActions` and map the component `removeAllCartItems` method to the store action of the same name. The `<script>` of the `CartList.vue` file will be updated to:

vuex/shopping_cart/src/app-complete/components/cart/CartList.vue

```
<script>
import {mapGetters, mapActions} from 'vuex';
import CartListItem from './CartListItem';

export default {
  name: 'CartList',
  computed: {
    ...mapGetters(['cartItems', 'cartTotal', 'cartQuantity'])
  },
  created() {
    this.$store.dispatch('getCartItems');
  },
  methods: {
    ...mapActions(['removeAllCartItems'])
  },
  components: {
    CartListItem
  }
};
</script>
```

Let's save this file and test it in the browser. By adding a list of items to the cart and clicking the `Remove all` icon, we should see everything removed from the cart and the expected 'Add some items' message displayed!

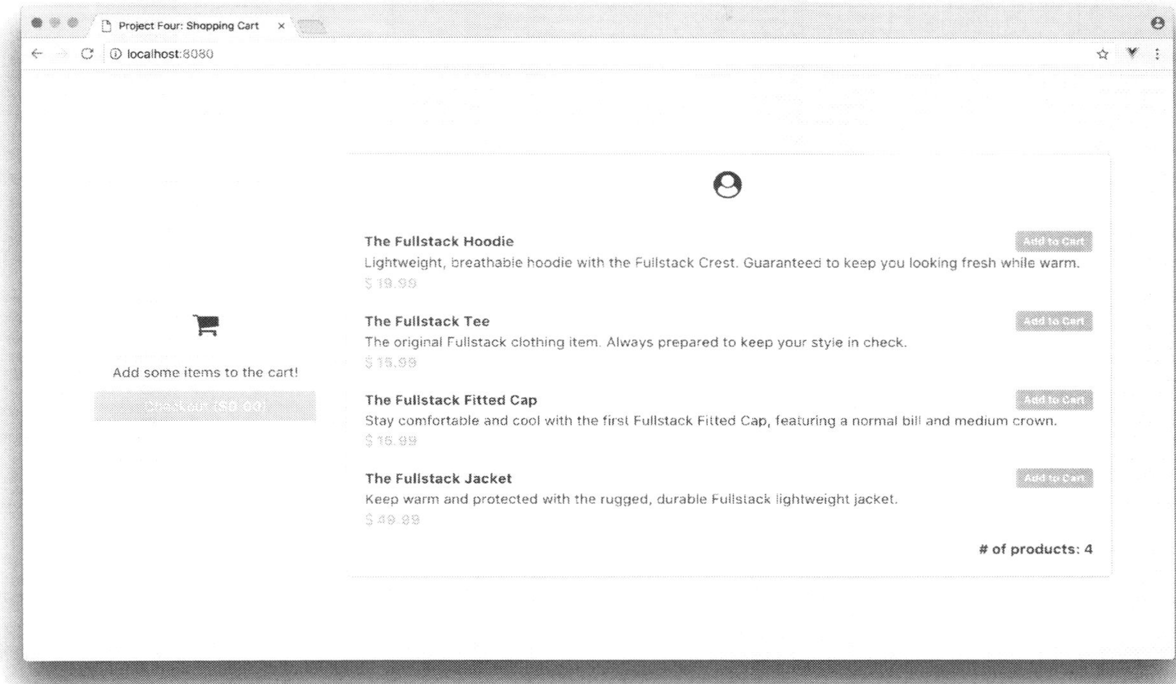

We've implemented everything we intended to build for this application. Our shopping cart has a fully functioning Vuex integration which persists to a server. This persistence allow changes to remain between app refreshes.

Vuex and medium to large scale applications

After some initial set-up and complexity with building our Vuex store, our app now neatly isolates responsibility.

Not only does this make the code easier to read, but it sets us up for scale significantly. Let's discuss some of the things we could've done differently and ways to now scale from here.

Mutation Types

In our application, we specified our mutations with a string type, and made our actions commit to these mutations by declaring the same string type:

```
const mutations = {
  UPDATE_CART_ITEMS (state, payload) {
    state.cartItems = payload;
  }
}

const actions = {
  getCartItems ({ commit }) {
    axios.get('/api/cart').then((response) => {
      commit('UPDATE_CART_ITEMS', response.data)
    });
  },
  ...
}
```

For large scale Flux implementations, a common standard is to often define mutation types as constants and to host them all in a separate file.

Let's see how we'd go about doing this. Addressing the `cartModule` alone, we'd create a `mutations-type.js` file within the `cart/` folder:

```
ls store/modules/cart
index.js
mutation-types.js
```

And have the `mutation-types.js` file export a `const` variable attached to a string handler for the UPDATE_CART_ITEMS mutation:

```
export const UPDATE_CART_ITEMS = 'UPDATE_CART_ITEMS';
```

In `cart/index.js`, we can import the `mutation-types.js` file as `types` and refer to the exported constant in our mutations and actions:

```
import * as types from './mutation-types';

const mutations = {
  [types.UPDATE_CART_ITEMS] (state, payload) {
    state.cartItems = payload;
  }
}

const actions = {
  getCartItems ({ commit }) {
    axios.get('/api/cart').then((response) => {
      commit(types.UPDATE_CART_ITEMS, response.data)
    });
  },
  ...
}
```

The [types.UPDATE_CART_ITEMS] declaration in the `mutations` object is an example of using ES6 computed property names to initialize object properties from variables.

Using constants for mutation types and keeping them in one file benefits larger applications by allowing collaborators to track and maintain all mutation types in a single file. The mutations section of the Vuex docs[77] states that this approach is completely optional and is simply a preference between different developers/teams.

Checkout feature

If we wanted to add a new action/mutation that constitutes the user *checking out* with his purchase, we wouldn't have to worry about logic as to where this would fit best. We'd initiate a new action in the `cartModule` that makes an asynchronous call and passes a payload, if necessary, to a mutation we'd like to commit.

This could look something like this:

[77]https://vuex.vuejs.org/en/mutations.html#using-constants-for-mutation-types

```
const state = {
  ...,
  checkout: false
}

const mutations = {
  ...,
  CHECKOUT_CART (state) {
    state.checkout = true;
  }
}

const actions = {
  ...,
  checkoutCart ({ commit }, cart) {
    axios.post('/api/cart/checkout').then((response) => {
      commit('CHECKOUT_CART');
    });
  }
}
```

In our CartList component, we'll simply map the action to a component method on click of the Checkout button.

```
<button
  @click="checkoutCart"
  :disabled="cartItems.length === 0"
  class="button is-primary">
    Checkout (<span class="has-text-weight-bold">
      {{ cartTotal }}$</span>)
</button>
...
methods: {
  ...mapActions([
    ...,
    'checkoutCart'
  ])
}
```

This example shows how the initial overhead of setting up a Vuex store becomes profitable when it's incredibly easy to create new state changes as an application grows.

File structure

Grouping actions, mutations, getters and state within a single `index.js` file for the `store/cart/` and `store/product/` folders suited our application well. However, if the number of state configurations/computations became hard to manage, we could separate the module pieces into separate files:

```
store/
  modules/
    cart/
      actions.js
      getters.js
      index.js // exports cartModule
      mutations.js
    product/
      actions.js
      getters.js
      index.js // exports productModule
      mutations.js
```

The `index.js` files would host `state`, import `actions`, `getters`, and `mutations`, and export the respective modules (`cartModule` or `productModule`).

A graphical representation of this:

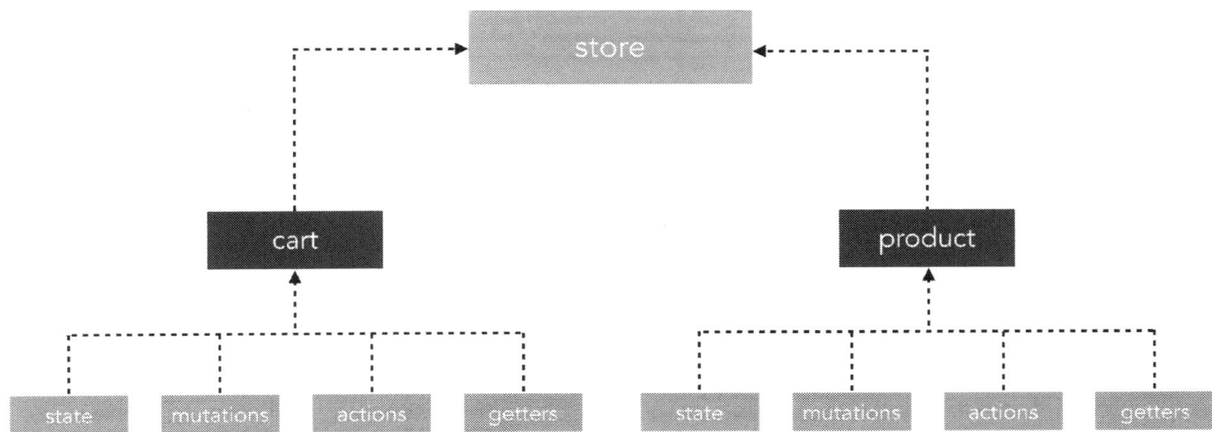

Say we wanted to add an entirely new piece of state to the system — like a notifications panel. We can create a `notificationsModule` that consists of the `state`, `mutations`, `actions` and `getters` respective of that domain. For the sake of keeping things consistent, we can group the major notification related components in a components sub-folder of its own as well:

```
components/
  cart/
  notifications/
  product/
store/
  modules/
    cart/
    notifications/
    product/
```

This approach isn't the only way to build a Vuex-powered Vue application. Though this clear separation of concerns helps greatly in managing the ever growing state of an application, it does have a few pitfalls - like difficulty in understanding where global functionality should fit in and how to group similar functionality between modules.

The decision on how Vuex can be integrated to a Vue app fully comes down to how different teams/developers aim to architect their entire application.

Recap

Let's recap how our Vuex store is implemented into the shopping cart application:

1. The Vuex store consists of the `cartModule` and `productModule`.
2. The `productModule` is primarily responsible in fetching all items in the product list. The `cartModule` provides the ability to fetch all items in the shopping cart as well as actions to add/delete items from the cart.
3. The `getProductItems` and `getCartItems` actions are dispatched, on page load, in the `ProductList` and `CartList` components `created` hooks.
4. The components compute store data with the help of `mapGetters` which maps component computed properties to the store getters.
5. The components contain click listeners that dispatch methods to store actions with the `mapActions` helper.

VI - Form Handling

Introduction

With the last few chapters, we've come to understand how Vue allows us to manage data within the components of an application. With these concepts, we managed to acquire a strong mindset in thinking how to architect and scale applications as they grow.

This chapter takes a deep dive on a crucial piece that we've come across and used without paying much attention to - **forms**. Forms are one of the most important parts of an application. While some interaction occurs through clicks and mouse moves, it's really through forms where we'll get the majority of rich input from users.

It's through forms that we often add payment info, search for results, edit profiles, upload photos, or even send messages. Forms are one of the key items that transform web **sites** into web **apps**.

Forms 101

On the surface, forms seem straightforward: we make an input tag, the user fills it out, and hits submit. How hard could it be? For simple applications, this could very well be the case. Forms, however, can become very complex *very quickly*. Here are some reasons why:

- Form inputs are meant to modify data, both on the page and the server.
- Changes often have to be kept in sync with data elsewhere on the page.
- Users can enter unpredictable values, some that we'll want to modify or reject outright.
- The UI needs to clearly state expectations and errors, if any
- Fields dependent on each other can have complex logic.
- Forms need to be testable, without relying on DOM selectors.

Thankfully, Vue provides us with tools that help with all of these things!

In this chapter, we'll first start simple and provide examples on how different form inputs are handled with Vue. We're then going to explore how to handle some of the challenges stated above by building a Vuex integrated form.

Preparation

Inside the code download that came with this book, navigate to the `form_handling` directory:

```
$ cd form_handling
```

This directory contains all the code examples for this chapter:

```
$ ls
01-basic-button/
02-basic-button/
03-basic-input/
04-data-input/
05-data-input-list/
06-data-input-multi/
07-basic-form-validation/
08-basic-field-validation/
09-remote-persist/
10-vuex-app/
app/
public/
```

For the beginning of this chapter, we'll be focusing solely on building simple form elements (`01-basic-button` to `05-data-input-list`). The rest of the chapter will involve building out a form, adding validation to said form, handling errors, persisting data asynchronously, and adapting the form to the Vuex paradigm.

The `app/` directory serves as the starting point for us to work with. Like every other folder, the directory contains an `index.html` and `main.js` file. The `index.html` file represents a barebones starting point:

form_handling/app/index.html

```
<!DOCTYPE html>
<html>

<head>
  <link rel="stylesheet" href="../public/semantic.min.css" />
  <title>Form App</title>
  <style>
    .ui.container {
      margin: 20px 0;
    }
  </style>
</head>

<body>
```

```
  <div id="app" class="ui container">
  </div>

  <script src="https://unpkg.com/vue"></script>
  <script src="./main.js"></script>
</body>

</html>
```

For styling in this chapter, we'll be using Semantic UI[78] with which we've installed locally in the `public/` folder and referenced in the `<head>` tag.

The `<body>` tag contains a `div` with `id` of `app` and two `<script>` tags that dictate which JavaScript files need to be loaded. The `div` with `id="app"` is where we'll be mounting our Vue application. The `<script>` tags load the latest version of Vue from a CDN and the internal JavaScript file (`main.js`) where we'll be writing all our Vue code.

The `main.js` file simply declares a new Vue instance that mounts to the DOM element with the id of `app`:

form_handling/app/main.js

```
new Vue({
  el: '#app',
})
```

For simplicity and to avoid unnecessary bloating, none of these code examples involve running Vue on a Webpack server. Since Vue is simply introduced as a CDN, we'll have to right click the `index.html` file within each code example and select `Open With > Google Chrome` to run the example/application.

Great! Let's get started!

The Basic Button

At their core, forms are a conversation with the user. Fields are the app's questions, and the values that the user inputs are the answers.

Let's ask the user what their favorite Fullstack clothing item is from the shopping cart built in the previous chapter.

[78] http://semantic-ui.com/

We could present the user with a text box, but we'll start even simpler. In this example, we'll constrain the response to just one of four possible answers. We want the user to pick between the "Hoodie", "Tee", "Fitted Cap" or "Jacket", and the simplest way to do that is to give them four buttons to choose from.

Here's what the first example looks like:

Basic Buttons

To get to this stage, we'll first have to set-up an HTML template that displays a `ui-header` title and a `button-row` component declaration:

form_handling/01-basic-button/index.html

```
<div id="app" class="ui container">
  <h2 class="ui header">What's your favorite Fullstack clothing item?</h2>
  <button-row></button-row>
</div>
```

The `button-row` component template needs to display the button elements and be declared in the Vue instance's `components` property, in the `main.js` file:

```
const ButtonRow = {
  template: `
    <div>
      <button @click="onHoodieClick" class="ui button">Hoodie</button>
      <button @click="onTeeClick" class="ui button">Tee</button>
      <button @click="onFittedCapClick" class="ui button">Fitted Cap</button>
      <button @click="onJacketClick" class="ui button">Jacket</button>
    </div>`
}

new Vue({
  el: '#app',
  components: {
    'button-row': ButtonRow
  }
})
```

So far this looks similar to how a form can be handled with vanilla HTML. The unique part to pay attention to is the `@click` (i.e. `v-on:click`) prop of the button elements. When a `button` is clicked, if it has a function set as its `@click` prop, that function will be called. We'll use this behavior to know what our user's answer is.

To know what our user's answer is, we pass a different function to each button (`onHoodieClick`, `onTeeClick`, etc.). We'll now need to set up functions within the `button-row` component's `methods` property to declare which button was clicked.

With this in mind, we'll create a `methods` property right after `template`:

```
const ButtonRow = {
  template: `
    <div>
      <button @click="onHoodieClick" class="ui button">Hoodie</button>
      <button @click="onTeeClick" class="ui button">Tee</button>
      <button @click="onFittedCapClick" class="ui button">Fitted Cap</button>
      <button @click="onJacketClick" class="ui button">Jacket</button>
    </div>`
  methods: {}
```

Within `methods`, we'll set-up a `console.log` for each of the event handlers to log which button was clicked.

form_handling/01-basic-button/main.js

```
  methods: {
    onHoodieClick(evt) {
      console.log('The user clicked button-hoodie', evt);
    },
    onTeeClick(evt) {
      console.log('The user clicked button-tee', evt);
    },
    onFittedCapClick(evt) {
      console.log('The user clicked button-fitted-cap', evt);
    },
    onJacketClick(evt) {
      console.log('The user clicked button-jacket', evt);
    }
  }
```

Notice that in the `@click` handlers, we pass the functions like `onHoodieClick` instead of `onHoodieClick()`.

What's the difference?

In the first case (without parens), we're passing the function `onHoodieClick`, whereas in the second case we're passing the *result* of calling the function `onHoodieClick` (which is not what we want right now).

This becomes the foundation of our app's ability to respond to a user's input. Our app can do different things depending on the user's response. In this case, we log different messages to the console depending on which button is clicked.

Events and Event Handlers

Note that our `@click` functions all accept an argument, `evt`. This is because these functions are **event handlers**. We've used event handlers in almost all the applications we've built thus far.

Event handling plays a central role to working with forms in JavaScript applications. When we provide a function to an element's `@click` prop (or `@keyup`, `@input`, etc.), that function becomes an event handler. The function will be called when that event occurs, and will *always* receive an **event object as its argument**.

In the above example, when the `button` elements were clicked, the corresponding event handler functions were called with a mouse click event object being passed in (`evt`). This object is the browser's native `MouseEvent`, and you'll be able to use it the same way you would a native DOM event.

Event objects contain lots of useful information about the action that occurred. A `MouseEvent` for example, will let you see the x and y coordinates of the mouse at the time of the click, whether or not the shift key was pressed, and (most useful for this example) a reference to the element that was clicked. We'll use this information to simplify things in the next section.

Instead, if we were interested in mouse movement, we could have created an event handler and provided it to the `onmousemove` event. In fact, Vue allows the use of any native event within the `v-on` directive: `click`, `dblclick`, `drag`, `drop`, `mousedown`, `mouseenter`, `mouseleave`, `mousemove`, `mouseout`, `mouseover`, `mouseup`, etc.

And those are only the mouse events. There are also clipboard, composition, keyboard, focus, form, selection, touch, ui, wheel, media, image, animation, and transition event groups. Each group has its own types of events, and not all events are appropriate for all elements. Here, we'll mainly work with the events `click`, `change`, `submit`, and `input` which are often used with form and input elements.

Back to the Button

In the previous section, we were able to perform different actions (log different messages) depending on the action of the user. However, with the way we've set it up, we needed to create separate functions for each action. Instead, it would be much cleaner if we provided the same event handler to all buttons, and used information from the event itself to determine our response.

To do this, we'll replace the separate event handlers `onHoodieClick`, `onTeeClick`, `onFittedCap`, and `onJacketClick` with a single event handler, `onButtonClick`. This would make our `button-row` component `methods` property become:

form_handling/02-basic-button/main.js

```
methods: {
  onButtonClick(evt) {
    const button = evt.target;
    console.log(`The user clicked ${button.name}: ${button.value}`);
  }
}
```

Our click handler function receives an event object, `evt`. `evt` has an attribute `target` that is a reference to the button that the user clicked. This way we can access the button the user clicked without creating a function for each button. With this we're able to log the button name and button value.

With the new `onButtonClick` event method declared, we need to update the `button` elements to use this event handler. In addition, we'll specify a `name` and `value` for each button that is used within the `onButtonClick` method to help dictate which button was clicked. This makes the `button-row` component template be:

form_handling/02-basic-button/main.js

```
template: `
  <div>
    <button @click="onButtonClick"
      name="button-hoodie"
      value="fullstack-hoodie"
      class="ui button">Hoodie</button>
    <button @click="onButtonClick"
      name="button-tee"
      value="fullstack-tee"
      class="ui button">Tee</button>
    <button @click="onButtonClick"
      name="button-fitted-cap"
      value="fullstack-fitted-cap"
```

```
      class="ui button">Fitted Cap</button>
    <button @click="onButtonClick"
      name="button-jacket"
      value="fullstack-jacket"
      class="ui button">Jacket</button>
  </div>`,
```

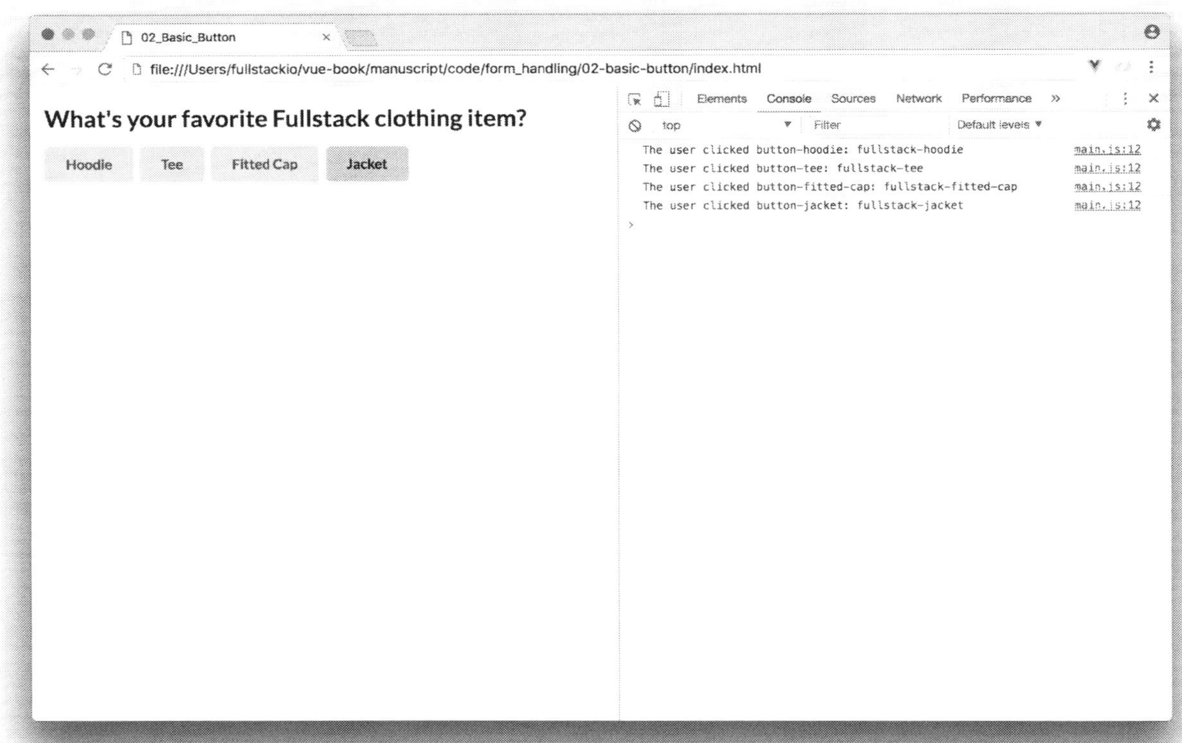

The `onButtonClick` event handler

By taking advantage of the event object and using a shared event handler, we could add 100 new buttons, and we wouldn't have to introduce any more methods to our app.

Text Input

In the previous example, we constrained our user's response to only one of four possibilities. Now that we know how to take advantage of event objects and handlers, we're going to accept a much wider range of responses and move on to a more typical use of forms: text input.

To showcase text input we'll create an inquiry form to allow the user to record a list of new clothing items to add to the Fullstack clothing list.

The app presents the user a text field where they can input a new clothing item and hit "Submit". When they enter an item, the following should occur:

- The item is added to a list
- The list is displayed/updated below the text input
- The text box is cleared so they can enter a new item.

Here's what that would look like:

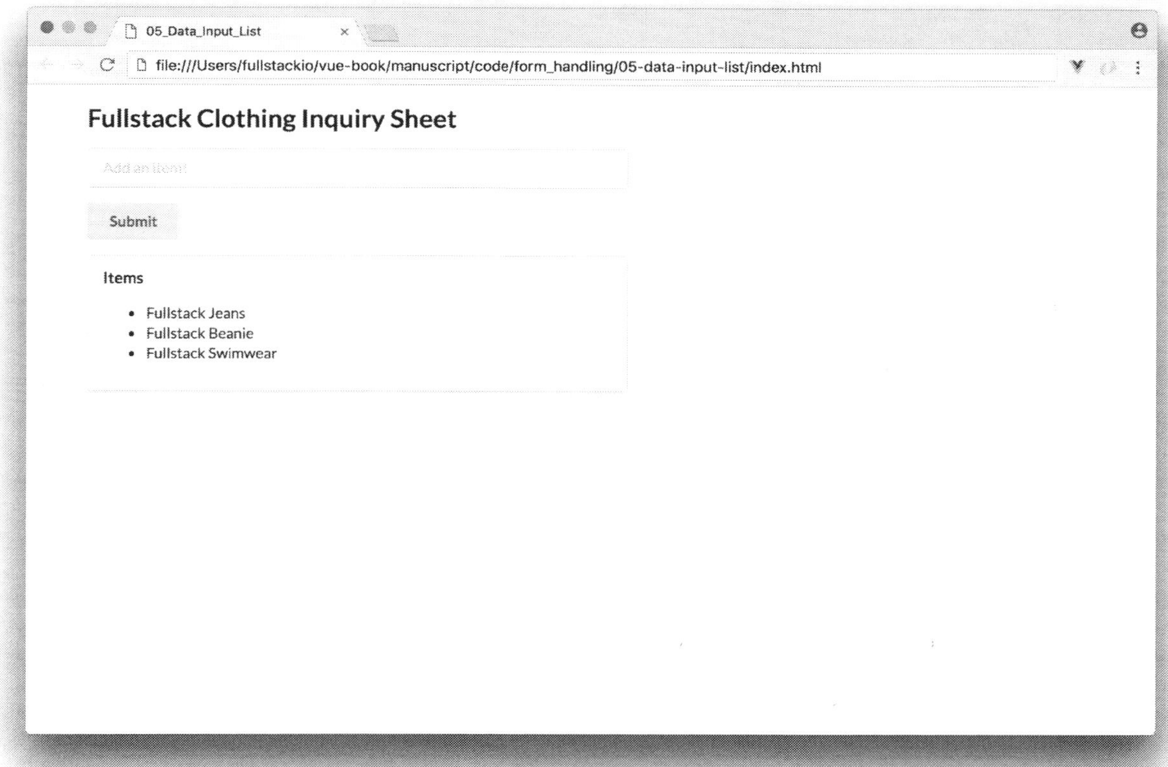

Adding to a List

Accessing DOM elements with `$refs`

To build the inquiry sheet we've displayed above, the first thing we need is to be able to read the contents of the text field when the user submits the form. A simple way to do this is to wait until the user submits the form, find the text field in the DOM, and finally grab its value.

To begin, we'll start with creating an HTML template that displays a title and an `input-form` component declaration:

form_handling/03-basic-input/index.html

```
<div id="app" class="ui container">
  <h2 class="ui header">Fullstack Clothing Inquiry Sheet</h2>
  <input-form></input-form>
</div>
```

The `input-form` should display a `form` that contains a text `input` and a submit button:

```
const InputForm = {
  template: `
    <div class="input-form">
      <form @submit="submitForm" class="ui form">
        <div class="field">
          <input ref="newItem" type="text" placeholder="Add an item!">
        </div>
        <button class="ui button">Submit</button>
      </form>
    <div>`
}

new Vue({
  el: '#app',
  components: {
    'input-form': InputForm
  }
})
```

Though similar to the previous example, we now instead have a `form` element that contains an `input` and `button` element.

There's two things to notice here. First, we've introduced an `@submit` event handler to the `form` element. Second, we've given the text `input` field a ref prop of 'newItem'.

The `@submit` event handler behaves a little differently than the examples we've had before. One change is that this handler is called either by clicking the "Submit" button, or by pressing "enter"/"return" while the form has focus. This is more user-friendly than forcing the user to click the "Submit" button.

Because our event handler is tied to the form, the event object argument to the handler is less useful than it was in the previous example since we're only interested in the text field's value.

One way to get the text field value upon submit would be to use the form event handler to look for a child input within, and find it's value. Though this may work, there is a simpler way.

Vue allows us to use `refs` (references) to easily access a DOM element in a component. Above, we gave our text field a `ref` property of `"newItem"`. Later when the `@submit` handler is called, we have the ability to access `this.$refs.newItem` to get a reference to that text field. Here's what that looks like if we create a `onFormSubmit()` event handler in the `methods` property of the component:

form_handling/03-basic-input/main.js

```
methods: {
  submitForm(evt) {
    evt.preventDefault();
    console.log(this.$refs.newItem.value)
  }
}
```

We use `preventDefault()` with the `@submit` handler to prevent the browser's default action of submitting the form.

With `this.$refs.newItem`, we gain a reference to our text field element and we can use it to access its `value` property. That `value` property contains the text that was entered into the field.

If we save our changes in `main.js` and reload the application, we'll be able to log the text input value upon form submit:

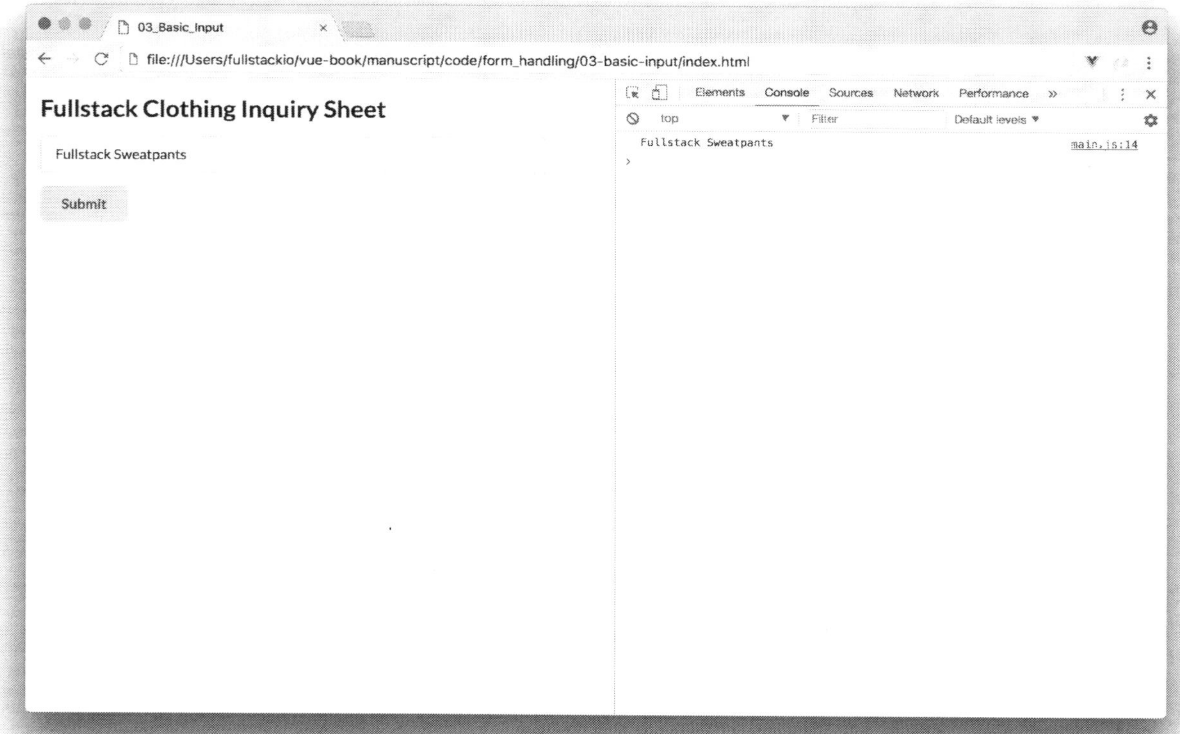

Logging the input value

Using User Input

Though the `ref` attribute enables us to expose DOM nodes for us to access and use, using `ref` opts out of a primary advantage of using Vue. With Vue, we'll hardly ever find the need to manipulate the DOM in this manner.

The next few steps of our application involve using the user input to display a list of items that the user enters. This is where it becomes more important to rely on Vue's ability to efficiently manipulate the DOM, based on the values in a components/instances `data` object. This would provide us with certainty that for any given value in `data`, we can predict what our component bound elements will look like.

First and foremost, we'll change our previous example to use Vue's `v-model` directive to get a reference to the text field element value. The ability of Vue's `v-model` directive to create two data binding between inputs and a data property is an important piece to keeping user input and application data consistent.

We'll change our `input-form` component to use `v-model` instead of `refs` to give us the value of the text `input` upon submit. In our text input, we'll change `ref="newItem"` to `v-model="newItem"`:

```
<input v-model="newItem" type="text" placeholder="Add an item!">
```

We'll now need to create the `newItem` data attribute within the components data model. In `input-component`, we'll add a data method that has a `newItem` property initialized with an empty string:

form_handling/04-data-input/main.js

```
data() {
  return {
    newItem: ''
  }
},
```

It's a good habit to provide sane defaults for any properties of `data` that will be used in a component. Since we probably want the field to be empty when the component is rendered, we set the default value to be an empty string, `''`.

In the `@submit` event handler, we'll now `console.log` the value of the `newItem` data property upon submit. Since two way data binding is established, the value of the data property is equal to the value of the input at all times:

form_handling/04-data-input/main.js

```
methods: {
  submitForm(evt) {
    evt.preventDefault();
    console.log(this.newItem)
  }
}
```

While our app didn't gain any new features in this section, we've both paved the way for better functionality (like validation and persistence) while also taking greater advantage of native Vue directives. The result at this point will appear the same:

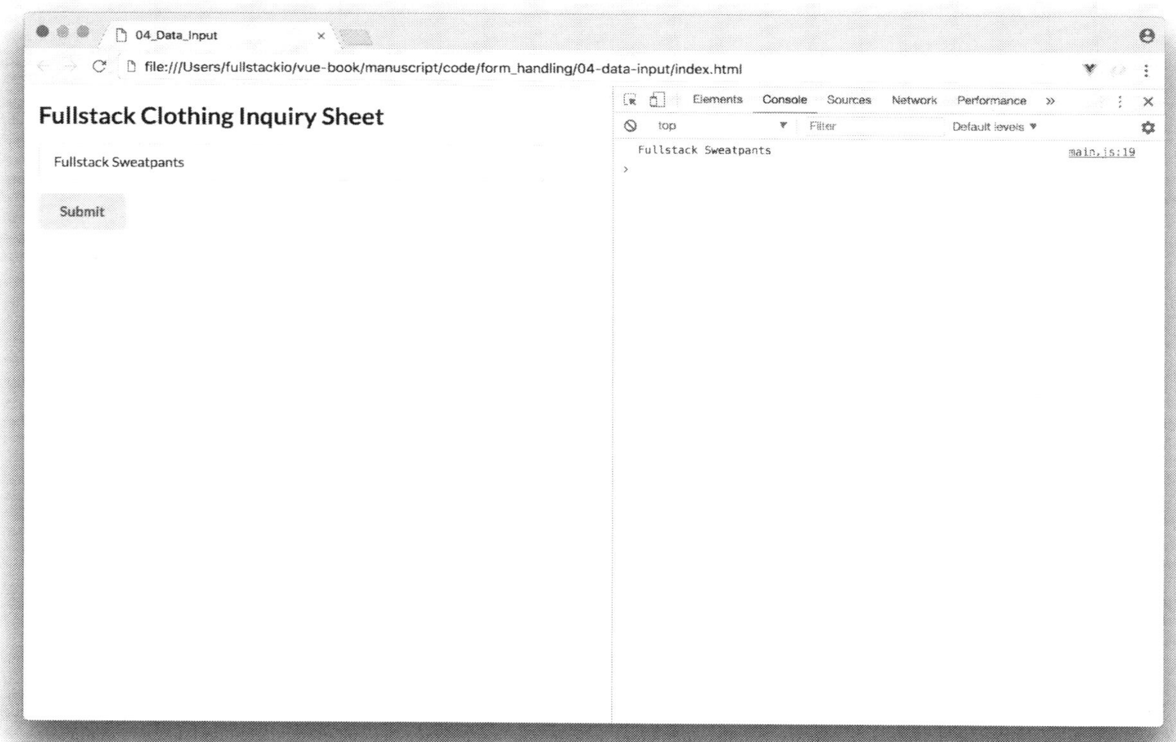

Logging the input value with `v-model`

With this, Vue makes it easy to reach our goal of showing a list of all items the user has entered. We'll need an array in our `data` object to hold the items, and in our component `template` we will use that array to populate a list.

When our app loads, the array will be empty, and each time the user submits a new name, we will add it to the array.

To do this, first we'll create an `items` array in the components `data` method. We'll set the initial value of `items` to be an empty array.

form_handling/05-data-input-list/main.js

```
data() {
  return {
    newItem: '',
    items: []
  }
},
```

Next, we'll modify the component `template` to show the list. When we think of rendering a list, the first thing that should come to mind is Vue's `v-for` directive.

Below our `form` element, we'll create a new `div` element. The `div` will contain a heading (`h4`) and our items list, a `ul` parent with a `li` child for each item. A `li` child element will be generated for each item with the help of `v-for=item in items`:

form_handling/05-data-input-list/main.js

```
template: `
  <div class="input-form">
    <form @submit="submitForm" class="ui form">
      <div class="field">
        <input v-model="newItem" type="text" placeholder="Add an item!">
      </div>
      <button class="ui button">Submit</button>
    </form>
    <div class="ui segment">
      <h4 class="ui header">Items</h4>
      <ul>
        <li v-for="item in items" class="item">{{ item }}</li>
      </ul>
    </div>
  </div>`,
```

Notice the `form` element and accompanying list markup are wrapped within a single `div` element. With Vue template declarations, it's a **must** to wrap templates in a single root element.

Now that the `template` is updated, the `submitForm()` method needs to update the `items` data array with a new item. We also want to clear the text field so that it's ready to accept additional user input. Since we have access to the text field via `v-model`, we can set its `value` to an empty string to clear it.

This is what `submitForm()` should look like now:

form_handling/05-data-input-list/main.js

```
methods: {
  submitForm(evt) {
    this.items.push(this.newItem);
    this.newItem = '';
    evt.preventDefault();
  }
}
```

At this point, our inquiry-sheet app is functional and displays a list of items submitted. Here's a rundown of the application flow:

1. User enters an item and clicks 'Submit'.
2. `submitForm` is called.
3. The `newItem` data value, bound to the text input, is added to the `items` data array.
4. The text field is cleared so that it is ready for more input.
5. The component re-renders and displays the updated list of `items`.

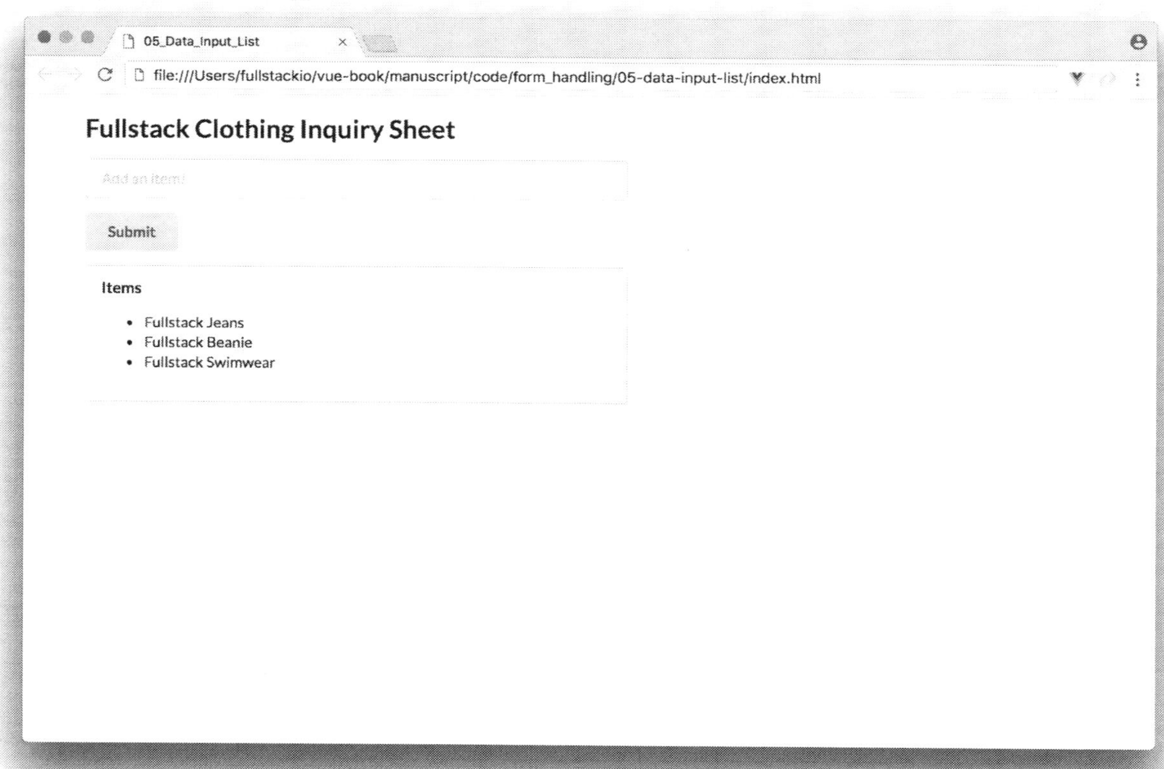

Awesome! In the upcoming sections, we'll be building our form out even further.

Multiple Fields

Our inquiry sheet is looking good, but what would happen if we wanted to add more fields? If our form is like most projects, it's only a matter of time before we want to add to it.

Let's explore how we can modify our app to allow for additional inputs in a clean, maintainable way. To illustrate this, let's first add an email address field to our inquiry sheet.

In the previous section our text `input` field had a dedicated property in the `data` object, `newItem`. If we were to do that here, we would add another property, `email`. To avoid adding a property for each input on `data`, let's instead add a `fields` object to store the values for all of our fields in one place. This makes our new `data` object become:

```
data() {
  return {
    fields: {
      newItem: '',
      email: ''
    },
    items: []
  }
}
```

The `fields` object can store data for as many inputs as we'd like. Here we've specified that we want to store data for `newItem` and `email`. In the component template, we now need to find those values at `fields.newItem` and `fields.email` instead of simply `newItem` and `email`.

In the template, let's create the new `email` input field and reference the input values appropriately. We'll also introduce `label` elements to now label each input field to make it evident what each field is to the user. The `form` element within the component `template` will be updated to:

```
<form @submit="submitForm" class="ui form">
  <div class="field">
    <label>New Item</label>
    <input v-model="fields.newItem" type="text" placeholder="Add an item!" />
  </div>
  <div class="field">
    <label>Email</label>
    <input v-model="fields.email" type="text" placeholder="What's your email?" />
  </div>
</form>
```

Let's add two more fields to the form that aren't text input fields. The first field would be a `select` dropdown for the user to select the urgency status of his inquiry. He/she will be able to select between the options urgent, moderate, and nonessential. This field in our template will look like this:

```
<div class="field">
  <label>Urgency</label>
  <select v-model="fields.urgency" class="ui fluid search dropdown">
    <option disabled value="">Please select one</option>
    <option>Nonessential</option>
    <option>Moderate</option>
    <option>Urgent</option>
  </select>
</div>
```

Select dropdowns are often set-up with the first option having an empty `value`, `""`, since that option isn't intended to be selected by the user. With Vue, it's recommended to set that empty value as `disabled` for iOS compatibility. `Select - Form Input Bindings`[79] in the Vue docs explains this some more.

We'll also introduce a `checkbox` input responsible for the user to accept some terms and conditions:

```
<div class="field">
  <div class="ui checkbox">
    <input v-model="fields.termsAndConditions" type="checkbox" />
    <label>I accept the terms and conditions</label>
  </div>
</div>
```

As you can see, we've used the `v-model` directive to bind the `select` and `checkbox` inputs to `fields.urgency` and `fields.termsAndConditions` data properties respectively. Just like text input fields, we can use `v-model` to create data bindings on both `select` and `input type="checkbox` elements.

> `v-model` always picks the correct way to update the element, based on the input type it's bound to.

For our application to load successfully, we'll need to initialize these data properties in the component's `data` object. We'll set a blank string for the dropdown initial value and since the checkbox value is a boolean, it's initial value will be `false`:

form_handling/06-data-input-multi/main.js

```
  data() {
    return {
      fields: {
        newItem: '',
        email: '',
        urgency: '',
        termsAndConditions: false
      },
      items: []
    }
  },
```

Our `form` element, in its entirety, becomes:

[79] https://vuejs.org/v2/guide/forms.html#Select

form_handling/06-data-input-multi/main.js

```
    <form @submit="submitForm" class="ui form">
      <div class="field">
        <label>New Item</label>
        <input v-model="fields.newItem" type="text"
          placeholder="Add an item!" />
      </div>
      <div class="field">
        <label>Email</label>
        <input v-model="fields.email" type="text"
          placeholder="What's your email?" />
      </div>
      <div class="field">
        <label>Urgency</label>
        <select v-model="fields.urgency" class="ui fluid search dropdown">
          <option disabled value="">Please select one</option>
          <option>Nonessential</option>
          <option>Moderate</option>
          <option>Urgent</option>
        </select>
      </div>
      <div class="field">
        <div class="ui checkbox">
          <input v-model="fields.termsAndConditions" type="checkbox" />
          <label>I accept the terms and conditions</label>
        </div>
      </div>
      <button class="ui button">Submit</button>
    </form>
```

Refreshing our application, we'll see an `email` input, a dropdown, and a checkbox that currently have no functionality:

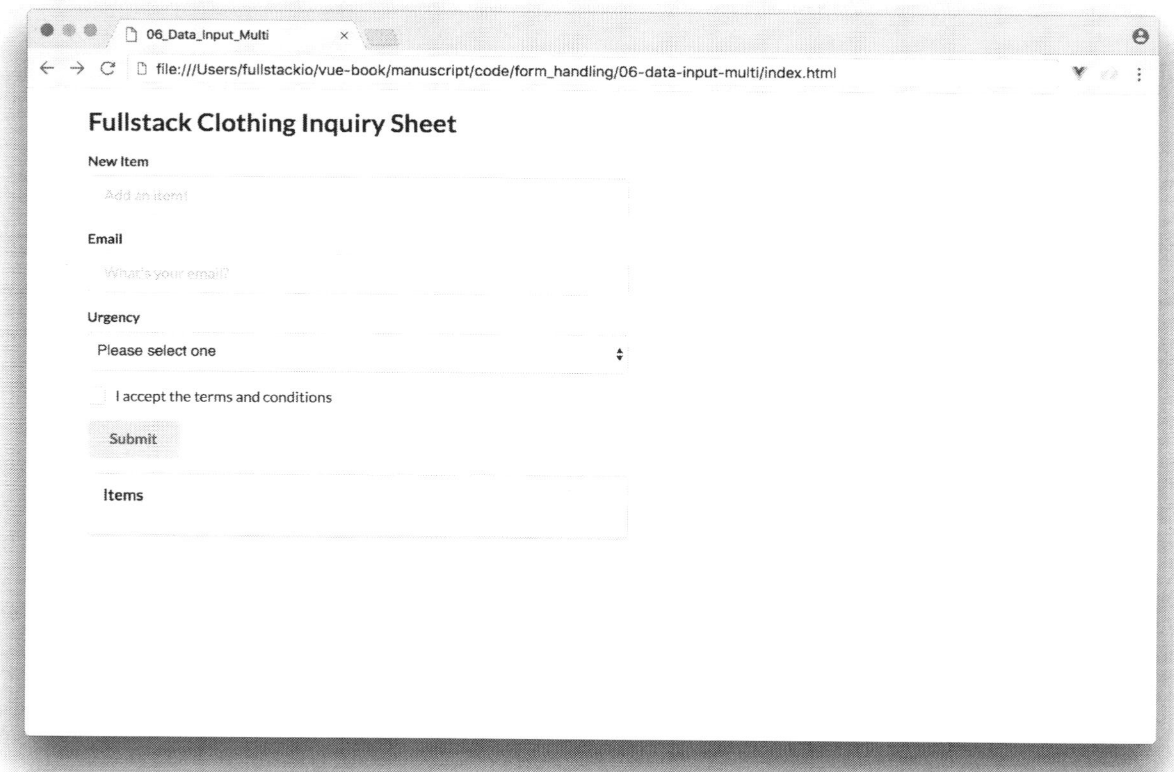

Thanks to the simplicity of `v-model`, there's no need for us to concern ourselves with creating methods to capture each user input separately. `v-model` makes sure that all data winds up in the right place by updating the appropriate data properties (`newItem` for item field, `email` for email field, `urgency` for dropdown, and `termsAndConditions` for checkbox) whenever there's a change to these inputs.

In the next section, we'll be enabling validation on the newly added fields. Our validations will prevent the form from being submitted until the relevant form elements are validated appropriately.

Validations

Validation is so central to building forms that it's rare to have a form without it. Validation can be both on the level of the **individual field** and on the **form as a whole**.

When you validate on an individual field, you're making sure that the user has entered data that conforms to your application's expectations and constraints as it relates to that piece of data.

For example, in a form, we're often expected to enter a password at least some minimum length.

Another example would be making sure that a zip code has exactly five (or nine) numerical characters.

Validation on the form as a whole is slightly different. Here is where we'll make sure that all required fields have been entered. This is also a good place to check for internal consistency between fields. For example ensuring the 'password' and 're-type password' fields are equal.

Additionally, there are trade-offs for "how" and "when" we validate. On some fields we might want to give validation feedback in real-time. For example, we might want to show password strength (by looking at length and characters used) while the user is typing. However, if we want to validate the availability of a username, we might want to wait until the user has finished typing before we make a request to the server/database to find out.

We also have options for how we display validation errors. We might style the field differently (e.g. a red outline), show text near the field (e.g. "Please enter a valid email."), and/or disable the form's submit button to prevent the user from progressing with invalid information.

For our app, let's begin with validation of the form as a whole by:

- Making sure the `New Item`, `Email`, and `Urgency` values are not blank and the terms and conditions checkbox is `checked`, upon form submit.
- Making sure that the email is a valid address.

Form Validation

To add form validation to our app, there's a few things we can do. We'll address these step by step.

`fieldErrors`

We'll first need to add a `fieldErrors` data object to store validation errors if they exist. In the component's `data` object, we'll introduce `fieldErrors` with an object of undefined values as defaults:

form_handling/07-basic-form-validation/main.js

```
data() {
  return {
    fields: {
      newItem: '',
      email: '',
      urgency: '',
      termsAndConditions: false
    },
    fieldErrors: {
      newItem: undefined,
```

```
      email: undefined,
      urgency: undefined,
      termsAndConditions: undefined
    },
    items: []
  }
},
```

Though it may seem that we don't have to initialize `undefined` values within `fieldErrors`, Vue best practices[80] state that it's necessary to declare properties that need to be reactive upfront to ensure consistent behaviour across browsers.

`template` errors

If an error arises we'll need to display it in the form. We'll do this up by showing a validation error message (if they exist) with red text next to each field.

With each `field` element in the form, we'll introduce a validation message like below:

```
<!-- New Item Field -->
<div class="field">
  <label>New Item</label>
  <input v-model="fields.newItem" type="text" placeholder="Add an item!" />
  <span style="color: red">{{ fieldErrors.newItem }}</span>
</div>

<!-- Email Field -->
<div class="field">
  <label>Email</label>
  <input v-model="fields.email" type="text" placeholder="What's your email?" />
  <span style="color: red">{{ fieldErrors.email }}</span>
</div>

<!-- Urgency Field -->
<div class="field">
  <label>Urgency</label>
  <select v-model="fields.urgency" class="ui fluid search dropdown">
    <option disabled value="">Please select one</option>
    <option>Nonessential</option>
```

[80]https://vuejs.org/2016/02/06/common-gotchas/#Why-isn%E2%80%99t-the-DOM-updating

```
    <option>Moderate</option>
    <option>Urgent</option>
  </select>
  <span style="color: red">{{ fieldErrors.urgency }}</span>
</div>

<!-- Terms and conditions checkbox -->
<div class="field">
  <div class="ui checkbox">
    <input v-model="fields.termsAndConditions" type="checkbox" />
    <label>I accept the terms and conditions</label>
    <span style="color: red">{{ fieldErrors.termsAndConditions }}</span>
  </div>
</div>
```

validateForm

It is after the user submits the form that we will check the validity of their input. So the appropriate place to begin validation is in the `submitForm()` method. However, we'll want to create a standalone function for that method to call. For that, we'll create a `validateForm()` method that takes a `fields` object as an argument.

```
methods: {
  submitForm(evt) {
    ...
  },
  validateForm(fields) {
  }
}
```

Our `validateForm()` method will have two goals. First, we want to make sure that the `newItem`, `email`, `urgency`, and `termsAndConditions` fields are present. By checking their truthiness we can know that they are defined and not empty strings. `validateForm` will either return an empty object if there are no issues, or if there are issues, it will return an object with keys corresponding to each field name and values corresponding to each error message:

```
methods: {
  submitForm(evt) {
    ...
  },
  validateForm(fields) {
    const errors = {};
    if (!fields.newItem) errors.newItem = "New Item Required";
    if (!fields.email) errors.email = "Email Required";
    if (!fields.urgency) errors.urgency = "Urgency Required";
    if (!fields.termsAndConditions) {
      errors.termsAndConditions = "Terms and conditions have to be approved";
    }

    return errors;
  }
}
```

Second, we want to know that the provided email address looks valid. This is actually a bit of a thorny issue, so we'll use a simple regular expression to detect the input is in the form `string@string.string`. We'll keep this regular expression check in a separate method denoted by `isEmail()`. With this in mind, our `methods` become:

```
methods: {
  submitForm(evt) {
    ...
  },
  validateForm(fields) {
    const errors = {};
    if (!fields.newItem) errors.newItem = "New Item Required";
    if (!fields.email) errors.email = "Email Required";
    if (!fields.urgency) errors.urgency = "Urgency Required";
    if (!fields.termsAndConditions) {
      errors.termsAndConditions = "Terms and conditions have to be approved";
    }

    if (fields.email && !this.isEmail(fields.email)) {
      errors.email = "Invalid Email";
    }

    return errors;
  },
  isEmail(email) {
```

```
    const re = /\S+@\S+\.\S+/;
    return re.test(email);
  }
}
```

It's important to note that email verification is important and the `regex` expression we've used only applies for very simple validation. Oftentimes, libraries like validator[81] is used to validate fields like email.

`submitForm`

When the form is submitted, we'll be using the `validateForm` method we've created to determine if the form is valid for submission. If the validation errors object has any keys (`Object.keys(fieldErrors).length > 0`) we know there are issues. In this case, we return early to prevent the new information from being added to the list. With that said, our `submitForm()` method will be changed to:

```
submitForm(evt) {
  evt.preventDefault();

  this.fieldErrors = this.validateForm(this.fields);
  if (Object.keys(this.fieldErrors).length) return;
},
```

However, If there are no validation issues, the logic is the same as in previous sections – we add the new item information and clear the fields. This makes the `submitForm()` method become:

form_handling/07-basic-form-validation/main.js

```
    submitForm(evt) {
      evt.preventDefault();

      this.fieldErrors = this.validateForm(this.fields);
      if (Object.keys(this.fieldErrors).length) return;

      this.items.push(this.fields.newItem);
      this.fields.newItem = '';
      this.fields.email = '';
      this.fields.urgency = '';
      this.fields.termsAndConditions = false;
    },
```

[81]https://github.com/chriso/validator.js

Let's give this a try! Save the `main.js` file and attempt to submit the form with all fields being empty:

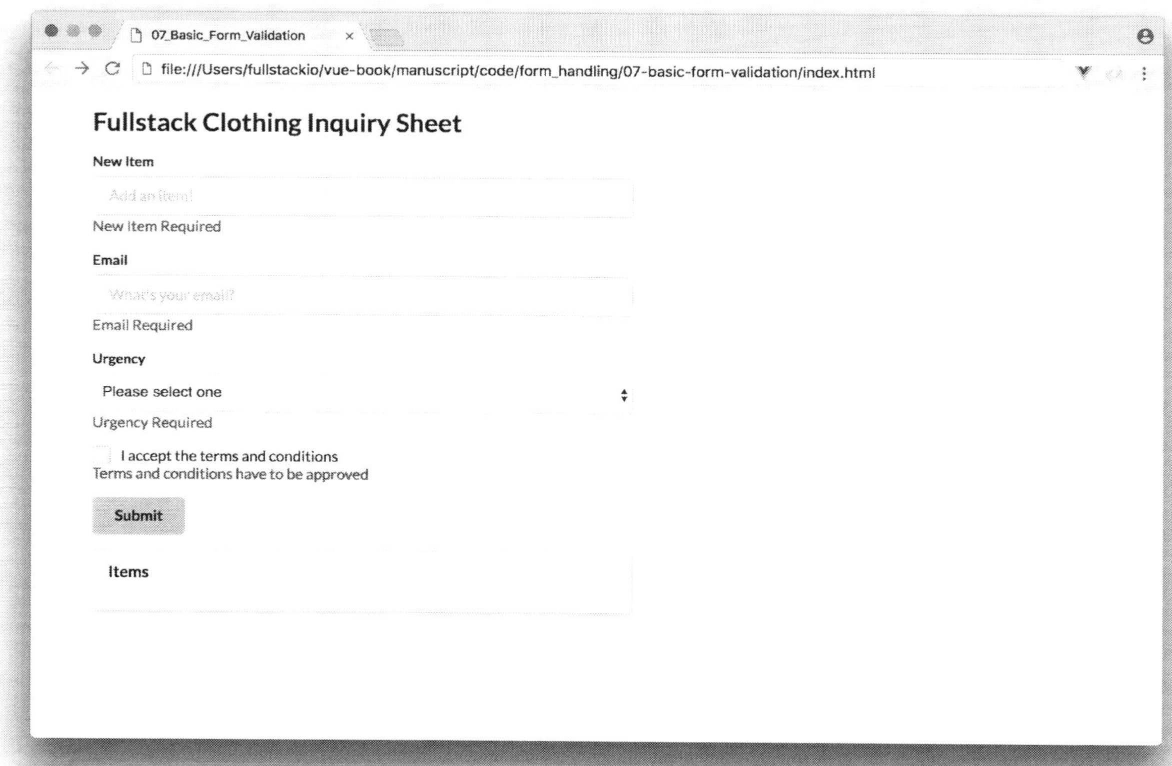

All fields required

Fill out the fields and input an invalid email address:

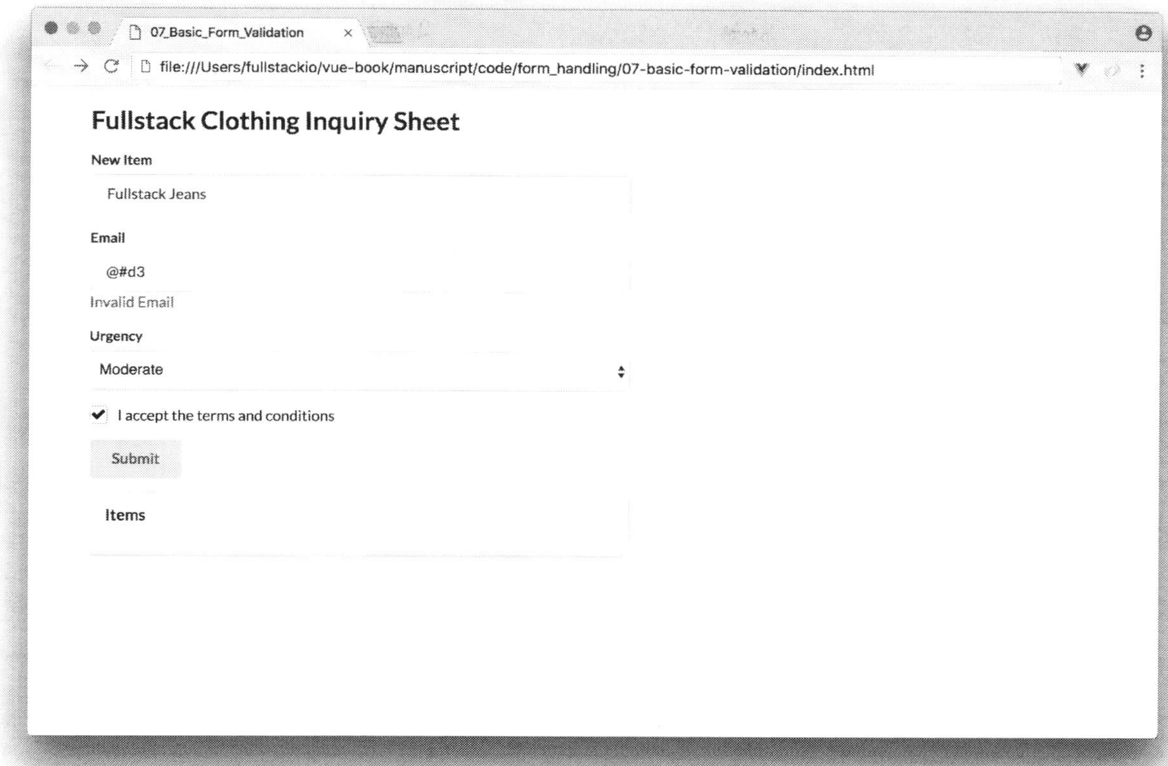

Email Invalid

Awesome! At this point we've covered the fundamentals of creating a form with validation in Vue. In the next section we'll take things a bit further and show how we can validate in real-time at the field level.

Field Validation

If you remember, we can employ two different levels of validation, one at the field level, and one at the form level. Field level validations are often important for two reasons:

- A field could check the format of it's input while the user types/selects in *real-time*.
- When the field incorporates its validation error message, it frees the parent form from having to keep track of it.

We'll assume the objective of `submitForm()` will remain the same. It is still responsible for either adding an item to the list, or preventing that behavior if there are form validation issues (e.g. any of the form fields are empty or the email input is invalid).

We'll now introduce two new field level validations:

- The new item input has to be under twenty characters.
- Urgency level has to be either Moderate or Urgent.

To invoke these validations, we can use `computed` properties and the `v-if` directive.

For the validation involving limiting the number of characters for the `newItem` input, we'll create a `computed` property called `isNewItemInputLimitExceeded` that returns `true` when the input has twenty or more characters:

```
computed: {
  isNewItemInputLimitExceeded() {
    return this.fields.newItem.length >= 20;
  }
}
```

In the `newItem` field within `template`, we'll simply introduce another text error `span` that's only displayed when `isNewItemInputLimitExceeded` is true. For this we'll use `v-if` to conditionally display the text. We'll also introduce a new span that tracks `fields.newItem.length` for the user to see in the UI. With this in mind, the `field` for the `newItem` input will now become:

form_handling/08-basic-field-validation/main.js

```
        <div class="field">
          <label>New Item</label>
          <input v-model="fields.newItem" type="text"
            placeholder="Add an item!" />
          <span style="float: right">{{ fields.newItem.length }}/20</span>
          <span style="color: red">{{ fieldErrors.newItem }}</span>
          <span v-if="isNewItemInputLimitExceeded"
            style="color: red; display: block">
            Must be under twenty characters
          </span>
        </div>
```

Within the `field`, we have the field `label` and `input`. Right below, we display the length of `fields.newItem` in the UI which will update in real-time as the user types in the input. The bottom two `span` elements are error messages with the first message only appearing and disappearing upon a successful submit. The second error message displays automatically when the user exceeds the input limit (with the help of the `v-if` directive) and is removed when the character length is less than the limit.

For the second field validation, we'll introduce another computed property `isNotUrgent` that returns true when `fields.urgency` is equal to `Nonessential`:

form_handling/08-basic-field-validation/main.js

```
  computed: {
    isNewItemInputLimitExceeded() {
      return this.fields.newItem.length >= 20;
    },
    isNotUrgent() {
      return this.fields.urgency === 'Nonessential';
    }
  },
```

Similar to what we've done earlier, we'll introduce a text error message when this computed property returns `true`, within the Urgency `field`:

form_handling/08-basic-field-validation/main.js

```
        <div class="field">
          <label>Urgency</label>
          <select v-model="fields.urgency" class="ui fluid search dropdown">
            <option disabled value="">Please select one</option>
            <option>Nonessential</option>
            <option>Moderate</option>
            <option>Urgent</option>
          </select>
          <span style="color: red">{{ fieldErrors.urgency }}</span>
          <span v-if="isNotUrgent"
            style="color: red; display: block">
            Must be moderate to urgent
          </span>
        </div>
```

For our field level validations, we'll take an extra step and prevent the user from submitting by *disabling* the submit button when either of the field error validations is present. To do this, we set the value of the button `disabled` prop to the return value of either `isNewItemInputLimitExceeded` or `isNotUrgent`. This updates the form button to:

form_handling/08-basic-field-validation/main.js

```
      <button :disabled="isNewItemInputLimitExceeded || isNotUrgent"
        class="ui button">
        Submit
      </button>
```

Let's test this out! Typing more than twenty characters in the `newItem` field and selecting the `Nonessential` option in the Urgency dropdown should now automatically display two field level validation errors *and* disable the Submit Button.

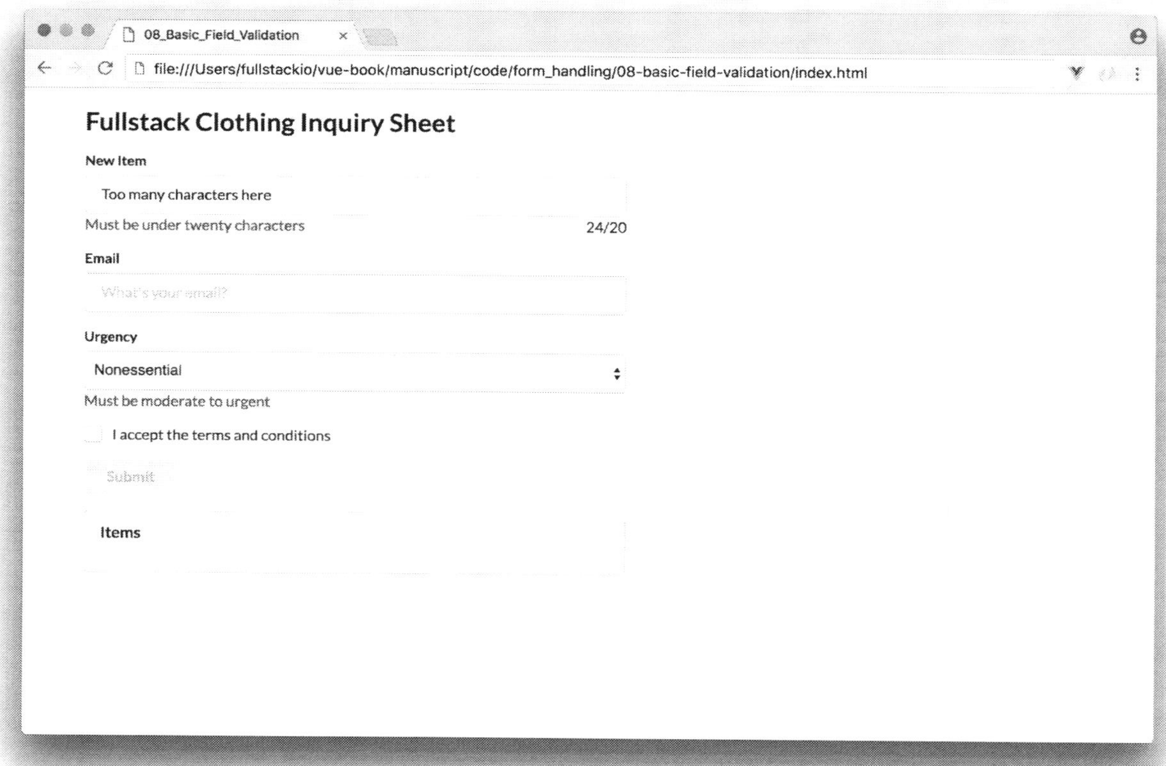

And that's it! We're now using `computed` properties to do field-level validation on the fly, and we use form-level validation to display form field errors upon submit.

Though we've used `computed` properties in our `v-if` directives, we could have very well achieved the same result using `methods` to dictate validations and instead have returned the result of these methods in `v-if` (e.g. `v-if="isNewItemInputLimitExceeded()"`). These are *identical* except for one strong distinction - **computed properties are cached and will only reevaluate when some of its dependencies have changed**. Method invocations, on the other hand, will always run when component re-rendering happens which can be expensive if the method functionality performs a lot of computations. For more information on this, check out the Vue docs[82].

Async Persistence

At this point our app is pretty useful. You could imagine having the app open on a kiosk where people can come up to it and add new items on a continuous basis. However, there's one big shortcoming: if the browser is closed or reloaded, all data is lost.

In most web apps, when a user inputs data, that data should be sent to a server for safekeeping in a database. When the user returns to the app, the data can be fetched, and the app can pick back up right where it left off. We saw how server persistence can work for a Vuex-integrated Vue app in the last chapter, Vuex and Servers.

In this chapter, we won't be sending the data to a remote server or storing it in a database but we'll be using `localStorage` instead. We'll cover three aspects of persistence: saving, loading, and handling errors and treat them as asynchronous operations to illustrate how almost any persistence strategy could be used.

The `localStorage` API allows you to read and write to a key-value store in the user's browser. You can store items to `localStorage` with `setItem()`:

`localStorage.setItem('gas', 'pop');`

And retrieve them later with `getItem()`:

```
`localStorage.getItem('gas');`
`// => 'pop'`
```

Note that items stored in `localStorage` have no expiry.

To persist the items in our inquiry sheet (`items`), we'll need to make a few changes to our component. At a high level they are:

1. Modify `data()` to keep track of persistence status. Basically, we'll want to know if the app is currently loading, is currently saving, or encountered an error during either operation.

[82] https://vuejs.org/v2/guide/computed.html#Computed-Caching-vs-Methods

2. Make a request using our API client to get any previously persisted data and load it into our `data()`.
3. Update our `submitForm()` event handler to trigger a save.
4. Change our component `template` so that the Submit button reflects the current save status *and* prevents the user from performing an unwanted action like a double-save, as well as display a loading indicator in the items list when data is still being fetched.

If this all doesn't make sense just yet, don't worry. We'll be addressing these step by step!

Modify `data()`

First, we'll want to modify our component `data()` to keep track of our "loading" and "saving" status. This is useful to both accurately communicate the status of persistence and to prevent unwanted user actions. For example, if we know that the app is in the process of "saving", we can disable the submit button. Let's introduce two new properties, `loading` and `saveStatus`, for the component to keep track of:

form_handling/09-remote-persist/main.js

```
data() {
  return {
    fields: {
      newItem: '',
      email: '',
      urgency: '',
      termsAndConditions: false
    },
    fieldErrors: {
      newItem: undefined,
      email: undefined,
      urgency: undefined,
      termsAndConditions: undefined
    },
    items: [],
    loading: false,
    saveStatus: 'READY'
  }
},
```

`saveStatus` is initialized with the value "`READY`", but we'll have four possible values: "`READY`", "`SAVING`", "`SUCCESS`", and "`ERROR`". If the `saveStatus` is "`SAVING`", we'll want to prevent the user from making an additional save.

`created()`

Next, when the component has just been created and is about to be added to the DOM, we'll want to request any previously saved data. To do this we'll use the lifecycle hook `created()` which is automatically called by Vue at the appropriate time.

To persist and retrieve data; we'll interact with an `apiClient` object that we'll create. We can add this object at the bottom of the file like so:

form_handling/09-remote-persist/main.js

```
let apiClient = {
  loadItems: function () {
    return {
      then: function (cb) {
        setTimeout(() => {
          cb(JSON.parse(localStorage.items || '[]'));
        }, 1000);
      },
    };
  },

  saveItems: function (items) {
    const success = !!(this.count++ % 2);

    return new Promise((resolve, reject) => {
      setTimeout(() => {
        if (!success) return reject({ success });

        localStorage.items = JSON.stringify(items);
        return resolve({ success });
      }, 1000);
    });
  },

  count: 1,
}
```

`apiClient` is a simple object that holds the responsibility in simulating asynchronous loading and saving. In the code example above, we can see that the "load" and "save" methods are thin async wrappers around `localStorage` that we'll use to retrieve and persist data.

In the app's `created()` hook, we'll use `apiClient` to retrieve stored data. Here's what that looks like:

form_handling/09-remote-persist/main.js

```
  created() {
    this.loading = true;
    apiClient.loadItems().then((items) => {
      this.items = items;
      this.loading = false;
    });
  },
```

Before we start the fetch with `apiClient`, we set `loading` to `true`. We'll use this in our component `template` to show a loading indicator. Once the fetch returns, we update component `items` with the previously persisted list and set `loading` back to `false`.

If you're developing in Safari, the browser may throw a `SecurityError (DOM Exception 18)` when `localStorage` is attempting to be accessed through a simple HTML file. To work around this, disable local file restrictions with `Develop > Disable Local File Restrictions`.

At this point our app doesn't yet have a way to persist data so there won't be any data to load. However, we can fix that by updating `submitForm()`.

Update `submitForm()`

As in the previous sections, we'll want our user to be able to fill out each field and hit "Submit" to add an item to the list. When they do that, `submitForm()` is called. We'll make a change so that we not only perform the previous behavior (validation, updating `items`, clearing form fields), but we *also* persist that list using `apiClient.saveItems()`:

form_handling/09-remote-persist/main.js

```
    submitForm(evt) {
      evt.preventDefault();

      this.fieldErrors = this.validateForm(this.fields);
      if (Object.keys(this.fieldErrors).length) return;

      const items = [...this.items, this.fields.newItem];

      this.saveStatus = 'SAVING';
      apiClient.saveItems(items)
        .then(() => {
```

```
        this.items = items;
        this.fields.newItem = '';
        this.fields.email = '';
        this.fields.urgency = '';
        this.fields.termsAndConditions = false;
        this.saveStatus = 'SUCCESS';
      })
      .catch((err) => {
        console.log(err);
        this.saveStatus = 'ERROR';
      });
  },
```

In the previous sections, if the data passed validation, we would just update our `items` list to include it. This time we *only* want to update our component `items` *if* `apiClient` can successfully persist. The order of operation in `submitForm` looks like this:

1. We prevent the browser's default action of submitting the form with `preventDefault()`.
2. If the form has field errors upon submission, we return early to prevent `apiClient` from being called.
3. If no field errors exist, we create a new array called `items` which contains the existing component `items` array and the new `field.newItem` value.
4. We then use `apiClient` to begin persisting the new `items` array with `apiClient.saveItems()`.
5. If `apiClient` is successful, we update the component data with our new `items` array, empty fields, and `saveStatus: 'SUCCESS'`. If `apiClient` is not successful, we leave everything as is but set `saveStatus` to '`ERROR`'.

Put simply, we set the `saveStatus` to '`SAVING`' while the `apiClient` request is 'in-flight'. If the request is successful, we set the `saveStatus` to '`SUCCESS`' and perform the same actions as before. If not, the only update is to set `saveStatus` to '`ERROR`'. This way, our local state does not get out of sync with our persisted copy. Also, since we don't clear the fields, we give the user an opportunity to try again without having to re-input their information.

> To test our error use case, we've set up the `apiClient` persistence (`apiClient.saveItems()`) to error in every 2nd consecutive attempt.

For this example we are being conservative with our UI updates. We only add the new item to the list if `apiClient` is successful. This is in contrast to an optimistic update, where we would add the `item` to the list locally first, and later make adjustments if there was a failure.

Update `template`

Our last change is to modify the component `template` so that the UI accurately reflects our status with respect to loading and saving. As mentioned, we'll want the user to know if we're in the middle of a load or a save, or if there was a problem saving. We can also control the UI to prevent them from performing unwanted actions such as a double save.

First off, we want the submit button to communicate the current save status.

- If no save request is in-flight, we want the button to be enabled if the field data is valid.
- If we are in the process of saving, we want the button to read "Saving..." and to be disabled.
- The user will know that the app is busy, and since the button is disabled, they won't be able to submit duplicate save requests.
- Finally, if the save request completes successfully, we use the button text to communicate that. The button will remain enabled (if the input data is still valid) to allow the user to add more items.

Here's how we can conditionally display the Submit button under different save statuses:

form_handling/09-remote-persist/main.js

```
<button v-if="saveStatus === 'SAVING'"
  disabled class="ui button">
  Saving...
</button>
<button v-if="saveStatus === 'SUCCESS'"
  :disabled="isNewItemInputLimitExceeded || isNotUrgent"
  class="ui button">
  Saved! Submit another
</button>
<button v-if="saveStatus === 'ERROR'"
  :disabled="isNewItemInputLimitExceeded || isNotUrgent"
  class="ui button">
  Save Failed - Retry?
</button>
<button v-if="saveStatus === 'READY'"
  :disabled="isNewItemInputLimitExceeded || isNotUrgent"
  class="ui button">
  Submit
</button>
```

What we have here are four different buttons – one for each possible `saveStatus`. Each button has a different button text corresponding to its status (e.g. `SUCCESS` - Saved! Submit Another). The button displayed when the form is saving (`saveStatus === 'SAVING'`) is set to `disabled` to prevent a double save. The other buttons all present the user the option to save under the condition the field level validations (`isNewItemInputLimitExceeded` and `isNotUrgent`) are not present.

We've used `v-if` directives for every possible button state. Vue also allows us to perform conditional rendering with `v-else` and `v-else-if`. Though the outcome is usually the same, the `v-else` and `v-else-if` blocks must follow a `v-if` (or `v-else-if`) statement in the template.

The second change we would like to make to the `template` is a simple loading indicator, within the items list, to indicate the persisted items are being fetched upon page load. The Semantic UI[83] CSS library we're using provides a loading indicator that we can use. We just need to display the indicator only under the condition that the `loading` data property is `true` (i.e. `apiClient` is still fetching data). So within the `ui segment` element, we'll introduce this indicator in the `ul` list:

form_handling/09-remote-persist/main.js

```
      <div class="ui segment">
        <h4 class="ui header">Items</h4>
        <ul>
          <div v-if="loading" class="ui active inline loader"></div>
          <li v-for="item in items" class="item">{{ item }}</li>
        </ul>
      </div>
```

And that's it! Our app currently persists information asynchronously to `localStorage` and fetches it upon page load.

[83] https://semantic-ui.com

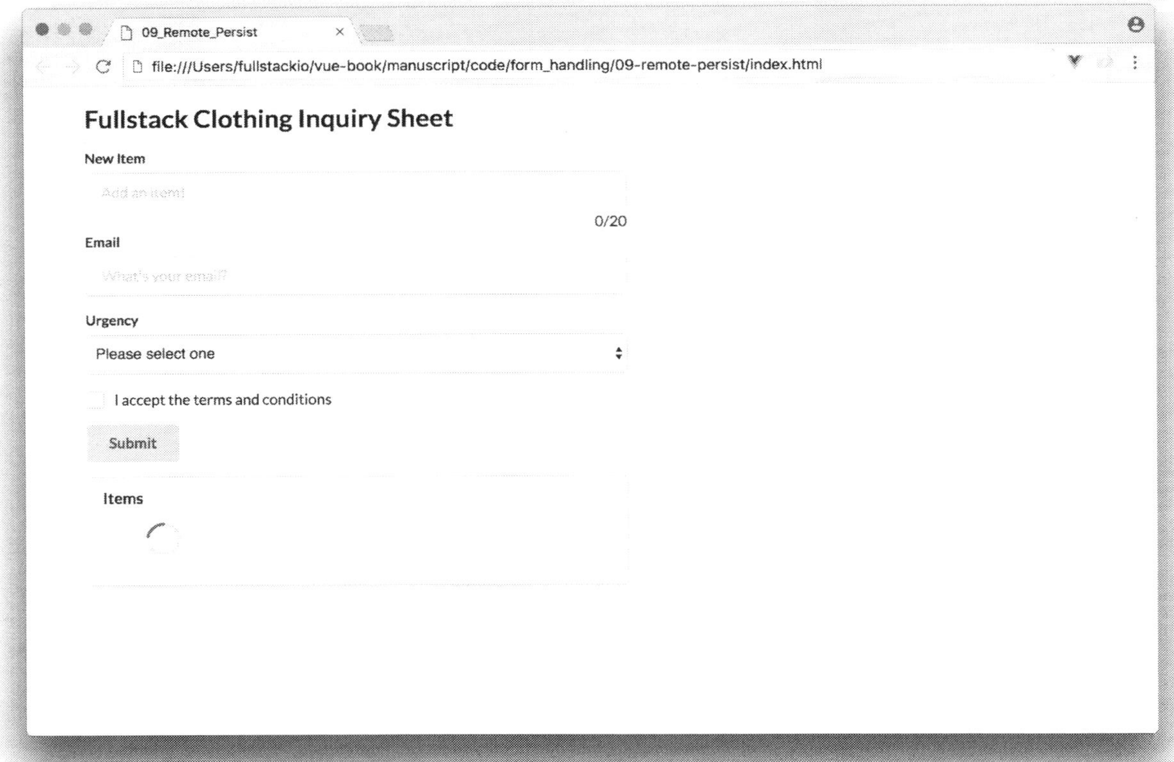

Loading Indicator

At this point our inquiry app is a nice illustration of the features and issues that you'll want to cover in your own forms using Vue. The next section entails how forms work slightly differently when using Vuex store data.

Vuex

In this section we'll see how we'll have to modify the form app we've built so that it can work within a larger app using Vuex.

Chronologically we've talked about Vuex in the last chapter and the one before. If you're unfamiliar with Vuex and you've started this chapter before covering the earlier chapters, hop over to those chapters and come back here to be better prepared.

We'll adapt our form to fit within the Vuex paradigm. At a high level, this involves moving state and functionality from our form component to Vuex store and actions/mutations. For example, we will no longer call API functions from within the form component - we dispatch async actions for that instead. Similarly, data that used to be held as part of the components `data()` will be held in the Vuex store.

As we've mentioned before in the earlier chapters, when building with Vuex it's helpful to start by thinking about the "shape" our state will take. In our case, we have a pretty good idea already since our functionality has already been built.

For this example, we'll move all field level information and persisted data properties (`fields` and `items`) to the Vuex store *but* keep the other data within the component. We'll assume the field information and persisted items array is needed for the entirety of the application while validation errors (`fieldErrors`), the loading status (`loading`), and the button save state (`saveState`) will only be required within the form component itself.

Let's set up the Vuex package and create the store before we begin integrating Vuex into our form. In the `body` element of the `index.html` file, we'll introduce Vuex with a CDN and reference a new internal `store.js` file as well:

form_handling/10-vuex-app/index.html

```
<body>
  <div id="app" class="ui container">
    <h2 class="ui header">Fullstack Clothing Inquiry Sheet</h2>
    <input-form></input-form>
  </div>

  <script src="https://unpkg.com/vue"></script>
  <script src="https://unpkg.com/vuex"></script>
  <script src="./store.js"></script>
  <script src="./main.js"></script>
</body>
```

Within the `app/` directory, we'll create the `store.js` file:

```
$ ls app/
index.html
main.js
store.js
```

In `store.js`, we'll establish a blank slate for the different pieces of a Vuex store and globalize the store with `window.store` for it to be accessed elsewhere. We'll also move `apiClient` to the store since store actions will now be responsible in calling the `apiClient` async methods. Our `store.js` file will be set up like this:

```
const state={}

const mutations={}

const actions={}

const getters={}

window.store = new Vuex.Store({
  state,
  mutations,
  actions,
  getters
})

let apiClient = {
  loadItems: function () {
    return {
      then: function (cb) {
        setTimeout(() => {
          cb(JSON.parse(localStorage.items || '[]'));
        }, 1000);
      },
    };
  },

  saveItems: function (items) {
    const success = !!(this.count++ % 2);

    return new Promise((resolve, reject) => {
      setTimeout(() => {
        if (!success) return reject({ success });

        localStorage.items = JSON.stringify(items);
        return resolve({ success });
      }, 1000);
    });
  },

  count: 1,
}
```

In `main.js`, we'll declare and pass the `store` property to the Vue instance, to integrate our soon to be implemented Vuex store to our Vue app:

form_handling/10-vuex-app/main.js

```
new Vue({
  el: '#app',
  store,
  components: {
    'input-form': InputForm
  }
})
```

We're now all ready to start building our store. We've stated that all field level information and persisted items should be part of the application state. This makes our `state` object in `store.js` become:

form_handling/10-vuex-app/store.js

```
const state = {
  fields: {
    newItem: '',
    email: '',
    urgency: '',
    termsAndConditions: false
  },
  items: []
}
```

This leaves our components `data()` object to involve only `fieldErrors`, `loading`, and the `saveStatus`:

form_handling/10-vuex-app/main.js

```
  data() {
    return {
      fieldErrors: {
        newItem: undefined,
        email: undefined,
        urgency: undefined,
        termsAndConditions: undefined
      },
      loading: false,
      saveStatus: 'READY'
    }
  },
```

Vuex and `v-model`

The next thing we may be inclined to do is *bind* the store data with the appropriate input fields since we already have the `v-model` directive set-up. So for instance, with regards to the `newItem` field; we may aim to do something like this:

```
template: `
  ...
  <input v-model="newItem" type="text"
    placeholder="Add an item!" />
  ...
`,
computed: Vuex.mapGetters({
  newItem: 'newItem',
})
```

Though this is the appropriate way of binding `input`'s in Vue, **this won't work well with Vuex state**. With this, `v-model` aims to directly mutate the state property it's bound to. When Vuex is in it's *strict* mode (i.e. can't modify state directly), it's a requirement to adhere to a flux-like pattern of using a mutation to modify the state. So if we aimed to do the above, we'll generate an error.

With Vuex, there's often two ways to invoke form binding. One method involves binding the `value` of the input to the data property, *listening* for any changes in the input, and invoking an action/mutation when a change is made. Something like this:

```
template: `
  ...
  <input :value="newItem" @input="onInputChange"
    type="text" placeholder="Add an item!" />
  ...
`,
computed: Vuex.mapGetters({
  newItem: 'newItem',
}),
methods: {
  onInputChange(evt) {
    this.$store.commit('UPDATE_INPUT', evt.target.value);
  }
}
```

The other alternative is keeping the use of `v-model` but instead using a two-way computed property approach with `get()` and `set()`:

```
template: `
  ...
  <input v-model="newItem" type="text"
    placeholder="Add an item!" />
  ...
`,
computed: {
  newItem: {
    get() {
      return this.$store.state.fields.newItem;
    },
    set(val) {
      this.$store.commit('UPDATE_INPUT', value);
    }
  }
}
```

Both approaches result in the same outcome but the first is often understood to be the "standard" Vuex way of managing form data, albeit being more verbose. We'll be using the first approach to make our form work with Vuex state.

Mutations

Since we know `mutations` have to be created to manipulate Vuex form data, we can create a `mutation` for every input change that needs to be made in the form.

Each mutation handler will receive a `payload` of the data we'd want to update a particular property with:

```
const mutations = {
  UPDATE_NEW_ITEM (state, payload) {
    state.fields.newItem = payload;
  },
  UPDATE_EMAIL (state, payload) {
    state.fields.email = payload;
  },
  UPDATE_URGENCY (state, payload) {
    state.fields.urgency = payload;
  },
  UPDATE_TERMS_AND_CONDITIONS (state, payload) {
    state.fields.termsAndConditions = payload;
  }
}
```

When a form is submitted, we'll also need a mutation that involves updating the `items` array with the newly added item and another mutation that's responsible in clearing all the fields of the form. Naming these mutations `UPDATE_ITEMS` and `CLEAR_FIELDS` respectively, our `mutations` object will be:

form_handling/10-vuex-app/store.js

```
const mutations = {
  UPDATE_NEW_ITEM (state, payload) {
    state.fields.newItem = payload;
  },
  UPDATE_EMAIL (state, payload) {
    state.fields.email = payload;
  },
  UPDATE_URGENCY (state, payload) {
    state.fields.urgency = payload;
  },
  UPDATE_TERMS_AND_CONDITIONS (state, payload) {
    state.fields.termsAndConditions = payload;
  },
  UPDATE_ITEMS (state, payload) {
    state.items = payload
  },
  CLEAR_FIELDS () {
    state.fields.newItem = '';
    state.fields.email = '';
    state.fields.urgency = '';
    state.fields.termsAndConditions = false
  }
}
```

We'll now move towards creating the `getters` and mapping them to the form prior to creating our `actions`.

Getters

We'll use `getters` to map all relevant state information to the form like below:

form_handling/10-vuex-app/store.js

```
const getters = {
  newItem: state => state.fields.newItem,
  newItemLength: state => state.fields.newItem.length,
  isNewItemInputLimitExceeded: state => state.fields.newItem.length >= 20,
  email: state => state.fields.email,
  urgency: state => state.fields.urgency,
  isNotUrgent: state => state.fields.urgency === 'Nonessential',
  termsAndConditions: state => state.fields.termsAndConditions,
  items: state => state.items
}
```

Instead of only computing data from `getters`, Vuex also allows us to retrieve store state directly from within components. We've simply conformed to using `getters` to map *all* state information.

Updating the form

With our `mutations` and `getters` established, we can update the form to work with these new changes. First and foremost, let's update the `computed` property of our component to now map directly to the store `getters`, with the use of the `mapGetters` helper:

form_handling/10-vuex-app/main.js

```
  computed: Vuex.mapGetters({
    newItem: 'newItem',
    newItemLength: 'newItemLength',
    isNewItemInputLimitExceeded: 'isNewItemInputLimitExceeded',
    email: 'email',
    urgency: 'urgency',
    isNotUrgent: 'isNotUrgent',
    termsAndConditions: 'termsAndConditions',
    items: 'items'
  }),
```

With the `getters` now mapped to the component computed properties, we can manually bind each property to its respective input. Without displaying our entire `template` code, our form inputs will be bound like below:

```
<!-- New Item Input -->
<input :value="newItem" type="text" placeholder="Add an item!" />

<!-- Email Input -->
<input :value="email" type="text" placeholder="What's your email?" />

<!-- Urgency Dropdown -->
<select :value="urgency" class="ui fluid search dropdown">
  <option disabled value="">Please select one</option>
  <option>Nonessential</option>
  <option>Moderate</option>
  <option>Urgent</option>
</select>

<!-- Terms and Conditions Checkbox -->
<input :checked="termsAndConditions" type="checkbox" />
```

Notice how we've bound the `checked` attribute for the checkbox, instead of it's value. The checked attribute will be the boolean (`true`/`false`) that we'll use to update the `termsAndConditions` state property.

With the `mutations` already created, we now need to create the event handlers for each of these field items to commit to these mutations when a change occurs.

For the sake of cleanliness, we'll use a single event handler, `onInputChange`, to capture the changes made to each field. Just like we did in the beginning of the chapter, we'll use the inputs `name` attribute to reference which input has been changed. Since our mutation handlers are in all CAPS, we'll set the names of each input to follow a similar format. Our input fields now become:

```
<!-- New Item Input -->
<input :value="newItem" @input="onInputChange"
  name="NEW_ITEM" type="text" placeholder="Add an item!" />

<!-- Email Input -->
<input :value="email" @input="onInputChange"
  name="EMAIL" type="text" placeholder="What's your email?" />

<!-- Urgency Dropdown -->
<select :value="urgency" @change="onInputChange"
  name="URGENCY" class="ui fluid search dropdown">
  <option disabled value="">Please select one</option>
  <option>Nonessential</option>
  <option>Moderate</option>
```

```
  <option>Urgent</option>
</select>

<!-- Terms and Conditions Checkbox -->
<input :checked="termsAndConditions" @change="onInputChange"
  name="TERMS_AND_CONDITIONS" type="checkbox" />
```

Notice how we've used the `@input` event for the `<input type="text" />` elements and the `@change` event for the `select` and `<input type="checkbox" />` elements. `@input` occurs when the text content of an element is changed while the `@change` event is fired when the selection or the checked state change.

Let's now create the `onInputChange` method, within the `methods` property, to commit to the correct mutation when a field element is changed:

form_handling/10-vuex-app/main.js

```
    onInputChange(evt) {
      const element = evt.target;
      const value =
        element.name === "TERMS_AND_CONDITIONS"
          ? element.checked
          : element.value;
      this.$store.commit(`UPDATE_${element.name}`, value);
    },
```

We use a ternary statement to send the input event's `checked` value if the checkbox field element is the one that's been changed. Since all our mutations start with `UPDATE_`, we use the element name to commit to the right mutation.

In the previous Vuex related chapters, we followed a strict format of making our component's dispatch actions that then commit to mutations. Since the actions for our input changes here will only be directly committing to mutations, we've omitted them to save having an extra step.

Actions

We now need to focus on creating the actions that get the items list from the server *and* persist the newly added item to the server upon a successful form submit. In both cases, we need to keep the Vuex state (`items`) and the server state in sync. When either call is made, we'll need to commit to the `UPDATE_ITEMS` mutation to maintain this synchronicity.

When the page loads, it needs to fetch the persisted `items` array from the server. For this to happen, an action has be to created that calls `apiClient.loadItems` on page load. When this data is fetched, the `UPDATE_ITEMS` mutation is then called to update the `items` application state array. Naming this action `loadItems`, our `actions` object in the store can initially be set-up with:

```
const actions = {
  loadItems (context, payload) {
    apiClient.loadItems().then((items) => {
      context.commit('UPDATE_ITEMS', items);
    });
  }
}
```

The other action we'll need involves creating the asynchronous call to persist the newly updated items to the server, upon submission of the form. When this persistence is done successfully, we'll also need to update the `items` application state (to keep the UI in sync) **and** clear all fields in the form. As a result, this action (to be named `saveItems`) will commit to two mutations, `UPDATE_ITEMS` for updating the `items` state, and `CLEAR_FIELDS` for clearing the field inputs:

```
const actions = {
  loadItems (context, payload) {
    apiClient.loadItems().then((items) => {
      context.commit('UPDATE_ITEMS', items);
    });
  },
  saveItems (context, payload) {
    const items = payload;
    apiClient.saveItems(payload).then(() => {
      context.commit('UPDATE_ITEMS', items);
      context.commit('CLEAR_FIELDS');
    });
  }
}
```

In our component, let's dispatch the `loadItems` action the moment the component is created (i.e. in the `created()` hook). Similar to how it was done before, we'll need to change the component's `loading` status to `false` *after* the dispatch is complete:

form_handling/10-vuex-app/main.js

```
  created() {
    this.loading = true;
    this.$store.dispatch('loadItems')
      .then((response) => {
        this.loading = false;
      })
      .catch((error) => {
        console.log(error);
      })
  },
```

Though this may appear to be okay, it won't currently work as intended. This is because Vuex actions are *asynchronous* as well.

When the component is created, the `loadItems` action will be called. Prior to the action being complete, the `loading` status will change back to `false`, making it seem like `loading` was never `true` in the first place. We need to let the calling function (`this.$store.dispatch`) know when the action is complete **by returning a `Promise` and then resolving it.**

Since both of our actions need to behave this way, our `actions` object will be updated to:

form_handling/10-vuex-app/store.js

```
const actions = {
  loadItems (context, payload) {
    return new Promise((resolve, reject) => {
      apiClient.loadItems().then((items) => {
        context.commit('UPDATE_ITEMS', items);
        resolve(items);
      }, (error) => {
        reject(error);
      });
    });
  },
  saveItems (context, payload) {
    return new Promise((resolve, reject) => {
      const items = payload;
      apiClient.saveItems(payload).then((response) => {
        context.commit('UPDATE_ITEMS', items);
        context.commit('CLEAR_FIELDS');
        resolve(response);
      }, (error) => {
```

```
        reject(error);
      });
    });
  }
}
```

The actions now return a `Promise` object to the dispatcher which then either gets resolved or rejected depending on the success of the asynchronous server calls. With this, our store dispatcher will set the component's `loading` data to `false` *only* after the Promise is resolved successfully.

At this point, everything in our app should work as expected except for a successful submission of a new item. We need to modify the `submitForm()` method to dispatch the `saveItems` action when the form is submitted. Since the clearing of fields is handled in the Vuex store, our `submitForm()` method is simply changed to:

form_handling/10-vuex-app/main.js

```
    submitForm(evt) {
      evt.preventDefault();

      this.fieldErrors = this.validateForm(this.$store.state.fields);
      if (Object.keys(this.fieldErrors).length) return;

      const items = [
        ...this.$store.state.items,
        this.$store.state.fields.newItem
      ];

      this.saveStatus = 'SAVING';

      this.$store.dispatch('saveItems', items)
        .then(() => {
          this.saveStatus = 'SUCCESS';
        })
        .catch((err) => {
          console.log(err);
          this.saveStatus = 'ERROR';
        });
    },
```

Just like we've done before, we've set `saveStatus` to '`SUCCESS`' when the request is successful, and to '`ERROR`' otherwise.

And that's it! Our form now fits neatly inside a Vuex-based data architecture. Notice how things are more verbose when using forms in a Vuex related app?

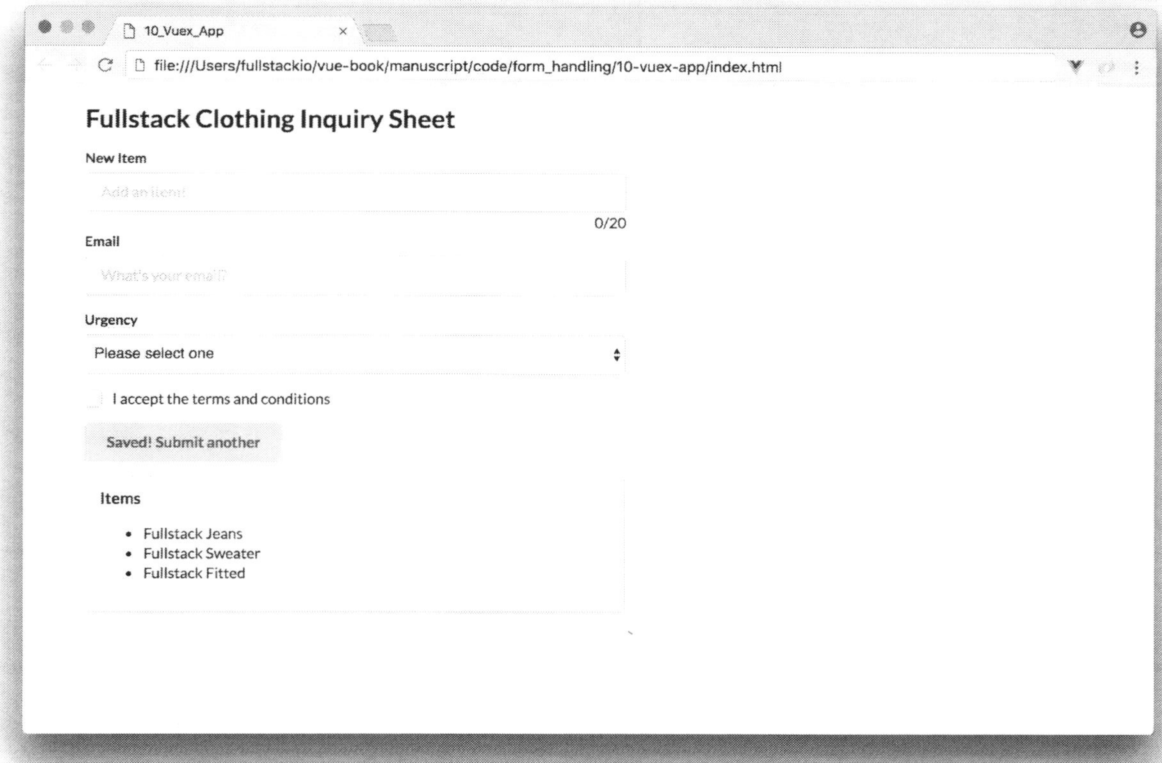

Vuex integrated form

After reading this chapter, you should have a good handle on the fundamentals of forms in Vue. That said, if you'd like to outsource some portion of your form handling to an external module, there are several available. Read on for a list of some of the more popular options.

Form Modules

vee-validate

http://vee-validate.logaretm.com/[84]

A simple plugin that focuses on input validation on the template (HTML) itself. `vee-validate` introduces a `v-validate` directive that assigns validation rules based on the information given to the directive.

[84]http://vee-validate.logaretm.com/

`vee-validate` provides more than 20 rules out of the box but also allows the creation of custom rules.

vuelidate

https://monterail.github.io/vuelidate/[85]

A lightweight library that decouples validations from the template and instead require them declared within a component's/instance's model.

`vuelidate` works by specifying a `validations` property where validations (e.g. `name: { required, minLength: minLength(4) }`) can be introduced. In the template, the `validations` result object can then be accessed to configure the template depending on whether the validation is/isn't met.

vue-multiselect

https://github.com/vue-generators/vue-form-generator/[86]

With no jQuery dependency, `vue-multiselect` allows for a customizable `select` box with support for single select, multiple select, tagging, dropdowns, filtering, etc.

`vue-multiselect` works by using the `Multiselect` component from the library and specifying its `data()`, `methods`, and attributes to enable unique features to `select` elements.

vue-form-generator

https://github.com/vue-generators/vue-form-generator/[87]

If the idea of defining forms and fields entirely with JSON sounds useful, `vue-form-generator` might be for you. With `vue-form-generator`, you sketch out your entire form in a JSON schema. The schema is a large object where you can define things like labels, validation requirements, and field types.

`vue-form-generator` works by declaring a component with `VueFormGenerator.component` and passing the JSON schema to the component as a `schema` prop.

[85]https://monterail.github.io/vuelidate/

[86]https://github.com/vue-generators/vue-form-generator/

[87]https://github.com/vue-generators/vue-form-generator/

VII - Routing

What is routing?

In web development, *routing* often means splitting the application into different areas usually based on rules that are derived from the current browser URL.

Imagine clicking a link and having the URL go from `https://website.com` to `https://website.com/about/`. *That's routing.*

When we visit the `/` path of a website, we intend to visit the home route of that website. If we visit `/about` we want to render the "about page", and so on.

Many applications can technically be written *without* routing but this can get messy as an application grows. Defining routes in an application is useful since one can separate different areas of an app **and** protect areas of the app based on certain rules.

URL

A URL is a reference (i.e. address) to a resource on the Internet and is often made up of:

- The protocol identifier.
- The hostname (i.e. domain name).
- A pathname.

Let's break down a sample URL, for instance:

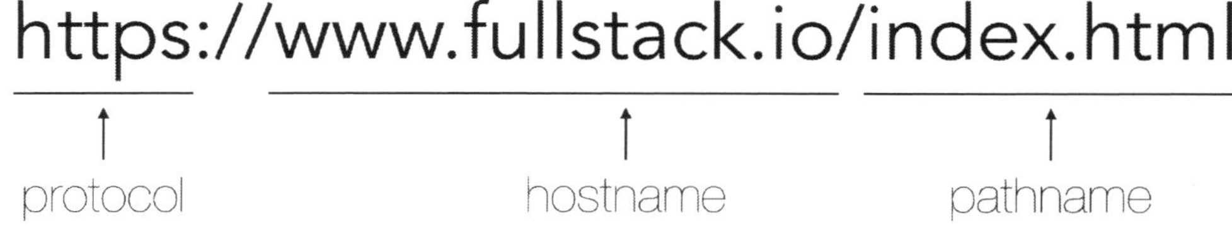

The **protocol** and the **hostname**, combined, help direct us to a certain website. The **pathname** is the indicator that helps us reference a specific resource (i.e. location) on that site.

An app often maintains its **context state in the URL**. For example, let's consider a fake URL of an online clothing store:

```
https://example.com/category/02/item/12
```

This location refers to a specific clothing item for a particular category (e.g. shoes). The numbers `02` and `12` denote the identifiers for both the category and the specific item:

```
https://example.com/category/:categoryId/item/:itemId
```

With the URL we're now able to refresh the page and keep our location in the app, bookmark to come back to it later, and share the URL with others. These are some of the benefits of creating routes within an application.

URL Requests

In a server-driven application, requests to a URL often follow a pattern:

1. The client (i.e. browser) makes a request to the server for the particular page.
2. The server uses the identifiers in the URL pathname to retrieve the relevant data from its database.
3. The server populates a template (HTML document) with this data.
4. The server returns the template along with other assets like CSS/images to the client.
5. The client renders these assets.

Server-side routing is often set up to retrieve and return different information depending on the incoming URL. Writing server-side routes with Express.js[88] generally looks like:

```
const express = require('express');
const router = express.Router();

// define the about route
router.get('/about', function(req, res) {
  res.send('About us');
});
```

Or using Ruby on Rails[89], a similar route definition might look like this:

[88] http://expressjs.com/en/guide/routing.html
[89] http://guides.rubyonrails.org/routing.html

```
# routes.rb
get '/about', to: 'pages#about'

# PagesController.rb
class PagesController < ActionController::Base
  def about
    render
  end
end
```

Whether it's Express.js[90], Ruby on Rails[91], or any other server-side framework, the pattern often remains the same. The **server** accepts a request and *routes* to a **controller** and the controller runs a specific **action** (e.g. return specific information), depending on the path and parameters.

Though client-side routing appears similar in concept, it's different in implementation. With client-side routing, **we don't make a request to the server** on every URL change. Instead we let the client handle defining what to present. Client-side routing is where the term **Single-page applications** (or **SPAs** for short) comes in.

Single-page applications

Single-page applications (SPAs) are web apps that load only once (server provides a single template) and JavaScript is used to dynamically render different pages. Every application we've built so far has been a type of a SPA.

The benefits to SPAs come after the initial page load. Once the initial load is complete, JavaScript is used to provide a much better user experience. Since the entire application is available, the browser does not fetch a brand new page with every call to the server. This helps avoid the unpleasant "blink" between page loads.

---

[90] http://expressjs.com/en/guide/routing.html

[91] http://guides.rubyonrails.org/routing.html

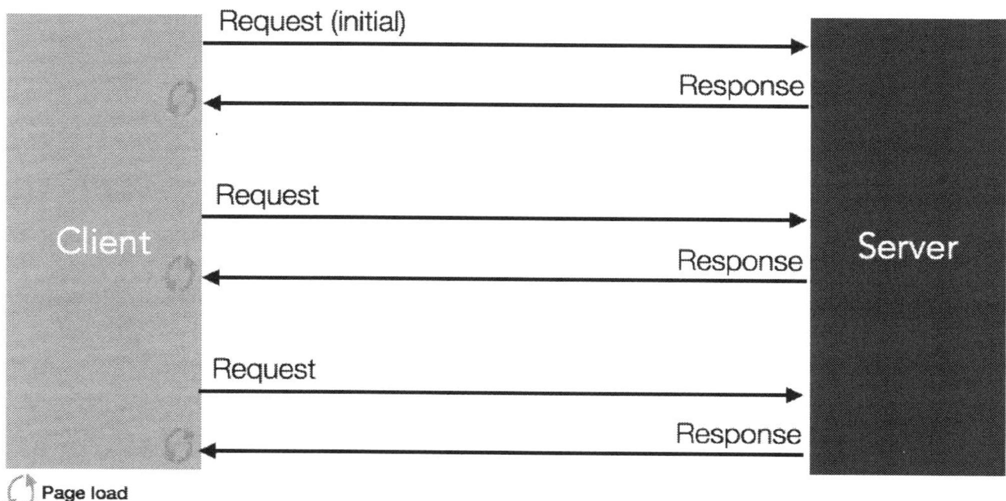

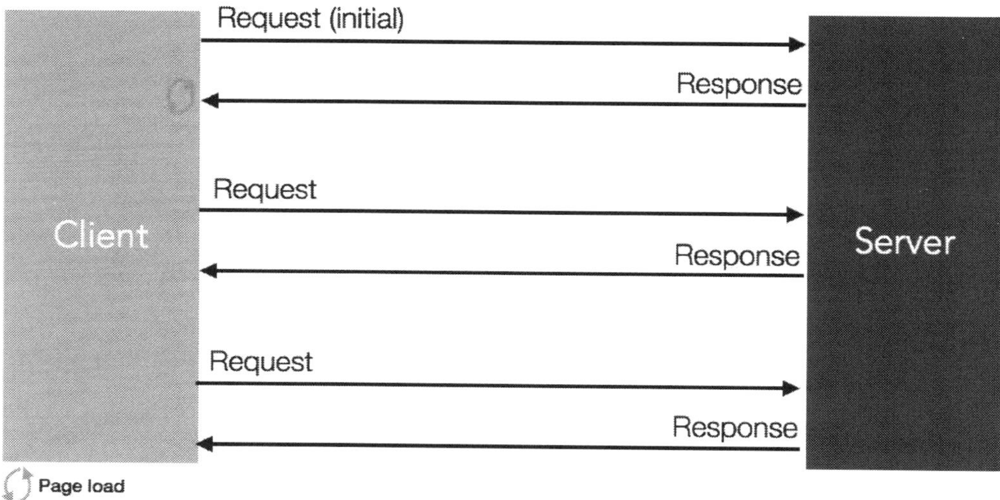

Though the apps we've built so far have been fluid and dynamic, they've all had **a single route (/)**.

For instance, the shopping cart app we built in Chapter 5 had a single view that displayed the list of product items and the cart. What if we wanted to move the cart UI to a separate page, with a location of `/cart` that can be accessed with the click of a 'Cart' button? Let's visit how this request flow would look like:

1. A user clicks on the 'Cart' button which links to `/cart`.
2. The browser makes a request to `/cart`.

3. The server in this case **does not care about the pathname**. The client already has the same `index.html` that includes the full Vue app and static assets.
4. As the Vue app is being created and mounted, it checks the URL and sees that the user is looking at the `/cart` page.
5. The top-level Vue component, (e.g. `App`), will map certain components to certain routes and will switch the current component to a `Cart` component based on the URL (`/cart`).

When the user clicks on the 'Cart' button, the browser already contains the full application. There's no need to have the browser make a new request to fetch the same app again from the server and re-mount it. The Vue app just needs to update the URL and render the correct component. This is the basic functionality of any **JavaScript** router.

Routing in single-page Vue applications involve two pieces of functionality:

1. modifying the location (URL) of the app
2. determining what Vue component to render at a given location.

To handle this functionality, we'll be using Vue's official router plugin, **`vue-router`**[92]. Since Vue applications are usually composed of separate components, building an SPA with Vue and Vue Router is a fairly *easy* process.

Basic Vue Router

Before we begin diving in to how `vue-router` works, we'll first start by building a basic router from scratch. Our simple client-side router will be fully-functional and will help us gain a good understanding of how a simple JavaScript router works in a Vue component-driven paradigm.

We'll then swap out our components for those provided by the `vue-router` library.

The completed app

All the example code for this chapter is inside the folder `routing` in the code download. We'll start off with the `basics` app:

```
$ cd routing/basics
```

Taking a look inside this directory, we see `basics/` is a simple Webpack-configured application:

[92]https://github.com/vuejs/vue-router

```
$ ls
README.md
index.html
package.json
public/
src/
webpack.config.js
```

The hidden files `.babelrc` and `.gitignore` are also present in the application scaffold.

In `basics/`, our Vue app lives inside `src/`:

```
$ ls src/
app/
main.js
```

`app/` contains each iteration of `app.js` that we'll build up throughout this section.

`main.js` is where the completed app is currently being imported and rendered in the Vue instance:

routing/basics/src/main.js

```
import Vue from 'vue';
import App from './app/app-complete';
import { router } from './app/app-complete';

new Vue({
  el: '#app',
  router,
  render: h => h(App)
});
```

We're also importing a `router` object that's being passed in to the Vue instance.

Let's install the npm packages:

```
$ npm i
```

If we boot the app, we'll see the completed version at `http://localhost:8080/`:

```
$ npm run dev
```

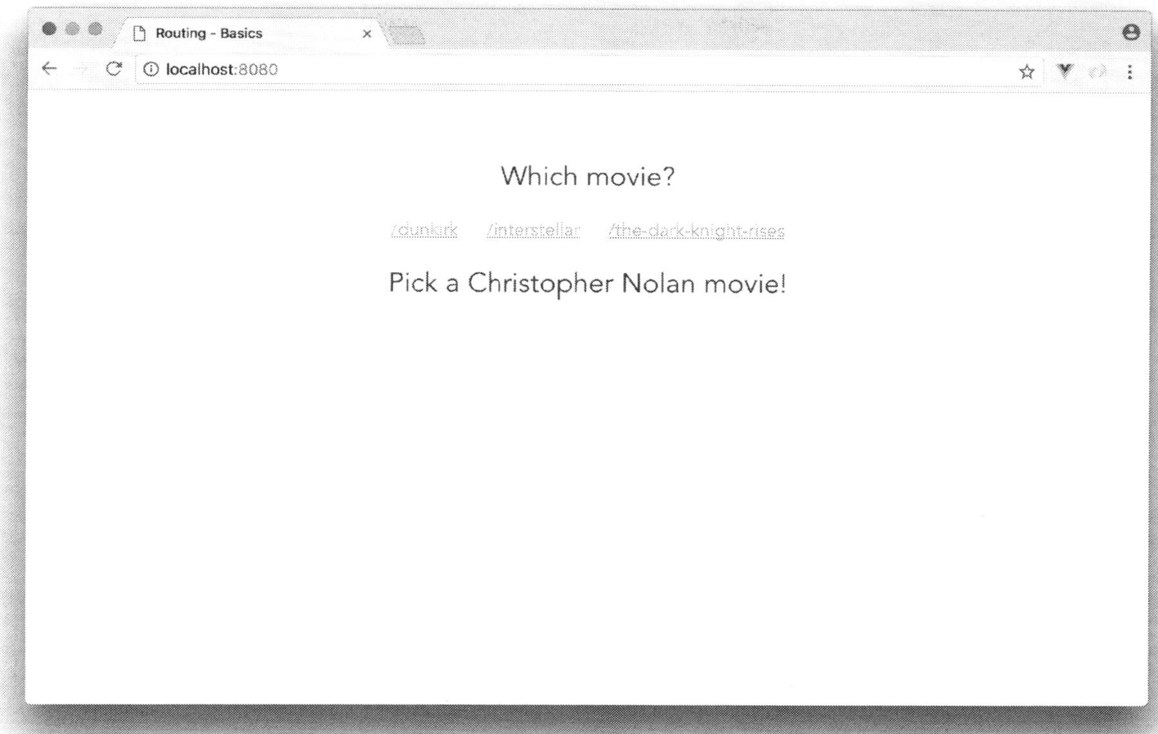

The app contains three links `/dunkirk`, `/interstellar`, and `/the-dark-knight-rises`. Clicking on a link displays a description blurb about each particular movie.

Notice that clicking on a link changes the location of the app. Clicking on the link `/interstellar`, for example, updates the URL to `/interstellar`. Importantly, **the browser does not make a request when we click on a link (i.e. there is no page reload)**. The description about Interstellar simply appears and the browser's URL bar updates to `/interstellar` instantly.

The routing in this app is powered by the `vue-router` library. We'll build a version of the app ourselves by constructing our own simple router before switching over to `vue-router`.

Building a simple router

Since we'll be working inside the `app.js` file, let's reference `app.js` as the app that's mounted in our Vue instance. We'll need to import `App` from `./app/app` in line 2 of the `main.js` file.

Let's also remove the `router` import and it's injection to the Vue instance. We'll re-add it once we create our `router` object. This updates the `src/main.js` file to:

```
import Vue from 'vue';
import App from './app/app';

new Vue({
  el: '#app',
  render: h => h(App)
});
```

Since our Webpack server is hot-reloaded, our application should automatically update. We'll notice the three links are still rendered on the page but with some static text now displayed below. When we click any of the links, we also notice the browser now makes a page request each time. Though the URL bar is updated with each request, we can see nothing in the app changes:

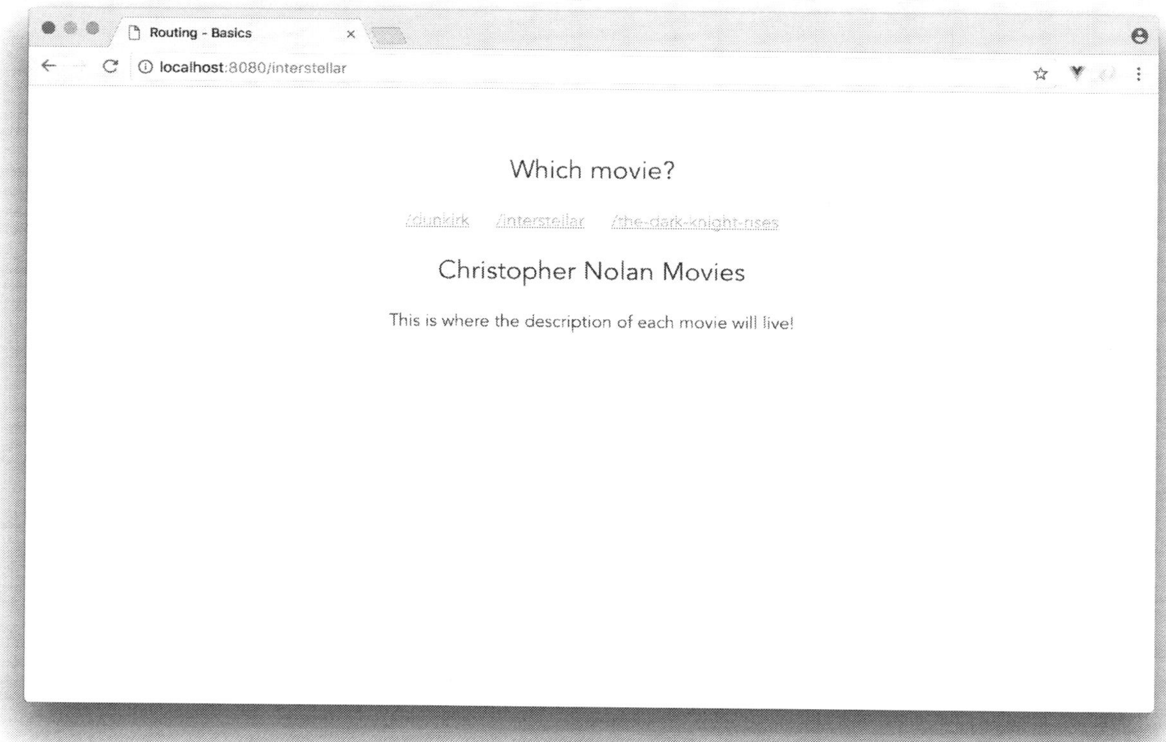

At this moment, our app doesn't care about the state of the URL pathname. No matter what path the browser requests from our server, the server will return the same `index.html` with the same exact JavaScript bundle. This is good since we want our browser to load Vue in the same way in each location and defer to Vue on what to show and how to render the page.

Let's have our app render appropriate components, `DunkirkBlurb`, `InterstellarBlurb`, or `TheDark-KnightRisesBlurb`, based on the location of the app (`/dunkirk`, `/interstellar`, or `the-dark-knight-rises`). To implement this behaviour, we'll write and use a `router-view` component.

In vue-router, router-view is a component that **renders a specified component based on the app's location**.

Let's look at how we might use this component before we write it. In the template of the App component in app/app.js, we'll remove the static text below the links and reference router-view like so:

routing/basics/src/app/app-1.js

```
const App = {
  name: 'App',
  template: `<div id="app">
    <div class="movies">
      <h2>Which movie?</h2>
      <a href="/dunkirk">/dunkirk</a>
      <a href="/interstellar">/interstellar</a>
      <a href="/the-dark-knight-rises">/the-dark-knight-rises</a>

      <router-view></router-view>
    </div>
  </div>`,
```

It's important to remember that router-view is a component, like any other Vue component. router-view matches the correct component based on a particular route. This matching will be dictated in a routes array that we'll create. We'll create this array right above the App component:

routing/basics/src/app/app-1.js

```
const routes = [
  {
    path: '/',
    component: {
      name: 'index-blurb',
      template: `<h2>Pick a Christopher Nolan movie!</h2>`
    }
  },
  {path: '/dunkirk', component: DunkirkBlurb},
  {path: '/interstellar', component: InterstellarBlurb},
  {path: '/the-dark-knight-rises', component: TheDarkKnightRisesBlurb}
];
```

We've set each movie path to their own respective component and the root path / to a component that displays a <h2> element stating 'Pick a Christopher Nolan movie!'.

Movie Blurbs

Before we create our `router-view` component, let's set up each of the movie blurb components that our routes would render. We'll create these components as simple `templates` that display a title and description blurb for each movie.

Let's create these components above our `routes` array:

routing/basics/src/app/app-1.js

```
const DunkirkBlurb = {
  name: 'dunkirk-blurb',
  template: `<div>
    <h2>Dunkirk</h2>
    <p class="movies__description">Miraculous evacuation of Allied soldiers from
      Belgium, Britain, Canada, and France, who were cut off and surrounded by
      the German army from the beaches and harbor of Dunkirk, France, during the
      Battle of France in World War II.</p>
  </div>`
};

const InterstellarBlurb = {
  name: 'interstellar-blurb',
  template: `<div>
    <h2>Interstellar</h2>
    <p class="movies__description">Interstellar chronicles the adventures of a
      group of explorers who make use of a newly discovered wormhole to surpass
      the limitations on human space travel and conquer the vast distances
      involved in an interstellar voyage.</p>
  </div>`
};

const TheDarkKnightRisesBlurb = {
  name: 'the-dark-knight-rises-blurb',
  template: `<div>
    <h2>The Dark Knight Rises</h2>
    <p class="movies__description">Batman encounters the mysterious Selina Kyle
      and the villainous Bane, a new terrorist leader who overwhelms Gotham's
      finest. The Dark Knight resurfaces to protect a city that has branded him
      an enemy.</p>
  </div>`
};
```

The name property within a component isn't a hard requirement but is often useful to have for debugging purposes. Specifying a name will help in showing more helpful error messages as well as ensuring the component is displayed appropriately in Vue Devtools.

The Vue docs[93] explains this some more.

router-view

With our routes and movie blurb components set up, we can begin to create our router-view component. We'll build router-view as a constant variable named View which we'll create right after our routes array, making our entire app.js file currently laid out like below:

```
import Vue from 'vue';

const DunkirkBlurb = {
  ...
};

const InterstellarBlurb = {
  ...
};

const TheDarkKnightRisesBlurb = {
  ...
};

const routes = [
  ...
];

const View = {
  name: 'router-view'
};

const App = {
  ...
};

export default App;
```

[93]https://vuejs.org/v2/api/#name

Our `router-view` component (i.e. `View`) needs to be built as a mounting point for **Dynamic Components**[94].

Dynamic components constitute the ability to dynamically change (i.e. switch) between components based on a data attribute. There are two ways dynamic components can be implemented, using the `is` attribute or binding directly to component objects.

Let's use the first approach by binding an `is` attribute to the reserved `<component>` element. To get a better understanding of how this can work, let's set up `router-view` (i.e. the `View` constant object) like below:

```
const View = {
  name: 'router-view',
  template: `<component :is="currentView"></component>`,
  data() {
    return {
      currentView: DunkirkBlurb
    }
  }
};
```

We're using the reserved `<component>` element as the *mounting* point of our `router-view` component. `<component>` will render whatever component the `is` attribute is bound to (which is currently `DunkirkBlurb`). To test the above functionality, we need to declare the `router-view` component property in `App`:

routing/basics/src/app/app-1.js

```
const App = {
  // ...
  components: {
    'router-view': View
  }
};
```

After saving the file, our updated app should now display the `DunkirkBlurb` component regardless of which link is clicked:

[94] https://vuejs.org/v2/guide/components.html#Dynamic-Components

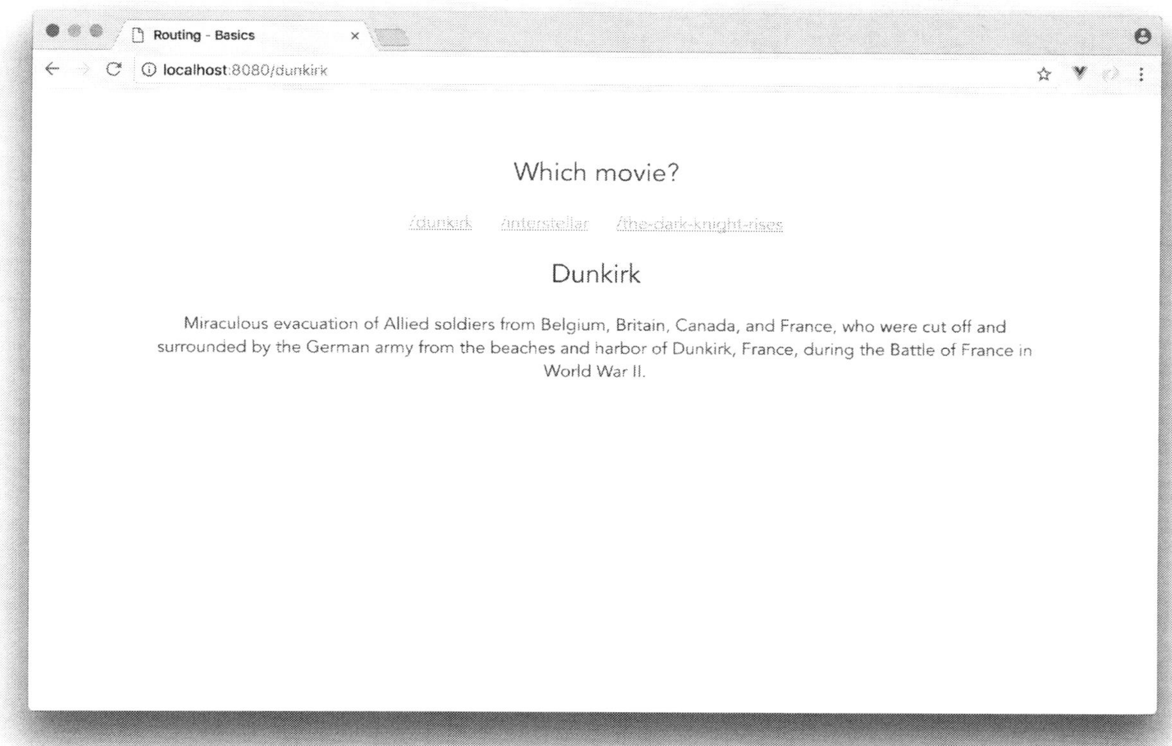

Though our `router-view` component is appropriately rendered within `App`, it's not currently dynamic. We need `router-view` to display the correct component based on the URL pathname, *upon page load*. To do this, we'll use the `created()` hook to filter the `routes` array and return the component that has a `path` that matches the URL path:

```
const View = {
  name: 'router-view',
  template: `<component :is="currentView"></component>`,
  data() {
    return {
      currentView: {}
    }
  },
  created() {
    this.currentView = routes.find(
      route => route.path === window.location.pathname
    ).component;
  }
};
```

In `data()`, we're now instantiating `currentView` with an empty object. In the `created()` hook, we're using JavaScript's native `find()` method to return the first object from `routes` that matches `route.path === window.location.pathname`. From this we get the component with `object.component` (where `object` is the returned object from `find()`).

Inside a browser environment, `window.location` is a special object containing the properties of the browser's current location. We grab the `pathname` from this object which is the path of the URL.

Let's take a look at the app at this stage.

Save `app.js`. Ensure the Webpack development server is still running and head to `http://localhost:8080`. Notice we're now rendering the appropriate component when we visit each location:

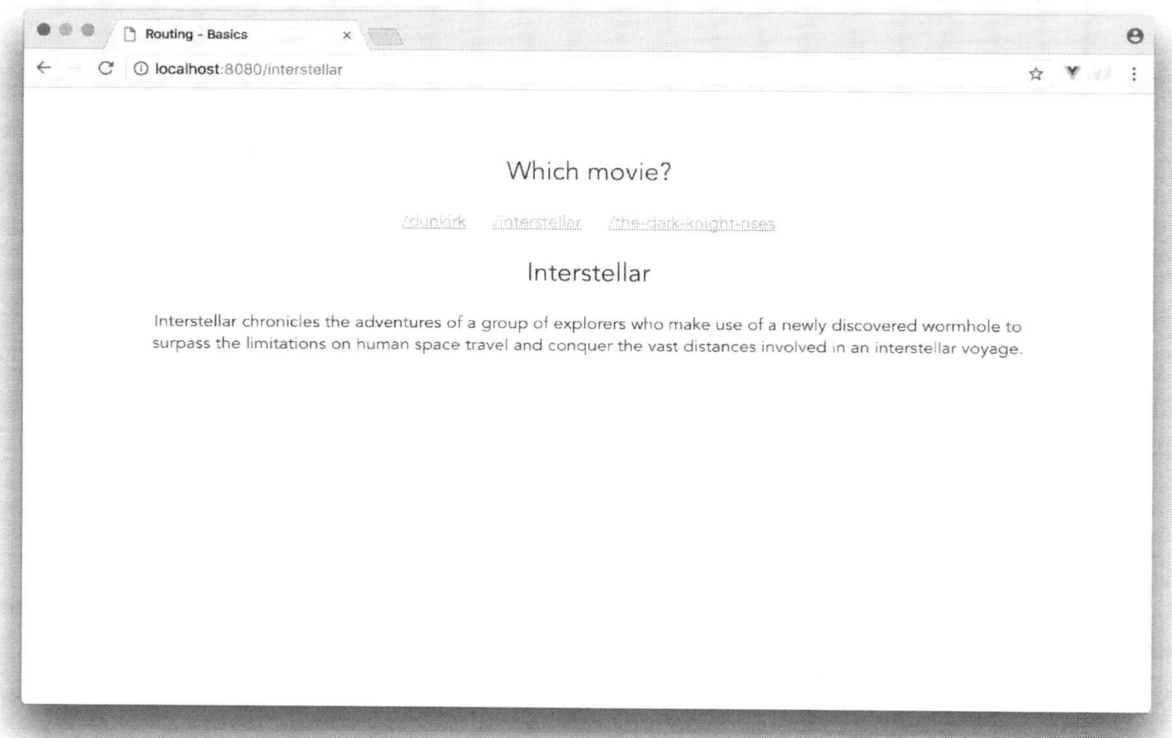

If a random URL `pathname` is entered, our app will currently error and present nothing to the view except for the links. To avoid this, let's introduce a simple check to display a 'Not Found' template if the URL `pathname` doesn't match any `path` existing in the `routes` array. We'll separate out the `find()` method to a component method, `getRouteObject()`, to avoid repetition.

routing/basics/src/app/app-1.js

```
const View = {
  // ...
  created() {
    if (this.getRouteObject() === undefined) {
      this.currentView = {
        template: `<h2>Not Found :(. Pick a movie from the list!</h2>`
      };
    } else {
      this.currentView = this.getRouteObject().component;
    }
  },
  methods: {
    getRouteObject() {
      return routes.find(
        route => route.path === window.location.pathname
      );
    }
  }
};
```

If the `getRouteObject()` returns `undefined`, we display the 'Not Found' template. If `getRouteObject()` returns an object from `routes`, we bind `currentView` to the component of that object. Now if a random URL is entered, the user will be notified:

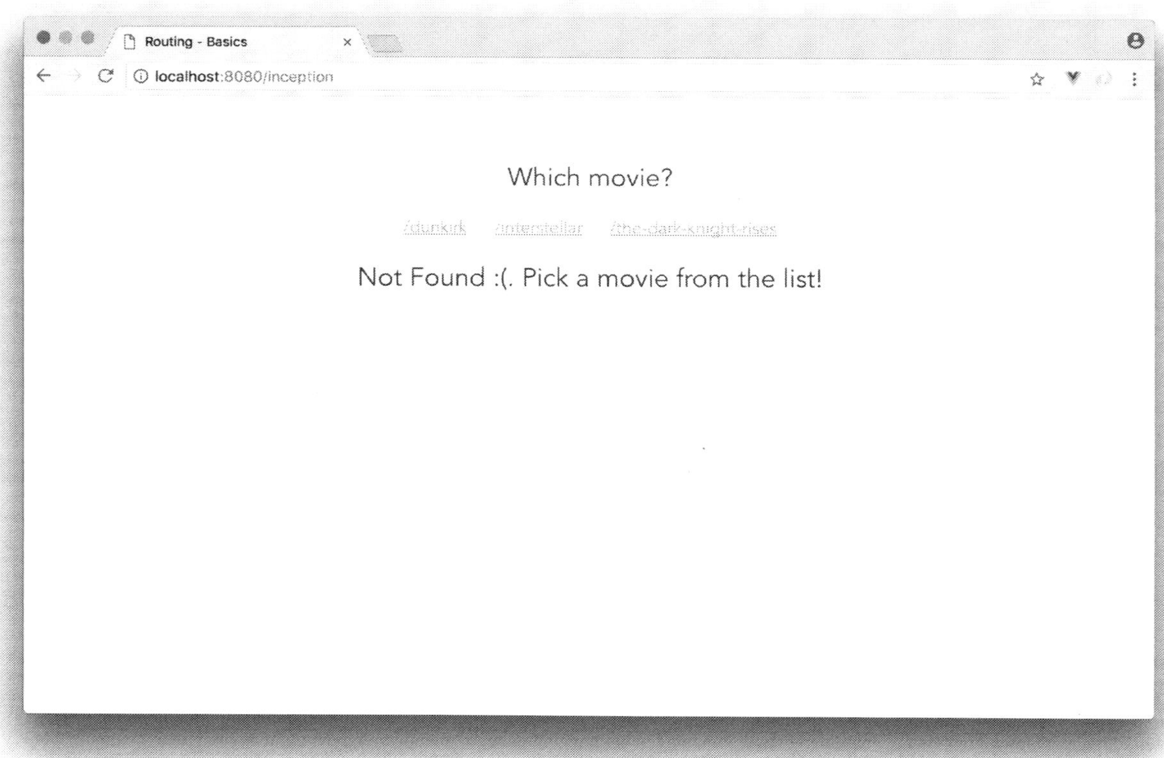

`/inception` returns the 'Not Found' template

Awesome, our app is now responding to some external state, the location of the browser. `router-view` determines which component should be displayed based on the app's location.

When we click on a link, though the app displays the correct component, we see that the browser currently does a full page load upon each click:

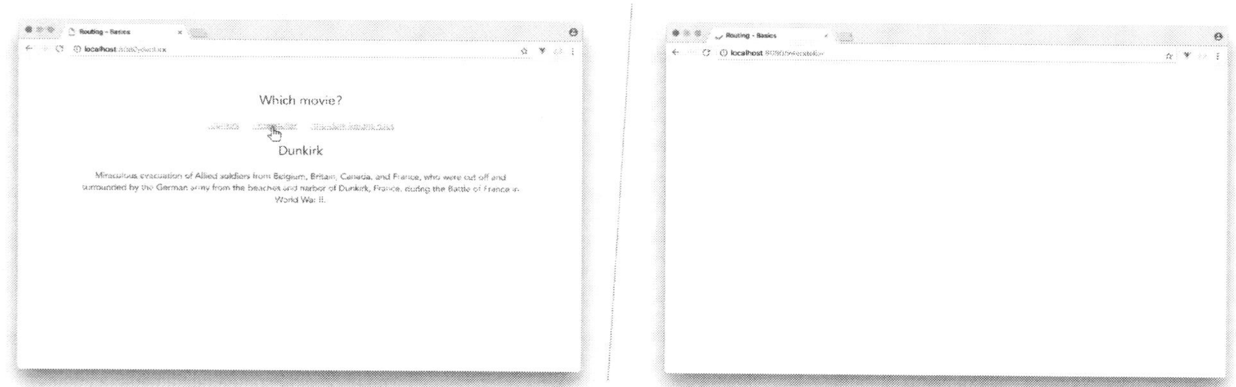

Clicking on `/interstellar` triggers a full page load

By default, our browser makes a fresh request to the Webpack development server every time we click a link. The server returns the `index.html` and our browser needs to perform the work of mounting the Vue app again.

As highlighted in the intro, this cycle is unnecessary. When switching between the links, there's no need to involve the server. Our client app already has all the components prepared and ready to go. We just need to swap in the right components for the right links.

What we'll need to do is construct navigation links that will **change the location of the browser without making a web request**. With the location updated, we can re-render our Vue app and rely on `router-view` to appropriately determine which component to render.

We'll label these links as `router-link` components.

`router-link`

In web interfaces, we use HTML `<a>` tags to create links. What we want here is a special type of `<a>` tag. When the user clicks on this tag, we'll want the browser to skip its default routine of making a web request to fetch the next page. Instead, we just want to manually update the browser's location.

Most browsers supply an API for managing the history of the current session, `window.history`. We encourage trying it out in a JavaScript console inside the browser. It has methods like `history.back()` and `history.forward()` that allow you to navigate the history stack. Of immediate interest, it has a method `history.pushState()` which allows you to navigate the browser to a desired location.

For more detailed info on the history API, check out the docs on MDN[95].

Let's compose a `router-link` component that produces an `<a>` tag with a special `click` binding. When the user clicks on the `router-link` component, we'll want to prevent the browser from making a request. Instead, we'll use the history API to update the browser's location.

Just like we did with `router-view`, let's see how we'll use this component before we build it.

In the template of the `App` component, let's replace the `<a>` tags with our upcoming `router-link` component. Rather than using the `href` attribute, we'll specify the desired location of the link using a `to` attribute. We'll also declare the upcoming `router-link` component (as `Link`) in the components property of `App`:

[95] https://developer.mozilla.org/en-US/docs/Web/API/History_API

routing/basics/src/app/app-2.js

```
const App = {
  // ...
  template: `<div id="app">
    <div class="movies">
      <h2>Which movie?</h2>
      <router-link to="/dunkirk"></router-link>
      <router-link to="/interstellar"></router-link>
      <router-link to="/the-dark-knight-rises"></router-link>

      <router-view></router-view>
    </div>
  </div>`,
  components: {
    'router-view': View,
    'router-link': Link
  }
};
```

Notice how we've removed the inner text content within each `router-link`. Our `router-link` component will render the appropriate text based on the given prop, with which we'll see shortly.

We'll create the `Link` object that represents `router-link` right above the `App` component:

```
const View = {
  ...
};

const Link = {
  name: 'router-link',
};

const App = {
  ...
};
```

We've established the `router-link` component should always be given a `to` attribute (i.e. prop) that has a value of the target location. We can enforce this prop validation requirement like so:

```
const Link = {
  name: 'router-link',
  props: {
    to: {
      type: String,
      required: true
    }
  }
};
```

If `router-link` is declared without a `to` prop or a `to` prop that is not a `string`, Vue will emit warnings.

Prop validation doesn't have to be enforced, but is often useful in maintaining strict component declarations. You can read more about them in the Vue docs[96].

The `template` of `router-link` will consist of an `<a>` tag with an `@click` handler attribute:

```
const Link = {
  name: 'router-link',
  props: {
    to: {
      type: String,
      required: true
    }
  },
  template: `<a @click="navigate" :href="to">{{ to }}</a>`,
};
```

When a user clicks a traditional `<a>` tag, the browser uses `href` to determine the next location to visit. In the `<a>` tag of `router-link`, we've bound the `href` attribute to the value of the `to` prop. Though this wouldn't be used in navigation of our app, this enables a user to hover over our links and see where they lead:

[96]https://vuejs.org/v2/guide/components.html#Prop-Validation

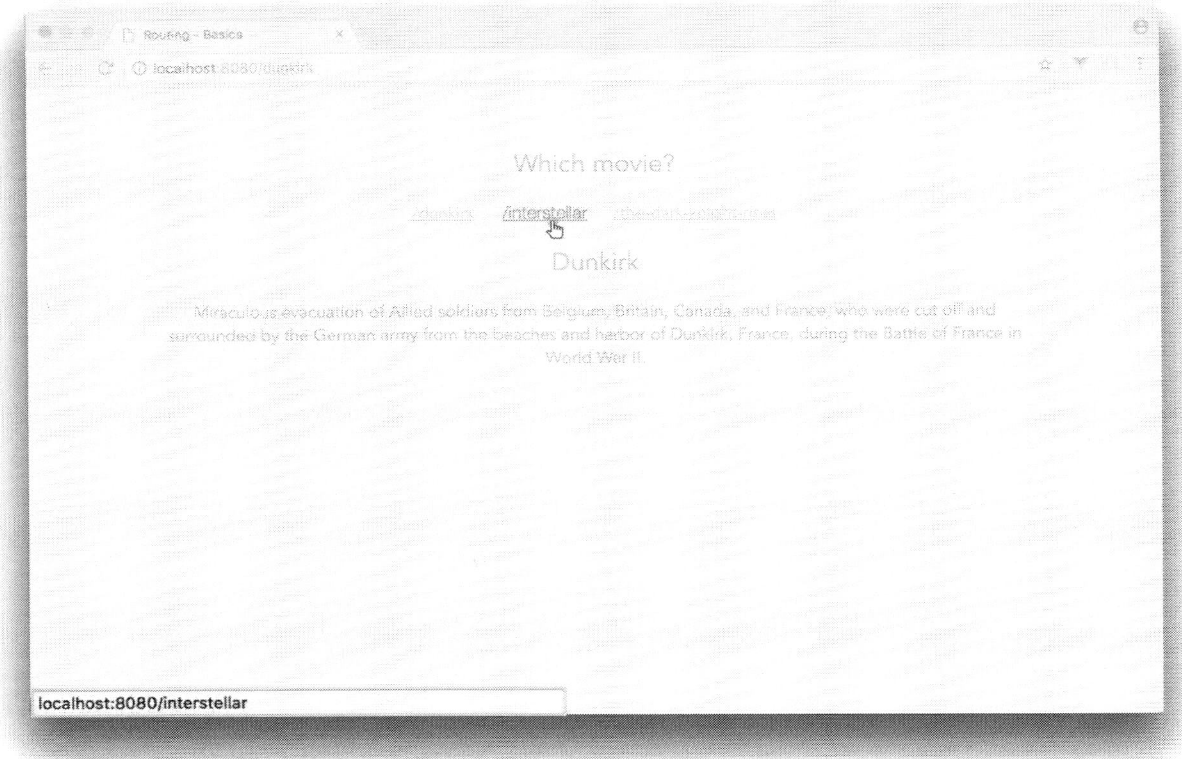

Within the <a> tag, we've also bound the value of the `to` prop to the element content text with `{{ to }}`. This is to simply render the `router-link` element text as to whatever the target location is. In our case, this will either be - `/dunkirk`, `/interstellar`, or `/the-dark-knight-rises`.

To finalize our `router-link` component, we'll need to create the `navigate()` handler method that navigates the browser to the desired location:

routing/basics/src/app/app-2.js

```
const Link = {
  name: 'router-link',
  props: {
    to: {
      type: [String],
      required: true
    }
  },
  template: `<a @click="navigate" :href="to">{{ to }}</a>`,
  methods: {
    navigate(evt) {
      evt.preventDefault();
```

```
      window.history.pushState(null, null, this.to);
    }
  }
};
```

Recall that the first argument passed to an `@click` handler is always the event object. `navigate()` first calls `preventDefault()` on the event object to prevent the browser from making a web request for the new location. Finally, we're "pushing" the new location onto the browser's history stack with `history.pushState()`.

The `history.pushState()` method takes three arguments

1. a state object to pass serialized state information
2. a title
3. the target URL

In our case, there is no state information that's needed to be passed so we leave the first argument as `null`. Some browsers (e.g. Firefox) currently ignore the second parameter, `title`, hence we've left that as `null` as well.

The target location, the `to` prop, is passed in to the third and last parameter. Since the `to` prop contains the target location in a relative state, it will be resolved relative to the current URL (i.e. in our case, `/dunkirk` will resolve to `http://localhost:8080/dunkirk`).

The MDN Web Docs[97] explains the `pushState()` method, as well as the other browser history methods, in a lot more detail.

If we click any of the links now, we'll notice our browser updates to the correct location without a full page reload. However, our app will not update and render the correct component. This unexpected behaviour happens because **when `router-link` is updating the location of the browser, our Vue app is not alerted of the change**. We'll need to trigger our app (or simply just the `router-view` component) to re-render whenever the location changes.

Though there's a few ways to accomplish this behaviour, we'll do this by using a custom `EventBus`. At the beginning of the file, right after the Vue `import`, let's create an `EventBus` with a new `Vue()` instance:

[97] https://developer.mozilla.org/en-US/docs/Web/API/History_API#The_pushState()_method

routing/basics/src/app/app-3.js

```
const EventBus = new Vue();
```

Chronologically we've talked about custom events and the `EventBus` in Chapter 3: Custom Events.

If you're unfamiliar with the Event Bus and you've started this chapter before covering that chapter, hop over there and come back here when you get a better understanding.

When a link has been clicked, we need to notify the necessary part of the application (i.e. `router-view`) that the user is navigating to a particular route. To do this, we'll create an event emitter in the `navigate()` method of `router-link` with a name of `navigate`:

routing/basics/src/app/app-3.js

```
const Link = {
  // ...
  methods: {
    navigate(evt) {
      evt.preventDefault();
      window.history.pushState(null, null, this.to);
      EventBus.$emit('navigate');
    }
  }
};
```

We can now set the event listener/trigger in the `created()` hook of `router-view`. We'll set the event trigger outside of the `if/else` statement.

This makes the `created()` hook of the `View` constant become:

routing/basics/src/app/app-3.js

```
const View = {
  // ...
  created() {
    if (this.getRouteObject() === undefined) {
      this.currentView = {
        template: `<h2>Not Found :(. Pick a movie from the list!</h2>`
      };
    } else {
      this.currentView = this.getRouteObject().component;
```

```
    }

    // Event listener for link navigation
    EventBus.$on('navigate', () => {
      this.currentView = this.getRouteObject().component;
    });
  },
  // ...
};
```

When the browser's location changes, this listening function will be invoked, re-rendering `router-view` to match against the latest URL!

Try it out

Let's save our updated `app.js` and visit the app in the browser. Notice that the browser doesn't perform any full page loads as we navigate between any of the three routes.

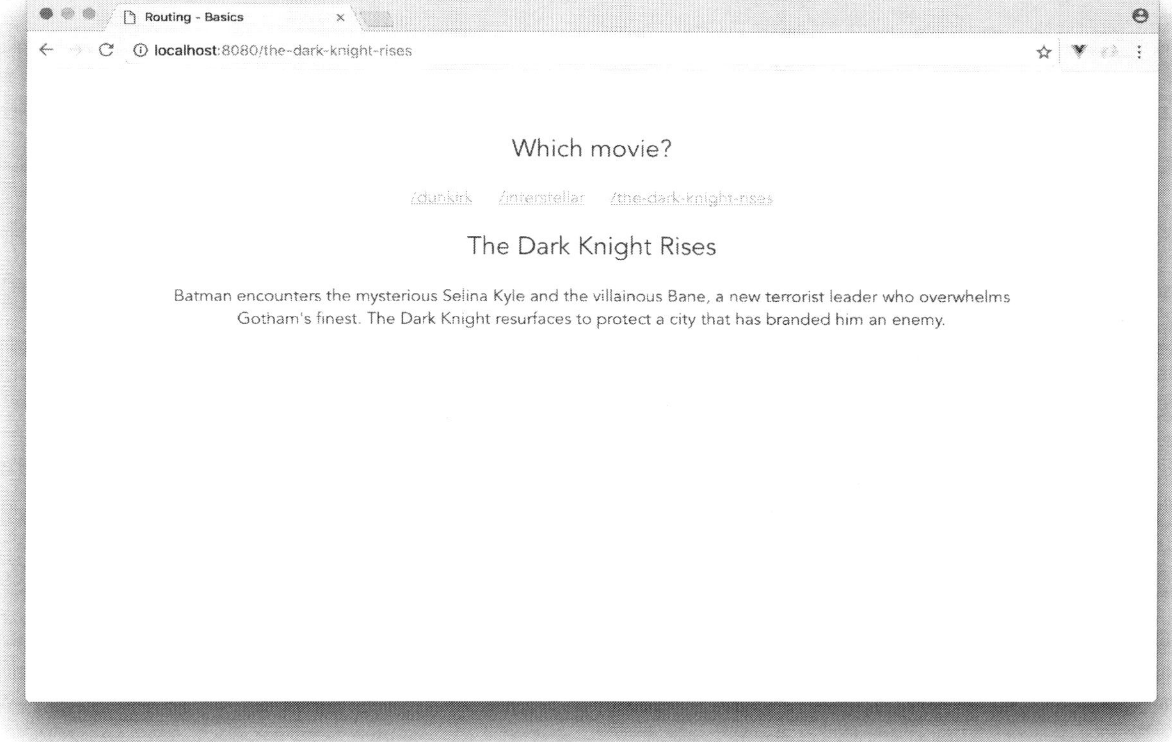

As of now, our app navigates appropriately as we click each of the links. However, if we try to use the browser back/forward buttons to navigate through the browser history, our application will not currently re-render correctly. Although unexpected, this occurs because no event notifier is emitted when the user clicks browser back or browser forward.

To make this work, we'll use the `onpopstate`[98] event handler. The `onpopstate` event is fired each time the active history entry changes. A history change is invoked by clicking on the back or forward buttons (or calling `history.back()` or `history.forward()` programmatically).

Right after our `EventBus` creation, let's set up the `onpopstate` event listener to emit the `navigate` event when a history change is invoked:

routing/basics/src/app/app-3.js

```
window.addEventListener('popstate', () => {
  EventBus.$emit('navigate');
});
```

Our application will now respond appropriately even when the browser navigation buttons are used. Awesome!

Even with the tiny size of our app we can enjoy a noticeable performance improvement. Avoiding a full page load saves hundreds of milliseconds and prevents our app from "blinking" during the page change.

Given this superior user experience now, it's easy to imagine how these benefits scale as the size and complexity of our app does.

Using `vue-router`

Now that our basic router works well, we'll import the components that we want to use from the `vue-router` package and remove the ones we've written so far.

The `vue-router` package is already included in this project's `package.json`.

The first thing we'll do is remove all unnecessary code that `vue-router` will take care of. This involves the `popstate` event listener, the custom `EventBus`, `View`, `Link`, and the `components` property of `App`. In addition, we'll input the necessary text information within each `router-link` since `vue-router` doesn't natively display each link with the text in the `to` prop.

This would make our `app.js` file be laid out like this:

[98] https://developer.mozilla.org/en-US/docs/Web/API/WindowEventHandlers/onpopstate

```
import Vue from 'vue';

const DunkirkBlurb = {
  ...
};

const InterstellarBlurb = {
  ...
};

const TheDarkKnightRisesBlurb = {
  ...
};

const routes = [
  ...
];

const App = {
  name: 'App',
  template: `<div id="app">
    <div class="movies">
      <h2>Which movie?</h2>
      <router-link to="/dunkirk">
        /dunkirk
      </router-link>
      <router-link to="/interstellar">
        /interstellar
      </router-link>
      <router-link to="/the-dark-knight-rises">
        /the-dark-knight-rises
      </router-link>

      <router-view></router-view>
    </div>
  </div>`
};

export default App;
```

Let's add an `import` statement to import the `vue-router` library:

routing/basics/src/app/app-complete.js

```
import Vue from 'vue';
import VueRouter from 'vue-router';
```

Since our application is a Webpack bundled Vue app, the `vue-router` library must be explicitly installed with `Vue.use()`:

routing/basics/src/app/app-complete.js

```
import Vue from 'vue';
import VueRouter from 'vue-router';

Vue.use(VueRouter);
```

In our custom router, our `router-view` component was able to return a 'Not Found' template if the URL pathname didn't match any path existing in the `routes` array. To do this in `vue-router`, all we'll need to do is add the 'Not Found' template to a path of `*` in `routes`:

routing/basics/src/app/app-complete.js

```
const routes = [
  {
    path: '/',
    component: {
      name: 'index-blurb',
      template: `<h2>Pick a Christopher Nolan movie!</h2>`
    }
  },
  {path: '/dunkirk', component: DunkirkBlurb},
  {path: '/interstellar', component: InterstellarBlurb},
  {path: '/the-dark-knight-rises', component: TheDarkKnightRisesBlurb},
  {
    path: '*',
    component: {
      name: 'not-found-blurb',
      template: `<h2>Not Found :(. Pick a movie from the list!</h2>`
    }
  }
];
```

Any route entered in the URL that does not exist will return the 'Not Found' `<h2>` element.

The only thing now left to do is to inject a `router` object to the Vue instance to make our whole app router aware.

The `vue-router` library provides a declaration for creating a router instance, `VueRouter({ routes })`. With our `routes` array already established, we'll create the `router` instance object right after `App`:

```
const router = new VueRouter({
  routes
});
```

`vue-router`'s default mode is `hash`. Hash mode URLs always contain a hash symbol (#) after the hostname. The `hash` mode basically means our application routes will be displayed like this - `http://localhost:8080/#/dunkirk`. The benefit to this often lies with allowing us to have multiple client side routes without having to provide the necessary server side fallbacks.

Traditionally, hash links are how web browsers navigate on a page because everything after the hash symbol is *never sent to the server.*

Since our application is a simple client-side app and we don't want the hash in our URLs, we can get rid of it. To remove hashes in our URLs, we'll specify the `history` mode property in our router:

```
const router = new VueRouter({
  mode: 'history',
  routes
});
```

Our routes will now be rendered like we've had before - `http://localhost:8080/dunkirk`.

To make the entire app router-aware, we now need to inject the `router` instance object to the Vue instance. First, we'll need to export our `router` from the `src/app/app.js` file:

routing/basics/src/app/app-complete.js

```
export const router = new VueRouter({
  mode: 'history',
  routes
});
```

Then import and inject `router` to the Vue instance in `main.js`:

```
import Vue from 'vue';
import App from './app/app';
import { router } from './app/app';

new Vue({
  el: '#app',
  router,
  render: h => h(App)
});
```

After saving both the `main.js` and `app.js` files, we'll see that everything is still working as it was before we switched to using `vue-router`.

Recap

Though this was a fairly simple introduction, we're now familiar with the main concepts of `vue-router`. We map our components to routes and we let `router-view` control where to render them at a given location. `router-link` gives us the ability to modify the location of the app without a full-page load.

Though the outcome of the simple router we've built matches that of `vue-router`, **`vue-router` is built differently and in a more advanced manner**. For simplicity, we've used the concepts we've already acquired in this book (custom events, lifecycle-hooks, etc.) to demonstrate how a router can dynamically display components based on the URL route.

The actual `vue-router` library ensures browser consistency and introduces incredibly useful routing capabilities with which we'll see in the next section!

Dynamic Route Matching

In this half of the chapter, we'll apply all the fundamentals we've covered to a more complex application. We'll see how `vue-router`'s fundamental components work together inside of a larger app, and explore a few different strategies for programming in its unique component-driven routing paradigm.

The app in this section will be an adaptation/continuation of the shopping cart app built in Chapter 5. The final app will have multiple pages with the main page, `/products`, only listing the list of products that can be purchased. The cart screen will now be placed in a different page - `/cart`. A user will also be able to select a particular product from the product list to see more information of said product - `/product/:id`.

The server that our app communicates with is now protected by a token that requires a login. While not a genuine authentication flow, the setup will give us a feel for how `vue-router` can be used inside of an application that requires users to login.

Though we'll be refreshing certain concepts in this section, the majority of points involving Vuex and server persistence will not be repeated for the sake of brevity. Feel free to hop back to Chapter 5 anytime you may need to get a quick refresher!

The completed app

The code for this section is inside `routing/shopping_cart`. From the root of the book's code folder, navigate to that directory:

```
$ cd routing/shopping_cart
```

Let's take a look at this project's structure:

```
$ ls
README.md
build/
config/
index.html
node_modules/
package.json
public/
server-cart-data.json
server-product-data.json
server.js
src/
```

This project's structure is identical to the shopping cart app built in Chapter 5. When in development, we boot two servers: `server.js` and the Webpack development server.

- The Webpack development server serves our Vue app.
- Our Vue app interfaces with `server.js` to fetch data about product items and cart items. `server.js` in turn communicates with the two `json` files, `server-cart-data.json` and `server-product-data.json`, to get and persist data.

Communication diagram

Let's install the dependencies:

```
$ npm i
```

We can boot the app with `npm run start` in the top-level directory. This uses `concurrently`[99] to boot both servers simultaneously:

```
$ npm run start
```

We'll be able to find the app at `http://localhost:8080` in the browser.

The app will prompt you with a login button. If we click login to "log in", we'll notice we're not prompted for a username or password.

After logging in, we can see a list of product items in the main page:

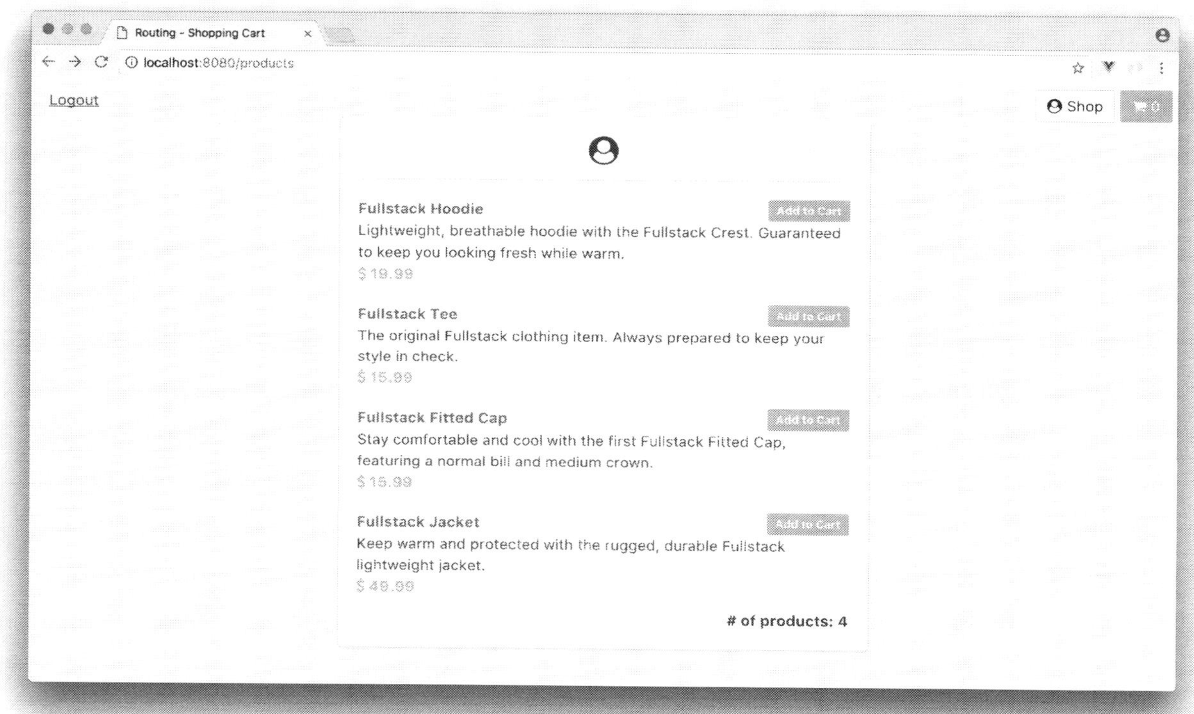

Clicking on one of these products directs us to a new screen that displays further details of the product. Furthermore, the URL of the app is updated:

[99] https://github.com/kimmobrunfeldt/concurrently

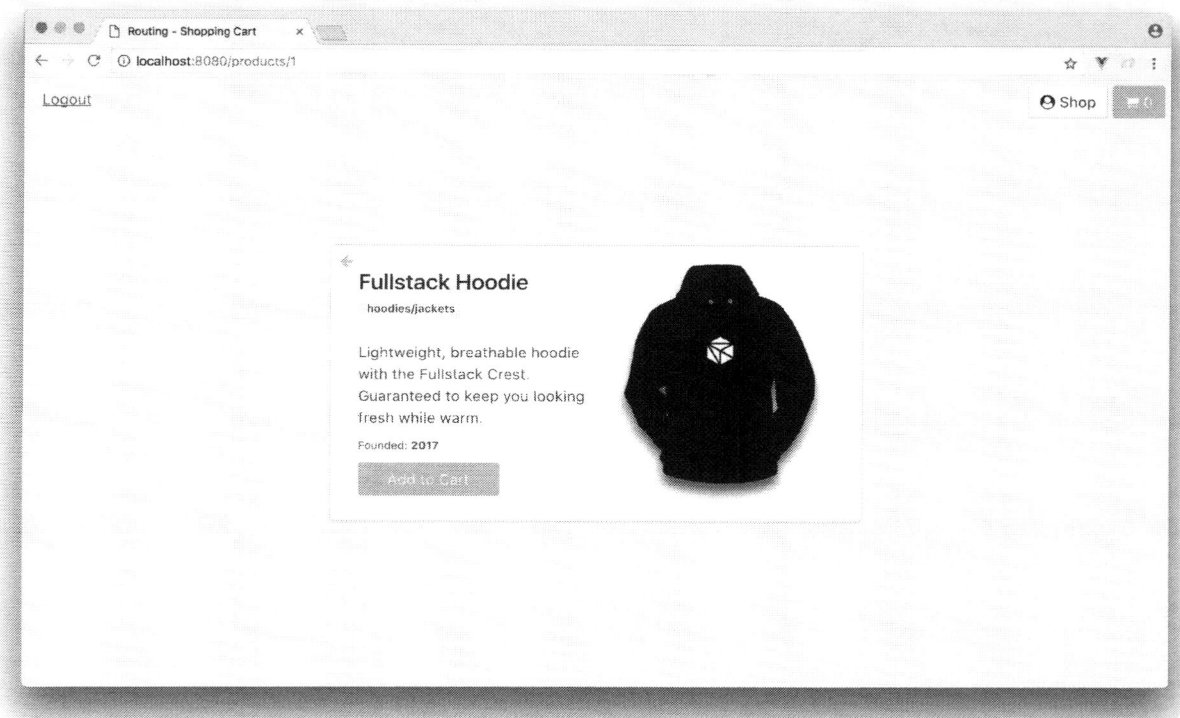

The URL follows the scheme `/products/:id` where `:id` is the **dynamic part** of the URL.

Clicking the "Add to Cart" button in this screen will add the product and direct us to the cart page at `/cart`:

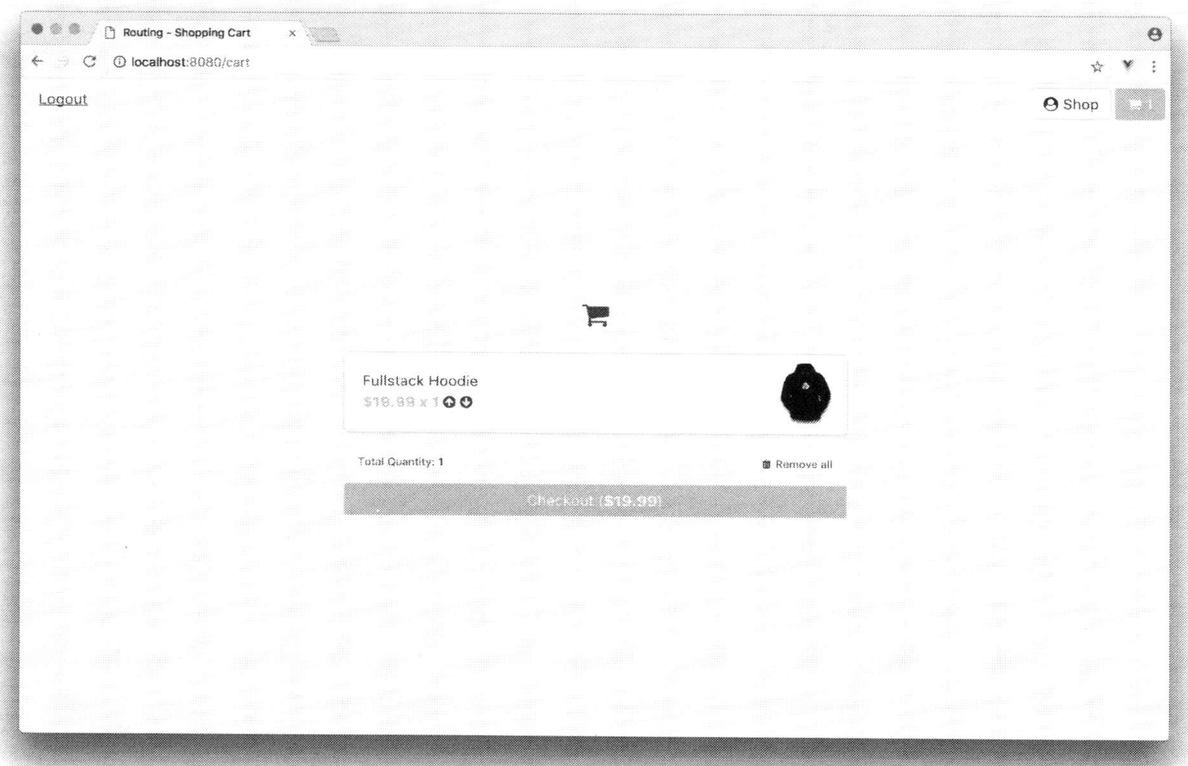

At any location, clicking the "Logout" button in the top left will redirect us to the login page at `/login`. If we try to manually navigate back to `/products` or `/cart` in the logged out state by typing that address into the URL bar, we are prevented from reaching that page. Instead, we are redirected back to `/login`.

Before digging into the Vue app, let's take a look at the updated server API for this section.

The Server API

`POST /login`

The server provides an endpoint for retrieving an API token, `/login`. This token is required for *retrieving* information on both endpoints, `/products` and `/cart`.

Unlike a real-world login endpoint, the `/login` endpoint does not require a user name or a password. `server.js` will always return a hard-coded API token when this endpoint is requested. That hard-coded token is a variable inside `server.js`:

routing/shopping_cart/server.js

```
// A fake API token our server validates
const API_TOKEN = 'D6W69PRgCoDKgHZGJmRUNA';
```

To test this endpoint yourself, with the server running you can use curl to make a POST request to that endpoint:

```
$ curl -X POST http://localhost:3000/login
{
  "success": true,
  "token": "D6W69PRgCoDKgHZGJmRUNA"
}
```

The Vue app stores this API token in `localStorage`. Our app will include this token in the `GET /products` and `GET /cart` requests to the server. Clicking the "Logout" button in the app removes the token from `localStorage`. The user will have to "login" again to access the app.

> In real-world applications, an authentication token is often implemented to a majority (if not all) of API requests to a server. In this application, we'll only implement authentication to the `/GET` calls.

Security and client-side API tokens

Security on the web is a huge topic and managing client-side API tokens is a delicate task. To build a truly secure web application, it's important to understand the intricacies of the topic. Unfortunately, it's far too easy to miss subtle practices which can end up leaving giant security holes in your implementation.

While using `localStorage` to store client-side API tokens works fine for hobby projects, there are significant risks. Your users' API tokens are exposed to cross-site scripting attacks. And tokens stored in `localStorage` impose no requirement on their safe transfer. If someone on your development team accidentally inserts code that makes requests over `http` as opposed to `https`, your tokens will be transferred over the wire exposed.

As a developer, you are obligated to be careful and deliberate when users entrust you with sensitive data. There are strategies you can use to protect your app and your users, like using JSON Web Tokens (JWTs) or cookies or both. Should you find yourself in this fortunate position, take the necessary time to carefully research and implement your token management solution.

`GET /products`

The `/products` endpoint returns a list of all product items from the `server-product-data.json` file.

The first thing to recognize is the product data within the `json` file now has additional data properties like `product_type`, `image_tag`, and `created_at` that didn't exist in Chapter 5:

```
{
  "id": 1,
  "title": "Fullstack Hoodie",
  "description": "Lightweight, breathable hoodie with the Fullstack Crest...",
  "product_type": "hoodies/jackets",
  "image_tag": "hoodie.png",
  "created_at": 2017,
  "price": 19.99
},
```

The `/products` endpoint now also expects the API token to be included as the query param `token`:

```
/products?token=<token>
```

Here's an example of querying the `/products` endpoint on the browser:

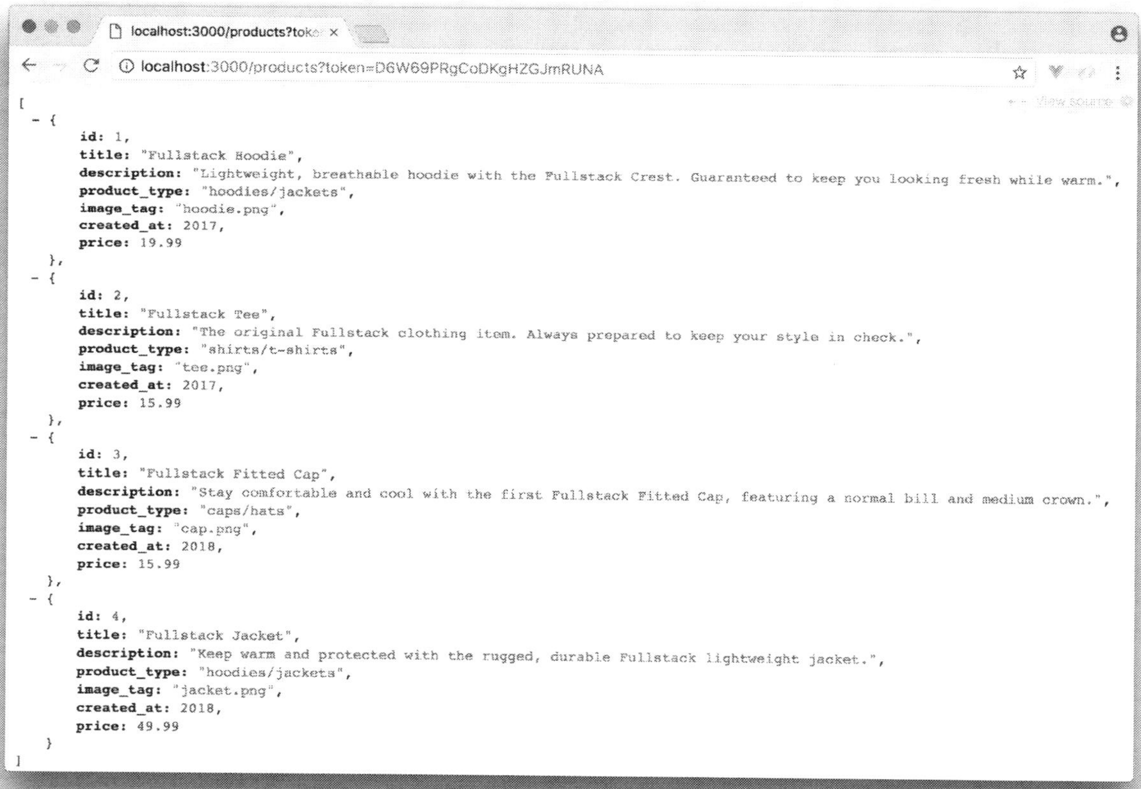

Without the token, an error object will return stating no token is present:

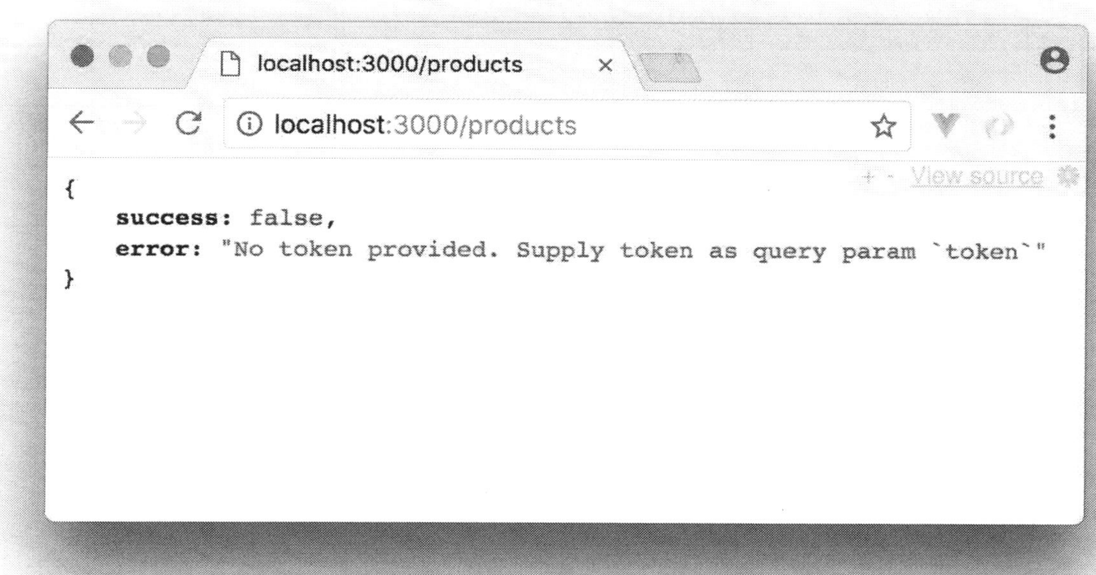

We're using the JSONView[100] Chrome extension to "humanize" the raw JSON on the browser, for easier readability.

GET /cart

The `/carts` endpoint works similarly to `/products` by expecting an API token param as well.

POST /cart, /cart/delete, and /cart/delete/all

The `POST` calls have remain unchanged from Chapter 5 and are as follows:

`POST /cart`: Inserts new item object to the cart. If the cart item already exists, this call will increment the quantity of the existing cart item by 1.

`POST /cart/delete`: Maps through the cart store and decrements the quantity of the cart item with the matching `id` by 1. If the quantity of that item is equal to 1 when the call is made, the cart item object is removed.

`POST /cart/delete/all`: Removes all items in the cart.

Starting point of the app

We'll be writing all the code for the rest of this chapter in `routing/shopping_cart/src`. Let's survey the directories within `src/`:

[100] https://chrome.google.com/webstore/detail/jsonview/chklaanhfefbnpoihckbnefhakgolnmc

```
$ ls src/
app/
app-1/
app-2/
app-3/
app-complete/
main.js
```

`app/` constitutes the shopping cart application in the completed state from Chapter 5 and will be the starting point of this section.

`app-complete/` denotes the completed application for this section with each significant step we take along the way included in `app-1/`, `app-2/` and `app-3/`.

Before we dive in to `app/`, we'll first take a look at the `main.js` file:

main.js

routing/shopping_cart/src/main.js

```
import Vue from 'vue';
import App from './app-complete/App.vue';
import store from './app-complete/store';
import router from './app-complete/router';

new Vue({
  el: '#app',
  store,
  router,
  render: h => h(App)
});
```

`main.js` imports the necessary modules of the application (`store`, `router`), wires it to the Vue instance that's mounted to `#app`, and renders the `App` component from the `app-complete/` directory.

To not reference `app-complete` anymore, let's change the import of `App` and `store` from `./app-complete/` to `./app/`. Since a `router` module doesn't currently exist in `app/`, we'll remove it for now. Our updated `main.js` file becomes:

```
import Vue from 'vue';
import App from './app/App.vue';
import store from './app/store';

new Vue({
  el: '#app',
  store,
  render: h => h(App)
});
```

app/

Surveying the folders within `app/`, we'll notice a new `assets/` folder has been introduced:

```
$ ls src/app/
assets/
components/
store/
App.vue
```

`assets/` holds the product images, in `.png` format, with which we'll be using in our app shortly.

The rest of the application is exactly as it was laid out in Chapter 5. Here's a quick refresher:

- `components/` host the components of the application
  - `components/` is broken down to the `cart/` and `product/` domain. Each domain has a `List.vue` component and a `ListItem.vue` component.
  - Components *get* information from the store with the help of getters.
  - Components *dispatch* relevant actions to the store to manipulate store state.
- `store/` hosts the Vuex store of the application
  - The Vuex store is broken into modules for each domain, `cart/` and `product/`, for easier maintainability.
  - Each module consists of `state`, `mutations`, `actions`, and `getters`.
- `App.vue` is the root level parent component of the application

Ensuring that we've saved the `main.js` file after our initial change and that our server is still running, we'll head to `http://localhost:8080/` to see our application in its starting point:

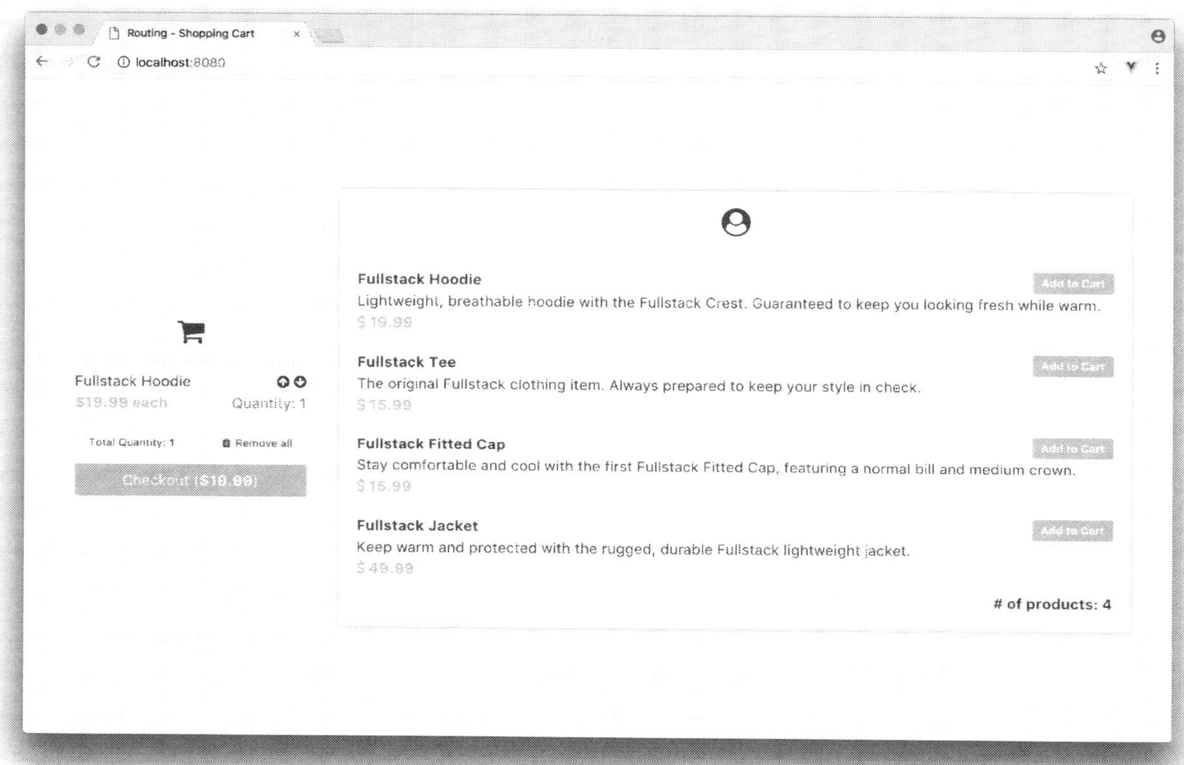

Functionality works as intended and we're able to add and remove items from and to the cart. We can now begin scaling our application with `vue-router`.

Integrating `vue-router`

The `vue-router` package is already included in this project's `package.json`. Like we saw in the first section, we need to explicitly install it with `Vue.use(vue-router)` and integrate it to the Vue instance.

As an application grows, the number of routes and router configurations often grow to an extent to warrant having the application router within its own file (or folder). To facilitate this, we'll create a `router/` directory that contains a single `index.js` file:

In `src/app`:

```
$ ls src/app/
assets/
components/
router/
store/
App.vue
```

And in `src/app/router`:

```
$ ls src/app/router/
index.js
```

In `router/index.js`, let's import the `vue` and `vue-router` libraries:

routing/shopping_cart/src/app-1/router/index.js

```
import Vue from 'vue';
import VueRouter from 'vue-router';
```

Since our router will map routes to components, we'll have to import the two components, `CartList` and `ProductList` that need to be mapped:

routing/shopping_cart/src/app-1/router/index.js

```
import Vue from 'vue';
import VueRouter from 'vue-router';
import CartList from '../components/cart/CartList.vue';
import ProductList from '../components/product/ProductList.vue';
```

Right after the `import` declarations, we'll call `Vue.use(vue-router)` to use the `vue-router` plugin:

routing/shopping_cart/src/app-1/router/index.js

```
Vue.use(VueRouter);
```

As we saw in the first section of the chapter, a `vue-router` instance is created with `new VueRouter({ routes })` with `routes` being the array that maps the components to their route paths. Let's start creating the router by specifying the router should be in `history` mode (i.e. no hashes in the URL). We'll set this router instance to a `const` variable named `router`:

```
const router = new VueRouter({
  mode: 'history',
  routes: []
});
```

We'll map the url path `/products` to the `ProductList` component and `/cart` to the `CartList` component. This indicates that we want `ProductList` and `CartList` to only render when we visit the app at `/products` and `/cart` respectively:

```
const router = new VueRouter({
  mode: 'history',
  routes: [
    {
      path: '/products',
      component: ProductList
    },
    {
      path: '/cart',
      component: CartList
    }
  ]
});
```

In this instance, the only two routes in our application will be `/products` and `/cart`. Since the root route (/) is usually the main route users first use to visit an application, let's specify a redirect from `/` to `/products` should this happen:

```
const router = new VueRouter({
  mode: 'history',
  routes: [
    {
      path: '/products',
      component: ProductList
    },
    {
      path: '/cart',
      component: CartList
    },
    {
      path: '/',
      redirect: '/products'
    }
```

```
  ]
});
```

This redirect specifies that when the user visits the / path in their browser, he/she will be *redirected* to /products.

> In vue-router a **redirect** is different than an **alias**. A **redirect** changes the URL path *and* redirects the user to the target path. An **alias** redirects the user *but* keeps the URL to what the original path was intended for.

It's often good to have a 404 error (or a 'not found') page that's displayed to the user when the user attempts to access a route that doesn't map to any of the component paths of the router. Let's create a simple component file called NotFound.vue in the components/ folder for this purpose:

```
$ ls src/app/components/
cart/
product/
NotFound.vue
```

The NotFound component would be a simple template that displays a title and some text:

routing/shopping_cart/src/app-1/components/NotFound.vue

```
<template>
  <div class="has-text-centered">
    <h1 class="title">Sorry. Page Not Found :(</h1>
    <p>Use the navigation links above to navigate between the product and
      cart screens.</p>
  </div>
</template>

<script>
export default {
  name: 'NotFound',
}
</script>

<style scoped>
</style>
```

We can now import the NotFound component in the router/index.js file:

routing/shopping_cart/src/app-1/router/index.js

```
import NotFound from '../components/NotFound.vue';
```

And map it to path `*`. We'll also finally export the `router` from the file:

routing/shopping_cart/src/app-1/router/index.js

```
const router = new VueRouter({
  mode: 'history',
  routes: [
    {
      path: '/products',
      component: ProductList
    },
    {
      path: '/cart',
      component: CartList
    },
    {
      path: '/',
      redirect: '/products'
    },
    {
      path: '*',
      component: NotFound
    }
  ]
});

export default router;
```

We can now inject the `router` object to the Vue instance to make our whole app router aware. In `src/main.js`, we'll import the newly created router and pass it within the already declared Vue instance:

```
import Vue from 'vue';
import App from './app/App.vue';
import store from './app/store';
import router from './app/router'; // importing router

new Vue({
  el: '#app',
  store,
  router, // injecting router
  render: h => h(App)
});
```

At this moment, our application should load successfully but will appear to remain unchanged. This is because we've yet to use `vue-router`'s `router-view` component in the template to dictate which component should render at a given location.

In the `template` of the parent component `App.vue`, we'll remove the use of the `<CartList>` and `<ProductList>` elements and simply use `<router-view>`. Since we're not directly referencing the components anymore, we can also remove the import declaration and `components` property of the component. This would make the `<template>` and `<script>` elements of `App.vue` be changed to:

```
<template>
  <div id="app">
    <div class="container">
      <div class="columns">
        <div class="column is-6 column--align-center">
          <router-view></router-view>
        </div>
      </div>
    </div>
  </div>
</template>

<script>
export default {
  name: 'App'
}
</script>
```

As always, the `<div>` elements and CSS classes throughout the app are present just for structure and styling. As in other projects, this app uses Bulma[101].

[101]https://bulma.io/

At this moment, when we launch the app with the root route `/`, we'll be redirected to `/products` which is responsible in displaying the product list (i.e. `ProductList`).

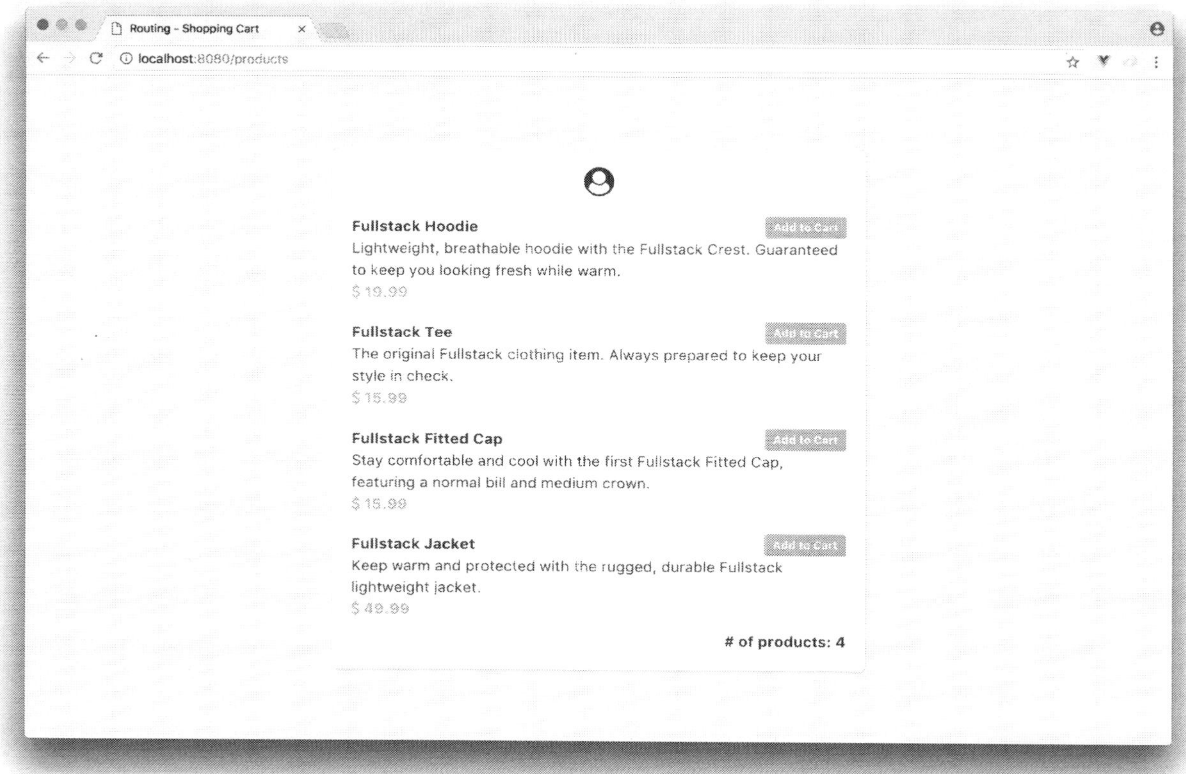

If we change the URL path to `/cart`, we'll visit the cart screen (`CartList`):

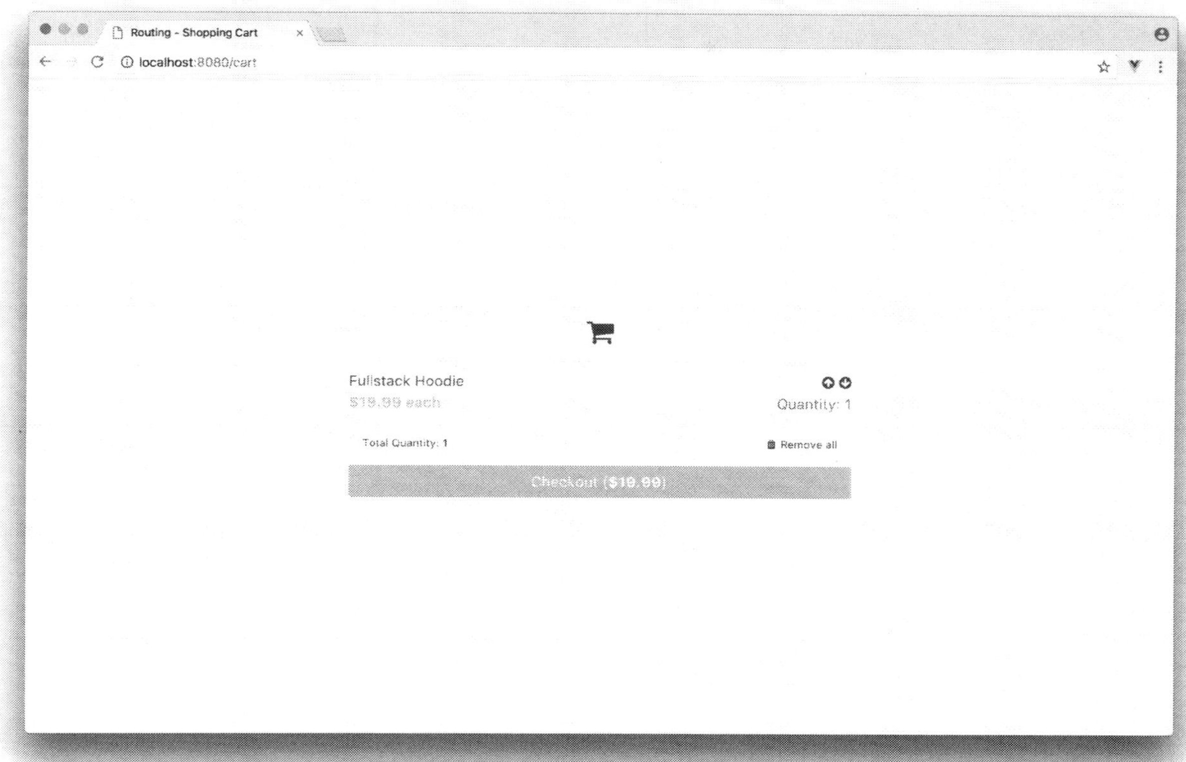

Finally, if we enter a random address in the URL bar, we're presented with the `NotFound` component.

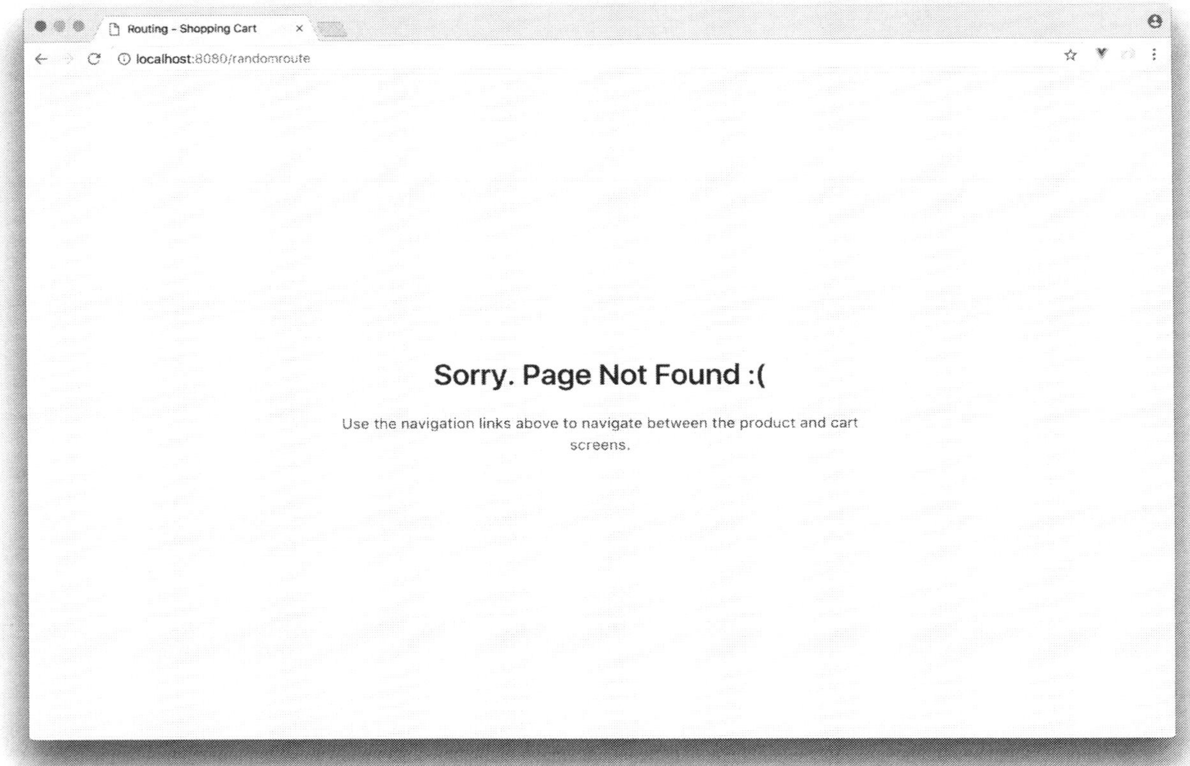

Currently the user has no means in navigating between the desired components apart from entering the relevant route paths in the URL. To address this, we'll create two `<router-link>` elements in `App.vue`. These `<router-link>` elements would allow the user to navigate to either `/products` or `/cart`:

routing/shopping_cart/src/app-1/App.vue

```
<template>
  <div id="app">
    <div class="navigation-buttons">
      <div class="is-pulled-right">
        <router-link to="/products" class="button">
          <i class="fa fa-user-circle"></i><span>Shop</span>
        </router-link>
        <router-link to="/cart" class="button is-primary">
          <i class="fa fa-shopping-cart"></i><span>{{ cartQuantity }}</span>
        </router-link>
      </div>
    </div>
    <div class="container">
```

```
      <div class="columns">
        <div class="column is-6 column--align-center">
          <router-view></router-view>
        </div>
      </div>
    </div>
  </div>
</template>
```

The first <router-link> element we've specified displays a button with a `fa-user-circle` icon and the text of "Shop".

The second <router-link> element displays a cart icon and the value of a `cartQuantity` property. The aim of this `cartQuantity` is to show the number of products the user currently has in their cart without having the need to navigate to the cart screen.

Currently, the `cartQuantity` property in the <router-link to="/cart"></router-link> element will generate an error since `cartQuantity` has not been defined in the `App` component. We already have the number of items persisted to the cart as a `cartQuantity getter` in our Vuex store. We can use Vuex's `mapGetters` helper to map the getter to a component property of the same name:

We'll update the <script> element of `App` to reflect this:

```
<script>
import { mapGetters } from 'vuex';

export default {
  name: 'App',
  computed: {
    ...mapGetters([
      'cartQuantity'
    ]),
  }
}
</script>
```

This will work as intended which will remove the error generated in our app. However, if we take a look at our application now, we'll notice something peculiar. The `cartQuantity` value in the nav-bar button will always be zero (and not reflect the actual number of cart items) until we navigate to the cart screen. This "bug" occurs because the call to the server to get a list of cart items (and update our Vuex state) doesn't occur only *until the `CartList` component is created*:

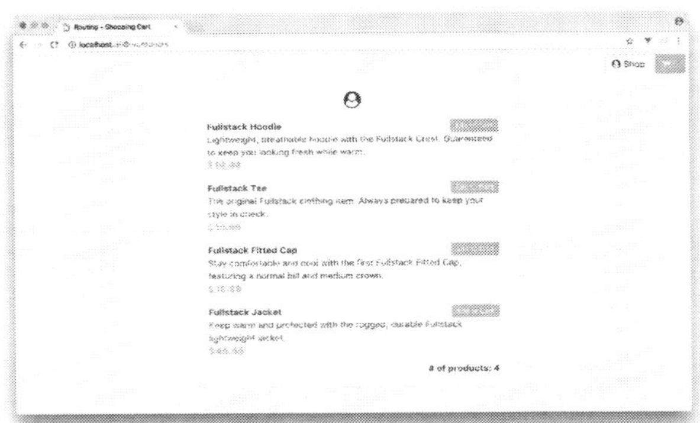

dispatch('getCartItems') **is not** called

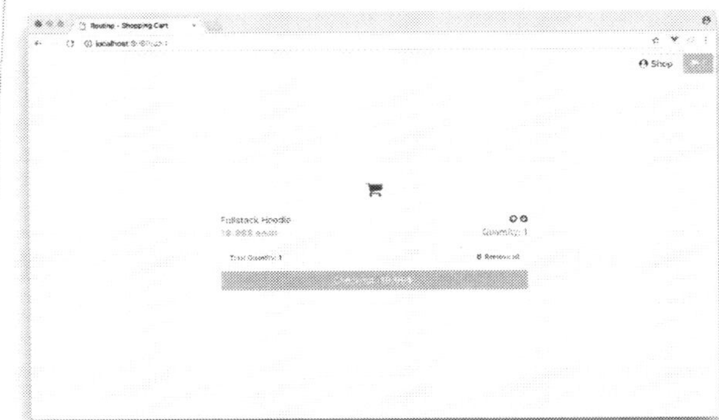

dispatch('getCartItems') **is** called

We can see that this functionality is reflected in the `dispatch('getCartItems')` call that only gets called in the `created()` hook of the `CartList` component. Prior to integrating `vue-router` in our application, this worked fine because it made sense to contain the call to retrieve the list of cart items from the server within the component that it mattered to - `CartList`.

With `vue-router` however and how our current application is arranged, the `<router-view>` element in the parent `App` dictates which component to render - `ProductList` or `CartList`. We need to move the `dispatch('getCartItems')` call from the `created()` hook of the `CartList` component to the root `App` component.

In the `CartList.vue` file, removing the `created()` hook will result in our `<script>` element looking like this:

routing/shopping_cart/src/app-1/components/cart/CartList.vue

```
<script>
import { mapGetters, mapActions } from 'vuex';
import CartListItem from './CartListItem';

export default {
  name: 'CartList',
  computed: {
    ...mapGetters([
      'cartItems',
      'cartTotal',
      'cartQuantity'
    ])
  },
  methods: {
    ...mapActions([
      'removeAllCartItems'
    ])
```

```
  },
  components: {
    CartListItem
  }
}
</script>
```

The <script> of `App` should be updated to now have the `dispatch('getCartItems')` in *its* `created()` hook:

```
<script>
import { mapGetters } from 'vuex';

export default {
  name: 'App',
  computed: {
    ...mapGetters([
      'cartQuantity'
    ]),
  },
  created() {
    this.$store.dispatch('getCartItems');
  }
}
</script>
```

The cart icon in the navigation bar will now reflect the appropriate number of items in the cart regardless of which route we're in.

Similarly, `ProductList` has the `dispatch('getProductItems')` call in its created hook. To keep things consistent, we'll remove it from `ProductList` and move it to `App` as well.

Our `ProductList` <script> becomes:

routing/shopping_cart/src/app-1/components/product/ProductList.vue

```
<script>
import { mapGetters } from 'vuex';
import ProductListItem from './ProductListItem';

export default {
  name: 'ProductList',
  computed: {
    ...mapGetters([
      'productItems'
    ])
  },
  components: {
    ProductListItem
  }
}
</script>
```

The `created()` method of `App` will now also dispatch the action that retrieves the list of products items from the server and updates the Vuex state (`getProductItems`):

routing/shopping_cart/src/app-1/App.vue

```
<script>
import { mapGetters } from 'vuex';

export default {
  name: 'App',
  computed: {
    ...mapGetters([
      'cartQuantity'
    ]),
  },
  created() {
    this.$store.dispatch('getCartItems');
    this.$store.dispatch('getProductItems');
  }
}
</script>
```

Awesome. Before we move onwards to creating dynamic routes for every product item, let's update the UI of each cart list item. *This isn't a hard requirement but more of a style change.*

Since the `CartListItem` component is responsible in the display of every cart item, let's change its template. In the `CartListItem.vue` file, we'll update the `<template>` to the following:

```
<template>
  <div class="box">
    <div class="cart-item__details">
      <p class="is-inline">{{ cartItem.title }}</p>
      <div>
        <span class="cart-item--price has-text-primary has-text-weight-bold">
          {{ cartItem.price }}$ x {{ cartItem.quantity }}
        </span>
        <span>
          <i @click="addCartItem(cartItem)"
            class="fa fa-arrow-circle-up cart-item__modify"></i>
          <i @click="removeCartItem(cartItem)"
            class="fa fa-arrow-circle-down cart-item__modify"></i>
        </span>
      </div>
    </div>
  </div>
</template>
```

Each cart list item will currently look like this:

Single `CartListItem`

Since it looks a little bare, let's introduce an image of the cart item in the right hand side of the element. As we've mentioned earlier, the `assets/` directory within `app/` hosts the image of each product. In addition, each product has an `image_tag` property which we'll use to help us map every product to the right image.

In `vue-cli` Webpack projects, assets are usually handled in two ways:

- Keeping asset files in a `static/` folder that is *not processed by Webpack* and must be referenced using *absolute* paths.
- Keeping asset files within the `src/` folder and referenced using *relative* paths.

Since our assets are within `src/` we'll be going with the second approach. In the `<template>` of `CartListItem`, let's introduce a new `<div>` element with `class="cart-item__image"` that's responsible in displaying a single `<img>` tag. As a starting point, we'll set the `<img>` `src` to the image of the Fullstack Hoodie:

```
<template>
  <div class="box">
    <div class="cart-item__details">
      ...
    </div>
    <div class="cart-item__image">
      <img src="../../assets/hoodie.png" />
    </div>
  </div>
</template>
```

With this, our `CartListItem` will always display the `hoodie.png` image regardless of what item it is:

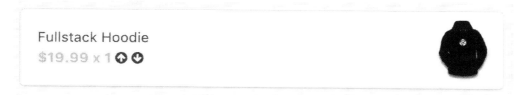

Since we need to dynamically bind the image `src` to the right item, our first instinct would be to do something like this:

```
<img :src="`../../assets/${cartItem.image_tag}`" />
```

Even though this makes perfect sense, **this wouldn't work**. This limitation is due to how Webpack handles static assets. If we employ Javascript (we're doing that with ES6 template literals here) to get an asset path, we'll need to use `require` like this: `require('./relative/path/to/file.png')`. This `require` call gets processed by `file-loader` appropriately and returns the correct Webpack resolved URL.

To employ this, our `<img>` element becomes:

```
<img :src="require(`../../assets/${cartItem.image_tag}`)" />
```

Our `CartListItem` now displays the correct image for each product item added to the cart:

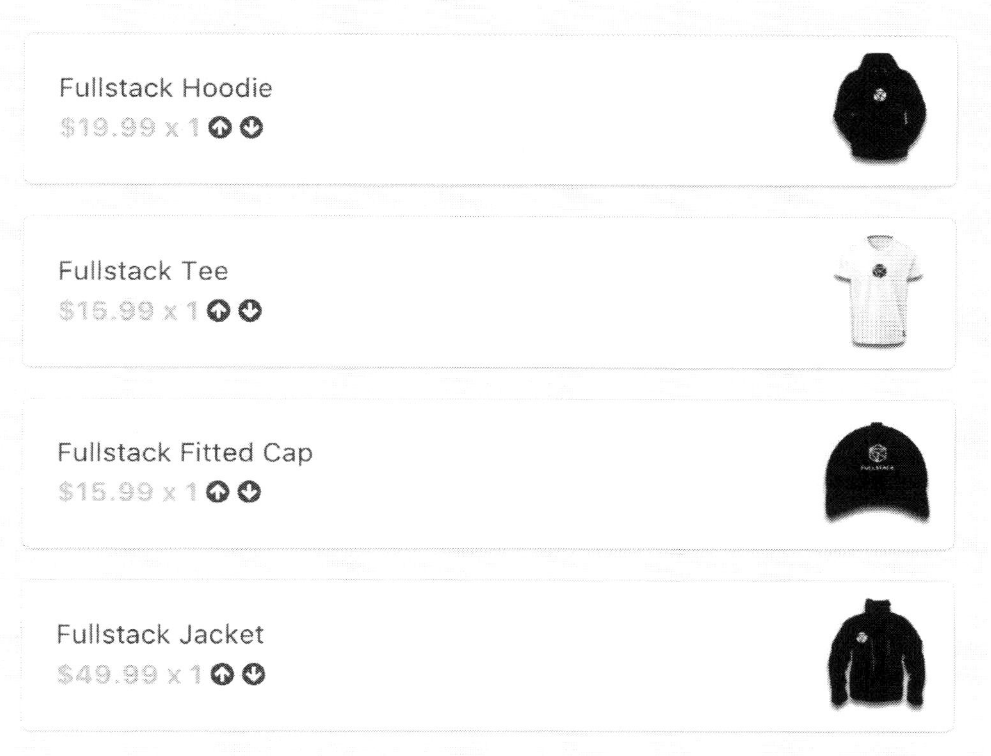

`CartListItem` for all product items

Instead of `require`, we could `import` the images directly to our component and bind it as a data value for it to be used in the template. In both cases, the images are treated as modules with which Webpack can return the correct asset path.

For more reading on how Webpack handles static assets in a Vue-Webpack project, check out the Handling Static Assets[102] section of the vuejs-template docs.

Our app is getting somewhere! We'll introduce dynamic routes for each product item next.

Dynamic Routing

As we saw earlier, our app will have a new screen responsible in displaying all details of a product. To navigate to this screen, a user would have to click the title of a product in the product list *or* navigate to a URL path of `/products/:id` where `id` is the product identifier.

Let's first create a starting point for a new component labelled `ProductItem`. We'll create this component in a `ProductItem.vue` file within the `components/product/` folder:

[102]https://vuejs-templates.github.io/webpack/static.html

```
ls src/components/product
ProductItem.vue
ProductList.vue
ProductListItem.vue
```

Though they are similarly named - `ProductItem` is a “parent” component that `<router-view>` will display depending on the route. `ProductListItem` is the child item `ProductList` iterates over.

Let’s populate the `ProductItem.vue` file with some initial code:

```
<template>
  <section id="product-item" class="box">
    <div class="product-item__details">
      Product Item
    </div>
    <div class="product-item__image">
    </div>
  </section>
</template>

<script>
export default {
  name: 'ProductItem'
}
</script>

<style scoped>
#product-item {
  display: flex;
  width: 100%;
  position: relative;
}

.return-icon {
  position: absolute;
  top: 5px;
  left: 10px;
  color: #00d1b2;
  cursor: pointer;
}
```

```
.product-item__details {
  max-width: 50%;
  padding-left: 10px;

  display: flex;
  flex-direction: column;
  justify-content: center;
}

.product-item__image {
  display: flex;
  flex-direction: column;
  justify-content: center;
}

.product-item__description {
  padding-bottom: 10px;
}

.product-item__created_at {
  font-size: 12px;
  padding-bottom: 10px;
}

.product-item__button {
  max-width: 150px;
}
</style>
```

`ProductItem` is a simple template as of now. Before we continue updating it, let's set up the route path and link that will allow us to navigate to this component.

In `router/index.js`, let's import `ProductItem`:

routing/shopping_cart/src/app-2/router/index.js

```
import ProductItem from '../components/product/ProductItem.vue';
```

We can now specify a new route path for `ProductItem`. Since we want this component to render for all product items *but* with different product ids, we need to create a **dynamic route path**:

```
routes: [
  ...,
  {
    path: '/products/:id',
    component: ProductItem
  },
  ...
]
```

Where we place the route path objects in the `routes` array will have no effect in how components get routed.

The path we're matching for `ProductItem` is `/products/:id`. The `:` is how we indicate to `vue-router` that this part of the URL is a **dynamic parameter**.

Keep in mind, **any value** will match this dynamic parameter.

Our end goal is to use the `id` parameter in the URL to display and render the correct product item. The `ProductItem` component will access its route params to obtain the `id`. `vue-router` allows us to use the `$route` object in our component to access params. The other way that's often advised[103] is to instead use `props`.

`vue-router` gives us the ability to use `props` to access URL params dynamically in components. Using `props` is sometimes preferred for easier testing and reusability of components. To enable `props`, we first have to specify `props: true` in our route path object:

```
routes: [
  ...,
  {
    path: '/products/:id',
    component: ProductItem,
    props: true
  },
  ...
]
```

In `ProductItem`, we're now able to access `id` like any other prop that might be given to it. Let's declare the `id` prop in the `<script>` element of `ProductItem`:

[103]https://router.vuejs.org/en/essentials/passing-props.html

```
<script>
export default {
  name: 'ProductItem',
  props: ['id']
}
</script>
```

In the `template` - we'll bind the `id` to text to see if everything will work as intended (i.e. we have access to the `id` URL param):

```
<div class="product-item__details">
  Product Item {{ id }}
</div>
```

If we currently enter an appropriate route that directs us to `ProductItem`, we will see the component rendering as intended *with the id URL param displayed in the view.* The Vue Devtools also tells us the `prop` is accessible within the component:

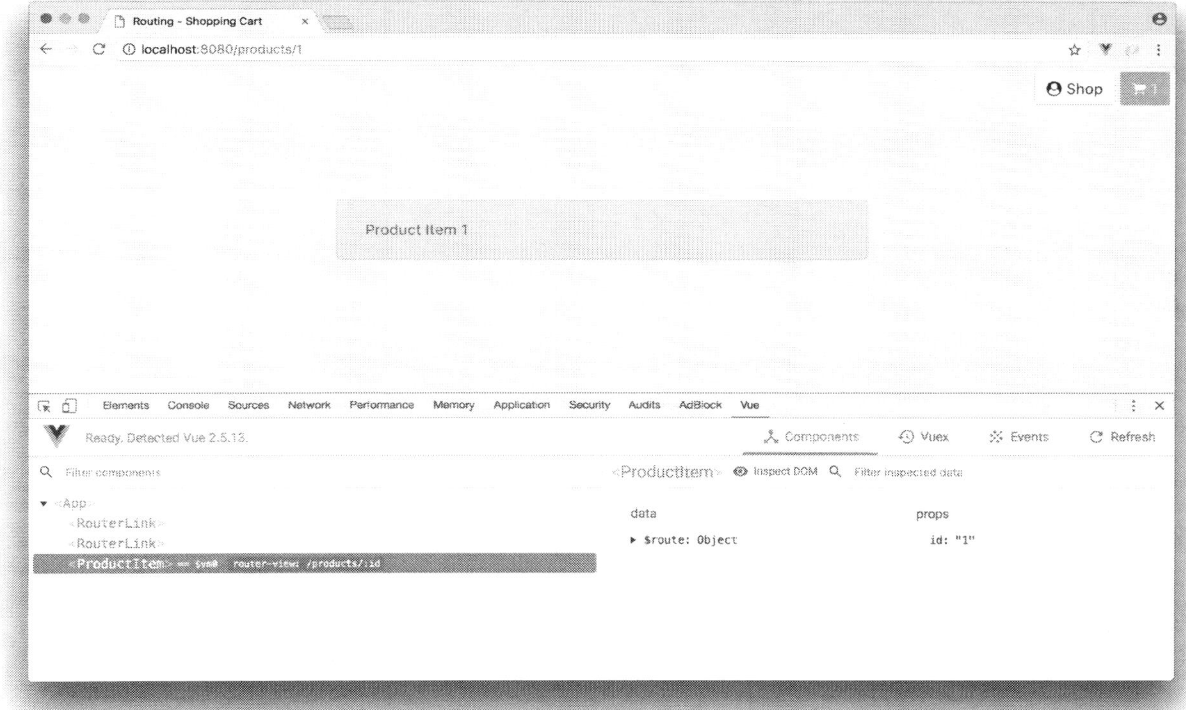

`products/1`

Now that we have the `id` prop within `ProductItem`, we can use it to obtain the appropriate product item object. Though there's a few ways we can get access to the product item, we'll delegate this task to a new `getter` method that returns a product item based on an `id` parameter given.

In the `getters` object of the product module in the Vuex store (i.e. in `store/modules/product/index.js`), let's introduce a new method called `productItemFromId`:

routing/shopping_cart/src/app-2/store/modules/product/index.js

```
const getters = {
  productItems: state => state.productItems,
  productItemFromId: (state) => (id) => {
    return state.productItems.find(productItem => productItem.id === id)
  }
}
```

Getters don't accept payloads except for the `state` object. What we've done above is return a *function* in the getter with which we're able to pass a parameter to! We then use the `Array.find()` method to return the first object that has the matching `id`.

We now need to map a computed property within the `productItem` component to the `productItemFromId` getter method. The Vuex `mapGetters` helper doesn't inherently allow us to pass arguments and often requires some unintuitive syntax to enable this. This is where it'll be easier to map a computed property explicitly like this:

```
<script>
export default {
  name: 'ProductItem',
  props: ['id'],
  computed: {
    productItem () {
      return this.$store.getters.productItemFromId(Number(this.id));
    }
  }
</script>
```

Route param data are often set as strings so we've simply converted the string `id` to a number before passing it to the getter method.

The `productItem` property will now return the appropriate product item object. With this, we can now lay out the template of `ProductItem` to display all the details of the product:

```
<template>
  <section id="product-item" class="box">
    <div class="product-item__details">
      <h1 class="title is-4">
        <p>{{ productItem.title }}</p>
        <span class="tag product-item__tag">{{ productItem.product_type }}</span>
      </h1>
      <p class="product-item__description">{{ productItem.description }}</p>
      <p class="product-item__created_at">
        Founded:
        <span class="has-text-weight-bold">
          {{ productItem.created_at }}
        </span>
      </p>
      <button class="button is-primary product-item__button">Add to Cart</button>
    </div>
    <div class="product-item__image">
      <img :src="require(`../../assets/${productItem.image_tag}`)" />
    </div>
  </section>
</template>
```

We've displayed the majority of product information in the `<div class="product-item__details"></div>` element while displaying the product item image within the `<div class="product-item__image"></div>` element. If we refresh our screen (assuming we're still on a route that displays `productItem`), we'll now see the updated component template:

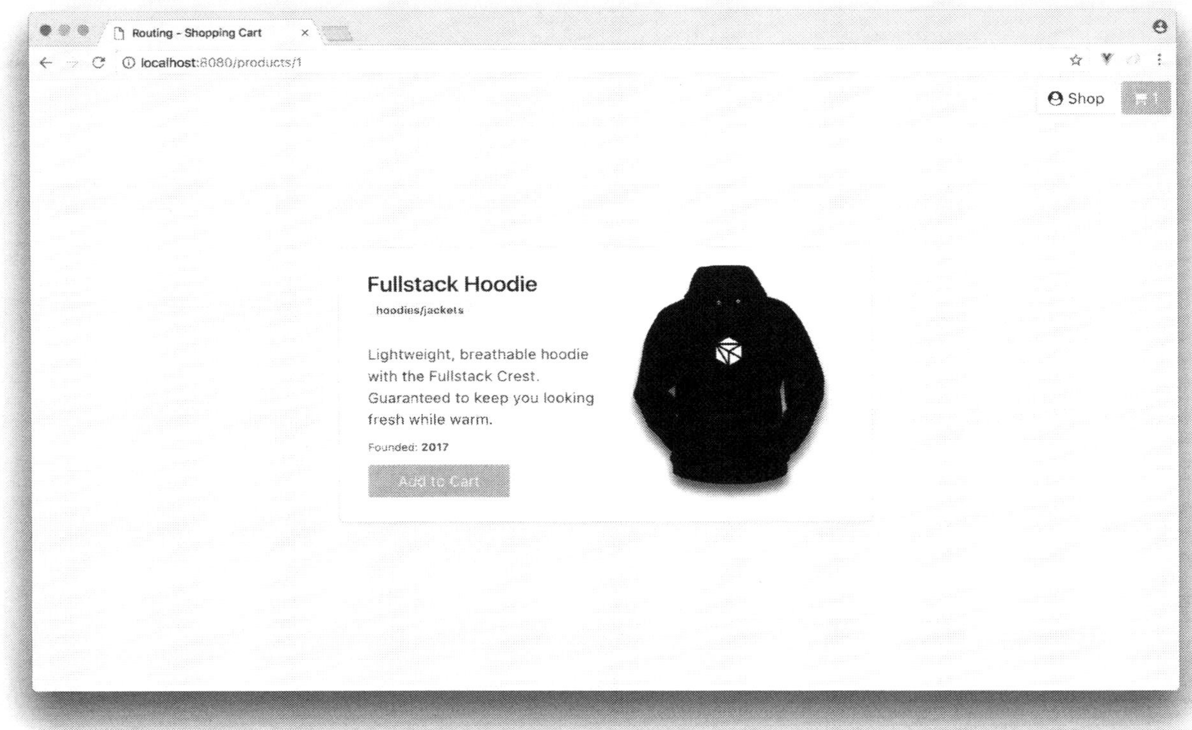

products/1

Our productItem component displays all the appropriate information of the product item. As in most e-commerce websites, we've introduced an "Add to Cart" button on the product item screen. When the user clicks the "Add to Cart" button, we want the item to be added to the cart *and* the user to navigate directly to the cart.

Let's introduce a click listener that calls an addAndGoToCart() method to the "Add to Cart" button. We'll pass the productItem property as a parameter:

routing/shopping_cart/src/app-2/components/product/ProductItem.vue

```
<button
  class="button is-primary product-item__button"
  @click="addAndGoToCart(productItem)">
    Add to Cart
</button>
```

We'll set up a methods property in the component with an addAndGoToCart() method that dispatches the action that involves adding an item to the cart (the addCartItem action) when called:

```
methods: {
  addAndGoToCart(productItem) {
    this.$store.dispatch('addCartItem', productItem);
  }
}
```

We could have used `mapActions` to directly map the component method to the store action to achieve the above result. However, once the item is added to the cart, we *then* need to use the router object to navigate to `/cart`. To navigate within this method, we'll employ **programmatic navigation**[104].

So far we've only used the `<router-link>` element to navigate between routes. `vue-router` allows us to specify navigation programmatically with the application wide `$router` object. A simple navigation to a URL with:

```
<router-link to="/url"></router-link>
```

Can be rewritten as:

```
this.$router.push('/url')
```

Clicking on a `<router-link>` element calls `router.push()` internally which *pushes* a new entry to the history stack after the browser navigates.

In addition to `router.push()`, we're able to use `router.go()` to navigate forwards/backwards in the window history stack, or `router.replace()` to navigate without pushing an entry to the history stack.

In the `addAndGoToCart()` method, let's introduce a `router.push()` with a target url of `/cart` after the `addCartItem` action is dispatched:

```
methods: {
  addAndGoToCart(productItem) {
    this.$store.dispatch('addCartItem', productItem);
    this.$router.push('/cart');
  }
}
```

Clicking on the button will now add the item and navigate us directly to the cart! Everything works well since the `addCartItem` action is completed just in time as we arrive to the `/cart`. If the asynchronous call to the server took some time longer, the user may navigate to the next screen *before* the item gets added. That's not the best user experience we can hope for.

[104]https://router.vuejs.org/en/essentials/navigation.html

To avoid the potential of this case happening, we need to navigate the user to `/cart` *only after* the `addCartItem` action is complete.

One way of doing is to modify the `addCartItem` action in the store to **return a `Promise`** with which upon resolving we'll then direct the user to `/cart`.

`axios`, the http library we're using, already returns a Promise so we don't have to create one. In the cart module of the store (`store/modules/cart/index.js`), we just need to update the `addCartItem` action to return the result of the Promise:

routing/shopping_cart/src/app-2/store/modules/cart/index.js

```
const actions = {
  // ...
  addCartItem ({ commit }, cartItem) {
    return axios.post('/api/cart', cartItem).then((response) => {
      commit('UPDATE_CART_ITEMS', response.data)
    });
  },
  // ...
}
```

Now in our `addAndGoToCart()` method in `ProductItem`, we can specify the change in route to occur *only after* the `addCartItem` action is successfully completed:

routing/shopping_cart/src/app-2/components/product/ProductItem.vue

```
  methods: {
    addAndGoToCart(productItem) {
      this.$store
        .dispatch('addCartItem', productItem)
        .then(() => {
          this.$router.push('/cart');
        });
    }
  }
```

For the sake of simplicity, we're assuming all our async server calls will resolve successfully. Good practice would involve making store actions commit to unique mutations under the conditions that server calls *fail*. These mutations should update the state accordingly which would display information to the view specifying a call was unsuccessful.

To finalize our `ProductItem` component, let's introduce a "back" element to allow the user to navigate back to where they came from.

To navigate back once in the history stack, we'll call `router.go(-1)` with `-1` dictating going back by one record. Since this action is the only one we'd need to perform when the element is clicked, we can add this functionality directly in the template:

```
<template>
  <section id="product-item" class="box">
    <!-- The new return icon element -->
    <span class="return-icon" @click="$router.go(-1)">
      <i class="fa fa-arrow-left is-primary"></i>
    </span>
    <!--  -->
    <div class="product-item__details">
      ...
    </div>
    <div class="product-item__image">
      ...
    </div>
  </section>
</template>
```

Another suitable option would involve navigating the user directly to `/products` when the `return-icon` is clicked.

Our `ProductItem` component is now complete! We just need to create the `<router-link>` element on the product list to allow the user to navigate to `ProductItem` from the main page. Since we want to add the navigation link on each product item list, we'll alter the `ProductListItem` component.

In the `<template>` of the `ProductListItem.vue` file, we can introduce the `<router-link>` element on `{{ productItem.title }}` like so:

routing/shopping_cart/src/app-2/components/product/ProductListItem.vue

```
    <h2 class="has-text-weight-bold">
      <router-link
        :to="'/products/' + productItem.id">
          {{ productItem.title }}
      </router-link>
      <span
        @click="addCartItem(productItem)"
        class="tag is-primary is-pulled-right has-text-white">
          Add to Cart
      </span>
    </h2>
```

Notice how we're dynamically binding the target destination, `:to`, to `'/products/' + productItem.id`. The target URL is dependent on the `id` of the `productItem` being clicked.

There are different ways we can specify the value of a dynamic `:to` prop in `<router-link>`. We could've resorted to using ES6 templates with:

```
<router-link :to="`/products/${productItem.id}`">
  {{ productItem.title }}
</router-link>
```

In addition, `<router-link>` allows the possibility of passing a location descriptor object instead of a string:

```
<router-link
  :to="{ name: 'products', params: { id: productItem.id }}">
    {{ productItem.title }}
</router-link>
```

The above will only work if we've specified a `name` property of 'products' in the route object path. All the above examples would achieve the same result - `/products/:id`.

Head over to the `<router-link>`[105] section of the `vue-router` docs to read more on the different possible value formats of the `:to` prop.

Each of the product item titles in the main screen, `/products`, is now a link to the product item details screen!

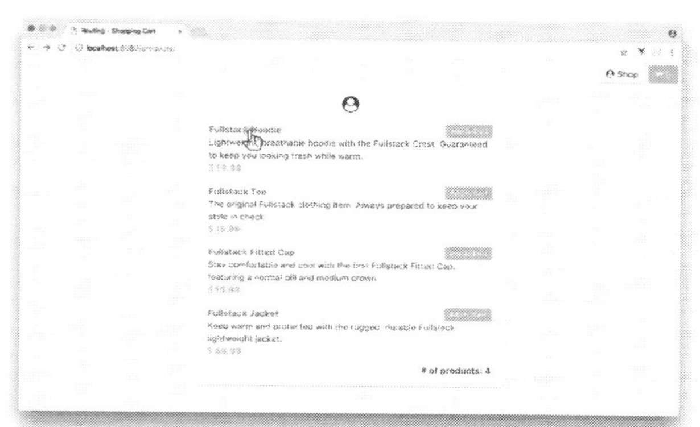

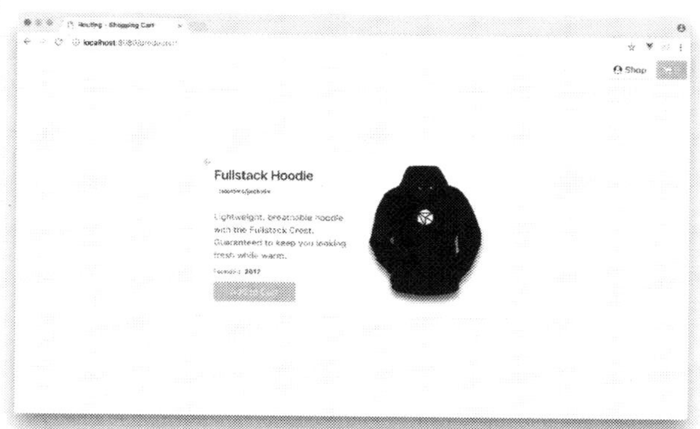

Great. When we click the title of a product in the `ProductList`, we should be directed to the appropriate `ProductItem`. If we refresh the page when we're in the `ProductItem` screen, data will be loaded appropriately, but we'll be given this interesting error:

[105]https://router.vuejs.org/en/api/router-link.html

```
[Vue warn]: Error in render:
  "TypeError: Cannot read property 'title' of undefined"
```

Vue is telling us that the `productItem` property is `undefined` when we refresh the page directly, though everything is displayed normally.

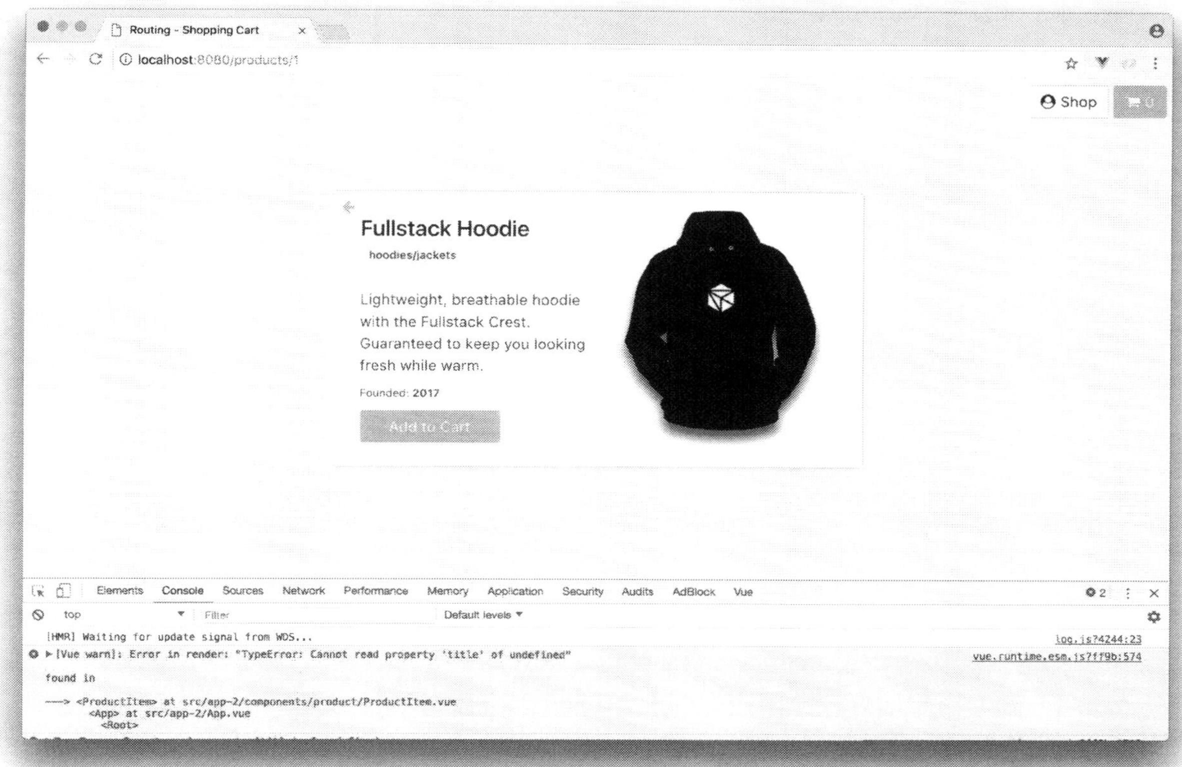

Remember, all data in our application is loaded from the server *asynchronously*. When we load the page from `/products`, then click a product item, all product items are appropriately stored in state and available. However, when we refresh the page directly, by the time the computed property is accessed - the data is not quite ready (i.e. the async calls have not been completed) and the error is generated. Only once the async call is complete, the template is then rendered appropriately.

The first thought that may come to mind to resolve this is to change the `getProductItems` action (the action that gets the list of product items from the server) call to a `Promise` and arrange the `productItem` property to compute *asynchronously* only after the `Promise` is complete. **This would not work since `computed` properties are entirely synchronous**.

Another *simpler* approach is to wrap the template of the `ProductItem` component with a `v-if` statement:

```
<template>
  <section id="product-item" class="box" v-if="productItem">
    ...
  </section>
</template>
```

Now, the `productItem` will only render when the `productItem` property is available! If we try and refresh the page when in the `/products/:id` route, we'll see no errors.

Recap

We've gotten to see some of `vue-router`'s components at work inside a slightly more complex interface:

- We created separate routes for `/products` and `/cart`
- We created a redirect from `/` to `/products`
- We moved our dispatch calls to populate our initial Vuex state to `App`
- We matched a component against a dynamic URL - `/products/:id`
- We used programmatic navigation to add an item and navigate the user to cart, in the product item screen

Let's take our application a bit further. We'll now look into implementing a fake authentication system for our app. We'll explore a strategy for elegantly preventing a user from accessing certain locations without logging in first.

Supporting authenticated routes

As we saw when we explored the API endpoint `/products` earlier, making a `GET` request to this endpoint (as well as `/cart`) requires a token to access. Since we don't yet have the login and logout functionality implemented in the app, we've been cheating by setting the token manually before making our requests.

We can see this at the `getProductItems` action in `store/modules/product/index.js`:

routing/shopping_cart/src/app-2/store/modules/product/index.js

```
  getProductItems ({ commit }) {
    axios.get('/api/products?token=D6W69PRgCoDKgHZGJmRUNA').then((response) => {
      commit('UPDATE_PRODUCT_ITEMS', response.data)
    });
  }
```

And the `getCartItems` action in `store/modules/cart/index.js`:

routing/shopping_cart/src/app-2/store/modules/cart/index.js

```
  getCartItems ({ commit }) {
    axios.get('/api/cart?token=D6W69PRgCoDKgHZGJmRUNA').then((response) => {
      commit('UPDATE_CART_ITEMS', response.data)
    });
  },
```

This token is the same token expected by `server.js`:

routing/shopping_cart/server.js

```
const API_TOKEN = 'D6W69PRgCoDKgHZGJmRUNA';
```

To mimic a more real-world authentication flow, we want to remove the token string literal from our server requests. Instead, we should have our app make a request to the API's `/login` endpoint to retrieve the authentication token.

We can then store the token locally and use it in subsequent requests. To keep things simple, our `/login` API doesn't require a user name or password.

As we've specified in the API proxying section in Chapter 5, we're proxying requests to `/api/` in the client to `http://localhost:3000/` (the server port). Though our server API calls are set with `/products`, `/cart`, and `/login`, our client makes requests to these calls with `/api/products`, `/api/cart`, and `/api/login` due to the proxy setup.

`login` module

Our app currently doesn't have any functionality associated with logging in/logging out. Since we'll be interacting with an api call (`/api/login`) in a domain that doesn't match `cart` or `product`, we'll create a new store module called `login` to hold this responsibility.

We'll have the `login/` folder set up in `store/modules`:

```
ls src/app/store/modules
cart/
login/
product/
```

`login/` will only contain a single `index.js` file:

```
$ ls src/app/store/modules/login/
index.js
```

Just like the other store modules, our `login` will have all the pieces (`state`, `mutations`, `actions`, and `getters`) of a Vuex store. To get things started, let's establish empty objects for each of these pieces, wire them to the module and export it. We'll import the `axios` library to the file since we'll need it to make our `api/login` request.

With that said, our `store/modules/login/index.js` file will start with this:

```
import axios from 'axios';

const state = {
  // ...
}

const mutations = {
  // ...
}

const actions = {
  // ...
}

const getters = {
  // ...
}

const loginModule = {
  state,
  mutations,
  actions,
  getters
}

export default loginModule;
```

Before we build our `login` module, let's import it to the `store/index.js` file and introduce it to the global store instance.

Our Vuex store in `store/index.js` will now be updated to:

routing/shopping_cart/src/app-3/store/index.js

```
import Vue from 'vue';
import Vuex from 'vuex';
import product from './modules/product';
import cart from './modules/cart';
import login from './modules/login';

Vue.use(Vuex);

export default new Vuex.Store({
  modules: {
    product,
    cart,
    login
  }
});
```

Now we can begin to handle authentication. Our authentication flow will look like this:

- When the app loads for the first time, it will be in the unauthenticated state and the user will be presented with a login screen.
- When the user logs in, a request will be made to `/api/login`. The returned token from this request is stored in `localStorage` and the Vuex state. The user is then redirected to the `/products` screen.
- The calls to retrieve product and cart list data from the server will now have the appropriate token passed in.
- When the user logs out, the token is *removed* from `localStorage` and the user is taken back to `/login`.
- If the user aims to access any app route in the unauthenticated state, he/she will be automatically redirected to `/login`.

We'll address these one-by-one.

At some point (with which we'll see shortly) we're going to need to *watch* our Vuex state to determine whether a token has been added/removed from our application. Therefore we need to keep our Vuex state and `localStorage` in sync. We'll add a `token` property to the state of `login` module and initialize it with a value of `null`:

```
const state = {
  token: null,
}
```

When we need to update the `token` property in state, we'll need to specify a mutation to do so. We'll call this mutation `SET_TOKEN` that directly updates the state `token` value with a payload provided:

```
const mutations = {
  SET_TOKEN (state, token) {
    state.token = token;
  }
}
```

There are going to be two major `actions` that our components will dispatch with regards to the `login` module, `login()` and `logout()`.

Our `login()` action performs a request to `/api/login`, stores the token with `localStorage`, and persists the token value to the state. Since we'll need to know when the async call is complete, we'll return the Promise `axios` returns:

```
const actions = {
  login ({ commit }) {
    return axios.post('/api/login').then((response) => {
      localStorage.setItem("token", response.data.token);
      commit('SET_TOKEN', response.data.token);
    });
  }
}
```

Our `logout()` action can be simpler since no api call needs to be made. `logout()` will simply remove the token value from `localStorage` and set the state `token` value to `null`. Since this action doesn't perform an api call and we'll need to know when this action is complete, we'll wrap this action in a `Promise`:

```
const actions = {
  login ({ commit }) {
    ...
  },
  logout ({ commit }) {
    return new Promise((resolve) => {
      localStorage.removeItem("token");
      commit('SET_TOKEN', null);
      resolve();
    });
  }
}
```

We'll have a single `getter` method that returns a state `token` value that can be accessed from our components:

```
const getters = {
  token: state => state.token
}
```

As mentioned earlier in the book, simple state computations don't need to be in `getters`. Store state can be directly retrieved (or mapped with the use of the `mapState`[106] helper).

We've conformed to using `getters` to map *all state information* to stick to a general pattern.

With our `login` module established, let's begin by adding a new login component.

Implementing login

As we saw in the completed version of the app, the login component displays a single "Login" button. Clicking this button fires off the login process. We also want to display the loading indicator while the login is in process:

[106]https://vuex.vuejs.org/en/state.html#the-mapstate-helper

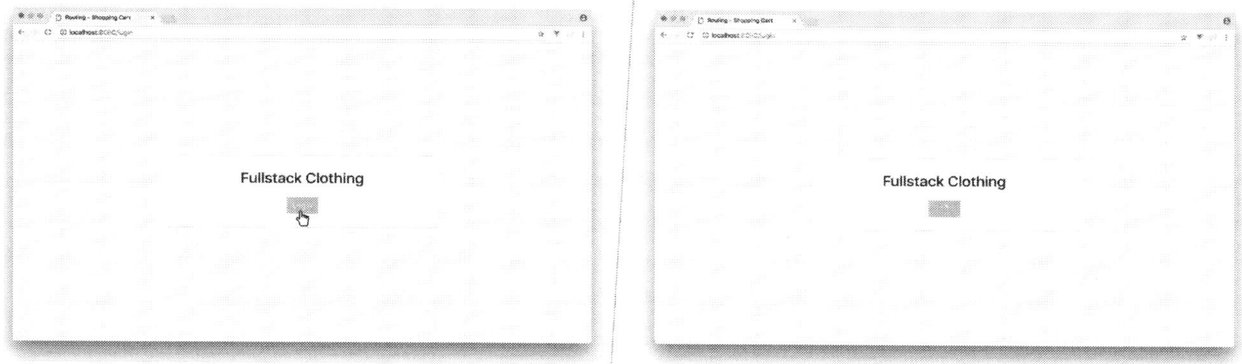

Clicking the "Login" button

For this, we're going to create a new component named `LoginBox`. We'll create this component in a `LoginBox.vue` file contained in a new `components/login` folder.

In `components/`:

```
$ ls src/app/components
cart/
login/
product/
```

In `components/login`:

```
$ ls src/app/components/login
LoginBox.vue
```

Let's create a simple static scaffold as a starting point for `LoginBox` by adding the following code to the `LoginBox.vue` file:

```
<template>
  <div id="login" class="box has-text-centered">
    <h2 class="title">Fullstack Clothing</h2>
    <button class="button is-primary">Login</button>
  </div>
</template>

<script>
export default {
  name: 'LoginBox'
}
```

```
</script>

<style scoped>
.box {
  padding: 30px;
}
</style>
```

Let's now create the route path that maps to this component. In `router/index.js`, we'll import `LoginBox` and specify that this component should be rendered with a route path of `/login`.

We'll import `LoginBox` at the top of of the `router/index.js` file:

routing/shopping_cart/src/app-3/router/index.js

```
import LoginBox from '../components/login/LoginBox.vue';
```

We can then specify the desired route path in the `routes` array of our router instance:

```
routes: [
  ...,
  {
    path: '/login',
    component: LoginBox
  },
  ...
]
```

When we enter `http://localhost:8080/login`, we'll now be presented with the login screen!

When the “Login” button is clicked, we want a request to be made to `/api/login` and upon success, redirect the user to the main page - `/products`. Let’s add a component method called `login()` to handle the login button.

Let’s attach a click listener, to call the `login()` method when fired, in the `<button>` element of the `LoginBox` component:

```
<button @click="login" class="button is-primary">Login</button>
```

We’ll now create the `login()` method in a components `methods` property to dispatch the `login` action, and subsequently redirect the user:

routing/shopping_cart/src/app-3/components/login/LoginBox.vue

```
  methods: {
    login() {
      this.$store.dispatch("login").then(() => {
        this.$router.push({ path: '/products' });
      });
    }
  }
```

Clicking on the "Login" button will now direct us from the `/login` screen to `/products`. If we take a look at the Vuex section of our Vue Devtools, we'll also see that the `token` value in state is populated with the token value.

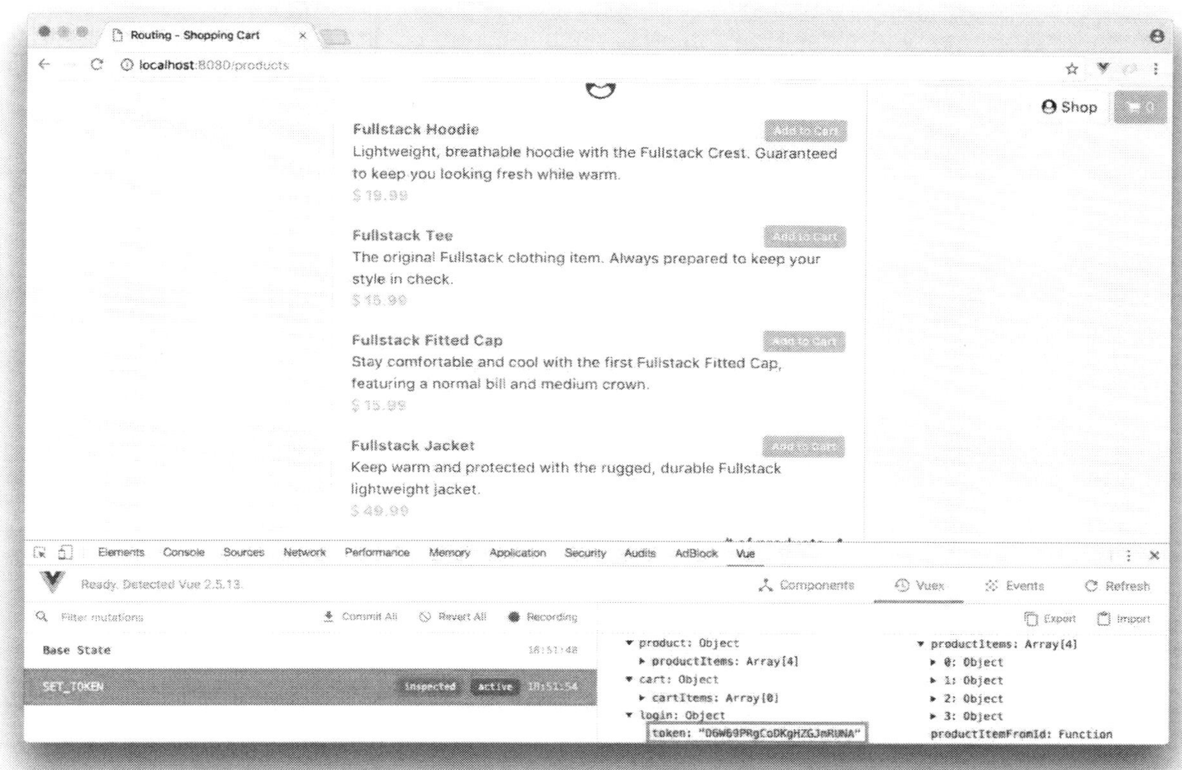

This verifies that our `login()` action appropriately calls `api/login` and sets the return token to our Vuex state. We should now be able to use the token in our GET `/products` and `/cart` server calls.

In the `created()` hook of the parent component `App`, let's introduce the `token` value as a parameter to each of the dispatch calls made (`getCartItems` and `getProductItems`). In this case, **we'll retrieve the `token` from `localStorage` instead of our `Vuex` state**. We'll explain why shortly.

The `created()` hook in our `App.vue` file becomes:

```
created() {
  const token = localStorage.getItem("token");
  if (token) {
    this.$store.dispatch('getCartItems', token);
    this.$store.dispatch('getProductItems', token);
  }
}
```

When the app loads, `App` tries to load the token from `localStorage`. If the token exists in `localStorage`, the token is passed to the dispatch calls that need it. The token is kept in `localStorage` indefinitely and has no expiry.

It's important to note the token in this case needs to be retrieved from `localStorage`, **not our Vuex state**. When `App` is created for the first time (i.e. the application is launched), the `token` in our state is always initialized with **`null`**. Only when the user logs in, does the token value in our state get updated.

In our `getProductItems()` and `getCartItems()` actions, we can now remove the hard coded token value in our query and reference the appropriate payload provided.

Updating `getProductItems()` action in `store/modules/product/index.js`:

routing/shopping_cart/src/app-3/store/modules/product/index.js

```
getProductItems ({ commit }, token) {
  axios.get(`/api/products?token=${token}`).then((response) => {
    commit('UPDATE_PRODUCT_ITEMS', response.data)
  });
}
```

And updating `getCartItems()` in `store/modules/cart/index.js`:

routing/shopping_cart/src/app-3/store/modules/cart/index.js

```
getCartItems ({ commit }, token) {
  axios.get(`/api/cart?token=${token}`).then((response) => {
    commit('UPDATE_CART_ITEMS', response.data)
  });
},
```

If we refresh our app in the `/products` and `/cart` routes, our app will render normally. This behaviour tells us the token from `localStorage` is being passed correctly to the actions upon app load.

Let's add the logout button to our application to give the user the ability to log out and log in at will. In the template of `App.vue`, we'll introduce a new button in the `<div class="navigation-buttons"></div>` element that calls a `logout()` method when clicked:

```
<div id="app">
  <div class="navigation-buttons">
    <button @click="logout" class="button is-text is-pulled-left">Logout</button>
    <!-- ... -->
  </div>
  <!-- ... -->
</div>
```

We'll now introduce the `logout()` method to the component. This method dispatches the `logout()` action then subsequently directs the user *back* to the `/login` route. We'll add the following to the `<script>` section of the `App` component:

```
methods: {
  logout() {
    this.$store.dispatch("logout").then(() => {
      this.$router.push("/login")
    }).catch((error) => {
      console.log(error);
    });
  }
}
```

When the user clicks the logout button, the token stored in `localStorage` will be removed and the user will be navigated back to the login screen. If we save our files, refresh our browser; we'll be able to log back in and forth.

However if we log out, refresh our browser and *then* log in; we'll be presented with an app with **no data** despite having no errors:

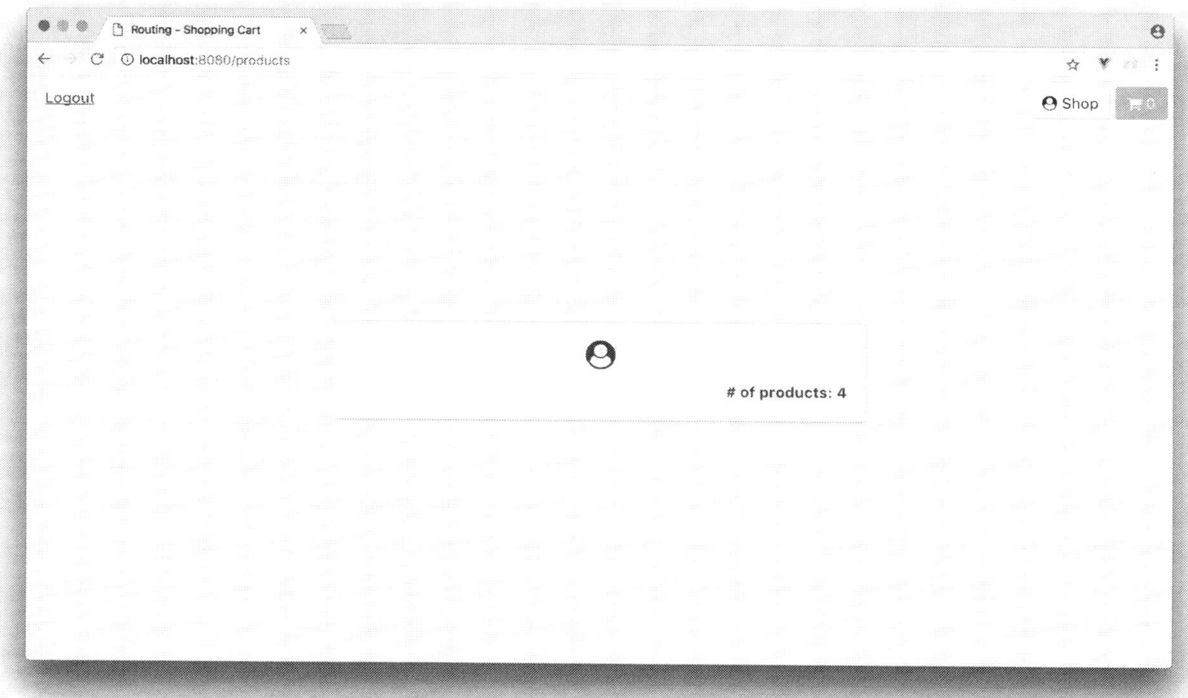

This unexpected behaviour happens because our `App` `created()` hook only gets called **once** when the app is loaded for the first time. The `created()` hook of `App` is where we dispatch the actions necessary to populate Vuex state.

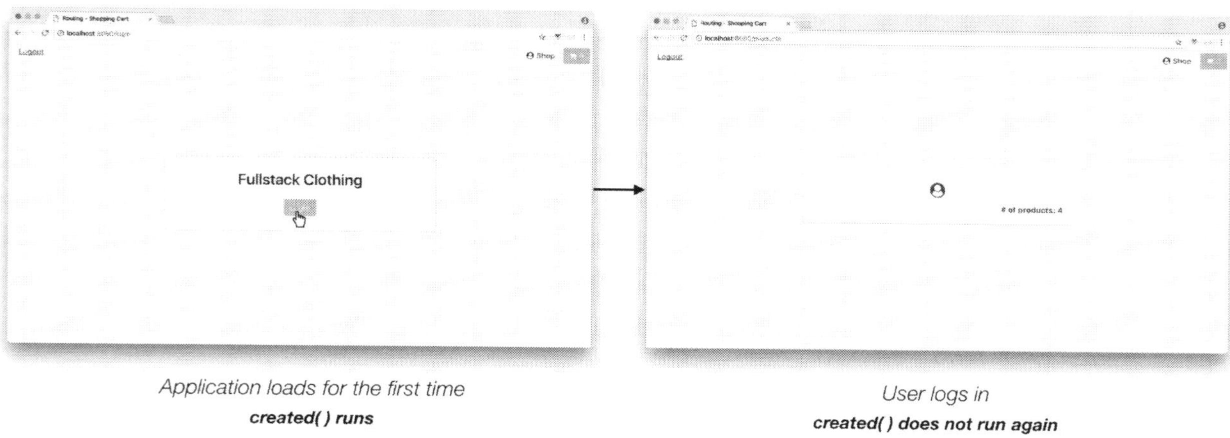

When the user launches the application in the login page, the `created()` hook runs. Since no token exists in `localStorage`, the dispatch calls don't get fired.

When the user logs in, despite persisting the token and storing it in our state, our dispatch actions *don't get fired again*. This case is where it becomes important to sync the Vuex state with `localStorage`. `localStorage` is not reactive, so Vue is unable to pick up changes that happen there. The Vuex state however can be watched with the help of a Vue **watch** property.

Vue `watch`

The Vue **watch**[107] property allows us to *react* in response to data changes. Let's see how this would work in our case.

Though it's possible to 'watch' the store `token` value directly from `App`, it's not advisable to do so. Just like how store state should never be mutated directly, store state properties should never be *watched* directly. We'll instead watch a mapped component property.

In `App`, let's map a `token` computed property to the `token getter` in our store:

We'll do this within the `mapGetters` helper in the `App.vue` file:

```
computed: {
  ...mapGetters([
    'token', // new computed property
    'cartQuantity'
  ])
},
```

We'll now introduce a new property labelled `watch` to our component. In our `watch` property, we'll watch the `token` data value in our component:

```
name: 'App',
computed: {
  ...mapGetters([
    'token',
    'cartQuantity'
  ])
},
created() {
  ...
},
watch: {
  token() {

  }
},
```

[107]https://vuejs.org/v2/guide/computed.html#Watchers

```
methods: {
  ...
}
```

Watch properties provide a payload of the new value upon change and the old value prior to the change:

```
watch: {
  token(newVal, oldVal) {
    // ...
  }
}
```

We don't need access to the old value, and the new value in this case **is** the token computed property. In this instance we don't need to use any of these parameters.

Now that our `watch` watches for changes in the computed `token` property, all we need to do is specify that when a change occurs and the token value exists; call the dispatchers that will update our Vuex `cartItems` and `productItems` state:

```
watch: {
  token() {
    if (this.token) {
      this.$store.dispatch('getCartItems', this.token);
      this.$store.dispatch('getProductItems', this.token);
    }
  }
}
```

Since we're repeating these dispatchers in both the `created()` hook and the `watch` property, we can delegate this to a component method that takes a `token` parameter. Our component `created()`, `watch`, and `methods` property now all look like this:

routing/shopping_cart/src/app-3/App.vue

```
  created() {
    const token = localStorage.getItem("token");
    if (token) {
      this.updateInitialState(token);
    }
  },
  watch: {
    token() {
      if (this.token) {
        this.updateInitialState(this.token);
      }
    }
  },
  methods: {
    logout() {
      this.$store.dispatch("logout").then(() => {
       this.$router.push("/login")
      });
    },
    updateInitialState(token) {
      this.$store.dispatch('getCartItems', token);
      this.$store.dispatch('getProductItems', token);
    }
  }
```

Let's try it out

Save `App.vue`. With the app running, log out, and head back to `/login`. If we refresh from here then click "Login", we'll be directed to the `/products` page with all data populated appropriately.

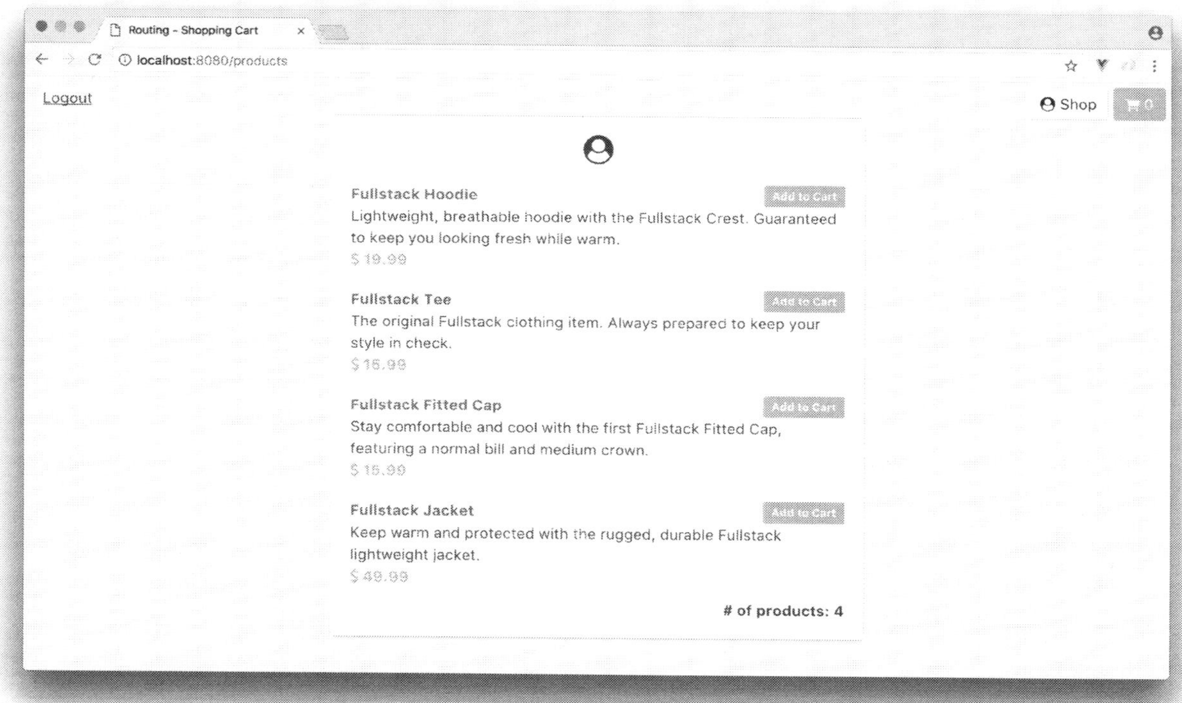

The dispatchers in `created()` will only run when the app is refreshed in the `/products` or `/cart` state **and** the user is in the authenticated state. The dispatchers in the `watch` property however will only run when the user moves from the unauthenticated state to the authenticated state (i.e. logs in).

Though the `watch` property allows us to react to data changes, oftentimes a Vue `computed` property will do the job just fine. Certain cases like we've just seen, it becomes imperative when a custom watcher is necessary.

`pending` login and navigation buttons

There are a few things left to make our login process how we want it. First, we don't need the "Logout" button when the user is logged out. Neither do we want the user to click either the "Shop" or "Cart" buttons when he/she is logged out.

Since the "Logout", "Shop", and "Cart" buttons are all contained within the `<div class="navigation-buttons"></div>` element, we can safely say we don't want this entire element to render when the user is logged out. We'll use `v-if` to state this `<div>` element should only render if the `route.params` is not equal to `/login`.

In App, we'll specify the `v-if` clause in the `class="navigation-buttons" <div>`:

```
<template>
  <div id="app">
    <div v-if="$route.path !== '/login'" class="navigation-buttons">
    </div>
    <div class="container">
      <!-- ... -->
    </div>
  </div>
</template>
```

Now, the user is unable to see the navigation buttons when logged out:

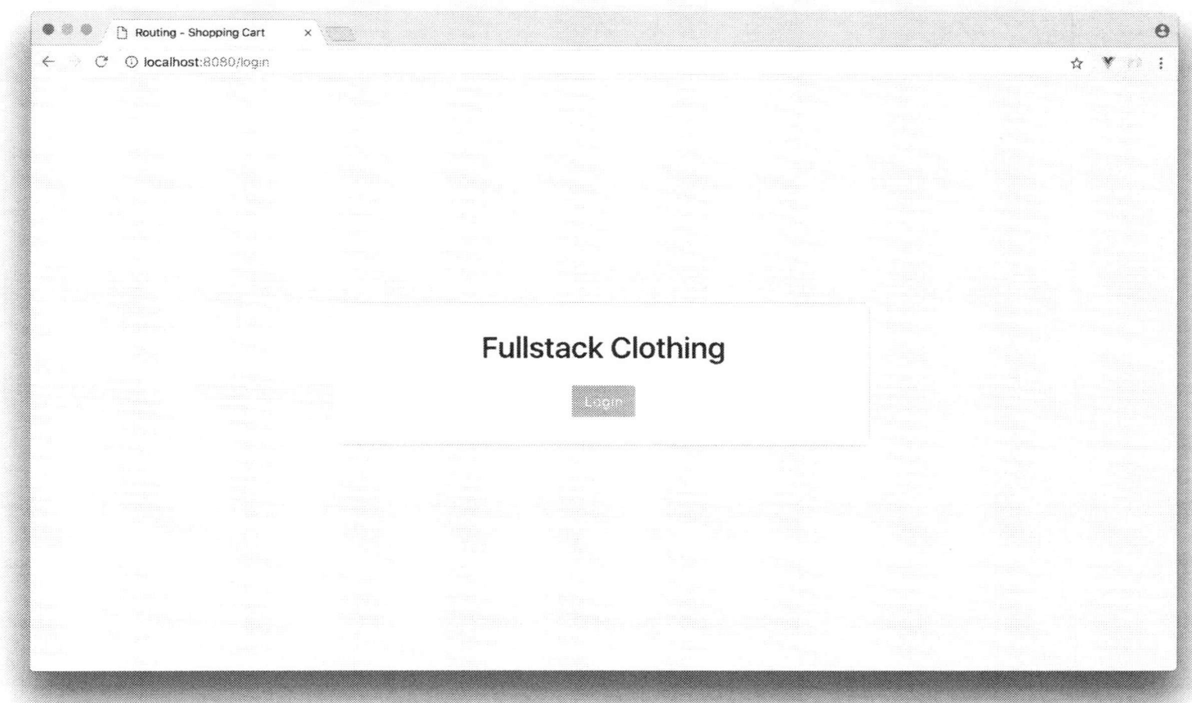

Perfect. We'll add another improvement to the login flow by introducing a simple loading indicator at the moment when the user is attempting to login and the asynchronous call is still being made.

To keep track of when the async `/api/login` call is being made, we'll add a few new items to the `login` module. First, we'll introduce a `loading` property to the state of our `login` module. This will be the property our `LoginBox` component will use to determine if the loading indicator should be displayed.

In `store/modules/login`, we'll initialize this `loading` state property with false:

routing/shopping_cart/src/app-3/store/modules/login/index.js

```
const state = {
  token: null,
  loading: false
}
```

We'll then create two mutations, one that sets the `loading` property to `true` and the other to set it back to `false`. We'll label these mutations `LOGIN_PENDING` and `LOGIN_SUCCESS` respectively:

routing/shopping_cart/src/app-3/store/modules/login/index.js

```
const mutations = {
  SET_TOKEN (state, token) {
    state.token = token;
  },
  LOGIN_PENDING (state) {
    state.loading = true;
  },
  LOGIN_SUCCESS (state) {
    state.loading = false;
  }
}
```

In our `login()` action, we can commit to the `LOGIN_PENDING` mutation just before the `api/login` call is made. When the call gets resolved successfully, we'll then `commit` to the `LOGIN_SUCCESS` mutation:

routing/shopping_cart/src/app-3/store/modules/login/index.js

```
  login ({ commit }) {
    commit('LOGIN_PENDING'); // login pending
    return axios.post('/api/login').then((response) => {
      localStorage.setItem("token", response.data.token);
      commit('SET_TOKEN', response.data.token);
      commit('LOGIN_SUCCESS'); // login success
    });
  },
```

Now when the `login()` action is first called, the `loading` property will be set to `true`. Only when the call is successful, will `loading` be set back to `false`.

For the sake of simplicity, we won't create additional `mutations` and/or `state` properties to handle when logging in becomes *unsuccessful*. However, in a real production scale application - **unsuccessful login attempts should be appropriately addressed**.

We can now just introduce a `loading` `getter` that returns the value of the state property to be accessed from the `LoginBox` component:

routing/shopping_cart/src/app-3/store/modules/login/index.js

```
const getters = {
  token: state => state.token,
  loading: state => state.loading
}
```

In the `LoginBox` component we'll import the `mapGetters` helper and map the `loading` `getter` to a computed property of the same name:

This makes the `<script>` element of `LoginBox` now be entirely laid out like this:

routing/shopping_cart/src/app-3/components/login/LoginBox.vue

```
<script>
import { mapGetters } from 'vuex';

export default {
  name: 'Login',
  computed: {
    ...mapGetters([
      'loading',
    ])
  },
  methods: {
    login() {
      this.$store.dispatch("login").then(() => {
        this.$router.push({ path: '/products' });
      });
    }
  }
}
</script>
```

Bulma[108] offers an `is-loading` class as one of it's button states[109]. `is-loading` displays a loading spinner within a button, which is pretty much what we need right now.

In the `<template>` of `LoginBox`, we're going to specify a **conditional class binding**[110] to the Login button:

[108]https://bulma.io/

[109]https://bulma.io/documentation/elements/button/#states

[110]https://vuejs.org/v2/guide/class-and-style.html

routing/shopping_cart/src/app-3/components/login/LoginBox.vue

```
    <button @click="login"
      :class="[{'is-loading': loading}, 'button is-primary']">
      Login
    </button>
```

We've specified that the presence of the `is-loading` class depends on the truthiness of the `loading` computed property. The `button` and `is-primary` classes, however, will always be present.

Give it a try! If we log out and try to log back in, we'll be presented with the loading indicator on the "Log In" button for a brief period of time.

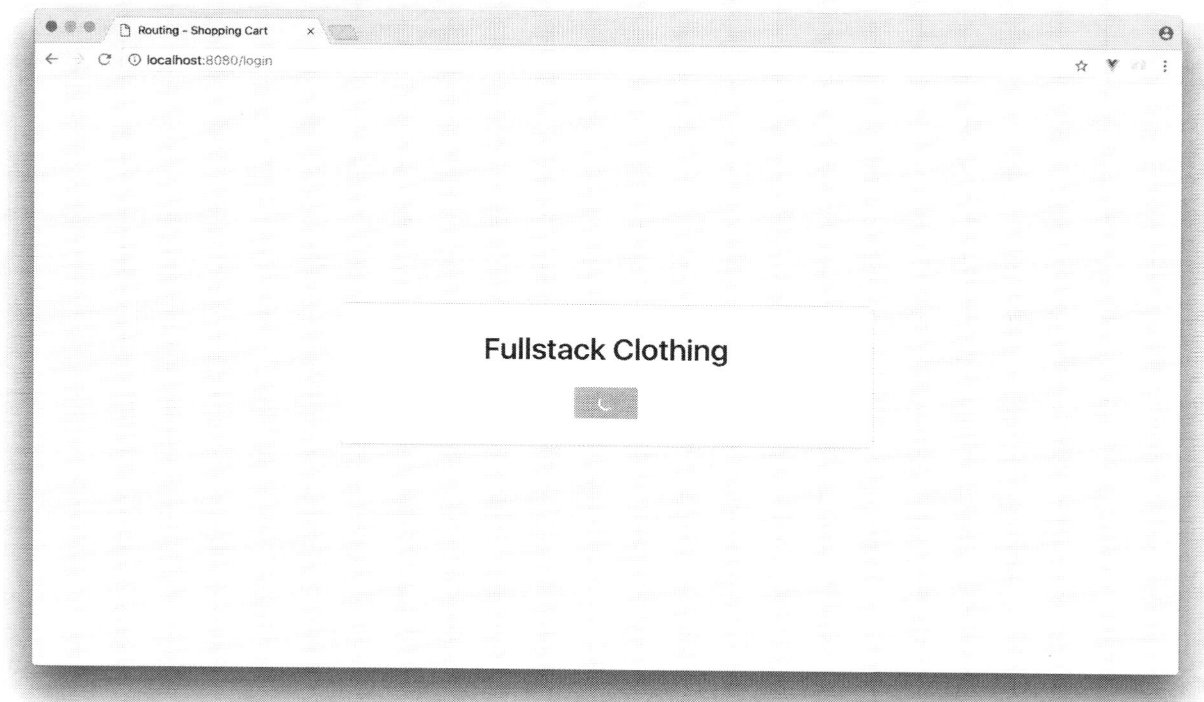

Loading indicator

We've almost finished tying everything together! Our login/logout flow works just as we intended. The last important piece left is to use `vue-router` to guard the authenticated pages from unauthenticated users.

Navigation Guards

If the user tries to visit a page on the site they can't access because they're not logged in, we need to redirect them to `/login`. In essence, we aim to *guard* navigations based on whether the user is authenticated or not.

`vue-router` allows us to specify navigation guards in three ways:

- Globally[111] - for all navigation routes
- Per-route[112] - for a single route
- Within components[113]

We're going to be using the first two in our application.

Global Route Guard

Global route navigation guards can be set up by specifying a `beforeEach` function on the entire `router` instance. All route navigation guard functions have access to three arguments.

1. `to` - the target route object.
2. `from` - the current route object.
3. `next()` - the function that must be invoked to complete routing the user.

In `router/index.js`, let's create a global guard on our `router` object prior to the `export` being made:

```
const router = new VueRouter({
  ...
});

// The global route guard
router.beforeEach((to, from, next) => {});

export default router;
```

Like `beforeEach`, an `afterEach` hook can be specified as well. `afterEach` occurs *after* a navigation is made and thus doesn't represent a navigation guard.

Our guard needs to specify that if the user is unauthenticated (i.e. `token` is `null`) and aims to access any route, he/she should be redirected back to `/login`. Once again, we'll be retrieving `token` from `localStorage` and not the Vuex state:

[111]https://router.vuejs.org/en/advanced/navigation-guards.html#global-guards
[112]https://router.vuejs.org/en/advanced/navigation-guards.html#per-route-guard
[113]https://router.vuejs.org/en/advanced/navigation-guards.html#in-component-guards

```
router.beforeEach((to, from, next) => {
  const token = localStorage.getItem("token");
  if (!token) next('/login');
  else next();
});
```

The `next()` function dictates how we want the hook to resolve. `next()` specifies to continue to the route the user intended to access while `next(/login)` forces the user to the `/login` route.

If we launched our application in the `/login` screen, we may see an error along the lines of `Maximum call stack size exceeded`. This is because our global navigation guard is being `run on every route`, including `/login`. In `/login`, an endless loop occurs since `vue-router` aims to redirect the user to `/login` over and over.

We just need to use the `to` parameter to dictate that the forced change in route should not occur when the user aims to access `/login`:

routing/shopping_cart/src/app-complete/router/index.js

```
router.beforeEach((to, from, next) => {
  const token = localStorage.getItem("token");
  if (!token && to.path !== '/login') next('/login');
  else next();
});
```

Let's verify that our navigation guard works as intended:

1. With the app open, click the "Logout" button.
2. If we attempt to visit `/products`, `/products/:id`, or `/cart`; we'll notice we're automatically redirected to `/login` each time.
3. When we do login, we're directed to `/products` appropriately.

Note, instead of having a global guard and specifying a check to see that the target route is not `/login`, we could've added individual route guards to everything *but* `/login`. The outcome will be the same.

Beautiful. Let's now create an additional navigation guard in the opposite sense. If the user is authenticated and aims to access the `/login` screen, he/she will be directed to `/products`.

`/login` route guard

We intend on specifying a single route guard on the `/login` route. To do this, we'll attach a `beforeEnter` guard directly on the `/login` route path object:

```
const router = new VueRouter({
  mode: 'history',
  routes: [
    ...,
    {
      path: '/login',
      component: LoginBox,
      beforeEnter: (to, from, next) => {
      }
    },
    ...
  ]
});
```

Similar to our global guard, we'll aim to retrieve the `token` from `localStorage`. If the `token` exists, we'll redirect the user to `/products`. If not, we'll let the route continue as intended to `/login`:

routing/shopping_cart/src/app-complete/router/index.js

```
    {
      path: '/login',
      component: LoginBox,
      beforeEnter: (to, from, next) => {
        const token = localStorage.getItem("token");
        if (token) next('/products');
        else next();
      }
    },
```

Let's try it out.

1. With the app open and in the logged in state, let's attempt to visit `/login` in the browser. We'll notice we're being automatically redirected to `/products`.
2. Click the 'Logout' button and attempt to visit `/login` in the browser (or refresh the page). We're not redirected and we continue (or remain) in the `/login` route.

We're almost there! There's one other route navigation guard we should handle before our app is complete.

`/products/:id` route guard

Our dynamic product item route, `/products/:id` works well when we enter a URL with an `id` that matches any of the products in our product list (i.e. `id` between 1 and 4). If we enter a URL of an id that doesn't match any of the products in our product item list, we're presented with a blank screen:

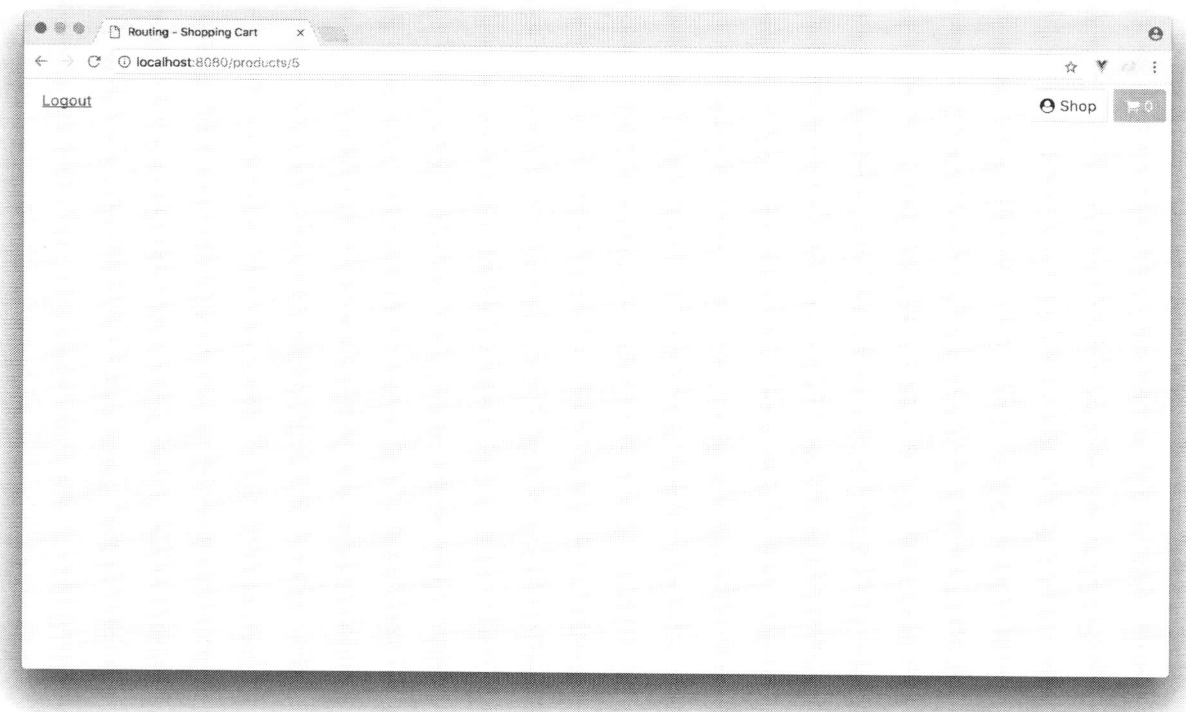

How is it that we're presented with a blank screen (apart from the navigation buttons) with no errors?

First, we're not being directed to the `NotFound` component because regardless of what `id` is specified, our dynamic route will be recognized as a route within our router instance.

Secondly, no errors are being displayed because we've added the clause (`v-if="productItem"`) to only render the `ProductItem` component when the `productItem` object exists. In this instance, we're not able to retrieve a product item from a non recognizable `id`.

To avoid this, let's introduce a navigation guard to the `/products/:id` route. We'll be able to get the `id` URL params from the `to` route object:

```
const router = new VueRouter({
  mode: 'history',
  routes: [
    ...,
    {
      path: '/products/:id',
      component: ProductItem,
      props: true,
      beforeEnter: (to, from, next) => {
        const id = to.params.id;
      }
    },
    ...
  ]
});
```

Our guard needs to specify that if the `id` doesn't match any of the `ids` that exist (i.e. `1`, `2`, `3`, or `4`), we can direct the user to the `NotFound` component. The `NotFound` component doesn't have a particular route attached to it but is instead rendered if a route that doesn't match any of the existing routes is accessed. So for this, we'll use a route like `/not-found` to be explicit:

routing/shopping_cart/src/app-complete/router/index.js

```
    {
      path: '/products/:id',
      component: ProductItem,
      props: true,
      beforeEnter: (to, from, next) => {
        const id = to.params.id;
        if (![1, 2, 3, 4].includes(Number(id))) next('/not-found');
        else next();
      }
    },
```

We're using ES6's `includes()`[114] method to determine whether the `id` param exists in the array of existing `id`'s. If it doesn't, we direct them to the `/not-found` route.

Let's give it a try. With the app open and in the logged in state, if we visit a dynamic products route with an `id` that doesn't match any existing product `id` (e.g. `http://localhost:8080/products/5`), we'll be directed to the `/not-found` route and hence shown the `NotFound` component:

[114]https://developer.mozilla.org/en-US/docs/Web/JavaScript/Reference/Global_Objects/Array/includes

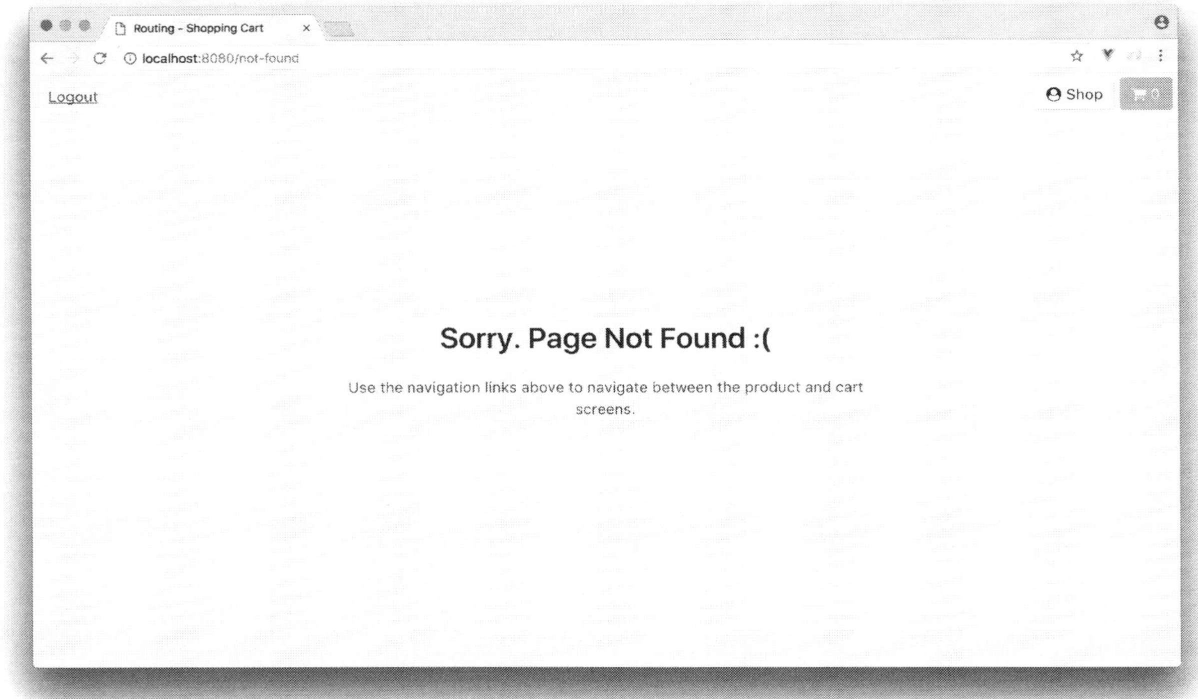

Great work! Our application is now complete!

Recap and further reading

In this chapter, we saw how we can use components from `vue-router` to provide fast, JavaScript-powered navigation in our web apps. We can prevent the user's browser from doing full page loads when navigating around our site. We can build user-friendly URLs that are shareable. And the added complexity to our application is **minimal**.

Though we've obtained a good understanding of routing within Vue's component-driven paradigm, the `vue-router`[115] docs contain even further advanced patterns of router configurations. At the time of writing, these features include transitions[116], data fetching[117] and lazy loading[118]. All those examples build on the foundations established in this chapter.

[115]https://router.vuejs.org/en/
[116]https://router.vuejs.org/en/advanced/transitions.html
[117]https://router.vuejs.org/en/advanced/data-fetching.html
[118]https://router.vuejs.org/en/advanced/lazy-loading.html

VIII - Unit Testing

Though we've yet to address testing in this book, **the importance of testing in front end web development can't be stressed enough**.

Testing can help reveal bugs before they appear, instill confidence in your web application, and make it easy to onboard new developers on an existing codebase. As an upfront investment, testing often pays dividends over the lifetime of a system.

The development community often specify *test-driven* development (i.e. writing tests first then building the implementation) as the appropriate way to handle testing. Whether we employ test-driven development or build tests to validate code that has already been written, focusing on building *testable* code is the vital aspect to always remember.

Testing individual pieces of code that are likely to change can double or triple the amount of work it takes to keep them up. In contrast, building applications in small components and keeping large amounts of functionality broken into several methods allows us to test the functionality of a part of the larger picture. This type of code is what we mean when we say *testable* code.

The decision of what to test will always be up to you and your team. We'll focus on *how* to test your Vue applications in this chapter.

End-to-end vs. Unit Testing

Application testing is often broken down into two main buckets: *end-to-end testing* or *unit testing*.

End-to-End Testing

End-to-end testing is a top-down approach where tests are written to determine whether an application has been built appropriately from start to finish. We write end-to-end tests as though we are a user's movement through our application.

Though different suites can be used, Nightwatch[119] is an end-to-end testing suite that is often used with Vue applications. Nightwatch[120] is Node.js based and allows us to write tests that mimic how a user interacts with an application.

> End-to-end tests are often labeled as integration tests since multiple modules or parts of a software system are often tested together.

[119]http://nightwatchjs.org/

[120]http://nightwatchjs.org/

Unit Testing

Unit testing is a confined approach that involves isolating each part of an application and testing it in isolation. Tests are provided a given input and an output is often evaluated to make sure it matches expectations.

In this chapter, we'll be focusing solely on unit testing.

Testing tools

Though numerous unit test environments/suites exist, we'll primarily use three popular tools: Karma[121], Mocha[122], and Chai[123].

Karma

Karma is a *test runner*, recommended[124] by the Vue.js team, that allows us to run tests in a test environment. Karma gives us the ability to run JavaScript code within a browser (Chrome/Firefox), or on a headless browser (browser that doesn't expose a user interface) like PhantomJS[125].

We'll be running tests in this chapter on PhantomJS.

Mocha and Chai

Mocha is a framework for writing JavaScript tests. It allows us to specify our test suites with `describe` and `it` blocks. We use the `describe` function to segment each logical *unit* of tests and inside that we can use the `it` function for each expectation we'd want to assert.

For instance, let's assume we wanted to test two methods, `sum()` and `subtract()`, in a `Calculator` object. With Mocha, we'll set it up like this:

[121]https://karma-runner.github.io/2.0/index.html
[122]https://mochajs.org/
[123]http://chaijs.com/
[124]https://vuejs.org/v2/guide/unit-testing.html
[125]http://phantomjs.org/

```
describe('Calculator', () => {
  it('sums 1 and 1 to 2', () => {
    // assertion for the sum() method
  });

  it('subtracts 5 and 3 to 2', () => {
    // assertion for the subtract() method
  });
});
```

Though Mocha creates the scaffold for us to write tests, it doesn't have a built-in assertion library. For writing assertions, we'll use the Chai library.

Chai is an assertion library that can be paired with any JavaScript testing framework. Chai provides three interfaces for creating assertions:

1. `should`
2. `expect`
3. `assert`

`should` and `expect` assertions follow a more **behavioural** aspect to testing by allowing us to chain together assertions.

Since we'll be employing a behaviour-driven approach to writing tests, we'll use the `expect` interface in this chapter.

Let's see how a Chai `expect` assertion works. In the example given above, an `expect` assertion for the `sum()` method of the `Calculator` object can look like this:

```
describe('Calculator', () => {
  it('sums 1 and 1 to 2', () => {
    var calc = new Calculator();
    expect(calc.sum(1,1)).to.equal(2);
  });

  // ...
});
```

In the test, we're *expecting* that `sum(1,1)` will return a value of `2`. Similarly, we can test that the `subtract()` method does as intended as well:

```
describe('Calculator', () => {
  it('sums 1 and 1 to 2', () => {
    var calc = new Calculator();
    expect(calc.sum(1, 1)).to.equal(2);
  });

  it('subtracts 5 and 3 to 2', () => {
    var calc = new Calculator();
    expect(calc.subtract(5, 3)).to.equal(2);
  });
});
```

Specifying a new `it` block for every expectation we want to assert isn't a hard rule. On occasion, we'll write an `it` block to contain several expectations.

Our `Calculator` object is simple enough for us to use one `describe` block for the whole class and one `it` block for each method. With more complex methods that produce different outcomes, it's often suitable to have nested `describe` functions: one for the object and one for each method. For example:

```
describe('Calculator', () => {
  describe('#sum', () => {
    it('sums 1 and 1 to 2', () => {
      ...
    });

    it('called at least twice', () => {
      ...
    });
  }

  describe('#subtract', () => {
    it('subtracts 5 and 3 to 2', () => {
      ...
    });

    it('called only once', () => {
      ...
    });
  }
});
```

We'll be looking at a lot of `describe` and `it` blocks throughout this chapter which might help clear up any confusion with this setup.

For more information, be sure to check out the documentation pages for Mocha[126] and Chai[127].

Testing a basic Vue component

To understand how units tests can be made in Vue, we're going to start by testing a basic single-file Vue component.

Setup

The example code for this entire chapter is in the `testing/` folder in the code download. Within `testing/`, there exists a `basics/` folder that we'll be looking at first. `basics/` is a Webpack configured Vue app created with the Vue command line interface[128] (i.e. the `vue-cli`).

Let's `cd` into `testing/basics`:

```
$ cd testing/basics
```

And install the necessary packages:

```
$ npm i
```

Note: Upon installation of application packages; you may be prompted with this message: `VUE-TEST-UTILS WARN: vue-test-utils has moved to a scoped package`. This is because the `vue-test-utils` library (i.e. the official Vue testing library with which we'll be using shortly) has very recently moved to a scoped package of its own. **Since the `vue-test-utils` library is to remain the same**; it's safe to continue to the rest of the chapter.

In the next book revision/update; the code samples from this chapter will be updated to reference the new `vue-test-utils` scoped package.

If we take a look at the project directory, we'll notice the project structure mimics the Webpack configured Vue applications we've built throughout the book:

[126]https://mochajs.org/#getting-started

[127]http://chaijs.com/guide/styles/#expect

[128]https://github.com/vuejs/vue-cli

```
$ ls
README.md
build/
config/
index.html
node_modules/
package.json
src/
static/
test/
```

We'll be focusing entirely in the `src/` and `test/` directories. Let's first take a look at the files within the `src/` directory:

```
$ ls src/
App.vue
main.js
```

We have a single component, `App.vue`, and a `main.js` file. The `App.vue` file is the component we'll be testing. Since the component is already in it's completed state, we won't be making any edits or changes to it.

App.vue

When we open `App.vue`, we'll see a fairly straightforward single-file component. We'll first take a look at the `<template>` portion of the file:

testing/basics/src/App.vue

```
<template>
  <div id="app" class="ui text container">
    <div class="ui text container">
      <table class="ui selectable structured large table">
        <thead>
          <tr>
            <th>Items</th>
          </tr>
        </thead>
        <tbody class="item-list">
          <tr v-for="item in items">
            <td>{{ item }}</td>
          </tr>
```

```
        </tbody>
        <tfoot>
          <tr>
            <th>
              <form class="ui form" @submit="addItem">
                <div class="field">
                  <input v-model="item"
                    type="text"
                    class="prompt"
                    placeholder="Add item..." value="" />
                </div>
                <button type="submit"
                  class="ui button" :disabled="!item">Add</button>
                <span @click="removeAllItems"
                  class="ui label">Remove all</span>
              </form>
            </th>
          </tr>
        </tfoot>
      </table>
    </div>
  </div>
</template>
```

The `<template>` is a `<div>` element that contains an HTML table with the following details:

- The table has a title of 'Items' specified in the header (`<thead>`).
- The body of the table, `<tbody>`, displays a list of items from an `items` array stored in the components data, with the help of the `v-for` directive.
- The footer consists of a form that upon submit calls an `addItem()` method. In the form exists an `input` field that is bound to an `item` data property. A `<button class="ui button"></button>` element is used to submit the form while a `<span class="ui label"></span>` element invokes a `removeAllItems()` method on click.

Taking a look at the components `<script>` section, we'll see the data values and methods that are being used in the `<template>`:

testing/basics/src/App.vue

```
<script>
export default {
  name: 'app',
  data() {
    return {
      item: '',
      items: []
    };
  },
  methods: {
    addItem(evt) {
      evt.preventDefault();
      this.items.push(this.item);
      this.item = '';
    },
    removeAllItems() {
      this.items = [];
    }
  }
};
</script>
```

`item` and `items` are initialized with an empty string and a blank array respectively. `item` is the data property tied to the controlled input while `items` is the list of items displayed in the table.

In `methods`, `addItem()` pushes a new item to the `items` data value and clears `item`. At the beginning of this method, `evt.preventDefault()` is called to prevent the default browser refresh upon form submit.

The `removeAllItems()` method simply sets the `items` array to empty, which clears all submitted items.

`<style>` consists of two simple custom CSS modifications. Like some of the chapters in this book, we're using Semantic UI[129] as the backbone of our application styling.

`main.js`

The `main.js` file imports and specifies `App` as the mounting point of our application:

[129]https://semantic-ui.com/

testing/basics/src/main.js

```
import Vue from 'vue';
import App from './App';

new Vue({
  el: '#app',
  render: h => h(App)
});
```

Let's see the application in the browser. We'll boot the app with:

```
$ npm run dev
```

And head over to `http://localhost:8080`:

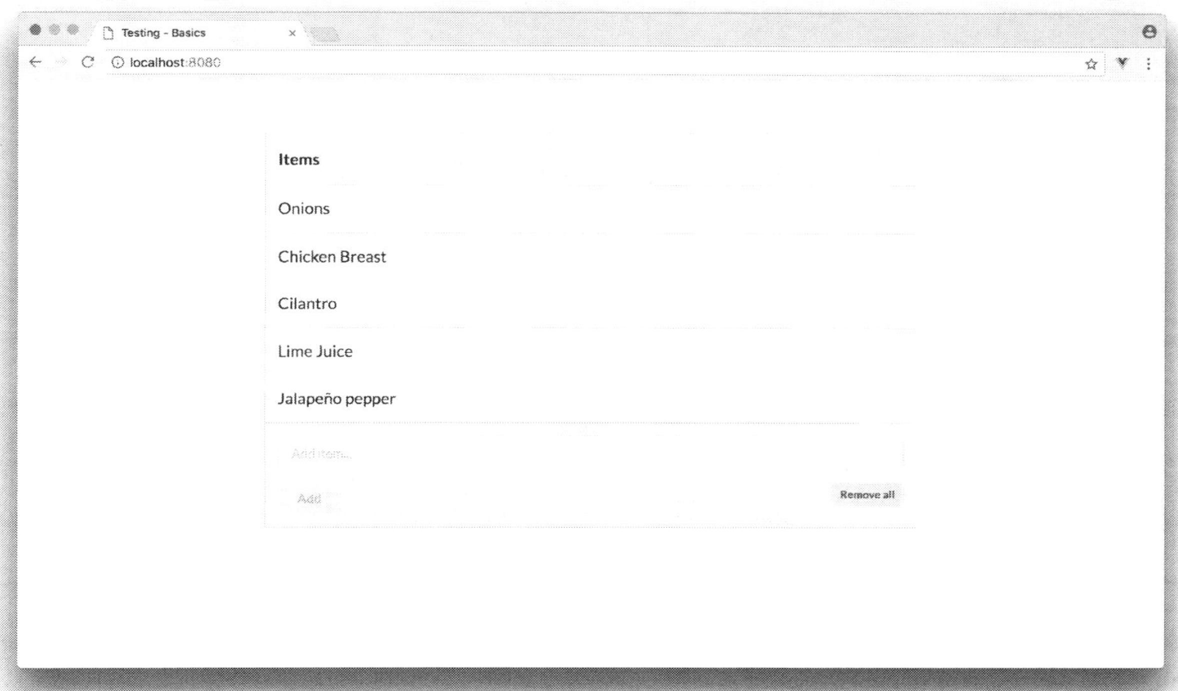

The app is simple. There is a field coupled with a button that adds items to a list. The "Remove all" label removes all items from the list when clicked.

`test/`

Before we begin writing tests for the `App` component, let's take a brief look at the files within the `test/` directory:

```
$ ls test/
index.js
karma.conf.js
specs/
```

`karma.conf.js` is the Karma configuration file for our Webpack project. It specifies `PhantomJS` as the environment our tests are to run in as well as the test frameworks that are to be used.

The `index.js` file specifies the location of the test files that should be included in the test suite. `karma.conf.js` references the `index.js` file in the *files* property of its configuration.

The `specs/` folder hosts the spec file we'll be working from, `App.spec.js`, as well as completed iterations along the way, `App.spec.1.js` to `App.spec.complete.js`.

```
$ ls test/specs/
App.spec.1.js
App.spec.2.js
App.spec.3.js
App.spec.4.js
App.spec.5.js
App.spec.complete.js
App.spec.js
```

Note: our test suite will currently *only* run tests from `App.spec.js` as specified in `test/index.js`. If there is a need to run tests from the completed iterations, the `test/index.js` file will have to be modified to reflect this.

In `test/index.js`, we specify that only the `.spec.js` file extensions, within the `specs/` folder, should be run in line 6:

testing/basics/test/index.js

```
const testsContext = require.context('./specs', true, /\.spec$/)
```

If, for example, we wanted to run tests from the `App.spec.complete.js` file, we'll modify the line to this:

```
const testsContext = require.context('./specs', true, /\.spec.complete$/)
```

Testing `App`

In `package.json`, we have a `test` script that boots Karma from our `karma.conf.js` file. We currently have a dummy test set up for us in `App.spec.js`. Let's execute Karma from inside `testing/basics` and see what happens:

```
$ npm run test
```

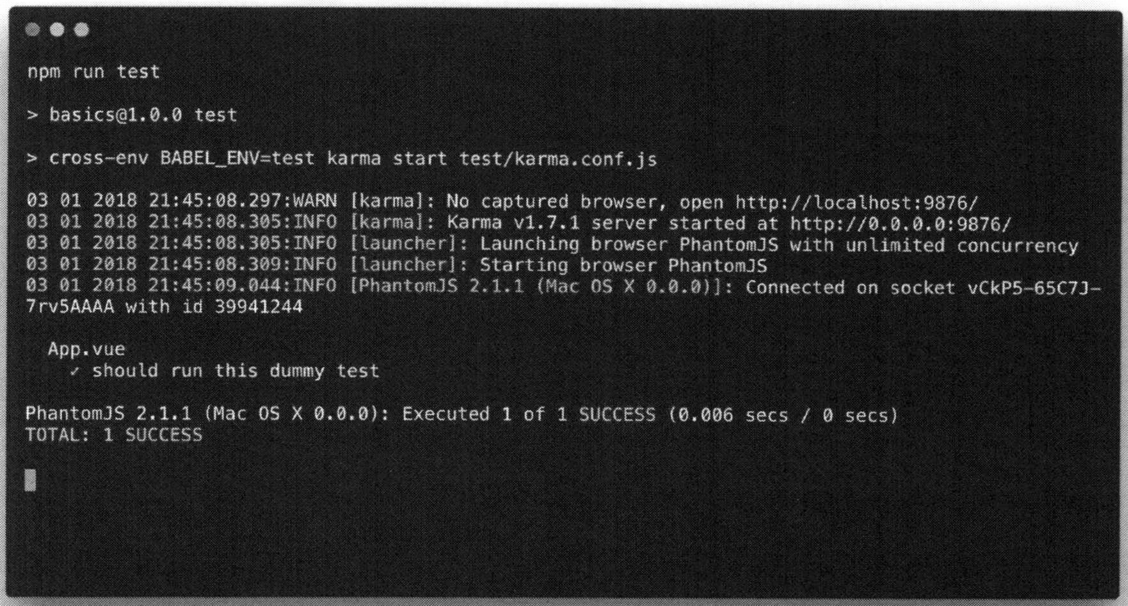

```
npm run test

> basics@1.0.0 test

> cross-env BABEL_ENV=test karma start test/karma.conf.js

03 01 2018 21:45:08.297:WARN [karma]: No captured browser, open http://localhost:9876/
03 01 2018 21:45:08.305:INFO [karma]: Karma v1.7.1 server started at http://0.0.0.0:9876/
03 01 2018 21:45:08.305:INFO [launcher]: Launching browser PhantomJS with unlimited concurrency
03 01 2018 21:45:08.309:INFO [launcher]: Starting browser PhantomJS
03 01 2018 21:45:09.044:INFO [PhantomJS 2.1.1 (Mac OS X 0.0.0)]: Connected on socket vCkP5-65C7J-
7rv5AAAA with id 39941244

  App.vue
    ✓ should run this dummy test

PhantomJS 2.1.1 (Mac OS X 0.0.0): Executed 1 of 1 SUCCESS (0.006 secs / 0 secs)
TOTAL: 1 SUCCESS
```

After the steps Karma takes to boot up, we can see information on the `describe` and `it` blocks that were run for the dummy test. In addition, we're given a summary of the overall test status at the end:

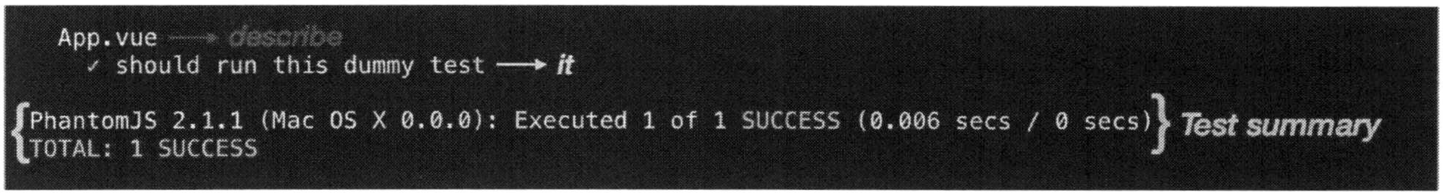

```
  App.vue ──→ describe
    ✓ should run this dummy test ──→ it

{PhantomJS 2.1.1 (Mac OS X 0.0.0): Executed 1 of 1 SUCCESS (0.006 secs / 0 secs)} Test summary
{TOTAL: 1 SUCCESS
```

A separate script in `package.json`, `test:watch`, allows us to **boot Karma in watch mode** as well:

testing/basics/package.json

```
    "test:watch": "cross-env BABEL_ENV=test karma start test/karma.conf.js",
```

In this mode, Karma does not quit after the test suite finishes. Instead, it watches the *whole project* for changes. When a change is detected, it re-runs the test suite.

To execute Karma in watch mode, we can run the following command in our terminal:

```
$ npm run test:watch
```

Throughout this chapter, we'll continue to mention to execute the test suite with `npm run test`. However, you can just keep a console window open with Karma running in watch mode if you'd like.

Writing our first spec

Let's take a look at the `App.spec.js` file and replace the existing dummy test with something more useful.

If we open `App.spec.js`, we'll see that it's currently laid out like this:

testing/basics/test/specs/App.spec.js

```
import Vue from 'vue';
import App from '@/App';

describe('App.vue', () => {
  it('should run this dummy test', () => {
    expect('Dummy' + ' Test!').to.equal('Dummy Test!');
  });
});
```

In the first two lines, we're importing the `vue` library and the `App` component. Though we can import `App` using the relative file path destination:

```
import App from '../../src/App';
```

Our Webpack configuration currently resolves the `@` symbol to import relatively from `src` anywhere in our app:

```
import App from '@/App';
```

Using the `@` character helps in readability when an application has a large number of `import` declarations.

Taking a look at our test, we can see we've titled our `describe` block after the module under test, `App.vue`. Let's remove the dummy test and create an actual test.

For our first spec, we'll assert that the application should render the *correct expected content*:

```
describe('App.vue', () => {
  it('should render correct contents', () => {
    // our assertion will go here
  });
});
```

The term "spec" is often used in JavaScript unit testing to refer to the *specification* (i.e. details of a feature) that must be fulfilled.

To test rendered content from our component, we need to mount our component. Before we mount, we'll first need to extend the `App` module like so:

```
describe('App.vue', () => {
  it('should render correct contents', () => {
    const Constructor = Vue.extend(App);
  });
});
```

`Vue.extend()` is the internal `Vue` method that is called when a component is created with `Vue.component()`. Unlike `Vue.component()`, `Vue.extend()` simply returns a constructor while `Vue.component()` associates the created constructor with a string ID for Vue to use in templates. We'll hardly ever find the need to use `Vue.extend()` in practice, but this differentiator makes it more suitable when writing unit tests.

With our constructor extended, we can now mount our component with the `$mount()` method:

```
describe('App.vue', () => {
  it('should render correct contents', () => {
    const Constructor = Vue.extend(App);
    const vm = new Constructor().$mount();
  });
});
```

`vm` references the mounted component that we can use to access rendered HTML. We can now inspect the rendered output and determine if the content matches what we expect.

To "look" for certain elements in the component template, we're going to be using CSS selectors with the native JavaScript `querySelector()`[130] method.

To see this in practice, let's first assert the presence of our table header:

[130]https://developer.mozilla.org/en-US/docs/Web/API/Document/querySelector

```
describe('App.vue', () => {
  it('should render correct contents', () => {
    const Constructor = Vue.extend(App);
    const vm = new Constructor().$mount();

    expect(
      vm.$el.querySelector('.ui.selectable thead tr th').textContent
    ).to.contain('Items');
  });
});
```

The component's HTML can be accessed with `vm.$el`. In this assertion we're using `querySelector()` to return the `<th>Items</th>` and *expecting* the element text content to contain the text 'Items'.

Though we can create multiple `it` blocks to test different assertions for rendering correct content; it also makes sense to keep it within the one spec we've created. Let's add two more assertions to verify the "Add" button and "Remove Items" label render the correct text content as well:

testing/basics/test/specs/App.spec.1.js

```
describe('App.vue', () => {
  it('should render correct contents', () => {
    const Constructor = Vue.extend(App);
    const vm = new Constructor().$mount();

    expect(
      vm.$el.querySelector('.ui.selectable thead tr th').textContent
    ).to.contain('Items');
    expect(
      vm.$el.querySelector('.ui.button').textContent
    ).to.contain('Add');
    expect(
      vm.$el.querySelector('.ui.label').textContent
    ).to.contain('Remove all');
  });
  // ...
});
```

CSS selectors

CSS files use selectors to specify which HTML elements a set of styles refers to. JavaScript applications also use this syntax to select HTML elements on a page.

Check out this MDN section[131] for more info on CSS selectors.

[131] https://developer.mozilla.org/en-US/docs/Learn/CSS/Introduction_to_CSS/Selectors

Try it out

Let's verify our first written spec. Save `App.spec.js` and run the test command from the console:

```
$ npm run test
```

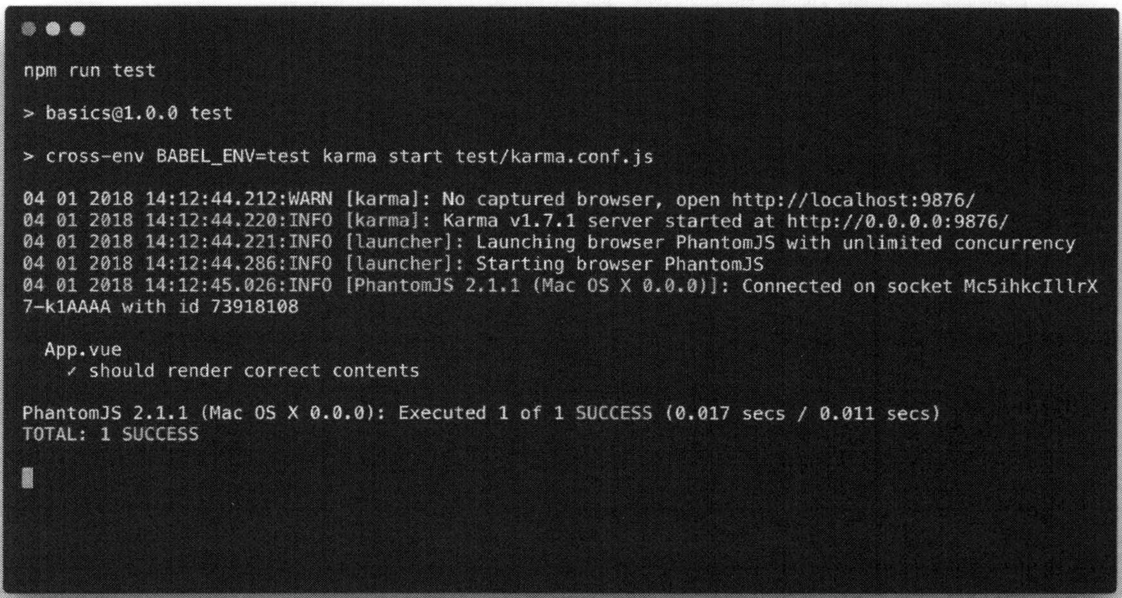

```
npm run test

> basics@1.0.0 test

> cross-env BABEL_ENV=test karma start test/karma.conf.js

04 01 2018 14:12:44.212:WARN [karma]: No captured browser, open http://localhost:9876/
04 01 2018 14:12:44.220:INFO [karma]: Karma v1.7.1 server started at http://0.0.0.0:9876/
04 01 2018 14:12:44.221:INFO [launcher]: Launching browser PhantomJS with unlimited concurrency
04 01 2018 14:12:44.286:INFO [launcher]: Starting browser PhantomJS
04 01 2018 14:12:45.026:INFO [PhantomJS 2.1.1 (Mac OS X 0.0.0)]: Connected on socket Mc5ihkcIllrX
7-k1AAAA with id 73918108

  App.vue
    ✓ should render correct contents

PhantomJS 2.1.1 (Mac OS X 0.0.0): Executed 1 of 1 SUCCESS (0.017 secs / 0.011 secs)
TOTAL: 1 SUCCESS
```

Awesome, our first test passes. Let's move on and create a test involving the initial component data.

Test initial data

We'll introduce a new spec that's responsible in asserting the component sets the correct default data:

```
describe('App.vue', () => {
  it('should render correct contents', () => {
    ...
  });

  it('should set correct default data', () => {
    // our assertion will go here
  });
});
```

The `data` property in components is a *function* that returns an object of key value pairs. We can access the component data by invoking said function. We'll do this and set the returned result to an `initialData` variable:

```
it('should set correct default data', () => {
  const initialData = App.data();
});
```

We can now create our assertions about the data. Our two assertions would expect that the `item` value and `items` array, in `initialData`, are a blank string and an empty array respectively:

testing/basics/test/specs/App.spec.1.js

```
  it('should set correct default data', () => {
    const initialData = App.data();

    expect(initialData.item).to.equal('');
    expect(initialData.items).to.deep.equal([]);
  });
```

Notice how we're specifying a `deep.equal` check for the `initialData.items`? Arrays are objects, and thus a simple equality operator checks if two arrays *are the same object*. Since we're only checking if the two arrays are *equivalent* (not identical), we use the deep[132] equality check.

Let's run our test suite again and verify that our new test passes:

```
$ npm run test
```

[132] http://chaijs.com/api/bdd/#method_deep

```
npm run test

> basics@1.0.0 test

> cross-env BABEL_ENV=test karma start test/karma.conf.js

04 01 2018 14:52:10.844:WARN [karma]: No captured browser, open http://localhost:9876/
04 01 2018 14:52:10.852:INFO [karma]: Karma v1.7.1 server started at http://0.0.0.0:9876/
04 01 2018 14:52:10.852:INFO [launcher]: Launching browser PhantomJS with unlimited concurrency
04 01 2018 14:52:10.857:INFO [launcher]: Starting browser PhantomJS
04 01 2018 14:52:11.609:INFO [PhantomJS 2.1.1 (Mac OS X 0.0.0)]: Connected on socket sXmZL-WOTkTj
88IEAAAA with id 86745532

  App.vue
    ✓ should render correct contents
    ✓ should set correct default data

PhantomJS 2.1.1 (Mac OS X 0.0.0): Executed 2 of 2 SUCCESS (0.018 secs / 0.011 secs)
TOTAL: 2 SUCCESS
```

Our specs pass

Our specs at this point assert that our component is initialized as expected. These fundamental specs assert that the elements we will be interacting with are present on the page to begin with.

Before we continue onwards however, we're going to refactor the current specs we have to use Vue's official unit testing library, `vue-test-utils`[133].

vue-test-utils

Though the way we've been writing our tests work just fine, there are significant advantages to using Vue's utility library, `vue-test-utils`.

The library provides us with useful methods that we can use to write our assertions. In general, these helper methods **help us traverse and select elements on the rendered DOM more easily**.

For instance, `vue-test-utils` allows us to mount a component in isolation simply using a `mount()` method. Here's an example of creating a `wrapper` using `mount()`:

```
const wrapper = mount(Component)
```

In the testing environment with `vue-test-utils`, a `wrapper` is an object that contains a mounted component *and* the accompanying methods to help test the component.

[133]https://github.com/vuejs/vue-test-utils

With the `wrapper` object, we're able to access the Vue instance with `vm`:

```
const vm = wrapper.vm;
```

We're also able to retrieve a component's HTML with the `html()` helper method:

```
const html = wrapper.html();
```

We could use the `find()` helper to return a wrapper for selected HTML elements:

```
const button = wrapper.find('button');
```

These are only some of the helper methods that `mount()` provides, while there are much more available.

In addition, `vue-test-utils` also allows us to mount a component *without rendering its children* using the `shallow()` method:

```
const wrapper = shallow(Component);
```

This wrapper now contains the shallow-rendered component. There are two primary advantages to shallow rendering:

It tests components in *isolation*

Isolated tests are preferable for unit tests. When we are writing tests for a parent component, we don't have to worry about dependencies on child components.

A change made to a child component might break the child component's unit tests but it won't break that of any parents.

It's *faster*

Components that contain many child components can have an extremely large rendered tree. With shallow rendering, we avoid rendering *all* child components.

Let's see how the `vue-test-utils` library works in practice.

At the time of writing, the `vue-test-utils`[134] library is still in **beta**. With that being said, the API and documentation[135] is almost complete so we're able to use the library effectively.

Refactoring the current specs

We'll start off with refactoring the current existing specs. Since we already have the `vue-test-utils` library installed in our application, let's import the `shallow()` method in `App.spec.js`. We won't have the need to use the `vue` library anymore so our `import` statements will now simply be:

[134] https://github.com/vuejs/vue-test-utils

[135] https://vue-test-utils.vuejs.org/en/

testing/basics/test/specs/App.spec.2.js

```
import App from '@/App';
import {shallow} from 'vue-test-utils';
```

Using `beforeEach`

Since we would need to shallow render the component (and declare a `wrapper` constant) in almost all `it` blocks, this would lead to some repetitive code. To avoid this repetition, the first thing that may come to mind is creating the `wrapper` at the top of the `describe` block:

```
describe('App.vue', () => {
  let wrapper = shallow(App);

  // specs
});
```

This approach works as expected since `wrapper` would now be available in each of our `it` blocks thanks to JavaScript's scoping rules.

However, if one of our tests needs to modify the shallow rendered component (e.g. changing the component's data or simulating an event), **this would cause state to leak between specs**. At the start of the next spec, our component's data would be *unpredictable*.

Instead, it is preferable to re-render the shallow component between each spec, ensuring that each spec is working with the component in a predictable, fresh state. We'll use a `beforeEach` function to set up this fresh state before every test:

`beforeEach` is a block of code, that exists in all popular JavaScript test frameworks, that will run **before each `it` block**.

We'll set up a `beforeEach` function like so:

```
describe('App.vue', () => {
  let wrapper;

  beforeEach(() => {
    wrapper = shallow(App);
  });

  // specs
});
```

We declare `wrapper` using a `let` declaration at the top of the describe block to ensure it's in scope for all of our assertions. If we declared `wrapper` inside the `beforeEach` block, it would not have been in scope for our specs.

Since our application only consists of a single component with fairly simple functionality, the `mount()` method works just as well in this case.

Now, let's refactor our first spec. Since our component is already rendered, we can remove `Vue.extend()` and the subsequent mounting. To determine whether the correct content has been rendered, we'll use the wrapper `html()` helper:

testing/basics/test/specs/App.spec.2.js

```
describe('App.vue', () => {
  // ...
  it('should render correct contents', () => {
    expect(wrapper.html()).to.contain('<th>Items</th>');
    expect(wrapper.html()).to.contain(
      '<input type="text" placeholder="Add item..." value="" class="prompt">'
    );
    expect(wrapper.html()).to.contain(
      '<button type="submit" disabled="disabled" class="ui button">Add</button>'
    );
    expect(wrapper.html()).to.contain(
      '<span class="ui label">Remove all</span>'
    );
  });
  // ...
});
```

`html()` returns the entire HTML of the component as a string. We've simply created our assertions to determine if the rendered template contains the expected markup elements. Though slightly different than testing for text content, the outcome is equivalent.

For our second spec ("should set correct default data"), we can access the data properties directly from the actual Vue instance with `wrapper.vm`:

testing/basics/test/specs/App.spec.2.js

```
  it('should set correct default data', () => {
    expect(wrapper.vm.item).to.equal('');
    expect(wrapper.vm.items).to.deep.equal([]);
  });
```

Try it out

Let's run our tests again to verify that our refactor hasn't broken any tests.

```
$ npm run test
```

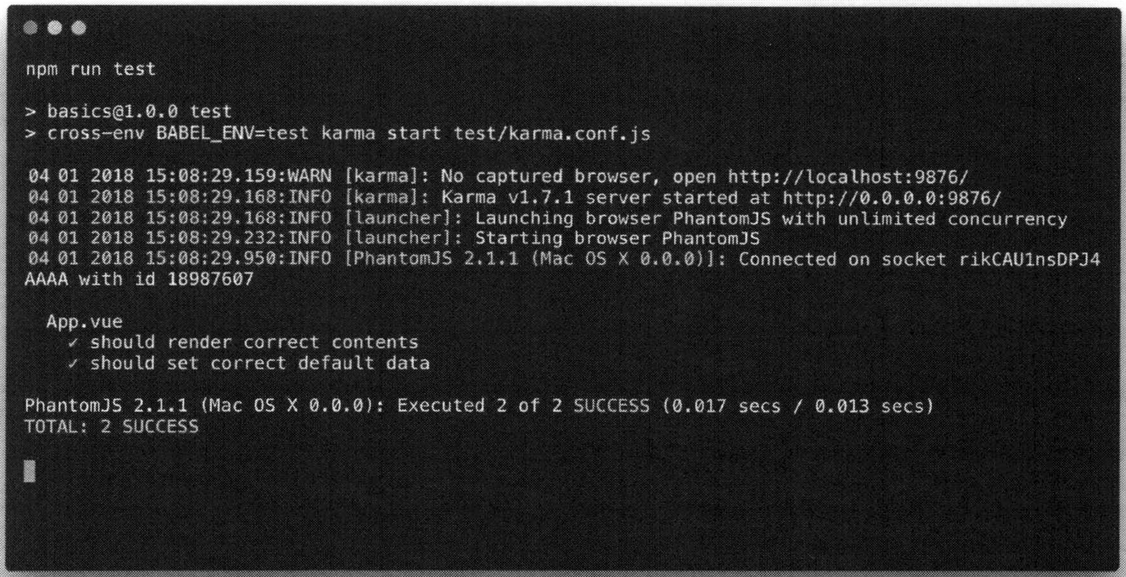

```
npm run test

> basics@1.0.0 test
> cross-env BABEL_ENV=test karma start test/karma.conf.js

04 01 2018 15:08:29.159:WARN [karma]: No captured browser, open http://localhost:9876/
04 01 2018 15:08:29.168:INFO [karma]: Karma v1.7.1 server started at http://0.0.0.0:9876/
04 01 2018 15:08:29.168:INFO [launcher]: Launching browser PhantomJS with unlimited concurrency
04 01 2018 15:08:29.232:INFO [launcher]: Starting browser PhantomJS
04 01 2018 15:08:29.950:INFO [PhantomJS 2.1.1 (Mac OS X 0.0.0)]: Connected on socket rikCAU1nsDPJ4
AAAA with id 18987607

  App.vue
    ✓ should render correct contents
    ✓ should set correct default data

PhantomJS 2.1.1 (Mac OS X 0.0.0): Executed 2 of 2 SUCCESS (0.017 secs / 0.013 secs)
TOTAL: 2 SUCCESS
```

Awesome, our refactor hasn't made our tests fail. We'll continue to explore the `vue-test-utils` API as we write more assertions.

More assertions for `App.vue`

Our next spec will involve asserting the components 'Add' button is `disabled` upon page load.

We'll specify this new assertion in a new `it` block. The first thing we'll need to do is "find" the button element. We'll use the `find()` helper with the appropriate button CSS selector to select this button element:

```
it('should have the "Add" button disabled', () => {
  const addItemButton = wrapper.find('.ui.button');
});
```

While the Vue instance wrapper contains a `vm` object, all elements returned by `find()` have an `element` property. Remember, `.find()` returns the *wrapper* of the DOM node. `element` will return the DOM node for us to access. As a result, we'll make an assertion on the element's `disabled` attribute:

testing/basics/test/specs/App.spec.2.js

```
  it('should have the "Add" button disabled', () => {
    const addItemButton = wrapper.find('.ui.button');

    expect(addItemButton.element.disabled).to.be.true;
  });
```

Try it out

Save `App.spec.js`. Run the test suite:

```
$ npm run test
```

```
npm run test

> basics@1.0.0 test

> cross-env BABEL_ENV=test karma start test/karma.conf.js

04 01 2018 19:34:10.432:WARN [karma]: No captured browser, open http://localhost:9876/
04 01 2018 19:34:10.441:INFO [karma]: Karma v1.7.1 server started at http://0.0.0.0:9876/
04 01 2018 19:34:10.442:INFO [launcher]: Launching browser PhantomJS with unlimited concurrency
04 01 2018 19:34:10.449:INFO [launcher]: Starting browser PhantomJS
04 01 2018 19:34:11.194:INFO [PhantomJS 2.1.1 (Mac OS X 0.0.0)]: Connected on socket XXpxwXVY3LMw
4NI6AAAA with id 59731056

  App.vue
    ✓ should render correct contents
    ✓ should set correct default data
    ✓ should have the "Add" button disabled

PhantomJS 2.1.1 (Mac OS X 0.0.0): Executed 3 of 3 SUCCESS (0.025 secs / 0.004 secs)
TOTAL: 3 SUCCESS
```

The specs we've written set the foundation for our next set of specs.

By asserting the presence of certain elements in the initial render as we have so far, we're asserting what the user will see on the page when the app loads. We have asserted that there will be a table header, an input, and a disabled button. We also asserted the initial values (`item` and `items`) in our template.

For our remaining assertions, we're going to use a **behavior-driven** style to drive how we lay out our `describe` and `it` blocks. With this style, we'll simulate interactions with the component much like we were a user navigating the interface.

After loading the app, the first thing we'd envision a user would do is fill in the input. When the input is filled, they will click the "Add" button. We would then expect the new item to be stored in the component data and on the page.

Populating the text input

The first interaction a user can have with our app is populating the input field to add a new item. We want to simulate this behavior in the next set of specs.

Since the next few specs we write fall within a particular group of tests, we can declare another `describe` block inside of our current one to group these together:

```
describe('App.vue', () => {
  // the assertions we've written so far

  describe('the user populates the text input field', () => {
    // our new assertions
  });
});
```

Our assertions in the new `describe` block all involve simulating how a user populates the text `input` DOM element. To avoid the repetition of finding the input, updating the value, and triggering an event in each test; we can extrapolate this set-up to a `beforeEach`:

```
describe('App.vue', () => {
  // the assertions we've written so far

  describe('the user populates the text input field', () => {
    let inputField;

    beforeEach(() => {
      inputField = wrapper.find('input');
      inputField.element.value = 'New Item';
```

```
      inputField.trigger('input');
    });

    // our new assertions
  });
});
```

The `beforeEach` that we write for our inner `describe` will be run after the `beforeEach` declared in the outer context. Therefore, the `wrapper` object will already be shallow rendered by the time this `beforeEach` function is executed. As expected, this `beforeEach` will only be run for `it` blocks inside our inner `describe` block.

In the `beforeEach`, we're doing a few things to simulate how a user will create an input event:

1. We first find the `input` wrapper with `.find()`. Since our component has a single input, we're able to use the actual `input` element as our selector.
2. We then set the value of the `input` DOM element to 'New Item'.
3. Finally, we use `trigger()` to simulate the actual user interaction.

The `trigger()` method accepts two arguments:

1. The event to *simulate* (e.g. `input`, `click`, etc.). This determines which Event handler gets dispatched (e.g. `oninput`, `onclick`).
2. An event object which is optional.

To manipulate the value of a DOM element, we **can't set the value of the event target in the optional event object argument**. We need to set the value *prior* to calling trigger like we've done above (`inputField.element.value = 'New Item'`).

With this setup written, we can now write specs related to the context where the user has just populated the input field. For this context, we'll write two new tests:

testing/basics/test/specs/App.spec.3.js

```
describe('the user populates the text input field', () => {
  let inputField;

  beforeEach(() => {
    inputField = wrapper.find('input');
    inputField.element.value = 'New Item';
    inputField.trigger('input');
  });
```

```
  it('should update the "text" data property', () => {
    expect(wrapper.vm.item).to.equal('New Item');
  });

  it('should enable the "Add" button when text input is populated', () => {
    const addItemButton = wrapper.find('.ui.button');

    expect(addItemButton.element.disabled).to.be.false;
  });
});
```

In the first test, we grab the `item` data property with `wrapper.vm.item` and simply test if it matches the `input` value after the event is triggered.

In the second, we find the 'Add' button like we've done earlier and test if the `disabled` attribute of the button is `false` (i.e the button is enabled).

To convey the behaviour-driven manner of our tests, at this moment we can envision our component in the following state:

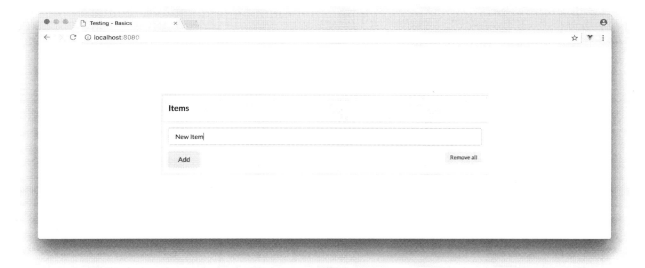

Before we run our test suite, let's write a test to determine how the button reacts when the user clears the input field.

Clearing the input field

When the user clears an input field that has been filled out, we expect the button to become disabled again. We can build on the context of the "the user populates text input field" `describe` by nesting a new `describe` inside of it.

Our entire `describe` hierarchy will now look like this:

```
describe('App.vue', () => {
  // ...

  describe('the user populates the text input field', () => {
    // ...

    describe('and then clears the input', () => {
      // assert the add item button is disabled
    });
  });
});
```

To create the scenario that the user clears the input field, we'll set the `input` element value to a blank string before calling `trigger()`. We'll find the 'Add' button and test the value of its `disabled` attribute like we've done before.

Since we'll have a single test in this `describe` block, we'll forego the use of a `beforeEach` and create our set-up within the test:

```
describe('the user populates the text input field', () => {
  // ...

  describe('and then clears the input', () => {
    it('should disable the "Add" button', () => {
      const addItemButton = wrapper.find('.ui.button');

      inputField.element.value = '';
      inputField.trigger('input');

      expect(addItemButton.element.disabled).to.be.true;
    });
  });
});
```

At the moment, we can envision this test in the following scenario of our application:

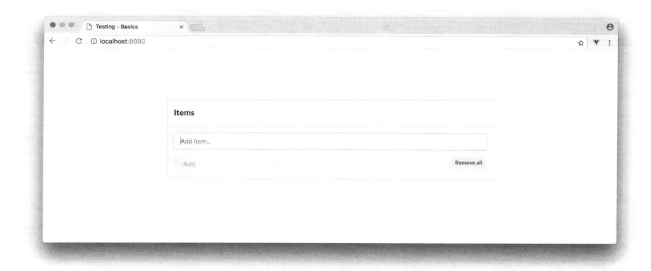

Try it out

Now will be a good time to verify the status of our test suite. We'll save `App.spec.js` and run the tests again:

```
$ npm run test
```

```
npm run test

> basics@1.0.0 test

> cross-env BABEL_ENV=test karma start test/karma.conf.js

05 01 2018 19:24:32.296:WARN [karma]: No captured browser, open http://localhost:9876/
05 01 2018 19:24:32.304:INFO [karma]: Karma v1.7.1 server started at http://0.0.0.0:9876/
05 01 2018 19:24:32.304:INFO [launcher]: Launching browser PhantomJS with unlimited concurrency
05 01 2018 19:24:32.308:INFO [launcher]: Starting browser PhantomJS
05 01 2018 19:24:33.045:INFO [PhantomJS 2.1.1 (Mac OS X 0.0.0)]: Connected on socket -fpmlkul_SLl
rUe1AAAA with id 88048677

  App.vue
    ✓ should render correct contents
    ✓ should set correct default data
    ✓ should have the "Add" button disabled
    the user populates the text input field
      ✓ should update the "text" data property
      ✓ should enable the "Add" button when text input is populated
      and then clears the input
        ✓ should disable the "Add" button

PhantomJS 2.1.1 (Mac OS X 0.0.0): Executed 6 of 6 SUCCESS (0.034 secs / 0.004 secs)
TOTAL: 6 SUCCESS
```

Our tests pass. Let's now move to creating tests for when the user submits the form.

Submitting the form

When a user submits the form we need to verify that:

1. The newly added item is in the data property `items` **and** is displayed in the rendered table.
2. The `item` data value is reverted to a blank string **and** the input field is cleared out.
3. The 'Add' button is disabled once again.

Each of these points will be a test spec of its own. These tests will live in a context inside the "the user populates the text input field" `describe` as a sibling to the "and then clears the input" `describe`. We'll name the new `describe` block with a title of "and then submits the form":

```
describe('App.vue', () => {
  // ...

  describe('the user populates the text input field', () => {
    // ...

    describe('and clears the input', () => {
      // ...
    });

    describe('and then submits the form', () => {
      // assertions for submitting the form
    });
  });
});
```

Since we'll be having multiple tests in this context that share a similar setup, we'll establish a `beforeEach` to mimic form submission.

To simulate a valid form submission, we need to click the add item button, "Add", with text present in the input field.

In this case, instead of simulating the input element value and calling `trigger()`, we'll directly update the `item` data value with the `setData()` method. Though this will achieve the same outcome, we'll use `setData()` to see how we can manipulate the component's `data` properties without always having to trigger events on template DOM nodes:

```
describe('and then submits the form', () => {
    let addItemButton;

    beforeEach(() => {
      wrapper.setData({item: 'New Item'});
      addItemButton = wrapper.find('.ui.button');
      addItemButton.trigger('click');
    });
});
```

`setData()` is a `wrapper` method that force updates the `wrapper vm` data object to set the `item` value to 'New Item'. This is equivalent to manipulating the input element value and calling `trigger()`.

With our setup in place, our first test will involve asserting that the new item is added to the `items` data property *and* the item is rendered in the table.

We'll create this test (and the following tests) within the "and then submits the form" `describe` block:

```
it('should add a new item to the "items" data property', () => {
  const itemList = wrapper.find('.item-list');

  expect(wrapper.vm.items).to.contain('New Item');
  expect(itemList.html()).to.contain('<td>New Item</td>');
});
```

We use `find()` to find the table body element from its CSS class `.item-list`. We check that the `items` array has a new item *and* the table body element contains the rendered item `<td>New Item<td>`.

Next, let's assert the `item` data property *and* the input element value is cleared out in the conceived template:

```
it('should set the "item" data property to a blank string', () => {
  const inputField = wrapper.find('input');

  expect(wrapper.vm.item).to.equal('');
  expect(inputField.element.value).to.equal('');
});
```

Finally, we'll assert that the add item button is again disabled:

```
it('should disable the "Add" button', () => {
  expect(addItemButton.element.disabled).to.be.true;
});
```

In its entirety, the "and then submits the form" `describe` block will be laid out like this:

```
describe('and then submits the form', () => {
  let addItemButton;

  beforeEach(() => {
    wrapper.setData({item: 'New Item'});
    addItemButton = wrapper.find('.ui.button');
    addItemButton.trigger('click');
  });

  it('should add a new item to the "items" data property', () => {
    let itemList = wrapper.find('.item-list');

    expect(wrapper.vm.items).to.contain('New Item');
    expect(itemList.html()).to.contain('<td>New Item</td>');
```

```
  });

  it('should set the "item" data property to a blank string', () => {
    let inputField = wrapper.find('input');

    expect(wrapper.vm.item).to.equal('');
    expect(inputField.element.value).to.equal('');
  });

  it('should disable the "Add" button', () => {
    expect(addItemButton.element.disabled).to.be.true;
  });
});
```

At this point, it might appear we have a minor refactor we can do. We can move all `.find()` declarations to the `beforeEach` method to simplify our specs:

testing/basics/test/specs/App.spec.5.js

```
    describe('and then submits the form', () => {
      let addItemButton;
      let itemList;
      let inputField;

      beforeEach(() => {
        addItemButton = wrapper.find('.ui.button');
        itemList = wrapper.find('.item-list');
        inputField = wrapper.find('input');

        wrapper.setData({item: 'New Item'});
        addItemButton.trigger('click');
      });

      it('should add a new item to the "items" data property', () => {
        expect(wrapper.vm.items).to.contain('New Item');
        expect(itemList.html()).to.contain('<td>New Item</td>');
      });

      it('should set the "item" data property to a blank string', () => {
        expect(wrapper.vm.item).to.equal('');
        expect(inputField.element.value).to.equal('');
      });
```

```
    it('should disable the "Add" button', () => {
      expect(addItemButton.element.disabled).to.be.true;
    });
  });
```

At this point, we're asserting how our app behaves in this condition:

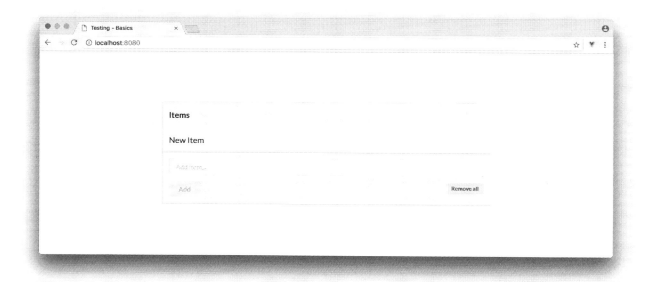

Try it out

Let's test our suite with our new `describe` context:

```
$ npm run test
```

```
npm run test

> basics@1.0.0 test

> cross-env BABEL_ENV=test karma start test/karma.conf.js

06 01 2018 12:53:33.411:WARN [karma]: No captured browser, open http://localhost:9876/
06 01 2018 12:53:33.420:INFO [karma]: Karma v1.7.1 server started at http://0.0.0.0:9876/
06 01 2018 12:53:33.420:INFO [launcher]: Launching browser PhantomJS with unlimited concurrency
06 01 2018 12:53:33.427:INFO [launcher]: Starting browser PhantomJS
06 01 2018 12:53:34.295:INFO [PhantomJS 2.1.1 (Mac OS X 0.0.0)]: Connected on socket IYwu1ry8gdda
5aRqAAAA with id 56263066

  App.vue
    ✓ should render correct contents
    ✓ should set correct default data
    ✓ should have the "Add" button disabled
    the user populates the text input field
      ✓ should update the "text" data property
      ✓ should enable the "Add" button when text input is populated
      and then clears the input
        ✓ should disable the "Add" button
      and then submits the form
        ✓ should add a new item to the "items" data property
        ✓ should set the "item" data property to a blank string
        ✓ should disable the "Add" button

PhantomJS 2.1.1 (Mac OS X 0.0.0): Executed 9 of 9 SUCCESS (0.044 secs / 0.004 secs)
TOTAL: 9 SUCCESS
```

Our tests pass. The last context we'll test involves asserting that clicking the "Remove all" label will remove all submitted items.

Removing all items

This particular context will live in its own `describe` block as a sibling to "the user populates the text input field" `describe`:

```
describe('App.vue', () => {
  // ...

  describe('the user populates the text input field', () => {
    // ...
  });

  describe('the user clicks the "Remove all" label', () => {
    // assertion for removing all items
  });
});
```

To create a spec for this particular context, we first need to have items submitted in the form as a starting point. We'll create this setup in the `beforeEach` of the new `describe` block:

```
describe('the user clicks the "Remove all" label', () => {
  beforeEach(() => {
    wrapper.setData({items: ['Item #1', 'Item #2', 'Item #3']});
  });
});
```

To simulate having three items already submitted in the form, we're using the `setData()` method to update the `items` data property directly with 'Item #1', 'Item #2', and 'Item #3'. With `setData()` we don't need to invoke a `trigger()` on the 'Add' button *multiple* times to ensure all three items are added to the `items` array.

Since we're using a `beforeEach` method for this context, let's establish the `find()` calls here as well. In the upcoming test, we'll need to have access to the item list body and the 'Remove all' label wrappers:

```
describe('the user clicks the "Remove all" label', () => {
  let itemList;
  let removeItemsLabel;

  beforeEach(() => {
    itemList = wrapper.find('.item-list');
    removeItemsLabel = wrapper.find('.ui.label');

    wrapper.setData({items: ['Item #1', 'Item #2', 'Item #3']});
  });
});
```

With our setup established, our test will simply involve triggering a click event on the 'Remove All' label and asserting that no items remain in the form. To assert no items exist, we'll verify that the `items` data property is a blank array *and* the rendered HTML does not contain any of the item cells in the table.

Our entire `describe` context will be:

testing/basics/test/specs/App.spec.complete.js

```
describe('the user clicks the "Remove all" label', () => {
  let itemList;
  let removeItemsLabel;

  beforeEach(() => {
    itemList = wrapper.find('.item-list');
    removeItemsLabel = wrapper.find('.ui.label');

    wrapper.setData({items: ['Item #1', 'Item #2', 'Item #3']});
  });

  it('should remove all items from the "items" data property', () => {
    removeItemsLabel.trigger('click');

    expect(wrapper.vm.items).to.deep.equal([]);
    expect(itemList.html()).to.not.contain('<td>Item #1</td>');
    expect(itemList.html()).to.not.contain('<td>Item #2</td>');
    expect(itemList.html()).to.not.contain('<td>Item #3</td>');
  });
});
```

Try it out

Let's make sure our new test passes successfully.

```
$ npm run start
```

```
npm run test

> basics@1.0.0 test

> cross-env BABEL_ENV=test karma start test/karma.conf.js

06 01 2018 13:59:40.215:WARN [karma]: No captured browser, open http://localhost:9876/
06 01 2018 13:59:40.224:INFO [karma]: Karma v1.7.1 server started at http://0.0.0.0:9876/
06 01 2018 13:59:40.224:INFO [launcher]: Launching browser PhantomJS with unlimited concurrency
06 01 2018 13:59:40.234:INFO [launcher]: Starting browser PhantomJS
06 01 2018 13:59:40.963:INFO [PhantomJS 2.1.1 (Mac OS X 0.0.0)]: Connected on socket WFQe6DSVYpLy
F43ZAAAA with id 88440153

  App.vue
    ✓ should render correct contents
    ✓ should set correct default data
    ✓ should have the "Add" button disabled
    the user populates the text input field
      ✓ should update the "text" data property
      ✓ should enable the "Add" button when text input is populated
      and then clears the input
        ✓ should disable the "Add" button
      and then submits the form
        ✓ should add a new item to the "items" data property
        ✓ should set the "item" data property to a blank string
        ✓ should disable the "Add" button
    the user clicks the "Remove all" label
      ✓ should remove all items from the "items" data property

PhantomJS 2.1.1 (Mac OS X 0.0.0): Executed 10 of 10 SUCCESS (0.047 secs / 0.008 secs)
TOTAL: 10 SUCCESS
```

Everything passes! We can try breaking various parts of the `App` component and witness the test suite catch these failures.

Our test suite for `App` is pretty comprehensive. We've established layers of context based on real-world workflows and with each context asserted the component's desired behavior.

We've managed to understand how a behavioural-driven approach to writing tests can be done with the `Mocha` testing library and `Chai` assertions. We've covered the benefits to using `vue-test-utils` and the importance of shallow rendering.

In the next section, we'll advance our understanding of writing Vue tests by looking into how tests can be done for an application that relies on a web request to an API and is integrated with Vuex and Vue Router.

Writing tests for a weather app

In this section, we're going to be writing tests for a weather application that tells us the current day's weather forecast in certain cities across the world (New York, Buenos Aires, Moscow, Tokyo, Sydney, and Lagos).

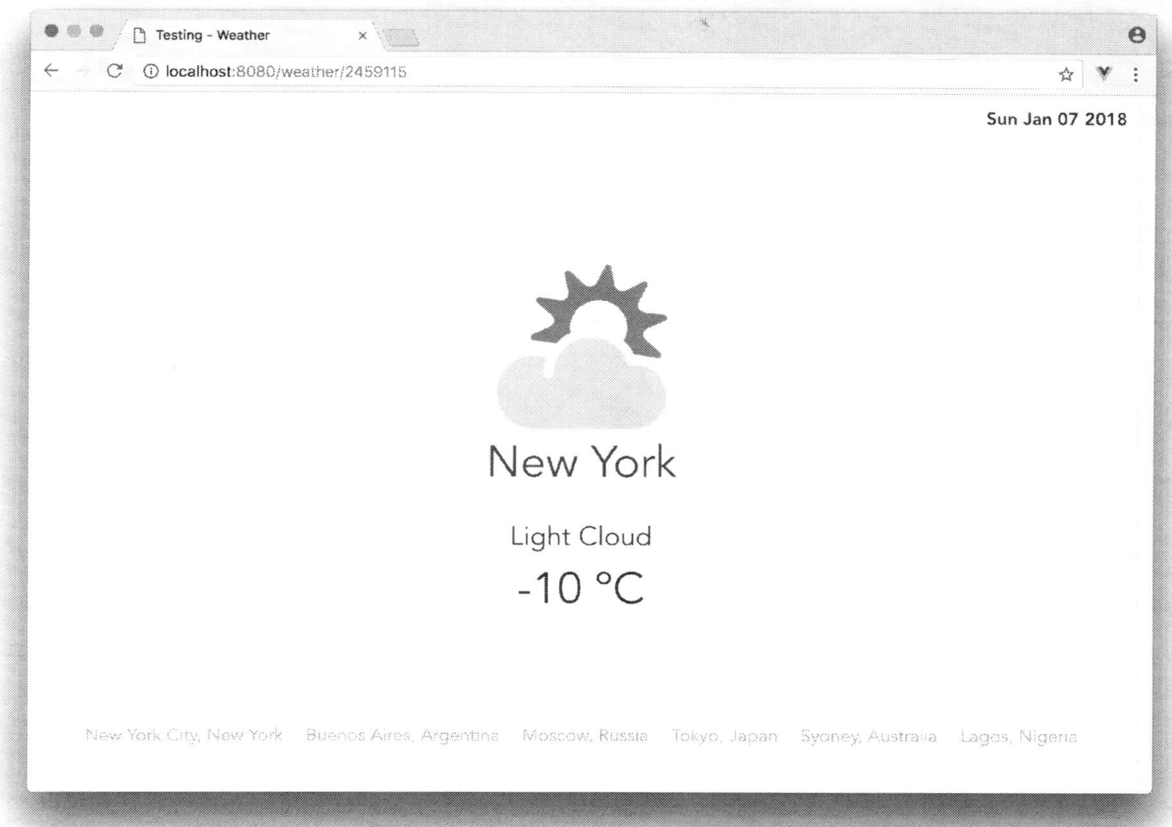

> Though we'll be describing the app's layout and structure, we won't be going into heavy detail on how Vuex and Vue Router was used to construct the app.
>
> If you're reading this chapter and are unfamiliar with these concepts, we discuss Vuex in depth in Chapters 4 and 5 and we cover routing in detail in Chapter 7.

Like the previous section, we'll be writing tests for an already completed application. To get into this app directory from the `testing/basics` folder, run the following command:

```
$ cd ../weather
```

We'll install the npm packages:

```
$ npm install
```

And start up the app with:

```
$ npm run start
```

Let's head over `http://localhost:8080` to find the running application. The first screen we'll be presented with will look like the following:

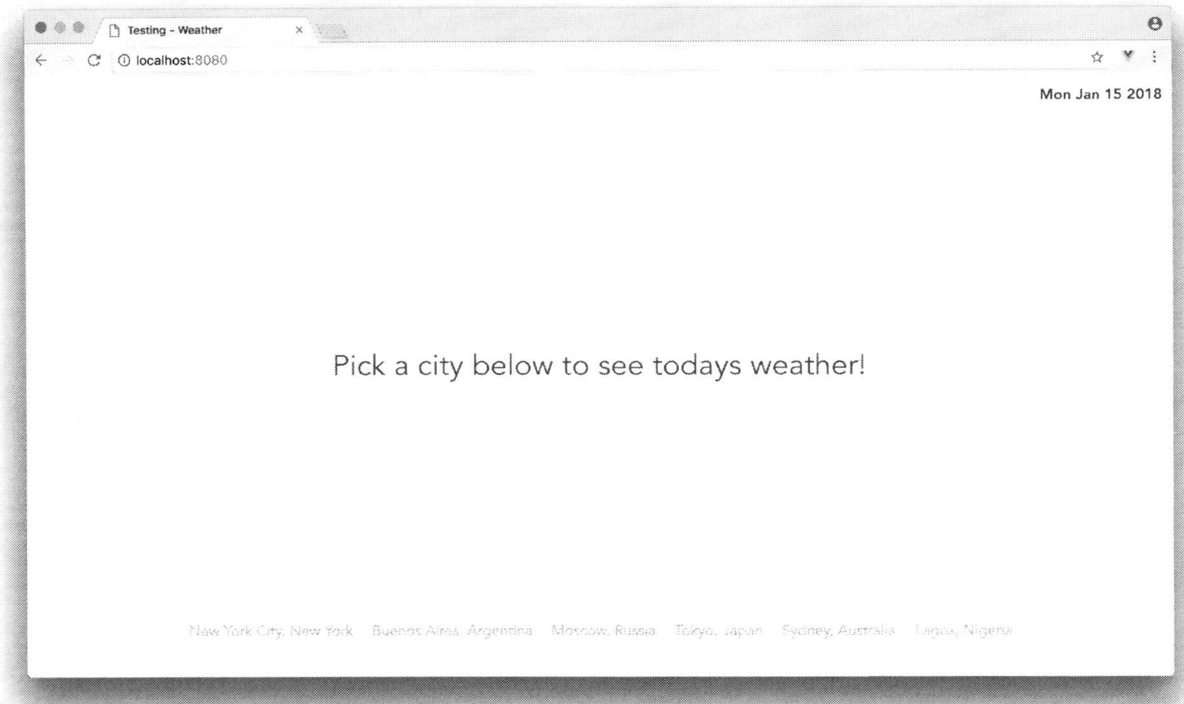

Clicking any of the links at the foot of the screen will *rerender* the 'Pick a city...' message to display weather details of the selected city:

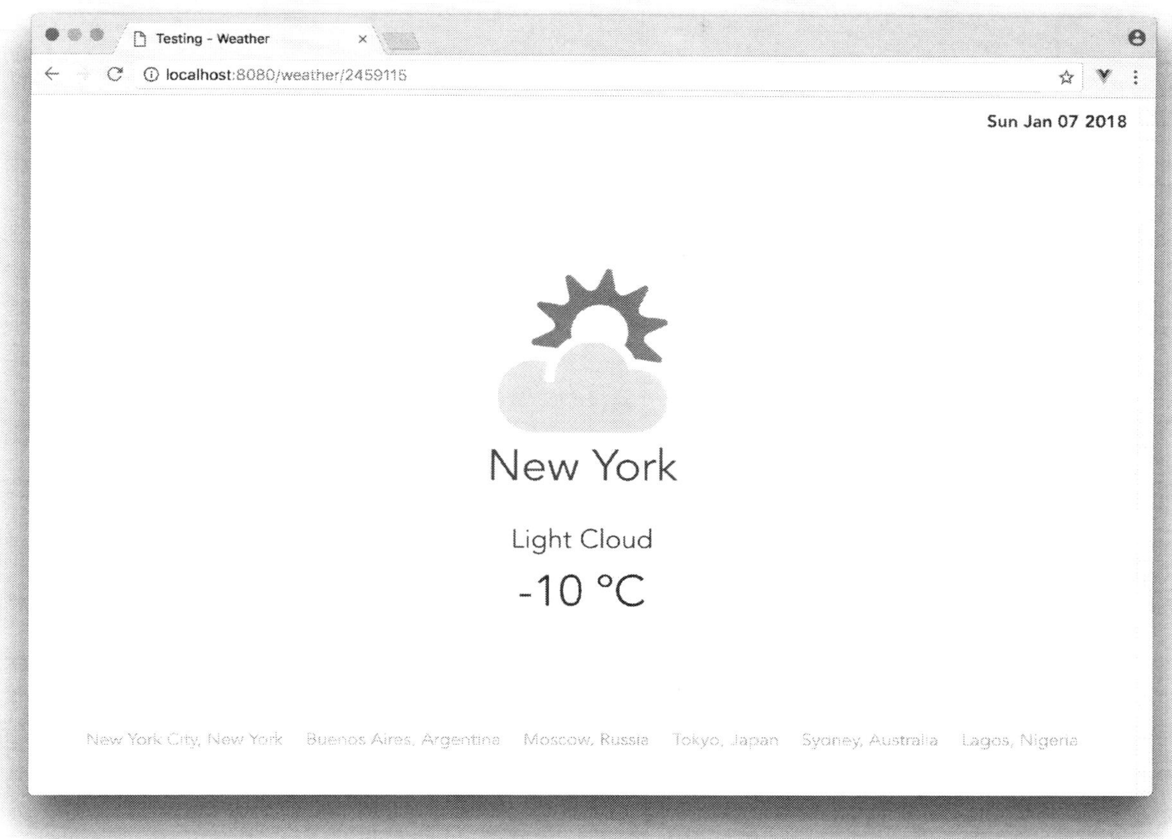

Let's understand how the app is broken down into components at a high-level:

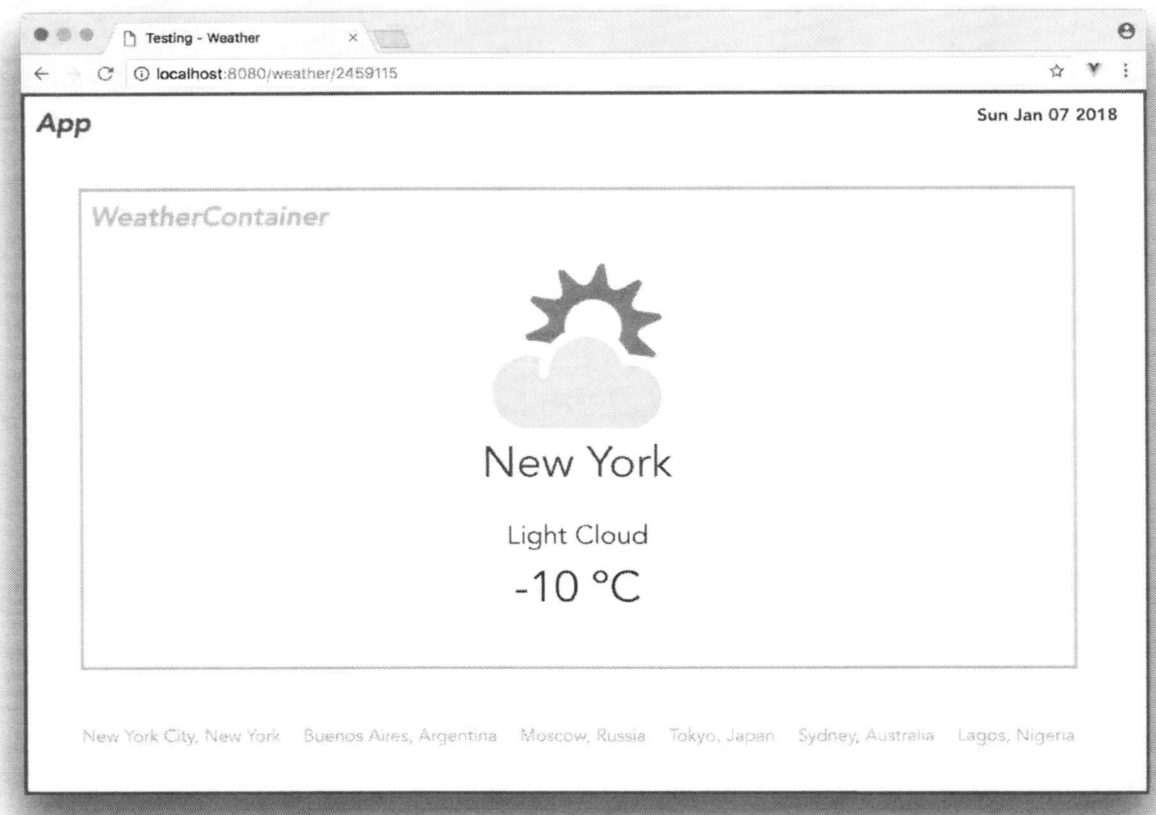

- **App**: The parent container for the application.
- **WeatherContainer**: The child component that displays weather details of a certain location based on the URL route

The links at the foot of application are `<router-link>` elements that upon click direct the user to a new route, which subsequently updates `WeatherContainer` with the weather details of the new location.

The "Pick a city…" message is the "Home" component (`HomeContainer`) that's displayed to the user when the URL route is at the root path, `/`. If we type an unknown pathname in the URL bar (e.g. `/not-found`), we'll be presented with the `NotFoundContainer` component instead:

/ — *HomeContainer*

/not-found — *NotFoundContainer*

This shows how `vue-router` is being used in our application. We'll get a better understanding of this when we look through the existing code.

App structure

The structure of the application matches that of the app we tested in the first section:

```
$ ls
README.md
build/
config/
index.html
node_modules/
package.json/
server.js
src/
static/
test/
```

The main difference with this application is the coexistence of a Node server and the client Webpack server. This Node server, which lives in `server.js` provides a single API call to the client:

testing/weather/server.js

```
app.get("/weather", (req, res) => {
  const id = Number(req.query.id);
  axios.get(`https://www.metaweather.com/api/location/${id}/`)
    .then(response => {
      res.setHeader("Cache-Control", "no-cache");
      res.json(response.data);
    })
    .catch(error => {
      console.log(error);
    });
});
```

When the `/weather` api call is made from the client side, the `id` from the request query is used to fetch real weather information with the help of the MetaWeather[136] API.

MetaWeather is a weather data aggregator that calculates the most likely outcome from predictions of different forecasters. Though they provide several endpoints to their API[137], we're only using the location[138] endpoint:

`/api/location/(woeid)/`

WOEID, or Where On Earth ID[139], is a location identifier that allows us find details about a specific location. For more detail on how exactly the MetaWeather API works, feel free to take a closer look at the documentation[140].

`concurrently`

When we start the application, the `concurrently` utility runs both the client at `http://localhost:8080/` and the server at `http://localhost:3000/` at the same time.

All API calls from the client to the server are proxied with `/api/` (for example, a call to `/api/weather` from the client is proxied to `http://localhost:3000/weather`).

`App.vue`

In the application code, let's first take a quick look at how the parent container, `App` is constructed. If we open the `App.vue` file, we'll notice the component's `<template>` and `<script>` elements constructed like so:

[136]https://www.metaweather.com/
[137]https://www.metaweather.com/api/
[138]https://www.metaweather.com/api/#location
[139]https://developer.yahoo.com/geo/geoplanet/guide/concepts.html
[140]https://www.metaweather.com/api/

testing/weather/src/App.vue

```
<template>
  <div id="app" class="flex-align has-text-centered">
    <p class="app__date has-text-weight-bold">{{ date }}</p>
    <router-view></router-view>
    <div class="app__cities">
      <router-link
        v-for="city in cities"
        :to="'/weather/' + city.id"
        :key="city.id"
        v-if="!loading">{{ city.name }}</router-link>
    </div>
  </div>
</template>

<script>
import { mapGetters } from 'vuex';

export default {
  name: 'app',
  data() {
    return {
      cities: [
        { id: 2459115, name: 'New York City, New York' },
        { id: 468739, name: 'Buenos Aires, Argentina' },
        { id: 2122265, name: 'Moscow, Russia' },
        { id: 1118370, name: 'Tokyo, Japan' },
        { id: 1105779, name: 'Sydney, Australia' },
        { id: 1398823, name: 'Lagos, Nigeria' }
      ]
    }
  },
  computed: {
    date() {
      return (new Date()).toDateString();
    },
    ...mapGetters([
      'loading'
    ])
  },
}
</script>
```

In the template, `date` is the computed property that simply gets the current day's date in a readable format. The `<router-view>` element declaration is where the child components are hoisted (e.g. `WeatherContainer`) depending on the URL route.

In the `<div class="app__cities"></div>` element, we're using the `v-for` directive to render a *list* of `<router-link>` elements from the component data array, `cities`. Here's an example of a single `<router-link>` element from the list:

```
<router-link
  :to="/weather/2459115"
  :key="city.id"
  v-if="!loading">New York City, New York</router-link>
```

Each link has a target URL of `/weather/:id` and is rendered to display as the name of the city from the `cities` array. A `v-if` statement exists to dictate that every link should *not* be displayed if the computed property `loading` is true. This `loading` property is mapped from a store getter with the help of the Vuex `mapGetters` helper.

Before we take a dive into the `components/` folder, let's first take a look at the `main.js`, `router.js`, and `store.js` files.

`main.js`

The `main.js` file integrates the `vuex` store and the `vue-router` router instance to the entire application. The application instance renders the parent component `App`, and is mounted on to an element with the id of `#app`:

testing/weather/src/main.js

```
import Vue from 'vue';
import App from './App';
import router from './router';
import store from './store';

new Vue({
  el: '#app',
  router,
  store,
  render: h => h(App)
});
```

`router.js`

The `router.js` file creates and exports the application router instance. The `router` instance object within the file looks like this:

testing/weather/src/router.js

```
const router = new VueRouter({
  mode: 'history',
  routes: [
    {
      path: '/',
      component: HomeContainer
    },
    {
      path: '/weather/:id',
      component: WeatherContainer,
      props: true,
      beforeEnter: (to, from, next) => {
        const id = to.params.id;
        if (
          ![
            2459115,
            468739,
            2122265,
            1118370,
            1105779,
            1398823
          ].includes(Number(id))
        ) {
          next("/not-found");
        } else {
          next();
        }
      }
    },
    {
      path: '*',
      component: NotFoundContainer
    }
  ]
});
```

In the routes array, the HomeContainer component is set to the root URL index /. The WeatherContainer component is displayed dynamically based on the id param of the URL route /weather/:id. To handle this dynamic route, we've added a beforeEnter guard to redirect the user to a /not-found route if the id param doesn't match any of the possible application ids.

Finally, the NotFoundContainer component is displayed if a URL route not present in the routes array (e.g. /not-found) is used.

store.js

If we open up the store.js file, we'll see a simple Vuex store with each store piece (state, mutations, actions, and getters) created in separate objects.

The state object of the store initializes the weather properties that's needed in the WeatherContainer component:

testing/weather/src/store.js

```
const state = {
  location: '',
  weatherDescription: '',
  imageAbbr: '',
  weatherTemp: 0,
  loading: false
};
```

Our store mutations specify the methods that update the state properties with the payloads provided:

testing/weather/src/store.js

```
const mutations = {
  UPDATE_LOCATION(state, payload) {
    state.location = payload;
  },
  UPDATE_WEATHER_DETAILS (state, payload) {
    state.weatherDescription = payload.weather_state_name;
    state.imageAbbr = payload.weather_state_abbr + '.png';
    state.weatherTemp = payload.the_temp.toFixed();
  },
  LOADING_PENDING (state) {
    state.loading = true;
  },
  LOADING_COMPLETE (state) {
    state.loading = false;
```

```
  }
};
```

The `actions` object has a single action labelled `fetchWeather`:

testing/weather/src/store.js

```
const actions = {
  fetchWeather ({ commit }, id) {
    commit('LOADING_PENDING');
    axios.get(`/api/weather`, {
      params: {
        id: id
      }
    }).then((response) => {
      const weather = response.data.consolidated_weather[0];
      commit('UPDATE_LOCATION', response.data.title);
      commit('UPDATE_WEATHER_DETAILS', weather);
      commit('LOADING_COMPLETE');
    });
  },
};
```

When the `fetchWeather` action is dispatched, it goes through the following steps:

- It first commits to the `LOADING_PENDING` mutation which sets the state loading property to `true`. This property is picked up in the view to display the loading indicator.
- A `GET` call is made to the server at `/api/weather` passing in an `id` param, which was provided to the action as a payload.
- When the asynchronous call is successful, commits are made to the relevant mutations passing in the necessary data from the response.
- It finally commits to the `LOADING_COMPLETE` mutation which resets the `loading` state to `false`.

The `getters` object creates the getter functions that return the necessary state properties:

testing/weather/src/store.js

```
const getters = {
  location: state => state.location,
  weatherDescription: state => state.weatherDescription,
  imageAbbr: state => state.imageAbbr,
  weatherTemp: state => state.weatherTemp,
  loading: state => state.loading
};
```

`src/components/`

With a good understanding of how the application store and router has been set up, let's survey the component files within `components/`:

```
$ ls src/components/
HomeContainer.vue
NotFoundContainer.vue
WeatherContainer.vue
```

The `HomeContainer.vue` and `NotFoundContainer.vue` component files are simple static templates that display a single `<h1>` element.

The `HomeContainer.vue` file:

testing/weather/src/components/HomeContainer.vue

```
<template>
  <h1 class="subtitle is-size-3">Pick a city below to see the weather!</h1>
</template>

<script>
export default {
  name: 'HomeContainer',
}
</script>
```

And the `NotFoundContainer.vue` file:

testing/weather/src/components/NotFoundContainer.vue

```
<template>
  <h1 class="subtitle is-size-3">Sorry, this route does not exist :(</h1>
</template>

<script>
export default {
  name: 'NotFoundContainer',
}
</script>
```

The `WeatherContainer.vue` file sets up the weather component by rendering the weather state data from the application store. Here are the `<template>` and `<script>` elements of the `WeatherContainer.vue` file:

testing/weather/src/components/WeatherContainer.vue

```
<template>
  <div>
    <div v-if="!loading" class="weather container">
      <img class="weather__image" :src="require(`../assets/${imageAbbr}`)" />
      <h1 class="subtitle weather__city">{{ location }}</h1>
      <p class="weather__description">{{ weatherDescription }}</p>
      <p class="weather__temperature">{{ weatherTemp }} ºC</p>
    </div>
    <div v-if="loading" class="loader"></div>
  </div>
</template>

<script>
import { mapGetters } from 'vuex';

export default {
  name: 'WeatherContainer',
  props: ['id'],
  computed: {
    ...mapGetters([
      'location',
      'weatherDescription',
      'imageAbbr',
      'weatherTemp',
      'loading'
```

```
    ])
  },
  watch: {
    id() {
      this.fetchWeather();
    }
  },
  created() {
    this.fetchWeather();
  },
  methods: {
    fetchWeather() {
      this.$store.dispatch('fetchWeather', Number(this.id));
    }
  }
}
</script>
```

In the `<template>`, we can see we have two `<div>` elements that are conditionally displayed based on the `loading` state value in the store. When `loading` is `false`, the appropriate weather details (`<div class="weather container></div>`) is shown. When `loading` is `true`, the `<div class="loader"></div>` element is shown which is the large loading indicator we notice in the middle of the screen.

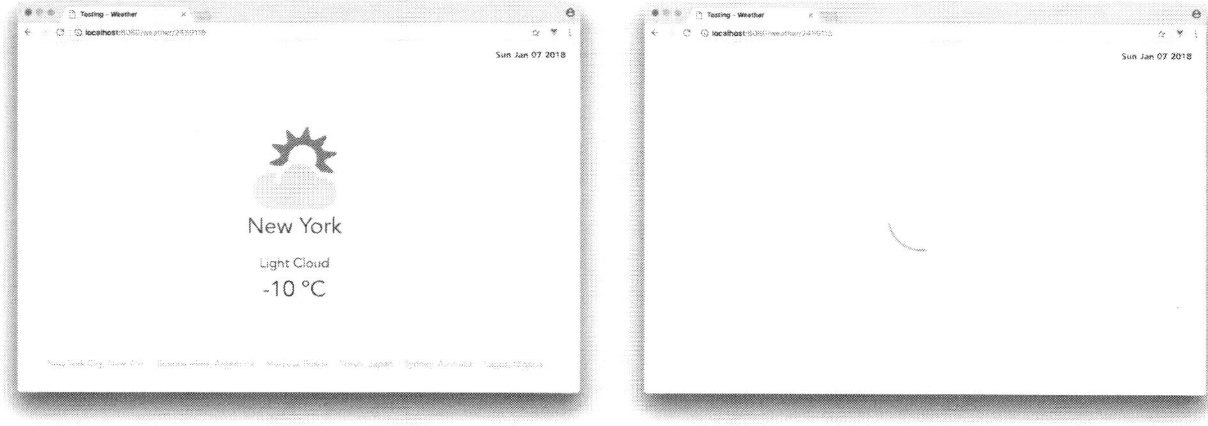

***loading**: false*

***loading**: true*

The `watch` and `created()` properties of `WeatherContainer` both call an internal `this.fetchWeather()` method when invoked:

testing/weather/src/components/WeatherContainer.vue

```
  watch: {
    id() {
      this.fetchWeather();
    }
  },
  created() {
    this.fetchWeather();
  },
  methods: {
    fetchWeather() {
      this.$store.dispatch('fetchWeather', Number(this.id));
    }
  }
```

The `watch` property specifies a *watch* on the component `id` prop. The `id` prop is dynamically linked to the route `id` param. So in essence, the watch states that **when any changes to the route occurs, the `this.fetchWeather()` method will be called.**

The `created()` hook invokes the same `fetchWeather()` method when the `WeatherContainer` component loads *for the first time.*

The `this.fetchWeather()` method dispatches the `fetchWeather` store action while passing in the route `id` as a payload.

When the `WeatherContainer` component loads for the first time, the `created()` hook is fired and the `fetchWeather` action is dispatched.

As the user routes to different URLS (i.e. clicks a `<router-link>` to navigate to another city), the `created()` hook **does not fire again.** This is the reason why we establish a **watch** option to *watch* for changes in the URL.

test/

In the `test/` directory, all test files are contained within the `test/specs/` folder. The test configuration is set up in the `test/index.js` and `test/karma.conf.js` files:

```
$ ls test/
index.js
karma.conf.js
specs/
```

The `test/specs/` folder hosts the test subfolder we'll be working from, `weather/`, as well as every iteration along the way (`weather-1/` to `weather-complete/`).

```
$ ls test/specs/
weather/
weather-1/
weather-2/
weather-3/
weather-complete/
```

In the `test/index.js` file, we've required our test suite to run tests only from the folder we'll be working from, `weather/`:

testing/weather/test/index.js

```
import Vue from 'vue'
import "es6-promise/auto"

Vue.config.productionTip = false

// require all test files within ./specs/weather
const testsContext = require.context('./specs/weather', true, /\.spec$/)
testsContext.keys().forEach(testsContext)
```

Line 7 of `test/index.js` will have to be changed to run tests from another folder. For example, if we intended to run tests from the `weather-complete/` folder, we'll have to update line 7 of `test/index.js` to reflect this:

```
// require all test files within ./specs/weather-complete
const testsContext = require.context('./specs/weather-complete', true, /\.spec$/)
```

If we take a look at the files within `test/specs/weather/`, we'll see that test files have been created for all the components in our application.

```
test/specs/weather/
  components/
    HomeContainer.spec.js
    NotFoundContainer.spec.js
    WeatherContainer.spec.js
  App.spec.js
```

Each component will be tested as an isolated *unit*. For each component, we'll feed the necessary inputs and assert the responses that we expect in the tests.

As a starting point, a single test has already been written in both the `HomeContainer.spec.js` and `NotFoundContainer.spec.js` files. Since these files are simple static components with no data, our tests just assert if the components render the expected `<h1>` elements.

The `HomeContainer.spec.js` file is set up like this:

testing/weather/test/specs/weather/components/HomeContainer.spec.js

```
import HomeContainer from '@/components/HomeContainer';
import {shallow} from 'vue-test-utils';

describe('HomeContainer.vue', () => {
  it('should display the appropriate index message', () => {
    const wrapper = shallow(HomeContainer);
    expect(
      wrapper.html()
    ).to.contain(
     '<h1 class="subtitle is-size-3">Pick a city below to see the weather!</h1>'
    );
  });
});
```

The `HomeContainer` component and the `shallow()` method from `vue-test-utils` is imported at the top of the file. We first shallow render the component and then assert the component rendered template contains the expected element, with the help of the wrapper `html()` helper.

The `NotFoundContainer.spec.js` file is laid out in the same way:

testing/weather/test/specs/weather/components/NotFoundContainer.spec.js

```
import NotFoundContainer from '@/components/NotFoundContainer';
import { shallow } from 'vue-test-utils';

describe('NotFoundContainer.vue', () => {
  it('should display the appropriate not found message', () => {
    const wrapper = shallow(NotFoundContainer);
    expect(
      wrapper.html()
    ).to.contain(
     '<h1 class="subtitle is-size-3">Sorry, this route does not exist :(</h1>'
    );
  });
});
```

Let's run our test suite to verify that our initial tests run correctly:

```
$ npm run test
```

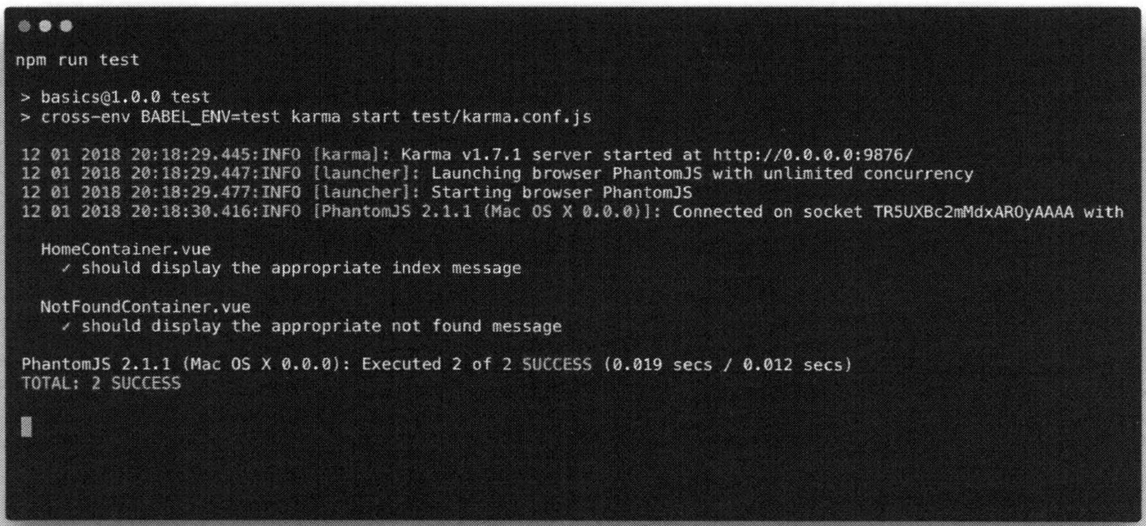

```
npm run test

> basics@1.0.0 test
> cross-env BABEL_ENV=test karma start test/karma.conf.js

12 01 2018 20:18:29.445:INFO [karma]: Karma v1.7.1 server started at http://0.0.0.0:9876/
12 01 2018 20:18:29.447:INFO [launcher]: Launching browser PhantomJS with unlimited concurrency
12 01 2018 20:18:29.477:INFO [launcher]: Starting browser PhantomJS
12 01 2018 20:18:30.416:INFO [PhantomJS 2.1.1 (Mac OS X 0.0.0)]: Connected on socket TR5UXBc2mMdxAROyAAAA with

  HomeContainer.vue
    ✓ should display the appropriate index message

  NotFoundContainer.vue
    ✓ should display the appropriate not found message

PhantomJS 2.1.1 (Mac OS X 0.0.0): Executed 2 of 2 SUCCESS (0.019 secs / 0.012 secs)
TOTAL: 2 SUCCESS
```

Our initial tests pass. Let's start writing tests for the `App.spec.js` file.

App.spec.js

There's a few things we'd want to assert for the App component:

- It correctly displays the current day's date.
- It should display the <router-link> elements when the application is not loading.
- It should *not* display the <router-link> elements when the application is loading.

We'll take each of these points and craft a test for each one.

Notice how we're not looking to test how the <router-view> component behaves under different route paths. The <router-view> component is a *separate* component and our focus is solely on how the App component behaves with different data values.

This concept of knowing where the boundaries of our application components start and end is important to start to develop as it will oftentimes determine the amount of extra work we'll accrue as we maintain our test suite. This skill becomes easier the more often we write tests.

Let's open the App.spec.js file and import the libraries/functions we would need:

```
import App from '@/App';
import { shallow, createLocalVue } from 'vue-test-utils';
import Vuex from 'vuex';

describe('App.vue', () => {
  // Our tests go here
});
```

We're importing the shallow() method and a createLocalVue() method from vue-test-utils. We're also importing the Vuex plugin.

createLocalVue

createLocalVue() is a method that is used to create a scoped Vue constructor, which allows us to render a component while integrating mixins/plugins like Vuex. Plugins are integrated onto this new Vue class, created with createLocalVue, in order to **not pollute the global Vue constructor**.

This point is an important note to remember; whenever external plugins (like Vuex or Vue Router) need to be integrated for tests, they need to be applied to a local copy of a Vue constructor in order to not pollute the global Vue instance. Using this scoped Vue constructor in turn, ensures that tests will not be affected by one another.

We *technically* don't need to integrate Vuex or use a local Vue copy for our first test. Our first test is a simple assertion that the component renders the current day's date correctly. With that said, let's write out the test and see how our test suite behaves:

```
import App from '@/App';
import { shallow, createLocalVue } from 'vue-test-utils';
import Vuex from 'vuex';

describe('App.vue', () => {
  let wrapper;

  beforeEach(() => {
    wrapper = shallow(App);
  });

  it("should display the current day's date", () => {
    const formattedDate = new Date().toDateString();
    expect(wrapper.html()).to.contain(formattedDate);
  });
});
```

We shallow render the `App` component in the `beforeEach` hook. Our test simply asserts if the components rendered html contains today's date in the formatted state we expect.

Let's run our suite:

```
$ npm run test
```

Like the first section of this chapter, `npm run test:watch` can also be used to boot Karma in watch mode.

```
App.vue
  ✗ "before each" hook for "should dislay the current day's date"
      undefined is not an object (evaluating 'this.$store.getters')
      mappedGetter@webpack:///node_modules/vuex/dist/vuex.esm.js:848:0 <- index.js:1106:61
      get@webpack:///node_modules/vue/dist/vue.runtime.esm.js:3111:0 <- index.js:8819:29
      evaluate@webpack:///node_modules/vue/dist/vue.runtime.esm.js:3218:0 <- index.js:8926:24
      computedGetter@webpack:///node_modules/vue/dist/vue.runtime.esm.js:3470:0 <- index.js:9178:25
      webpack:///src/App.vue?edc5:19:0 <- index.js:16440:22
      renderList@webpack:///node_modules/vue/dist/vue.runtime.esm.js:3668:0 <- index.js:9376:22
      render@webpack:///src/App.vue?edc5:18:0 <- index.js:16439:15
      _render@webpack:///node_modules/vue/dist/vue.runtime.esm.js:4470:0 <- index.js:10178:26
      updateComponent@webpack:///node_modules/vue/dist/vue.runtime.esm.js:2761:0 <- index.js:8469:28
      get@webpack:///node_modules/vue/dist/vue.runtime.esm.js:3111:0 <- index.js:8819:29
      Watcher@webpack:///node_modules/vue/dist/vue.runtime.esm.js:3100:0 <- index.js:8808:15
      mountComponent@webpack:///node_modules/vue/dist/vue.runtime.esm.js:2768:0 <- index.js:8476:14
      $mount@webpack:///node_modules/vue/dist/vue.runtime.esm.js:7891:0 <- index.js:13599:24
      mount@webpack:///node_modules/vue-test-utils/dist/vue-test-utils.js:4468:0 <- index.js:5664:14
      shallow@webpack:///node_modules/vue-test-utils/dist/vue-test-utils.js:4490:0 <- index.js:5686:15
      webpack:///test/specs/weather/App.spec.js:9:13 <- index.js:15828:41

HomeContainer.vue
```

Our test **fails**. Through a series of test logs, we can see that the main message given to us is `undefined is not an object (evaluating 'this.$store.getters')`.

Our test suite currently doesn't recognize the store instance being used in the `App` component. In order to test *anything* within `App`, **we need to create a mock store**.

Mock Store

The only thing the `App` component uses from the application store is the store getters (precisely the `loading` getter from the store).

In essence, when we create a mock store object, we only need to *mock* the `loading` getter in that store object. The `App` component doesn't care about any other properties in the store.

To create a mock store, we'll first declare a `store` and `getters` variable in our test, and integrate Vuex to a local copy of a Vue instance in the `beforeEach` hook:

```
describe('App.vue', () => {
  let wrapper;
  let store;
  let getters;

  beforeEach(() => {
    const localVue = createLocalVue();
    localVue.use(Vuex);

    wrapper = shallow(App);
```

```
  });

  it("should display the current day's date", () => {
    const formattedDate = new Date().toDateString();
    expect(wrapper.html()).to.contain(formattedDate);
  });
});
```

Remember, we're integrating Vuex to a local copy of a Vuex instance to avoid polluting the global Vue constructor.

In the `beforeEach` hook, we can now create a `getters` object that has a `loading()` method within. We'll also setup a Vuex store that has the `getters` object passed in:

```
describe('App.vue', () => {
  let wrapper;
  let store;
  let getters;

  beforeEach(() => {
    const localVue = createLocalVue();
    localVue.use(Vuex);

    getters = {
      loading: () => { return false }
    }
    store = new Vuex.Store({
      getters
    });

    wrapper = shallow(App);
  });

  it("should display the current day's date", () => {
    const formattedDate = new Date().toDateString();
    expect(wrapper.html()).to.contain(formattedDate);
  });
});
```

As we shallow render the component, we now need to pass in the new Vue options, `localVue` and `store`. The `shallow()` method call takes arguments in the format of `shallow(component, {options})`. In the `options` object of the argument, we'll pass in the **mock store** and **local Vue copy**.

In the `beforeEach`, our `shallow()` call can now be updated to:

testing/weather/test/specs/weather-1/App.spec.js

```
describe('App.vue', () => {
  let wrapper;
  let store;
  let getters;

  beforeEach(() => {
    const localVue = createLocalVue();
    localVue.use(Vuex);

    getters = {
      loading: () => { return false }
    }

    store = new Vuex.Store({
      getters
    });

    wrapper = shallow(App, {
      localVue,
      store
    });
  });

  it("should display the current day's date", () => {
    const formattedDate = new Date().toDateString();
    expect(wrapper.html()).to.contain(formattedDate);
  });
});
```

Though we've made no changes to our test, running our test suite should have all our tests pass.

```
$ npm run test
```

```
npm run test

> basics@1.0.0 test
> cross-env BABEL_ENV=test karma start test/karma.conf.js

13 01 2018 12:15:34.881:WARN [karma]: No captured browser, open http://localhost:9876/
13 01 2018 12:15:34.889:INFO [karma]: Karma v1.7.1 server started at http://0.0.0.0:9876/
13 01 2018 12:15:34.889:INFO [launcher]: Launching browser PhantomJS with unlimited concurrency
13 01 2018 12:15:34.915:INFO [launcher]: Starting browser PhantomJS
13 01 2018 12:15:35.845:INFO [PhantomJS 2.1.1 (Mac OS X 0.0.0)]: Connected on socket XueFW6rdA4-wdJADAAAA with
 id 78273035

  App.vue
    ✓ should dislay the current day's date

  HomeContainer.vue
    ✓ should display the appropriate index message

  NotFoundContainer.vue
    ✓ should display the appropriate not found message

PhantomJS 2.1.1 (Mac OS X 0.0.0): Executed 3 of 3 SUCCESS (0.027 secs / 0.004 secs)
TOTAL: 3 SUCCESS
```

Awesome! We can now move onwards to creating tests that actually depend upon the `loading` getter value.

The second test we'll create will assert that when the application is *not* loading, the footer `<router-link>` elements should be displayed. We'll create this test as a sibling to the previous test:

```
describe('App.vue', () => {
  // ...

  it("should display the current day's date", () => {
    // ...
  });

  it('should display the footer links when application is not loading', () => {
    // assertion for the presence of footer links
  });
});
```

Our `loading` getter currently returns a value of `false` so our test is already prepared. To create our test, we can find the footer links wrapper and assert whether this wrapper element contains the `<router-link>` elements we expect:

```
it('should display the footer links when application is not loading', () => {
  const footerLinks = wrapper.find('.app__cities');

  expect(footerLinks.html()).to.contain(
    '<router-link to="/weather/2459115">New York City, New York</router-link>'
  );
  expect(footerLinks.html()).to.contain(
    '<router-link to="/weather/468739">Buenos Aires, Argentina</router-link>'
  );
  expect(footerLinks.html()).to.contain(
    '<router-link to="/weather/2122265">Moscow, Russia</router-link>'
  );
  expect(footerLinks.html()).to.contain(
    '<router-link to="/weather/1118370">Tokyo, Japan</router-link>'
  );
  expect(footerLinks.html()).to.contain(
    '<router-link to="/weather/1105779">Sydney, Australia</router-link>'
  );
  expect(footerLinks.html()).to.contain(
    '<router-link to="/weather/1398823">Lagos, Nigeria</router-link>'
  );
});
```

Though we can abbreviate the test by only asserting the presence of one (or few) `<router-link>` elements, we're being explicit by asserting the presence of every single link.

Before we run our test suite, let's create the test in the opposite scenario - asserting that the footer links are *not* displayed when the application *is* loading.

```
describe('App.vue', () => {
  // ...

  it("should display the current day's date", () => {
    // ...
  });

  it('should display the footer links when application is not loading', () => {
    // ...
  });

  it('should not display footer links when application is loading', () => {
    // assertion for the absence of footer links
  });
});
```

In this test, we need to assert the component behaviour when the store `loading` getter value is `true`. However, in our `beforeEach` hook, we've simply always assigned `loading` to return `false`.

There are a few ways we can handle passing different `loading` state values to separate tests. A simple way to pass different values will be *removing* the `beforeEach` hook and using a method of our own, called `setUpWrapper` that takes a `loading` parameter and returns this parameter in the `loading` getter.

To see how our expectations can work, let's change the `beforeEach` to wrap this functionality into a `setUpWrapper` function instead:

```
describe('App.vue', () => {
  let wrapper;
  let store;
  let getters;

  const setUpWrapper = loading => {
    const localVue = createLocalVue();
    localVue.use(Vuex);

    getters = {
      loading: () => { return loading }
    }
    store = new Vuex.Store({
      getters
    });

    wrapper = shallow(App, {
      localVue,
      store
    });
  }

  // ...
});
```

Unlike the `beforeEach` hook, the `setUpWrapper` method would not automatically run prior to each test. We'll have to invoke the method in the beginning of each test.

Let's call `setUpWrapper` while passing in a boolean of `false` in the beginning of the first two tests. In our third test, we'll call `setUpWrapper(true)`:

```
describe('App.vue', () => {
  //..

  it("should display the current day's date", () => {
    setUpWrapper(false);

    // ...
  });

  it('should display the footer links when application is not loading', () => {
    setUpWrapper(false);

    // ...
  });

  it('should not display footer links when application is loading', () => {
    setUpWrapper(true);
  });
});
```

Now in our third test, we can test for the absence of the footer links similar to how we asserted their presence. We'll find the wrapper element that should contain the `<router-link>` elements and assert that the wrapper element *does not* contain these links. Once again, we'll be explicit and assert the absence of every link:

testing/weather/test/specs/weather-2/App.spec.js

```
  it('should not display footer links when application is loading', () => {
    setUpWrapper(true);
    const footerLinks = wrapper.find('.app__cities');

    expect(footerLinks.html()).to.not.contain(
      '<router-link to="/weather/2459115">New York City, New York</router-link>'
    );
    expect(footerLinks.html()).to.not.contain(
      '<router-link to="/weather/468739">Buenos Aires, Argentina</router-link>'
    );
    expect(footerLinks.html()).to.not.contain(
      '<router-link to="/weather/2122265">Moscow, Russia</router-link>'
    );
    expect(footerLinks.html()).to.not.contain(
      '<router-link to="/weather/1118370">Tokyo, Japan</router-link>'
    );
```

```
    expect(footerLinks.html()).to.not.contain(
      '<router-link to="/weather/1105779">Sydney, Australia</router-link>'
    );
    expect(footerLinks.html()).to.not.contain(
      '<router-link to="/weather/1398823">Lagos, Nigeria</router-link>'
    );
  });
```

Let's run our test suite!

```
$ npm run test
```

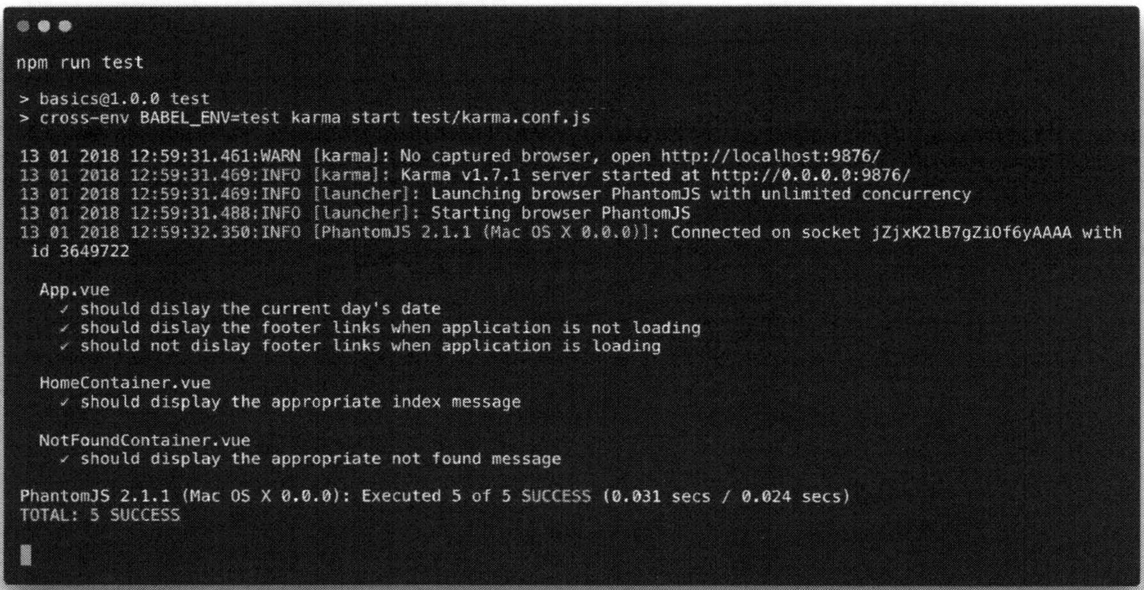

```
npm run test

> basics@1.0.0 test
> cross-env BABEL_ENV=test karma start test/karma.conf.js

13 01 2018 12:59:31.461:WARN [karma]: No captured browser, open http://localhost:9876/
13 01 2018 12:59:31.469:INFO [karma]: Karma v1.7.1 server started at http://0.0.0.0:9876/
13 01 2018 12:59:31.469:INFO [launcher]: Launching browser PhantomJS with unlimited concurrency
13 01 2018 12:59:31.488:INFO [launcher]: Starting browser PhantomJS
13 01 2018 12:59:32.350:INFO [PhantomJS 2.1.1 (Mac OS X 0.0.0)]: Connected on socket jZjxK2lB7gZiOf6yAAAA with
 id 3649722

  App.vue
    ✓ should dislay the current day's date
    ✓ should dislay the footer links when application is not loading
    ✓ should not dislay footer links when application is loading

  HomeContainer.vue
    ✓ should display the appropriate index message

  NotFoundContainer.vue
    ✓ should display the appropriate not found message

PhantomJS 2.1.1 (Mac OS X 0.0.0): Executed 5 of 5 SUCCESS (0.031 secs / 0.024 secs)
TOTAL: 5 SUCCESS
```

Our tests for the `App` component pass.

We've created assertions and expectations on how the `App` component should behave in slightly different conditions (when the `loading` getter is `true` or `false`).

For the purpose of these tests, we're not concerned with how the `getters` are established or what the `store` even looks like. We just need to know that our component is rendered correctly depending on what the `loading` getter returns. In essence, we're testing the `App` component **in isolation**.

We'll be using this same thinking process as we create tests for the `WeatherContainer` component:

`WeatherContainer.spec.js`

Let's list the expectations we have for the `WeatherContainer` component:

- It should display the appropriate weather content when the `loading` getter is equal to `false`.
- It should display the loading indicator when the `loading` getter is equal to `true`.
- It should fire the `fetchWeather` action from the store, when the component is created.
- It should fire the `fetchWeather` action from the store, when the URL route changes.

Each of these points can be asserted in a test of its own. Let's write these tests.

Since the `WeatherContainer` component uses both store actions and getters, we're going to need to mock a Vuex store that has mock `getters` *and* `actions` in the test file.

Let's create this mock store in a `setUpWrapper` function that takes a `loading` argument, similar to how we wrote one in `App.spec.js`.

Here's our entire starting point for `WeatherContainer.spec`:

```
import WeatherContainer from '@/components/WeatherContainer';
import { shallow, createLocalVue } from 'vue-test-utils';
import Vuex from 'vuex';

describe('WeatherContainer.vue', () => {
  let wrapper;
  let getters;
  let actions;
  let store;
  let localVue;

  const setUpWrapper = loading => {
    localVue = createLocalVue();
    localVue.use(Vuex);

    getters = {
      location: () => 'New York',
      weatherDescription: () => 'Light Cloud',
      imageAbbr: () => 'lc.png',
      weatherTemp: () => -10.0,
      loading: () => loading
    }

    actions = {
```

```
      fetchWeather: sinon.stub()
    }

    store = new Vuex.Store({
      getters,
      actions
    });

    wrapper = shallow(WeatherContainer, {
      localVue,
      store
    });
  };
});
```

Let's step through what we're doing above step-by-step:

We're importing the `WeatherContainer` component, the necessary test helper methods, and the Vuex library at the top of the file. We've declared the variables we'll be using in the `setUpWrapper` function (`wrapper`, `getters`, etc.) in the beginning of the test `describe` block.

We've created a `setUpWrapper` function that takes a `loading` argument. In the `setUpWrapper` function, we're creating a local Vue instance and integrating the Vuex package to that instance.

Before we shallow render the wrapper, we've set up a store that consists of a mock `getters` and `actions` objects. The methods in the mock `getters` object return data that we can expect from the MetaWeather api call.

In the mock `actions` object, we're using `sinon.stub()` to specify an anonymous stub function for the `fetchWeather` store action.

Sinon[141] is a testing library that gives us the ability to spy on, stub, and mock external dependencies and functions within our code. The benefits to using Sinon comes from reducing effort by allowing us to test what we only need to test, and allowing Sinon to mock any external dependency (Ajax requests, timeouts, database dependencies, etc.).

In our case, we're using `sinon.stub()` to create a mock function for `fetchWeather` since we'll only **assert whether the action was called** in certain scenarios. We're not concerned with what the action actually does, but only whether the `WeatherContainer` component calls the action when we expect it to.

Though we won't have the need to do so in this case, the Sinon stubs[142] documentation highlight several ways to manipulate how a function behaves in a test.

[141]http://sinonjs.org/

[142]http://sinonjs.org/releases/v1.17.7/stubs/

Finally, we've wired the local Vue instance and the store as part of the `options` argument within our `shallow()` method call. We can now begin to write our tests.

Our first two tests will simply assert whether the component renders the expected content when the application is or isn't loading. We'll create these tests side-by-side:

```
describe('WeatherContainer.vue', () => {
  // ...

  it('should render the correct content when the app is loading', () => {
    // assertion for rendering correct weather content when not loading
  });

  it('should render the correct content when the app is not loading', () => {
    // assertion for rendering the loading indicator when loading
  });
});
```

We'll declare `setUpWrapper(true)` in the beginning of the first test and `setUpWrapper(false)` in the beginning of the second to provide different `loading` getter values to each test. Like we've done so far, we'll use the `html()` wrapper function to retrieve the rendered HTML and assert whether the template contains the content we expect:

testing/weather/test/specs/weather-3/components/WeatherContainer.spec.js

```
  it('should render the correct content when the app is loading', () => {
    setUpWrapper(true);

    expect(
      wrapper.html()
    ).to.contain('<div class="loader"></div>');
    expect(
      wrapper.html()
    ).to.not.contain('<h1 class="subtitle weather__city">New York</h1>');
    expect(
      wrapper.html()
    ).to.not.contain('<p class="weather__description">Light Cloud</p>');
    expect(
      wrapper.html()
    ).to.not.contain('<p class="weather__temperature">-10 ºC</p></div>');
  });
  // ...
  it('should render the correct content when the app is not loading', () => {
```

```
    setUpWrapper(false);

    expect(
      wrapper.html()
    ).to.contain('<h1 class="subtitle weather__city">New York</h1>');
    expect(
      wrapper.html()
    ).to.contain('<p class="weather__description">Light Cloud</p>');
    expect(
      wrapper.html()
    ).to.contain('<p class="weather__temperature">-10 ºC</p></div>');
    expect(
      wrapper.html()
    ).to.not.contain('<div class="loader"></div>');
  });
```

When the application is loading, we assert the presence of the only element that exists in that case - the loading indicator, and the absence of any elements that are responsible for displaying weather details.

When the application finishes loading, we expect to see the rendered content that displays the weather details from our mock `getters`. In addition, we expect that no loading indicator is displayed in this scenario.

`fetchWeather`

Now that we've created tests for how our component renders content appropriately, we can begin to test whether the `fetchWeather` store action gets fired when we want it to.

The first test we'll write in this case is assert that the `fetchWeather` action is called once when the application loads. If we remember, we dispatch the action in the `created` hook of the `WeatherContainer` component:

```
import { mapGetters } from 'vuex';

export default {
  name: 'WeatherContainer',
  props: ['id'],
  // ...,
  created() {
    this.fetchWeather();
  },
  methods: {
```

```
    fetchWeather() {
      this.$store.dispatch('fetchWeather', Number(this.id));
    }
  }
}
```

So we'll want to test this actually occurs. In `WeatherContainer.spec.js`, we'll create the "should call the `fetchWeather` action once when created" test as a sibling to the previous tests:

```
describe('WeatherContainer.vue', () => {
  // ...

  it('should call the "fetchWeather" action once when created', () => {
    // assertion that fetchWeather is called once
  });
});
```

When we create the wrapper, the `WeatherContainer` component is shallow rendered (i.e. created) so the test is already prepared at that point. In the test, all we need to do is to call `setUpWrapper()` and simply assert whether the `fetchWeather` action is called once.

It won't matter what boolean we pass in the `setUpWrapper` call since the action is dispatched regardless of the value of the `loading` getter:

testing/weather/test/specs/weather-complete/components/WeatherContainer.spec.js

```
  it('should call the "fetchWeather" action once when created', () => {
    setUpWrapper(false);

    expect(actions.fetchWeather).to.have.been.calledOnce;
  });
```

Before we run our test suite, let's introduce the last test. The only other test we need to make is asserting that the `fetchWeather` action is called when the `id` prop of the component changes (i.e. when the route changes). We need to watch for this event because we've established the store dispatcher to occur in a `watch id` property.

When we declared our route, we used the props option to specify how the `id` param of the URL can be accessed in the `WeatherContainer` component. We can see this declaration in the `routes` array of the router instance, in the `src/router.js` file:

```
routes: [
  // ...,
  {
    path: '/weather/:id',
    component: WeatherContainer,
    props: true,
    beforeEnter: (to, from, next) => {
      // ...
    }
  },
  // ...
]
```

This gave us the ability to simply watch the `id` prop within the `WeatherContainer` component, with which we're able to see in the `src/component/WeatherContainer.vue` file:

```
<script>
  import { mapGetters } from 'vuex';

  export default {
    name: 'WeatherContainer',
    props: ['id'],
    // ...,
    watch: {
      id() {
        this.fetchWeather();
      }
    },
    // ...,
    methods: {
      fetchWeather() {
        this.$store.dispatch('fetchWeather', Number(this.id));
      }
    }
  }
</script>
```

This separation greatly simplifies testing since the component is now **decoupled** from the router. We just need to test the `fetchWeather` action is called when the `id` prop changes.

Let's create the test for this as a sibling to the other tests:

```
describe('WeatherContainer.vue', () => {
  // ...

  it('should also call the "fetchWeather" action when "id" is changed', () => {
    // assertion that fetchWeather action is also called when id prop is changed
  });
});
```

To test that the `fetchWeather` action is *also* called when the `id` prop is changed, we can simply assert that the `fetchWeather` action will be called *twice* in total; once for when the component is rendered, and the second time when the `id` prop is manipulated.

To change the component's `id` data value, we'll use the wrapper's `setData()` function to force update the `wrapper` `vm` data object. Our new test will be laid out like so:

testing/weather/test/specs/weather-complete/components/WeatherContainer.spec.js

```
  it('should also call the "fetchWeather" action when "id" is changed', () => {
    setUpWrapper(false);
    wrapper.setData({ id: '1398823'});

    expect(actions.fetchWeather).to.have.been.calledTwice;
  });
```

It doesn't matter what value we use to update `id` since the `watch` call gets fired as long as the `id` prop has changed. We've simply used the `id` `string` value for Lagos, Nigeria above.

Here's a summary of all the tests we've written for `WeatherContainer.spec.js`:

testing/weather/test/specs/weather-complete/components/WeatherContainer.spec.js

```
  it('should render the correct content when the app is loading', () => {
    setUpWrapper(true);

    expect(
      wrapper.html()
    ).to.contain('<div class="loader"></div>');
    expect(
      wrapper.html()
    ).to.not.contain('<h1 class="subtitle weather__city">New York</h1>');
    expect(
      wrapper.html()
    ).to.not.contain('<p class="weather__description">Light Cloud</p>');
    expect(
```

```
    wrapper.html()
  ).to.not.contain('<p class="weather__temperature">-10 ºC</p></div>');
});
// ...
it('should render the correct content when the app is not loading', () => {
  setUpWrapper(false);

  expect(
    wrapper.html()
  ).to.contain('<h1 class="subtitle weather__city">New York</h1>');
  expect(
    wrapper.html()
  ).to.contain('<p class="weather__description">Light Cloud</p>');
  expect(
    wrapper.html()
  ).to.contain('<p class="weather__temperature">-10 ºC</p></div>');
  expect(
    wrapper.html()
  ).to.not.contain('<div class="loader"></div>');
});
// ...
it('should call the "fetchWeather" action once when created', () => {
  setUpWrapper(false);

  expect(actions.fetchWeather).to.have.been.calledOnce;
});
// ...
it('should also call the "fetchWeather" action when "id" is changed', () => {
  setUpWrapper(false);
  wrapper.setData({ id: '1398823'});

  expect(actions.fetchWeather).to.have.been.calledTwice;
});
```

Now would be a good time to verify that all our tests pass.

Try it out

Save `WeatherContainer.spec.js` and let's run the test suite:

```
$ npm run test
```

```
npm run test

> basics@1.0.0 test
> cross-env BABEL_ENV=test karma start test/karma.conf.js

13 01 2018 15:54:13.683:WARN [karma]: No captured browser, open http://localhost:9876/
13 01 2018 15:54:13.692:INFO [karma]: Karma v1.7.1 server started at http://0.0.0.0:9876/
13 01 2018 15:54:13.692:INFO [launcher]: Launching browser PhantomJS with unlimited concurrency
13 01 2018 15:54:13.697:INFO [launcher]: Starting browser PhantomJS
13 01 2018 15:54:14.834:INFO [PhantomJS 2.1.1 (Mac OS X 0.0.0)]: Connected on socket hsZVWEjzINIhdlM2AAAA with
 id 45483759

  App.vue
    ✓ should display the current day's date
    ✓ should display the footer links when application is not loading
    ✓ should not display footer links when application is loading

  HomeContainer.vue
    ✓ should display the appropriate index message

  NotFoundContainer.vue
    ✓ should display the appropriate not found message

  WeatherContainer.vue
    ✓ should render the correct content when the app is loading
    ✓ should render the correct content when the app is not loading
    ✓ should call the 'fetchWeather' action once when created
    ✓ should also call the 'fetchWeather' action when 'id' is changed

PhantomJS 2.1.1 (Mac OS X 0.0.0): Executed 9 of 9 SUCCESS (0.059 secs / 0.045 secs)
TOTAL: 9 SUCCESS
```

We see that everything passes!

The tests for `WeatherContainer` involved asserting whether the correct content was rendered in the template and whether the `fetchWeather` action was called when we expect it.

We don't care about how the store looks like or what the actions inherently do. We just need to verify the actions are fired at the right times and the template renders the right content from the store.

We've covered how to test how each of our application's components work under different scenarios/situations. We've tested each component in isolation by feeding the necessary inputs and asserting the responses that we expect in each of the tests.

As we've seen, testing Vue components require us to traverse and select elements on the rendered DOM for us to make our assertions. This case highlights the benefits of using the `vue-test-utils` library. Though we won't be writing any more tests, we'll investigate and discuss how tests can be written for the pieces in a Vuex store.

Store

Though the Vuex store itself can be tested in isolation, writing tests for the store is different. Unlike Vue components, we're now not concerned with rendering and DOM manipulation.

In the Vuex docs[143], it's specified that **mutations** and **actions** of a Vuex store are the main pieces of a store that should often be tested.

Mutations

Mutations are the most straightforward functions to test in the Vuex store. `mutations` are just simple methods that rely on the parameters given.

For example let's look at the `UPDATE_LOCATION` mutation in the Vuex store of the weather app. It simply assigns the `location` property in `state` to the value of the payload provided.

```
UPDATE_LOCATION(state, payload) {
  state.location = payload;
}
```

We can create a test with a mock `state` object and assert that the location of the object is updated with the payload provided:

```
// import the mutation
const updateLocation = mutations.UPDATE_LOCATION;

// test the mutation
it('UPDATE_LOCATION', () => {
  const state = {location: ''};

  updateLocation(state, 'New York');

  expect(state.location).to.equal('New York');
});
```

In this example, we're directly importing the specific mutation we want to test, `UPDATE_LOCATION`. In the test, we create a mock state object, call the mutation on that object, and assert that the object has updated. All mutation tests are as similar and straightforward as this.

Actions

Creating tests for actions involve asserting whether the expected mutations, with the correct payloads, have been committed. For basic actions this is simple.

However, if an external API call is made within an action, it's not as straightforward. In this case, testing actions will involve mocking the API call made with a stub, resolving the API promise, and then asserting that the expected mutations are called.

Let's provide an example for the `fetchWeather` action in our application:

[143] https://vuex.vuejs.org/en/testing.html

```
fetchWeather ({ commit }, id) {
  commit('LOADING_PENDING');
  axios.get(`/api/weather`, {
    params: {
      id: id
    }
  }).then((response) => {
    const weather = response.data.consolidated_weather[0];
    commit('UPDATE_LOCATION', response.data.title);
    commit('UPDATE_WEATHER_DETAILS', weather);
    commit('LOADING_COMPLETE');
  });
}
```

The Testing Actions[144] section of the Vuex docs specifies a helper method to test an async action. Here is a summarized version of this helper method:

```
const testAction = (action, expectedMutations, done) => {
  let count = 0

  const commit = type => {
    const mutation = expectedMutations[count]

    try {
      expect(mutation.type).to.equal(type)
    } catch (error) {
      assert.fail(mutation.type, type, error.message)
      done()
    }

    count++
    if (count >= expectedMutations.length) {
      done()
    }
  }

  action({ commit })
}
```

This `testAction` helper method takes the expected action to test, an array of expected mutations, and the `done` callback as the helper arguments. A mock `commit` function is set up which iterates over the

[144] https://vuex.vuejs.org/en/testing.html#testing-actions

number of mutations within the `expectedMutations` array. For every mutation the function asserts the expectation that the `mutation.type` is equal to the `type` specified within the actual action. If not, `assert.fail()`[145] is fired which fails the test and generates the error message as to why.

A test for `fetchWeather` would involve importing the store `actions` object and the `axios` library, stubbing the `axios.get` call to resolve successfully, and using the `testAction` helper to assert the mutations we expect the action to commit to:

```
import { actions } from '@/store';
import axios from 'axios';

const testAction = (action, expectedMutations, done) => {
  // testAction helper
}

describe('actions', () => {
  it('fetchWeather', done => {
    sinon.stub(axios, 'get').resolves(
      // expected payload
    );

    testAction(actions.fetchWeather, [
      { type: 'LOADING_PENDING' },
      { type: 'UPDATE_LOCATION' },
      { type: 'UPDATE_WEATHER_DETAILS' },
      { type: 'LOADING_COMPLETE' }
    ], () => {
      done();
    })
  })
});
```

In the example above, the `testAction` helper is called with the `fetchWeather` action, the array of mutations we expect, and a callback function that when invoked tells our test suite that our asynchronous logic is complete.

This is a *simple* way of how to test Vuex actions and may not be a fully acceptable test for a production ready application. This is because:

- Our example test only involves asserting whether the *types* of the expected mutations have been called. We should also be asserting whether the correct *payloads* are passed to committed mutations.

[145]http://chaijs.com/api/assert/#method_fail

- The api call within the `fetchWeather` store action doesn't have a `catch()` clause to handle what happens when the call *fails*. For strong testing, we would also need to create accompanying tests that handle the *failure* cases of the API request.

The Vuex docs[146] provides a more detailed example for using a `testAction` helper to test an async action.

Getters

Store `getters` should be tested if complex manipulation is performed prior to returning computed store state. These tests are fairly straightforward since assertions will only be made as to whether the intended computations are done correctly.

In our weather application, the store `getters` are simple functions that directly return store values:

testing/weather/src/store.js

```
const getters = {
  location: state => state.location,
  weatherDescription: state => state.weatherDescription,
  imageAbbr: state => state.imageAbbr,
  weatherTemp: state => state.weatherTemp,
  loading: state => state.loading
};
```

As a result, tests for our application store `getters` would not really be needed. The Vuex docs does give an example of testing a getter that performs some calculation[147].

Further reading

In this chapter, we:

1. Demystified JavaScript testing frameworks by building from the ground up.
2. Introduced Mocha, a testing framework that allows us to categorize our tests in `describe` and `it` blocks.
3. Introduced Chai, an assertion library which gives us handy features like `expect`.
4. Learned how to organize and create tests in a behavior-driven style.
5. Introduced `vue-test-utils`, the official Vue library for working with Vue components in a testing environment.

[146] https://vuex.vuejs.org/en/testing.html#testing-actions

[147] https://vuex.vuejs.org/en/testing.html#testing-getters

Armed with this knowledge, we're now prepared to isolate Vue components in a variety of different contexts and effectively write unit tests for them.

A few resources outside of this chapter will aid you greatly as you compose unit tests:

`vue-test-utils`[148]

We explored a few methods for traversing the virtual DOM (e.g. `find()`) and making assertions on the virtual DOM's contents. `vue-test-utils` has many more methods/options that you may find useful:

- `setMethods(methods)`[149]: an option that sets new methods to the `wrapper vm` and forces an update.
- `emitted()`[150]: a wrapper method that returns an object containing the custom events previously emitted by the wrapper.
- `contains(selector)`[151]: a wrapper method that returns a boolean depending on whether the wrapper contains the specified selector. (This can be used instead of `wrapper.html().contains()` to determine if the rendered component contains the expected content).

Chai[152]

The chai docs provide, in detail, the various assertions that can be made. We've used some handy matchers in this chapter, like `contain` and `equal`. Here are a few more examples:

- `.exists`[153]: asserts that an item is neither `undefined` or `null`.
- `.isOk`[154]: asserts that an item is `truthy`.
- `.typeOf`[155]: asserts the type of an item is the name specified, as determined by `Object.prototype.toString`.

---

148 https://vue-test-utils.vuejs.org/en/
149 https://vue-test-utils.vuejs.org/en/api/wrapper/setMethods.html
150 https://vue-test-utils.vuejs.org/en/api/wrapper/emitted.html
151 https://vue-test-utils.vuejs.org/en/api/wrapper/contains.html
152 http://facebook.github.io/jest/docs/api.html
153 http://chaijs.com/api/assert/#exists
154 http://chaijs.com/api/assert/#method_isok
155 http://chaijs.com/api/assert/#method_isok

Made in the USA
Middletown, DE
25 April 2018